Intergroup Dialogue

Intergroup Dialogue

Deliberative Democracy in School, College, Community, and Workplace

Edited by David Schoem
and Sylvia Hurtado

Ann Arbor
THE UNIVERSITY OF MICHIGAN PRESS

2004   2003   2002   4   3   2

A CIP catalog record for this book is available from the British Library.

Library of Congress Cataloging-in-Publication Data

Intergroup dialogue : deliberative democracy in school, college,
    community, and workplace / edited by David Schoem and Sylvia
    Hurtado.
       p.   cm.
    Includes bibliographical references and index.
    ISBN 0-472-09782-2 (cloth : alk. paper) — ISBN 0-472-06782-6
(pbk. : alk. paper)
    1. Group relations training. 2. Intergroup relations. 3.
Intergroup relations—United States. I. Schoem, David Louis. II.
Hurtado, Sylvia, 1957–
HM1086.I55   2001
302'.14—dc21   2001001224

To All Those Working for Peace, Social Justice, and a Diverse Democracy

Acknowledgments

We wish to thank all the authors for their intellectual contributions to this book and for their tireless efforts to advance the practice of intergroup dialogue and create a more just world. For many of our authors (and friends) this is part of a continuing history of collaboration in social justice work, and we look forward with great anticipation to strengthening and continuing our ties with many of our new colleagues whose work is represented in these pages.

This idea for this book first arose out of discussions of the planning group for the Conference on Intergroup Dialogue on the College Campus convened at the University of Michigan in November 1997. That planning group consisted of several of the contributors to this book, including Mark Chesler, Sylvia Hurtado, David Schoem, Todd Sevig, and Stephen H. Sumida. The participants at that conference represented a remarkable gathering of deeply knowledgeable and highly experienced individuals dedicated to advancing our understanding and practice of intergroup dialogue. The discussions of that conference were so open, honest, and inspired that we felt even more convinced of the value of putting in writing some of the important ideas and lessons generated by our colleagues.

We were most gratified to have brought together for the first time the leading voices on intergroup dialogue in higher education. Jonathan Hutson and Rosemary Fennell, among others, urged us to broaden our scope even further in order to engage the world of intergroup dialogue in K–12 schools, community settings, and the corporate sector. We are most thankful to them for that very sound suggestion, and this book reflects our effort to address that broader vision. We also extend our appreciation to Pat McCune and Bess Chuang of UM's Dialogues on Diversity, who did so much to organize the January 2001 Conference, "In Search of Common Ground: Finding Our Way in a Diverse Democracy," based on the work of the authors of this book.

Mark Chesler has been of great assistance throughout this project in many ways, including helping to conceptualize the book (with the other members of the planning group) and organizing the case studies on the workplace. Chavella Pittman has been a core member of our working group from the start. She was of great assistance as a member of the planning group in helping to organize the conference and has helped with a great many of the details of making this book a reality. We are very appreciative of Pat Preston's work in compiling the subject index of this book.

We are thankful to Ruby Beale, Charles Behling, Teresa Graham Brett, Mark Chesler, Patricia Gurin, Diana Kardia, Ratnesh Nagda, Shari Saunders, Todd Sevig, Stephen Sumida, Monita Thompson, Jesús Treviño, and Ximena Zúñiga for all they have taught us over the years about intergroup dialogue. We also want to thank Robert Corcoran, Tina Fernandez, Marjorie Green, Karen Elliot Greisdorf, Gretchen Groth, Rita Hardiman, Jonathan Hutson, Scott Marshall, Michael McCormick, Martha McCoy, Joseph McKenna, Mike McQuillan, Cassandra Mitchell, Lester Monts, Maria Ramos, James Sauceda, Allison Smith, Lorraine Tiven, and Wayne Winborne for all their interest and support in the development of this project.

Beverly Tatum and Maurianne Adams were most valuable from the very start in helping us identify potential publishers. Martha McCoy and Joseph McKenna were particularly helpful in securing certain endorsements and they, along with Karen Elliot Greisdorf, Jonathan Hutson, and Lorraine Tiven, helped tremendously with dissemination of the book. We are very pleased to have this book published by University of Michigan Press and to have the opportunity to work again with their outstanding editors, Mary Erwin, Kelly Sippell and Christina Milton, and with other fine staff such as Mike Kehoe and Giles Brown. We also want to acknowledge our appreciation of the College of Literature, Science and the Arts and of Marvin Parnes for support from the Office of the Vice President for Research at the University of Michigan.

Finally, we wish to thank our families for their love and support during the process of bringing this book to print. Karyn, Adina, and Shana make all this worthwhile for David. Intergroup relations has been a part of Sylvia's daily life with Eric, who supports her research and diversity work in many ways.

Contents

Chapter 1

Intergroup Dialogue: Democracy at Work in Theory and Practice

David Schoem, Sylvia Hurtado, Todd Sevig, Mark Chesler, and Stephen H. Sumida

The issues range from race relations to family relations and from peace talks to schoolyard discipline. Today, people in all walks of life report they are confronted with problems of intergroup relations, and many seek some venue to join in dialogue about these issues. Why? Because every day in contemporary society we face conflicts rooted in the historical legacies of the social divisions of our country and because, at the same time, we embrace a pluralistic and democratic America that functions on deliberation, thrives on difference of opinion, and operates on principles of representation. How do we achieve our highest aspirations for a just society in the face of continuing segregation and social divisions in the United States? Each of us, in addition to our unique, individual identities, is a representation of our communities, be they organized by race and ethnicity, gender, sexual orientation, religion, or class. We must talk with each other to survive as a society. For individuals, success in an increasingly diverse society will depend on having the skills to bridge the spectrum of social differences to help create the type of society we aspire to be. Further, it is important to develop a vehicle for more individuals to deal comfortably with conflict, social differences, and sociohistorical legacies that shape their daily interactions.

Although the notion of bringing groups together to address long-standing conflict has been with us for a great many years, it has gained acclaim and renewed interest as the nation enters the twenty-first century. A small number of education, community, and business leaders have quietly fostered and advanced intergroup dialogue and other conversations at the local level for over a decade (Statham 1997). Media interest and public awareness rose to a new level when President Bill Clinton highlighted the notion of dialogue in the mid-1990s as part of his "Initiative on Race" (*One America* 1998). He and Hillary Clinton, masters of the town hall meeting, moderated televised conversations in auditoriums filled with thousands of adults and children. Others jumped on the bandwagon, offering what they referred to as "dialogues" to high school and college students, community and government leaders, and corporate managers (*Promising Practices* 1997). These dialogues came in forms that varied widely in format, including workshops; lectures; one-time, one-hour conversations about race and diversity; and peer-mediated, small, interactive, sustained face-to-face discussions between two groups in conflict (*Promising Practices* 1997; Statham 1997; Du Bois and Hutson 1997; Sherman et al. 1998).

We clearly embrace the notion of conversation and dialogue, and we applaud much of the work that has gone forward under this broad umbrella. However, we approach the topic with some particular notions as to what intergroup dialogue is and what it is not, and what are the conceptual underpinnings of this uniquely democratic practice. We also have a clear sense of the difficult practical, intellectual, and theoretical struggles that exist for those who engage in this activity and wish to bring about understanding among groups to bridge differences that are evident. In this chapter we present our framework for thinking conceptually and pragmatically about intergroup dialogue by discussing intergroup dialogue as deliberative democracy, defining what is intergroup dialogue, and exploring its place in a just and diverse democracy.

Intergroup Dialogue as Deliberative, Participatory Democracy

One of the greatest challenges facing democracy in the United States is for its citizens to learn how to live together across their different backgrounds without resorting to inequality, subjugation, and oppression. It is the challenge of how best to build upon difference and conflict in ways that are beneficial to the development and sustenance of a just society (West 1994; Young 1990). This challenge is bound to the history of humankind, not just the history of the United States. But it is an ideal that the American people have long held for the country and its democratic principles through our nation's history and into the present (Hughes 1992; Takaki 1993). The ideal speaks forcefully to the enormous amount of work yet to be done. And yet there are no other national examples to turn to that offer a sustained, successful model for the development of a just society. In fact, the negative models, precisely what we wish to reach beyond, continue to predominate throughout the world. The necessary vision, and the accompanying responsibility and work to see it to fruition, rests today with each and every citizen participating together in the best of democratic practice (Guarasci and Cornwell 1997).

In recent years a growing concern has been expressed for the strength and endurance of democracy in the United States. The uprisings/riots of 1992 in East Los Angeles, the growth of militia groups, and the widespread cynicism toward federal and state governments exemplified by the Clinton impeachment debates are symbolic of a deepening crisis facing the core of this nation (West 1994). Progress toward racial justice moves ever so slowly even in the best of economic times, assaults on separation of church and state are unceasing, violent hate crimes against gays are reported with increasing frequency, the gap between wealthy and poor seems impenetrable, and moves to reduce gender inequity are blamed for much of society's ills. The yuppies and "Me" generation of the 1980s, the enormous accumulations of assets by our wealthiest, and the growing influence of the corporate and special interest lobby groups all carry a message that is a far cry from President John Kennedy's famous words, "Ask not what your country can do for you, ask what you can do for your country."

The decline of the last quarter century in civic engagement and the deep cynicism toward public life have been publicly heralded by the "bowling alone" metaphor made popular by Robert Putnam (2000). The significant declines in voter turnout and political involvement, the very low interest in current events on the part of young people, the drastic drop in public trust of the federal government and government leaders, and the astonishingly negative turnabout in participation in public meetings for towns or schools lead many to worry deeply about the decline of civil society and democratic institutions (Dionne 1998). While others interpret the data in a somewhat less threatening manner (Wuthnow 1998), they still acknowledge a sense of porousness in society's civic life, a withdrawal from the traditional communal infrastructures and bonds toward a society that is held together only by "loose connections."

Skocpol and Fiorina (1999, 2) write, "Everyday Americans are increasingly mere spectators of public affairs. Much of the time they are benignly disinterested observers; at other moments angry or cynical. Either way, ordinary citizens have less and less involvement in shaping our common affairs." In turn, the very real danger to society is that our democracy is both increasingly organized by those who are more privileged and, as a result, increasingly serves the interests of those who are more privileged.

The decline in democratic *processes* is certainly one source of concern, but it is almost necessarily accompanied by a concern about democratic *outcomes*, in this case, continuing and growing inequality in society.

The alternative vision is that of a strong democracy with facilitating leaders building civic competence (Barber 1998), where individuals speak out spontaneously against ordinary injustice (Rosenblum 1998), and where engaged citizens act in a spirit of social justice and equality, doing *with* one another, not *for* one another (Skocpol 1998). This is not a new vision for the United States, but it is one that represents a significantly different ideal of the democratic community, one of difference, connection, and equality (Guarasci and Cornwell 1997). And the vision of a strong democracy may very well be one that is sustained by its citizens embracing community in small groups rather than enormous political organizations (Walzer 1998).

Intergroup dialogue is one significant and bold model of small groups of people coming together from various walks of life to build a strong democracy (Schoem 1995). Intergroup dialogue represents a grassroots effort that is a constructive response to the challenges facing our fragile democracy (Schoem 1991b). It is a positive effort on the part of the citizenry to take initiative and responsibility for talking about building a just, multicultural society (Du Bois and Hutson 1997).

In a sense, intergroup dialogue is a *diverse* twenty-first-century version of the *homogeneous* nineteenth-century town hall meeting: sleeves rolled up, talking directly, honestly, and sometimes quite harshly about the most difficult and pressing topics of the day, and then moving forward together with solutions to strengthen the community and the nation. It is local hands-on work to build community in schools, in neighborhoods, in the workplace, in government. However, in the age-old New England–style town hall meeting, there was an assumption of homogeneity of experience, including religion, race, and common goals and values among community members who came together to deliberate differences of opinion and resolve problems. This homogeneity, coupled with common problems and hardships (and even common enemies), served to maintain social cohesion among community members as they shared differences of opinion. Although intergroup dialogues can be arranged to address problems that must be resolved across groups, unlike a town hall meeting, there is no assumption of homogeneity or common goals among different group members. In fact, the assumption is that members who come together in a dialogue likely will have different sociohistorical legacies steeped in intergroup antagonisms due to unequal social relations, hold stereotypical views of each others' behaviors and values, and question whether they are members of the same community (Zúñiga et al. 1996).

This is the reality of many of the social differences that permeate our contemporary societal institutions (schools and colleges) and diverse communities. Thus, an important starting point for any intergroup dialogue is the assumption and acknowledgment of group differences. Through discussion, dialogue participants begin to understand why there may be group differences as well as to see that group members are more divergent in opinion and experience than group "stereotypes" convey (Lopez, Gurin, and Nagda 1998). Participants may begin to see that these differences deserve respect and that they are not as divisive or incompatible as they seemed on the surface. Eventually such contact and discussion can lead to the discovery of commonality of goals and values, which can lead to coalitions toward action on a community problem. However, this can only occur after a long process and hard work (Schoem and Stevenson 1990; Schoem 1995).

Many community groups and institutions have turned to intergroup dialogue as a means of addressing today's conflicts and advancing institutional values and culture (*Promising Practices* 1997). By itself, intergroup dialogue won't solve all of our nation's problems. But the open and honest exchange and serious face-to-face engagement that represents good dialogue provides the best opportunity to engage in the practice of deliberative democracy in order to address our institutional and national concerns. To choose not to join the process of intergroup dialogue when that opportunity is available would seem a certain path to worsening relations across group boundaries, leading to increasingly dangerous, even explosive ways of dealing with conflicts in our communities and in our nation.

And change *is* taking place. In our schools and colleges, children, teenagers, and young adults are coming together in dialogue-based programs to fight the tide of prejudice, separation, and injustice. They revisit their exclusive friendship patterns, challenge the status quo of socially biased and inequitable paradigms in school, and construct a vision for their futures that will take them, we hope, beyond the structural barriers that have marked the lives of the generations that have preceded them. In our communities, private citizens and civic leaders are coming together to work through neighborhood, marketplace, and governmental issues of concern to all, making sure that all voices are heard and represented in problem solving, decision making, and plans for the future. In the workplace, too, corporate leaders and line workers are engaging in difficult conversations about race and other intergroup relations. These dialogues are intended to build upon the rapidly changing demographic profile of American workers and corporate management to ensure profitability at home and in the global marketplace.

An indication of the powerful potential of intergroup dialogue is that it is sometimes used by powerful groups in a cynical or manipulative way in order to delay or cool out protest and civic participation. The negative use of intergroup dialogue is intended to encourage groups to focus strictly on the dialogue process rather than on substantive, structural issues; to emphasize talk above, and in place of, action; to focus exclusively on celebration rather than on power; and to frame issues restrictively as individually driven, rather than as a part of social group dynamics and social causation.

What Is Intergroup Dialogue?

Intergroup dialogue is a form of democratic practice, engagement, problem solving, and education involving face-to-face, focused, facilitated, and confidential discussions occurring over time between two or more groups of people defined by their different social identities.

1. Dialogue is a process, not an event. Dialogue takes place over time. It requires a commitment on the part of participants to listen, challenge, reflect, and continue to talk with one another. A dialogue that continues over weeks or months allows participants to work through stages of growth, change, conflict, friendship, and anger, uncovering new layers of understanding and insight (Adams, Bell, and Griffin 1997). The depth of meaning, the nuance of difference, and the fulfillment of connection and sharing only come through extended discussion. As trust between participants grows and is tested, people feel freer to probe issues, challenge self and others, express anger, offer comfort, and see beyond group boundaries to both structural conditions and intragroup concerns (Lopez, Gurin, and Nagda 1998).

Dialogue exercises and techniques also can be adapted to enhance and enrich other institutional activities, although they should not be confused with distinct intergroup dialogues (Adams, Bell, and Griffin 1997; Cox and Beale 1997; Schoem 1995). The college seminar class can truly become a setting for active, engaged learning with text and fellow students through incorporation of dialogue techniques. Faculty development activities and human resource workshops, social studies classes and student organizations, administrative policy meetings, staff training sessions, and community organization meetings can be transformed through the adaptation of dialogue activities for those settings.

2. Dialogue is about relationship building and thoughtful engagement about difficult issues. Dialogue involves in-depth conversations about competing perspectives. It requires face-to-face engagement and attention to relationship building across groups, within groups, and between individuals (Dalton 1995; Hubbard 1997). In addition, the purpose of dialogue, unlike debate, is not to declare winners and losers at the end of the day, but rather to engender deeper and broader understandings and insights, oftentimes leading to action, among all participants.

Intergroup dialogues can take place in many settings in schools, colleges, communities, and the workplace. They can include students, teachers, staff and administration, citizens and citizen groups, community and governmental leaders and their constituents, clerical staff, line workers, management and professional staff, and corporate CEOs.

Dialogues should be small, about twelve to eighteen participants, in order to increase the opportunity to build more trusting relationships, encourage more engaged interaction, provide greater safety and confidentiality, and make better use of the limited time (Nagda, Zúñiga, and Sevig 1995). With highly skilled facilitation, it also is possible, though not generally desirable because of the difficulty involved, to conduct dialogues with more participants.

Intergroup dialogue exercises and techniques can be constructively used to encourage in-depth interaction and conversation with groups ranging from thirty to three hundred participants. But in most cases these should not be considered dialogues per se; they are more like town hall meetings. These larger events also serve a very important purpose of bringing people together for focused and engaged discussion. However, town hall meetings are different from intergroup dialogues. Finally, gatherings of five hundred to ten thousand people or more about topics of race relations or intergroup dialogue can also be educational and even provocative for those in attendance, using dynamic speakers and panels, multimedia presentations, and performances. Nevertheless, however beneficial they may be, these events should not be confused with intergroup dialogues as described here.

3. Dialogue requires an extended commitment. Implicit in the definition of dialogue is the notion of a sustained activity (Sherman et al. 1998). Dialogue is more likely to be meaningful and successful when participants agree to participate for more than a few meetings. With commitment, people realize they can confront tough issues and know the conversation will continue and move forward the following week with the group intact. When people participate in an extended dialogue, they begin to realize that it is only through a long-term commitment that our racial and other divisions will be fully addressed. Over an extended time, trust slowly builds in the group to allow for more frank and difficult discussion (Schoem and Stevenson 1990).

The length of dialogues can vary widely, usually in categories of weekly meetings over three weeks, six weeks, three to six months, or a year or more. Our preference is for regular meetings of the dialogue group. Dialogues that meet just a few times can be intense and powerful, but most often fall short of the success of long-term engagement. Some dialogues may be organized in longer time blocks, such as intensive weekend retreats, and they may be deeply meaningful and even transformative. Nevertheless, while seeking a good balance between the numbers of meeting hours and the interval between meetings, we still value the commitment to dialogue over at least several weeks of time for the following reasons: (1) it allows for building more trusting relationships, (2) it provides time to process issues between sessions, (3) it permits attention to the complex layers of issues, (4) it provides opportunity for outside reading related to the topic, and (5) it teaches that change requires long-term commitment.

Those who organize dialogue-type discussions that meet once or twice also may find intense and often very positive reactions from participants. However, meeting just once or twice, in our minds, constitutes an "introduction to dialogue" rather than a true dialogue experience. These short-term experiences offer an opportunity to expose individuals and groups to the value of the dialogue process and techniques, but there are no shortcuts to the benefits of long-term engagement and commitment.

4. Dialogue takes place face-to-face. Face-to-face engagement is necessary to build and maintain the trust, confidentiality, and openness of the group. Without face-to-face interaction it is much more difficult to listen carefully, engage ideas and participants fully, and develop meaningful relationships. Meeting face-to-face also is required to create the safe environment needed for building trust and confidentiality for dialogue (Zúñiga et al. 1995). There is an important sense of "place" that is created when groups in dialogue come together over an extended time. Intergroup dialogue simply can't happen with hundreds of participants.

One of the key components of intergroup dialogue is its emphasis on listening (Guarasci and Cornwell 1997). While many dialogue participants come ready to tell their story, air their grievances, and explain their perspective, it is the emphasis on active listening that makes this process distinctive. People are always ready to talk, and they do, but there are few instances in which people listen, and listen intently, to their talk. Through the open acknowledgement of the importance of listening and, more importantly, the use of structured exercises that force and reinforce an emphasis on listening, dialogue participants finally begin to "hear" and understand one another's stories and perspectives. This experience is not only eye-opening to the listeners, who quickly find themselves deeply engaged in meaningful and forceful conversation, but it is equally valuable to the speakers, who almost always are struck by the difference that is made when another person actively and seriously listens to one's words.

With the advent of the internet there is increasing interest in virtual dialogue. Some find that virtual dialogue can complement and extend the work of an existing face-to-face dialogue, but the internet is fraught with problems of privacy and confidentiality and, alone, does not lend itself well to building trust and community among people engaging long-standing issues of conflict. Attempts at stand-alone, virtual intergroup dialogue are not recommended. On-line and other forms of distance communication can provide important support and can enhance and extend the value of a good dialogue, but face-to-face meetings will always be at the center of intergroup dialogue (Schoem 1998).

5. Dialogue takes place best in an atmosphere of confidentiality, and issues of sponsorship and context are important to its success. Precisely because dialogue is about relationship building, it requires confidence that what people say in the dialogue will not be reported to nonparticipants. A dialogue takes place in the moment, and what one says and hears is not for the purpose of gaining advantage with anyone outside the dialogue group. Practices such as revealing private comments to friends outside the group, attempting dialogue in big crowds, or looking for sound bites and photo opportunities for the six o'clock news don't make for good dialogue. In a dialogue, *listening* is essential, and saying words from both the heart and the mind is paramount (Schoem 1995).

Dialogues are most often organized because there are new or long-standing conflicts between more powerful groups and those groups in subordinate positions, most often arising from an imbalance of power and privilege between them. A dialogue may be sponsored by both or all of the parties involved, by a third-party convener acceptable to all participants, or by a single, "interested" party. The trust level of participants entering into the dialogue, and thus the subsequent success of the dialogue, is more likely to be deepened through cosponsorship or third-party sponsorship. Sometimes, however, it is only possible to obtain sponsorship from a single, "interested" party, and though more difficult, trust can be built and the dialogue still can be successful. In these cases it is important for information about sponsorship to be brought to the attention of all participants and discussed openly.

Among the dialogue participants themselves, there obviously also are issues of power relations to address. If participants come from the same organization, for example, a business, a college, or a school, to discuss issues of race or gender, there will be different intergroup dynamics when the participants hold the same status (all vice presidents, all faculty, all tenth graders) than when there are hierarchical relationships in the group. With considerable care such power imbalances can be addressed, but one must be very attentive to these dynamics and the possible ramifications in the setting outside the dialogue group.

The larger context in which dialogues take place influences the individual dialogue itself and, in turn, reflects the long-term impact of dialogue activity on the institutional or community setting. A distinct dialogue program that exists in a school, college, community, or corporation is more likely to have a secure presence, institutional commitment, and satisfactory resources than any one-time workshop or activity based on individual initiative. In some cases, an organization may make a strong commitment but choose to infuse dialogue-like activities throughout the workforce or curriculum instead of creating a distinct program. When dialogue "events" are offered as stand-alone events or part of a retreat or orientation program, although useful, they are more likely to be short term and without opportunity for follow-up.

6. Dialogues often may focus on race, but they also address multiple issues of social identity that extend beyond race. Intergroup dialogue brings together two or more groups of people with issues of conflict or potential for conflict (Zúñiga and Chesler 1995; Gadlin 1994). A dialogue may bring together Blacks and Whites, Hispanics and Native Americans, Christians, Moslems, Hindus, and Jews, women and men, multiracial/multiethnic people, or gays, lesbians, and heterosexuals (Zúñiga et al. 1995). There are also intragroup dialogues that bring together several subgroups within a larger identity group, such as Mexican Americans, Puerto Ricans, and Cuban Americans, or Orthodox Jews and

Reform Jews, or Asian/Pacific Americans of many different ethnic backgrounds. Dialogues also can bring together a wide range of community leaders from many backgrounds. Multigroup dialogues result in outcomes just as valuable as more topically focused dialogues or dialogues with just two groups, but may take longer to accomplish their goals (Schoem 1995). Because there are so many forces that constitute our individual identity and self, the most engaged dialogue participants will likely bring into any topic issues of race, gender, class, sexual orientation, and religion at some point in the discussion.

Intergroup dialogue contrasts with interpersonal dialogue just as intergroup relations differ from interpersonal relations, or an autoethnography may differ from an autobiography. In the United States an ideology of individualism tends to be overt. A definitive feature of intergroup dialogue, however, is its occurrence among people who are trying to see and speak of themselves as members of their groups, rather than as sole individuals. It is not that the individuals are to be considered representatives of their groups, but intergroup dialogue is sensitive to and expressive of participants' backgrounds in the values, customs, philosophies and beliefs, rites of passage, celebrations, struggles, and histories of their respective groups and communities. By actively considering groups and their interactions in the lives of participating individuals, intergroup dialogue can analyze structural relations among groups in society. These features of intergroup dialogue are stated as well as examined in many ways in what follows in this volume.

Intergroup dialogues cross the boundaries of individual and group identities and experiences. It is important for each participant (1) to acknowledge his or her social group identities and those groups' roles in society and, (2) at the same time, to affirm his or her own individuality within and across social groups, and (3) to recognize commonalties across social groups. A dialogue that focuses exclusively on the individual and intrapsychic processes ignores social structural conditions of power and place in society. At the same time, dialogue processes that ignore participants' individual identities by insisting exclusively upon group and/or subgroup identities also deny the unique character of people's lives and diminish opportunities for personal growth and change. It is important to keep in mind that what is addressed in a dialogue is an integration of individual, group, and societal issues and identities and, therefore, the participants may experience the dialogue as a mix of intellectual, political, conceptual, relational, and intrapsychic processes. However, intergroup dialogue groups should never be confused with therapy groups (Schoem and Stevenson 1990; Schoem 1995). Any individual who confuses these purposes or who wishes to use dialogue for therapy should be advised of the significant distinctions and referred elsewhere for counseling if that is what is desired.

7. **Dialogue focuses on both intergroup conflict and community building.** It is intense, difficult work, and only occasionally is it a "feel good" experience. The constructive use and management of conflict for building community and addressing issues of social justice is a core focus of intergroup dialogue. Clearly, conflict avoidance is not one of the goals of intergroup dialogue. Dialogue groups provide an opportunity for participants to engage issues of conflict in a safe, structured environment (Hubbard 1997). It is this rare opportunity to engage conflict safely and fully with groups that have histories of distance, separation, and power imbalance that often evokes great interest in building community among participants. Community building requires time for addressing conflict, time for celebration of both commonalities and differences, and attention to issues of power and social structures through problem solving and change making. Joint celebration across groups of holidays, foods, and accomplishments is an important social experience but does not alone constitute intergroup dialogue.

As individuals, we Americans are amazingly adept at not talking about race with people across different racial backgrounds and at talking superficially rather than substantively. As members of different social identity groups, we live in separate worlds from one another (Schoem 1991b). When people come together in dialogue, they first have to overcome this history of keeping apart from others, and they quickly confront the barriers that divide them, including their lack of awareness, skills, and knowledge. None of this is easy. People often feel anxious, fearful, and vulnerable during the dialogue. At the same time, as people realize how much progress they can make through dialogue, the hard work feels good and the relationships that develop can be heartwarming and enduring.

8. **Dialogues are led by skilled facilitators.** Dialogues are a difficult, complex social process, and without the careful attention of skilled facilitators they can go badly (Nagda, Zúñiga, and Sevig 1995). Facilitators can and should come from every sector of society. However, dialogue does require facilitation by skilled individuals, and the importance of in-depth training to develop such skills cannot be underestimated (Adams, Bell, and Griffin 1997; Zúñiga et al. 1998). Attempts to shortcut the training process

are likely to decrease the chances for the success of the dialogue group. Although not every organization or group wanting to organize dialogue groups has the resources to offer in-depth training, the principle that more training is better than less training applies in most cases.

There is considerable value in having the social group of participants represented by cofacilitators who can model constructive dialogic processes. Facilitators who also are peers of the participants offer them a greater sense of ownership and understanding in the dialogue, and often allow for greater engagement and relationship building. Successful cofacilitation requires careful coordination and preparation, constant review, and regular feedback.

9. Dialogue is about inquiry and understanding and the integration of content and process. The dialogue process involves challenging ideas, listening to other viewpoints, and gaining new insights. It requires intellectual, social, and personal reflection. It asks that one attempt to see issues from another's perspective and often to develop the ability to hold multiple and sometimes competing perspectives at the same time. Participants learn as much about their own personal beliefs, group identity, and their group's social history as they learn about other group(s), and they often report learning more than they do in school or any work setting (Franklin 1996; Zúñiga et al. 1998). This is because dialogue depends on the extended presence and engagement of a diverse group of individuals to make real what otherwise may be presented as "background information." They realize that groups are not monolithic and that there are considerable intragroup differences. They confront and leave behind the narrow lens through which they have previously viewed the world around them. They often come to recognize the inadequacies of their own schooling and the limitations of growing up in segregated neighborhoods and living in a segregated society (Hurtado 1996; Osajima 1995; Schoem 1991a, 1995).

Intergroup dialogue at its best integrates elements of content and process. There must be opportunity for presentation and discussion of information, theory, and perspectives of students and scholars in the field. Facilitators must not only be skilled in group processes and have a high degree of self-awareness of social identity group issues, but must also be knowledgeable about the content area of the dialogue. To proceed without content from the facilitator as well as outside readings and resources allows participants to go forward in the dialogue with the possibility that misinformation is being introduced and reinforced without question or challenge, and it allows individual experience to far outweigh social and historical experience. At the other extreme, by no means does a traditional lecture format constitute a dialogue. There needs to be a careful balance between content and process.

10. Dialogue involves talking, but taking action often leads to good talking, and dialogue often leads to action. At its very essence, intergroup dialogue involves communication, and it emphasizes communication primarily in the form of talking with one another. Many people find that communication is enhanced when groups of people work together on a joint task or project. Having a concrete experience in common allows people to bring the real-world activity of the task to enrich the dialogue and allows the frank discourse of the dialogue to enhance the work of the project.

In addition, some groups may intentionally enter into a dialogue to advance their work together, and some individuals may decide either at the outset or at the conclusion of a dialogue to continue to be together by engaging in a collaborative action project to effect social change. Policymakers or community groups are more likely to make informed decisions and work more cooperatively after having participated in related intergroup dialogues. In cases of action following dialogue, the foundation of dialogic processes already established will inform the continued collaborative processes of the action project.

Dialogues often are organized so that there is talk only. In these cases there may be important new understandings and deep insights gained, but participants may never move beyond the intellectual and abstract to personal change and collective action based on the dialogue discussions. Dialogues also can be tied to an action project as part of the conceptualization of the dialogue or in response to discussions within the dialogue or even as an outcome of the dialogue. These might include community service projects, social change projects, or coalition-based actions. These dialogues address the concern raised above regarding dialogues with talk only but, depending on the action taken, may also involve some personal and collective risk.

Intergroup Dialogue for a Just and Diverse America

Democracy is a powerful but fragile political arrangement, requiring careful maintenance, regular nurturance, and continuing advancement and improvement in the areas of social justice and equality. The American ideal, that people from all backgrounds can join together to live in a just and democratic society, will become even more of a necessity for our democratic survival as we proceed into the new century. Our nation increasingly will depend on the social, cultural, intellectual, and economic contributions of citizens from every social identity group.

Intergroup dialogue is a positive and powerful process in which different groups come together to discuss issues of community and conflict. Our societal task is not to end or resolve all conflicts, but to examine and understand conflict so communities can live together productively, even harmoniously, with conflict. Conflict is a natural phenomenon, one that exists in both good and bad relationships at multiple levels (Chesler 1995). If we can't talk openly with one another in a sustained way, we have little hope of achieving our national ideal, let alone maintaining the progress we have made thus far.

Maurianne Adams (1997) offers a valuable overview of the broader context of approaches to social justice education developed over many decades since the 1940s. Intergroup dialogues draw in a variety of ways from all these models. These models include laboratory and intergroup education (Lippitt 1949), human relations, intergroup, and multicultural education (Sleeter and Grant 1994; Schoem et al. 1995b), cross-cultural and international training (York 1994), experiential education (Joplin 1995), black studies and ethnic studies (Cole 1991), feminist pedagogies (Howe 1984), and critical pedagogies and liberatory education (Freire 1970). The intergroup dialogue model draws on all these important social justice education practices, including lessons drawn from social and cognitive development models.

Learning how to build and strengthen a just, democratic society that comprises a variety of cultural and racial groups does not take place without vehicles for learning, through community groups, high-quality education, and supportive institutional and corporate structures. Most Americans grow up in communities segregated by race, class, and religion and have little experience personally or through their schooling with people from backgrounds that differ from their own. Intergroup misunderstanding and unproductive conflict on personal and institutional levels are pervasive when members of these different groups come together at some point in schools, in the community, or in the workplace.

The global economy requires our citizens to have cross-cultural competence to remain competitive (Ellinor and Gerard 1998). Yet without the opportunity for dialogue, most of our young people lack experience even with their fellow citizens in the United States from different racial groups, let alone people from other countries. Many of the young people entering our colleges and professional schools have grown up in gated communities and segregated schools, and they continue that pattern of separation at college through membership in monoracial and monoclass fraternities and sororities. Through intergroup dialogue, students not only experience an extended and substantive interracial exchange, but they learn to traverse racial boundaries and build new and more inclusive "comfort zones."

In the intergroup dialogue, participants not only learn about the "other," but they learn just as much about their own group, about intragroup issues, and about themselves as individuals. In fact, one of the most compelling facets of dialogue is that while participants join in order to address issues between their own group and another group, they usually find that they learn as much about themselves as about the other group (Franklin 1996; Schoem 1997; Zúñiga et al. 1998). In part this occurs because unexplored areas of commonality across groups are identified, but also because participants often find it difficult to answer informatively questions about their own group from a sincere and interested "other." This results in a process of self-reflection and new and renewed exploration of one's own social identities.

Intergroup dialogues also move the central and often exclusive interracial focus from Black and White to the rich and complex racial mix that America comprises (Takaki 1993; Schoem 1991b). Although the dialogue framework may remain the same, it is very clear that the range of relationships requires multiple and varied dialogues. Further, any notion that a dialogue can maintain fixed boundaries in focusing on a single relationship, for example, race or gender, is quickly disposed of as issues of multiple and intersecting identities and varied positions of power emerge in discussion (McIntosh 1992; Lorde 1992). In addition, though the public focus of intergroup dialogue has often been about race, dialogues are often centered on other issues as well, such as religion, immigration, sexual orientation, gender, economic class, and national and international identities.

Within the confines of the dialogue, all participants have equal status (Stephan and Stephan 1996; Zúñiga et al. 1998). This fact requires participants to confront the possibilities of a relationship, a community, and a nation in which all people have equal standing. It encourages open discussions of equality, justice, and freedom both on a theoretical basis and a very real, practical basis. When people from different and historically unequal footing come together as equals to confront past and present conflict, they move to the very issues of democracy in the United States. How will communities of difference live and work together? What are the common bases upon which the national social contract can be made acceptable and sustained for all groups of people? What does a multicultural school, university, community, workplace, government, society look like, and how does it function day to day? How does one go about changing organizational and institutional structures to support a new vision of a just, diverse America? Progress on these questions, which are at the heart of American democracy, constitutes the promise of intergroup dialogue.

REFERENCES

Adams, Maurianne. 1997. "Pedagogical Frameworks for Social Justice Education." In Maurianne Adams, Lee Bell, and Pat Griffin, *Teaching for Diversity and Social Justice: A Sourcebook*. New York: Routledge.

Adams, Maurianne, Lee Bell, and Pat Griffin. 1997. *Teaching for Diversity and Social Justice: A Sourcebook*. New York: Routledge.

American Pluralism and the College Curriculum: Higher Education in a Diverse Democracy. 1995. Washington, D.C.: Association of American Colleges and Universities.

Barber, Benjamin. 1998. *A Passion for Democracy*. Princeton, N.J.: Princeton University Press.

Burbules, Nicholas. 1993. *Dialogue in Teaching: Theory and Practice*. New York: Teachers College Press.

Chesler, Mark. 1995. "Racetalk: Thinking and Talking about Racism." *Diversity Factor* 3, no. 3: 37–45.

Cole, J. B. 1991. "Black Studies in Liberal Arts Education." In *Transforming the Curriculum: Ethnic Studies and Women's Studies,* ed. J. E. Butler and J. C. Walter. Albany: SUNY Press.

Cox, Taylor, and Ruby Beale. 1997. *Developing Competency to Manage Diversity: Reading, Cases, and Activities*. San Francisco: Berrett-Koehler.

Crowfoot, James, and Mark Chesler. 1996. "White Men's Roles in Multicultural Coalitions." In *Impacts of Racism on White Americans*, ed. Benjamin Bowser and Raymond Hunt. Thousand Oaks, Calif.: Sage.

Dalton, Harlon. 1995. *Racial Healing: Confronting the Fear between Blacks and Whites*. New York: Doubleday.

Dionne, E. J., Jr., ed. 1998. *Community Works: The Revival of Civil Society in America*. Washington, D.C.: Brookings Institution Press.

The Drama of Diversity and Democracy: Higher Education and American Commitments. 1995. Washington, D.C.: Association of American Colleges and Universities.

Du Bois, Paul Martin, and Jonathan Hutson. 1997. *Bridging the Racial Divide: A Report on Interracial Dialogue in America.* Brattleboro, Vt.: Center for Living Democracy.

Ellinor, Linda, and Glenna Gerard. 1998. *Dialogue: Rediscover the Transforming Power of Conversation.* New York: John Wiley and Sons.

Franklin, Robert. 1996. "Conversations in Black and White: Let's Take Race." *Commonwealth,* February 23, 9–10.

Freire, Paulo. 1970. *Pedagogy of the Oppressed.* New York: Seabury.

Gadlin, Howard. 1994. "Conflict Resolution, Cultural Differences, and the Culture of Racism." *Negotiation Journal,* January, 33–47.

Guarasci, Richard, and Grant Cornwell. 1997. "Democracy and Difference: Emerging Concepts of Identity, Diversity, and Community." In *Democratic Education in an Age of Difference: Redefining Citizenship in Higher Education,* ed. Richard Guarasci, Grant Cornwell, and associates. San Francisco: Jossey-Bass.

Howe, F. 1984. "Women and the Power to Change." In *Myths of Coeducation,* ed. F. Howe. Bloomington: Indiana University Press.

Hubbard, Amy. 1997. "Face-to-Face at Arm's Length: Conflict Norms and Extra Group Relations in Grassroots Dialogue Groups." *Human Organization* 56, no. 3: 265–74.

Hughes, Langston. 1992. "Let America Be America Again." In Gary Columbo et al., *ReReading America: Cultural Concepts for Critical Thinking and Writing.* Boston: Bedford Books.

Hurtado, Sylvia. 1996. "How Diversity Affects Teaching and Learning." *Educational Record,* fall, 27–29.

Joplin, L. 1995. "On Defining Experiential Education." In *The Theory of Experiential Education,* ed. K. Warren, M. Sakofs, and J. S. Hunt, Jr. Dubuque, Iowa: Kendall/Hunt.

Lippitt, Ronald. 1949. *Training in Community Relations.* New York: Harper and Bros.

Lopez, Gretchen, Patricia Gurin, and Biren A. Nagda. 1998. "Education and Understanding Structural Causes for Group Inequalities." *Political Psychology* 19, no. 2: 305–29.

Lorde, Audre. 1992. "Age, Race, Class, and Sex: Women Redefining Difference." In *Women, Culture, and Society: A Reader,* ed. B. Balliet and D. Humphreys. Dubuque, Iowa: Kendall/Hunt.

McIntosh, Peggy. 1992. "White Privilege and Male Privilege." In *Race, Class, and Gender: An Anthology,* ed. Patricia Hill Collins and Margaret Anderson. Belmont, Calif.: Wadsworth.

Nagda, Biren A., Ximena Zúñiga, and Todd Sevig. 1995. "Bridging Differences through Peer Facilitated Intergroup Dialogues." In *Peer Programs on a College Campus: Theory, Training, and the Voices of the Peers,* ed. Sherry Hatcher. San Diego: New Resources.

One America in the Twenty-first Century: The President's Initiative on Race—One America Dialogue Guide. 1998. Washington, D.C.: The White House.

Osajima, Keith. 1995. "Creating Classroom Environments for Change." In *Practicing What We Teach: Confronting Diversity in Teacher Education,* ed. Renee Martin. New York: SUNY Press.

Promising Practices—The President's Initiative on Race. November 6, 1997. http://www.whitehouse.gov/Initiatives/OneAmerica/One America_Links.html.

Putnam, Robert. 2000. *Bowling Alone: The Collapse and Revival of American Community.* New York: Simon and Schuster.

Rosenblum, Nancy. 1998. *Membership and Morals: The Personal Uses of Pluralism in America.* Princeton, N.J.: Princeton University Press.

Schoem, David. 1991a. "College Students Need Thoughtful, in-Depth Study of Race Relations." *Chronicle of Higher Education,* April 3, A48.

———, ed. 1991b. *Inside Separate Worlds: Life Stories of Young Blacks, Jews, and Latinos.* Ann Arbor: University of Michigan Press.

———. 1995. "Teaching about Ethnic Identity and Intergroup Relations." In David Schoem et al., *Multicultural Teaching in the University.* Westport, Conn.: Praeger.

———. 1997. "Intergroup Relations, Conflict, and Community." In *Democratic Education in an Age of Difference: Redefining Citizenship in Higher Education,* ed. Richard Guarasci, Grant Cornwell, and associates. San Francisco: Jossey-Bass.

———. 1998. "The Intersection of Intergroup Dialogue and On-Line Communication." In *Diversity Web: Where Diversity and Learning are Linked Through the Web,* ed. Laura Blasi. Washington, D.C.: AACU.

Schoem, David, Linda Frankel, Ximena Zúñiga, and Edith A. Lewis. 1995a. "The Meaning of Multicultural Teaching." In *Multicultural Teaching in the University,* ed. David Schoem, Linda Frankel, Ximena Zúñiga, and Edith A. Lewis. Westport, Conn.: Praeger.

Schoem, David, Linda Frankel, Ximena Zúñiga, and Edith A. Lewis, eds. 1995b. *Multicultural Teaching in the University.* Westport, Conn.: Praeger.

Schoem, David, and Marshall Stevenson. 1990. "Teaching Ethnic Identity and Intergroup Relations: The Case of Blacks and Jews." *Teachers College Record* 91, no. 4: 579–94.

Sherman, Robert, Dayna Cunningham, Henry Ramos, Miguel Satut, and Lori Villarosa. 1998. "Foundation Initiatives and Dialogues on Race." *National Civic Review* 87, no. 2: 127–35.

Skocpol, Theda, 1998. "Don't Blame Big Government: America's Voluntary Groups Thrive in a National Network." In *Community Works: The Revival of Civil Society in America,* ed. E. J. Dionne, Jr. Washington, D.C.: Brookings Institution Press.

Skocpol, Theda, and Morris Fiorina. 1999. "Making Sense of the Civic Engagement Debate." In Theda Skocpol and Morris Fiorina, *Civic Engagement and American Democracy.* Washington, D.C.: Brookings Institution Press.

Sleeter, C., and C. Grant. 1994. "Education That Is Multicultural and Social Reconstructionist." In C. Sleeter and C. Grant, *Making Choices for Multicultural Education: Five Approaches to Race, Class, and Gender.* New York: Macmillan.

Statham, Mary Ann. 1997. *Interracial Dialogue Groups across America: A Directory.* Brattleboro, Vt.: Center for Living Democracy.

Stephan, Walter, and Cookie W. Stephan. 1996. *Intergroup Relations.* Boulder, Colo.: Westview Press.

Takaki, Ronald. 1993. *A Different Mirror.* Boston: Little, Brown.

Walzer, Michael. 1998. "The Idea of Civil Society." In *Community Works: The Revival of Civil Society in America,* ed. E. J. Dionne, Jr. Washington, D.C.: Brookings Institution Press.

West, Cornel. 1994. "Race and Social Justice in America." *Liberal Education* 80, no. 3: 32–39.

Wuthnow, Robert. 1998. *Loose Connections.* Cambridge: Harvard University Press.

York, D. 1994. *Cross-Cultural Training Programs.* Westport, Conn.: Bergin and Garvey.

Young, Iris Marion. 1990. *Justice and the Politics of Difference.* Princeton, N.J.: Princeton University Press.

Zúñiga, Ximena, and Mark Chesler. 1995. "Teaching with and about Conflict in the Classroom." In *Multicultural Teaching in the University,* ed. David Schoem, Linda Frankel, Ximena Zúñiga, and Edith A. Lewis. Westport, Conn.: Praeger.

Zúñiga, Ximena, Biren A. Nagda, Todd Sevig, Monita Thompson, and Eric Dey. 1995. "Speaking the Unspeakable: Student Learning Outcomes in Intergroup Dialogues on a College Campus." Paper presented at a meeting of the Association for the Study of Higher Education, November 2–5.

Zúñiga, Ximena, Biren A. Nagda, Todd Sevig, Carolyn Vasques, and Eric Dey. 1996. "Tearing down the Walls: Peer-Facilitated Intergroup Dialogue Processes and Experiences." Paper presented at a meeting of the American Educational Research Association, April 8–12.

Zúñiga, Ximena, Carolyn Vasques Scalera, Biren A. Nagda, and Todd Sevig. 1998. "Exploring and Bridging Race/Ethnic Differences: Developing Intergroup Dialogue Competencies in a Co-Learning Environment." Typescript.

Chapter 2

Research and Evaluation on Intergroup Dialogue

Sylvia Hurtado

As an increasing number of individuals engage in the practice of intergroup dialogue and invest in program development in many different settings, it becomes important to understand how many organizations have assessed the impact of their efforts. How do we know that intergroup dialogue works? What can be achieved if we introduce an intergroup dialogue program in our community? We are fortunate to witness a growing body of research that supports dialogue principles as well as actual studies on the process and outcomes of intergroup dialogue. This chapter discusses research related to the practice of intergroup dialogue, including long- and short-term assessments of individual participants. Much of the research on intergroup dialogue identifies thinking and citizenship skills necessary for participation in a diverse society with increasingly complex social problems that are too difficult for one person to solve. After experiencing intergroup dialogue, participants typically think and see the world differently, increase personal and social awareness of different group experiences and forms of oppression in society, and build confidence in working through differences with others. These skills are essential for cooperative problem-solving and the development of alliances to build a more just society. These are also necessary skills for a democracy that embraces difference and requires that commonality be constructed and negotiated by its participants (Guarasci, Cornwell, and associates 1997).

General Research Supporting Intergroup Dialogue

Many areas of social science research undergird the practice of intergroup dialogue. In some cases, familiarity with some of the research that supports the rationale for a sustained intervention like intergroup dialogue may be necessary before introducing a program in a school, community, or workplace. Several strands of research in business, education, psychology, and sociology support the rationale and practice of intergroup dialogue. For example, new intergroup relations skills are necessary for workers, students, and leaders in communities that are rapidly becoming demographically diverse in order to develop fair and culturally sensitive policies, or simply to better serve clients from diverse communities. Employers have articulated a need for a more diverse workforce and better-prepared graduates who have the skills to manage the diversity in the work environment. *Workforce 2000: Work and Workers for the 21st Century* projected that over the next few years, 85 percent of the net new entrants into the workforce will be women, immigrants, and racial/ethnic minorities (Johnston 1987). A recent study by the RAND Institute also showed the business community identified highly valued cognitive and social skills they desired among employees including: the ability to work effectively in groups with others of diverse backgrounds, openness to new ideas and perspectives, and empathy with other workers' perspectives (Bikson and Law 1994). Members of heterogeneous working groups offer more creative solution to problems, have the potential for critical thinking, and are less likely to mindlessly conform when confronted with challenges (Cox 1993). However, Cox (1993) contends that members must be skilled in managing diversity if they are to realize the potential benefits of people with diverse backgrounds, talents, and viewpoints. In short, new thinking and interacting skills are becoming highly desirable among employees in diverse workplaces.

However, some form of intergroup training and experience is necessary because schools and neighborhoods have become increasingly racially and socioeconomically segregated in this country. Gary Orfield and associates documented a deepening segregation in American public schools, with nearly three-quarters of Latino and two-thirds of African American students attending predominantly (50–100 percent) nonwhite schools (Orfield et al. 1997). This segregated educational experience often results in students' holding distinct perspectives about the world, harboring stereotypical views of groups outside of their own racial or socioeconomic group, and having very little experience in interacting with diverse peers. Indeed, when confronted with social differences, many individuals seek comfort in the familiarity of others who are like themselves, resulting in somewhat homogeneous friendship patterns, living arrangements, and associates. However, a more diverse workplace is inevitable, and our democracy calls for the participation of citizens in the solution of common problems. Each citizen needs to be better prepared to handle complex problems, engage in ethical decision-making, communicate across social differences, seek commonality, and build community with individuals who come from diverse social identity groups (in terms of social status, background, and history). The intergroup dialogue process allows for social interaction with diverse peers and facilitates learning about others, which in turn increases the probability that participants will develop these necessary skills.

Existing research supports the notion that interaction with someone from a different background, perspective, and experience can stimulate individual development. Classic psychological research and theory indicates that individual cognitive and social development occurs through social interaction, spurred by a disequilibrium that results when one tries to reconcile one's own embedded views with those of others (Piaget 1975). The development of the ability to see the world from someone else's perspective, for example, is facilitated by social interaction because one-sided and one-dimensional perceptions are challenged and must be reexamined in view of the ideas expressed by others. In reconciling the dissonance between one's own one-sided perspective and the point of view of others, the individual progresses to see several dimensions of an issue and learns to take another person's point of view. However, it is clear that the social interaction must be facilitated to provide a safe environment for reconciliation of different perspectives because most of us do not have significant experience handling conflict, nor does knowledge about differing worldviews come naturally. Some individuals prefer to avoid challenges to their own worldview or are in the habit of reducing complex issues to uncompromising dualisms where different perspectives are either "wrong or right," "good or evil," or "for or against" an issue. In contrast, cognitively complex thinkers (rather than dualistic thinkers) are able to demonstrate perspective-taking skills, more sociocentric behaviors, and develop in-depth and societal perspectives about situations and problems (Selman 1980; Perry 1970). These complex thinking and empathic skills can be developed among individuals in interaction with others from distinct group identities, histories, or perspectives.

Educational research also provides compelling evidence to support the premise that interaction with diverse peers enhances learning, civic outcomes, and a broad range of skills. In the National Study for Student Learning, first-year college students who reported interactions with diverse peers (in terms of race, interests, and values) showed a greater openness to diverse perspectives and a willingness to challenge their own beliefs (Pascarella et al. 1996). Researchers also found that students who interacted with diverse peers reported more frequent discussion of complex social issues, including such things as the economy and major social issues such as peace, human rights, equality, and justice (Springer 1995). These studies indicate that students who interact with diverse peers demonstrate more complex thinking that is linked with both cognitive and social development.

Utilizing three distinct longitudinal college student cohorts that participated in College Student Survey and the Cooperative Institutional Research Program's (CIRP) surveys, several studies show that student interaction with racially diverse peers is associated with increases in cultural knowledge and understanding, leadership abilities, and commitment to promoting racial understanding (Milem 1994; Hurtado 2000; Antonio 1998). These outcomes can be considered important values, skills, and knowledge for living in a diverse society. Another CIRP study conducted by Mitchell Chang (1996) identified a positive link between students engaged in dialogue activity (i.e., discussing racial issues) and student performance, persistence in college, intellectual self-confidence, and social self-confidence. Taken together, these findings derived from several different national databases provide consistent evidence for the educational value of interactions with diverse peers that can be facilitated through intergroup dialogue.

However, most of these outcomes can only be achieved when encounters and social interaction are positive in nature. Additional research literature suggests that particular conditions are necessary for intergroup relations to be effective in reducing stereotyping and prejudice, changing attitudes, and building support for policies that improve the circumstances of disadvantaged populations. Gordon Allport (1954) outlined the conditions necessary for positive intergroup relations as part of a "contact hypothesis." Allport hypothesized that prejudices are reduced when members of different groups have equal status in encounters with each other, find ways to work together in the pursuit of common goals, and have contact substantial enough to allow the perception of common interests and humanity among group members. Moreover, contact among members of different groups must be sanctioned by the support of institutional authorities (as in the case of schools, employers, or community leaders). Although the central hypothesis was developed during an era when legalized school segregation was initially contested and old-fashioned racism and prejudice were explicit, many of these conditions for social interaction among different groups remain important today in improving intergroup relations. A recent review of research concluded that "varied research supports the [contact] hypothesis—from field and archival studies to national surveys and laboratory experiments" (Pettigrew 1998, 80).

Subsequent research extends the conditions for contact among individuals from different social backgrounds and perspectives. Most prominent is the recognition of how affiliation with various groups is a part of every individual's social identity that comes into play in social interaction, which is distinct from personal identity. In encountering someone new and different, social identities predominate because expectations for behavior are based on cultural or sociological data (Miller and Steinberg 1975). One's own personal identity does not come into play until relationships become close (Gudykunst 1989). In short, different types of identities are activated in intergroup, as opposed to interpersonal, encounters. Gudykunst and Shapiro (1996) found that when individuals base their interaction on social identities, "they are distancing and differentiating themselves from noningroup members," which can lead to uncertainty and anxiety about interacting with others who are from very different backgrounds. These researchers conclude that uncertainty and anxiety must be managed for effective communication to take place. Pettigrew (1998) contends that the contact situation must have "friendship potential," allowing the personal identities of individuals to emerge. However, in order to extend the positive effects beyond the immediate situation and allow members to develop more positive perceptions of different groups in society, group membership (or social identity) must also be allowed to become salient after threat and anxiety is minimized in the contact situation. Understanding how social identities become activated is one way of managing anxiety, and this is among many of the concepts often taught in the intergroup dialogue process. Work by other researchers has also extended Allport's contact theory by indicating that bias among different social groups is reduced when individuals forge some common identity or seek superordinate group membership (e.g., identifying as American) in addition to their subgroup membership (Gaertner et al. 1994). In some cases, the formation of a new common identity has become a natural outgrowth of participation in intergroup dialogue, which is evident when participants form coalitions or new organizations engaged in social change activities.

This research suggests that attention to the conditions for social interaction among different groups is essential, and that we must create opportunities for sustained and positive intergroup contact if we want individuals to learn from each other and work together to build more vital communities. Many institutional environments have left social interaction among members of different groups to chance, believing that once our organizations became more diverse, we will achieve our goals for a more just society. In fact, increased contact among different groups who have had no previous contact experience can lead to misunderstanding and conflict (Allport 1954). Many intergroup dialogue programs emerged out of the need to proactively address the potential for conflict associated with the development of more diverse communities. In addition to focusing efforts on building more civil communities, specific programs have increasingly turned their attention to building important skills among individuals for thinking, interacting, and becoming a citizen in a diverse democracy. These are illustrated in actual studies of the intergroup dialogue process and its impact on individuals.

Studies of Intergroup Dialogue

The practice of intergroup dialogue and its development in many communities is based on principles derived from years of research conducted in many different settings and empirically tested theory. Many program directors have kept abreast of the latest research in intergroup relations in order to implement these principles and encourage participants to arrive at new understandings of themselves and others from different backgrounds. In addition, several dialogue initiatives have ongoing programs of research and evaluation on the process and its outcomes to gain a better understanding of program impact. Many of the programs featured in the case section of this book provide insights into what coordinators have learned through evaluation efforts.

Table 1 outlines areas for the study of intergroup dialogue. These areas have been categorized according to foci that include *actors, processes,* and *outcomes* of the programs. These areas can be studied across programs or within specific programs. It should be noted that despite a firm grounding in theory and research-based principles, actual research on intergroup dialogue is still in its infancy. The practice of intergroup dialogue has assumed somewhat different implementation models in various settings (Zúñiga and Nagda 2001), which has implications for what is studied, how it is studied, and presumably what conclusions are drawn about the impact of dialogue programs. In the near future, we can expect to learn more from standard methods of studying intergroup dialogue or information about the common features of programs that hold promise for achieving specific goals. Until the results of such cross-program studies are available, how-

TABLE 1. Areas for the Study of Intergroup Dialogue

	Actors	Processes	Outcomes
Across Programs	Coordinators	Institutional support	Overall impact
Within Program	Facilitators	Overall sequence of sessions	Improved climate
	Participants	Group dynamics or change in social interaction, individual change	Increased awareness, attitude change, communication, conflict management, commitment to action and social justice, complex thinking

ever, we know very little about how the programs develop institutional support, or whether slight differences across program processes, organization, or activity have distinct effects on outcomes.

Each program was developed as a solution to intergroup relations issues in its particular context. For this reason, most research on intergroup dialogues has taken place within program-specific contexts as part of an evaluation of the *actors* and of the *processes* that occur at the program and individual level, or of specific *outcomes* related to the goals of the program. Most studies focus on individual participants because researchers and program coordinators attempt to determine the impact of the program on individual dispositions and behavior (Zúñiga et al. 1995; Yeakley 1998; Gurin et al. 1999). A few studies have been conducted on facilitators of dialogue programs who are trained, guide the group learning of participants, and gain insight into improving the process of intergroup dialogue. At the same time, these facilitators or peer trainers grow and change as a result of their involvement in the dialogue activities (Nagda et al. 2001; Tiven 2001; Vasques Scalera 1999). However, no studies have focused on the coordinators as key actors in the development, implementation, and leadership of the programs as of this writing.

Coordinators and researchers have studied at least three different types of *processes* associated with intergroup dialogue. The first is the educational process or the sequence of dialogue sessions, focusing on what participants learn through each phase of activity and whether desired goals were achieved (Zúñiga et al. 1996; Nagda, Zúñiga, and Sevig 1995). Evaluative studies on "best practices" are also conducted to identify key elements of dialogue that appear to be effective in improving intergroup relations (see McCoy and McCormick 2001). Finally, gaps in the knowledge base among participants are sometimes evaluated at the beginning of a dialogue sequence to improve the program's educational process for participants who want or need to learn specific information during the intergroup experience (see Treviño 2001). Attention to the educational process is important because many participants are experiencing intergroup contact at a substantially personal level for the first time.

A second process evident in intergroup dialogue is group dynamics, the study of which involves observing changes in social interaction or collecting personal accounts that offer insight into what actually occurs interpersonally among participants (Yeakley 1998; Vasques Scalera 1999). Greater attention to group dynamics is typically part of the "curriculum" in intergroup dialogue, and more research is needed to understand how conflicts arise and are resolved when "hot button" issues are addressed in group discussions. Increasing individuals' skills to recognize group dynamics and to take responsibility to direct them toward positive ends is essential to resolving conflicts, negotiating solutions to many contemporary problems, and deepening the impact of the dialogue (see Zúñiga and Nagda 2001).

The third process most often studied is the individual change that occurs among participants in the dialogue activity. Personal accounts of the individual change process offer stunning revelations about how individuals come to terms with their own beliefs and fears, identify expectations for encounters with someone from another group, and engage in self-reflection (Zúñiga et al. 1996; Yeakley 1998; Vasques Scalera 1999). In a study of dialogue facilitators, Vasques Scalera (1999) describes the individual change process as a transformative learning process that involves three types of learning: personal (or building self-awareness), emotional (dealing with one's own and other people's feelings), and experiential— where dialogue programs are described as a place to learn by doing, to practice communication skills, to experiment, and to engage in social justice work with others.

In addition to a research focus on the multiple levels of process, many studies on intergroup dialogue have focused on documenting *outcomes* of the programs. At the community level, most dialogue programs seek to promote civility among members and to improve the overall climate for intergroup relations. While it might be well worth the effort to examine the impact of dialogue on the climate of a community, most studies have focused on the impact of the program on a wide array of outcomes for individual participants. This may be because programs wish to document what individuals take away from the experience and want to know if the dialogue experience is beneficial in people's professional or personal lives. Yeakley (1998) found that with increased opportunity for contact among different groups, positive and negative changes can sometimes occur. Positive outcomes resulted when the dialogue group encouraged individuals to share personal experiences and established norms for individuals to learn to disagree with respect.

Researchers have documented increased personal and social awareness regarding the importance of identity, affiliation, and difference, as well as increased knowledge about other groups and discrimination in society (Zúñiga and Sevig 1997; Geranios 1997; Vasques Scalera 1999; Gurin et al. 1999; Nagda et al. 2001). Different types of attitudes and attitude change have also been monitored among participants, including comfort in dealing with diversity or reduction in intergroup anxiety, reduction of stereotyping, and increased tolerance (Nagda 1993; Vasques Scalera 1999). Increased communication skills, ability to manage conflict, growth in perspective-taking skills, and complex thinking have also been noted in several studies (Zúñiga et al. 1995; Zúñiga and Sevig 1997; Gurin 1999; Gurin et al. 1999). These competencies are essential for living in a complex and diverse society.

Perhaps the most compelling evidence of program impact involves studies that have examined individual commitment to take action and participation in social justice issues after the dialogue experience. Researchers have found that participants are interested in taking action (Zúñiga et al. 1995), and long-term occupational outcomes often include social justice work (Vasques Scalera 1999). In one programmatic example (Treviño 2001), former participants of an intergroup dialogue program started an organization and declared themselves allies in seeking to address social justice issues. While it may be that participants entered the dialogue program with a proclivity for these behaviors, the dialogue program appears to provide a supportive environment for the development of social change agents.

Program Evaluation Approaches

The actors, processes, and outcomes of intergroup dialogue programs have been studied using a variety of approaches. The research approach may depend on the focus and goal of the study. For example, some programs require immediate feedback from participants during the sessions, and so they employ exercises, ask participants to turn in journals or essays, or initiate focus group discussions to obtain formative and summative evaluation information. Their goal is to obtain information about how participants experience the dialogue and to use the information as feedback for program design and improvement. In other cases, programs have hired external consultants to observe the dialogues, interview participants, and evaluate program impact. For example, the Study Circles Resource Center (McCoy and McCormick 2001) used external consultants to conduct focus group discussions about "best practices" and to assess successful elements of the dialogue process. The University of Michigan (Thompson, Brett, and Behling 2001) also invited intergroup relations "experts" to conduct an external review of their intergroup relations program, which provided additional validation of many of the internal studies that have been conducted over the years.

Although many studies on intergroup dialogue focus on obtaining information that is used immediately for program improvement, it is important to find a forum to share study results with wider audiences of both practitioners and scholars. The study of intergroup dialogue offers great possibilities for advancing the knowledge base about intergroup relations, conflict negotiation, and education for participation in diverse democracy. This is primarily because dialogue occurs in a natural setting, rather than a contrived or hypothetical situation that has been the basis of experimental and intergroup relations studies (Yeakley 1998). Most intergroup dialogues are formed in response to an actual conflict, and real problems are dealt with during the sessions. Therefore, studies on intergroup dialogue offer an important window on individual growth and group dynamics that can advance our recognition of human resources that come from diverse groups in our community and can help us work cooperatively to solve important social problems.

Some program directors actually wear two hats, one of coordinator of intergroup relations work and another of researcher. In this case, some of the evaluation work actually evolves into an action research approach—where attention to method is rigorous but the researcher does not pretend to be "disinterested," looks for indications that suggest modification of practice, avoids experimental methods that require "distancing" oneself, and is interested in making the most of the research to achieve social change. However, assuming such a dual role is difficult because of the high demands of both maintaining the vitality of the program and conducting ongoing studies of intergroup dialogue. More often than not, program directors find collaborators who have a keen interest in advancing the knowledge base that can be gleaned from the practice of intergroup dialogue.

If the focus of the study is attention to process, researchers have used qualitative approach techniques that include individual interviews with participants and facilitators, essays or self-reflective papers, and journals about the experience (Zúñiga et al. 1996; Yeakley 1998; Vasques Scalera 1999). Another approach is to ask participants to respond to scenarios to determine how they think about difference, conflict, and complex issues. Themes may be drawn across these sources of information to highlight experiences and personal accounts about the process, backgrounds of participants, reexamination of values and beliefs, and new outcomes of intergroup dialogue.

Survey research has been employed using information about a range of outcomes before beginning and typically some time after participation in intergroup dialogue. These longitudinal designs are best conducted on larger samples of participants to understand average change or the impact of the program on well-defined outcomes. Most typically, studies have also employed comparison groups to determine if the changes are greater among those who have participated in dialogue relative to nonparticipants. Several research approaches have followed up participants and comparison groups for up to four years. These studies confirm identity development, more comfort with conflict as a normal part of social life, more positive intergroup interactions, and long-term effects on participation in activities with members of other racial/ethnic groups among dialogue participants (Gurin et al. 1999; Zúñiga et al. 1995).

Longitudinal research designs are optimal for assessing change in individuals; however, several difficulties arise. Keeping track of participants is difficult for programs where community members are highly mobile. Minimizing response bias through high response rates is challenging given that surveys compete for attention with increasing junk mail and telemarketing firms. And over time, individuals may have additional positive or negative experiences in intergroup contact. Singling out the impact of intergroup dialogue is more difficult over time unless the study takes into account these intermediate experiences that can reinforce or negate participants' intergroup relations skills. Undoubtedly, various experiences can reinforce participants' learning processes in intergroup dialogue, as participants have related that it becomes "impossible to see the world in the same way" after an intensive dialogue experience. An astute researcher can help determine relevant experiences that must be taken into account to uncover how intergroup dialogue works and its overall impact on communities or individual participants over time.

Conclusion

The numerous studies detailed in this chapter are evidence of researchers' diligent work to uncover the positive impact of intergroup dialogue and share findings with educators, community representatives, and scholars from various fields of study. Intergroup relations issues are here to stay, and we continue to face difficult social problems that are the result of intergroup conflict, inequality, and violence. Continuing research and the practice of intergroup dialogue provide concrete ways to proactively address these issues and make changes in communities.

A final point on dialogue research is offered for readers who find the intergroup dialogue models in this book exciting and compelling enough to adopt in their communities. In initiating an intergroup dialogue program, it is important to lay out the goals or intended outcomes. Plans can be drawn for a sensitive and appropriate research approach that will help determine whether the goals are achieved by the program. Clear goals help keep the program focused and will clarify the information you wish to obtain through an appropriate research approach. At the same time, however, it is important to be flexible enough in one's approach to discover important but unintended outcomes. There is much we have yet to learn about intergroup relations in our society. The need for cooperation among members of different groups is paramount if we wish to build a just society, create an inclusive democracy, and make use of the vast reserves of human talent that misunderstanding and exclusion have kept hidden in our communities for so long.

REFERENCES

Allport, G. W. 1954. *The Nature of Prejudice.* Cambridge, Mass.: Addison-Wesley.

Antonio, A. L. 1998. "The Impact of Friendship Groups in a Multicultural University." Ph.D. diss., University of California, Los Angeles.

Bikson, T. K., and S. A. Law. 1994. *Global Preparedness and Human Resources.* Santa Monica, Calif.: RAND Institute.

Chang, M. 1996. "Racial Diversity in Higher Education: Does a Racially Mixed Student Population Affect Educational Outcomes?" Ph.D. diss., University of California, Los Angeles.

Cox, T., Jr. 1993. *Cultural Diversity in Organizations: Theory, Research, and Practice.* San Francisco: Berrett-Koehler.

Gaertner, S. L., M. C. Rust, J. F. Dovidio, B. A. Bachman, and P. A. Anastasio. 1994. "The Contact Hypothesis: The Role of Common In-Group Identity on Reducing Intergroup Bias." *Small Group Research* 25:224–49.

Geranios, C. A. 1997. "Cognitive, Affective, and Behavioral Outcomes of Multicultural Courses and Intergroup Dialogues in Higher Education." Ph.D. diss., Arizona State University, Tempe.

Guarasci, R., G. H. Cornwell, and associates. 1997. *Democratic Education in an Age of Difference: Redefining Citizenship in Higher Education.* San Francisco: Jossey-Bass.

Gudykunst, W. B. 1989. "Culture and Communication in Interpersonal Relationships." In *Communication Yearbook,* ed. J. Andersen, 12:315–54. Newbury Park, Calif.: Sage.

Gudykunst, W. B., and R. B. Shapiro. 1996. "Communication in Everyday Interpersonal and Intergroup Encounters." *International Journal of Intercultural Relations* 20, no. 1: 19–45.

Gurin, P. 1999. Expert witness report, "The Compelling Need for Diversity in Higher Education." Presented in *Gratz et al. v. Bollinger et al.,* No. 97–75231 (E.D. Michigan), and *Grutter et al. v. Bollinger et al.,* No. 97–75928 (E.D. Michigan).

Gurin, P., T. Peng, G. Lopez, and B. A. Nagda. 1999. "Context, Identity, and Intergroup Relations." In *Cultural Divides: Understanding and Overcoming Group Conflict,* ed. D. A. Prentice and D. T. Miller. New York: Russell Sage Foundation.

Hurtado, S. 2000. "Linking Diversity with Educational Purpose: How Diversity Impacts the Classroom Environment and Student Development." In *Diversity Challenged: Legal Crisis and New Evidence,* ed. G. Orfield. Cambridge, Mass.: Harvard Publishing Group.

Johnston, W. B. 1987. *Workforce 2000: Work and Workers for the 21st Century.* Indianapolis, In.: Hudson Institute.

McCoy, M., and M. McCormick. 2001. "Engaging the Whole Community in Dialogue and Action: Study Circles Resource Center." In this volume.

Milem, J. F. 1994. "College, Students, and Racial Understanding." *Thought and Action* 9, no. 2: 51–92.

Miller, G. R., and M. Steinberg. 1975. *Between People.* Chicago: Science Research Associates.

Nagda, B. A. 1993. "Dialogue across Difference: Toward Multicultural Integration." Paper presented at the Annual Meeting of the American Psychological Association, Toronto, August.

Nagda, B. A., S. Harding, D. Moise-Swanson, M. L. Balassone, M. Spearmon, and

S. de Mello. 2001. "Intergroup Dialogue, Education, and Action: Innovations in a School of Social Work." In this volume.

Nagda, B. A., X. Zúñiga, and T. D. Sevig. 1995. "Bridging Difference through Peer-Facilitated Intergroup Dialogues." In *Peer Programs on a College Campus: Theory, Training, and "Voice of Peers,"* ed. S. Hatcher. San Jose, Calif.: Resource Publications.

Orfield, G., M. D. Bachmeier, D. R. James, and T. Eitle. 1997. "Deepening Segregation in American Public Schools: A Special Report from the Harvard Project on School Desegregation." *Equity and Excellence in Education* 30, no. 2: 5–28.

Pascarella, E. T., M. Edison, A. Nora, L. S. Hagedorn, and P. T. Terenzini. 1996. "Influences on Students' Openness to Diversity and Challenge in the First Year of College." *Journal of Higher Education* 67, no. 2: 174–95.

Perry, W. 1970. *Forms of Intellectual and Ethical Development in the College Years: A Scheme.* New York: Holt, Rinehart and Winston.

Pettigrew, T. F. 1998. "Intergroup Contact Theory." *Annual Review of Psychology* 49:65–85.

Piaget, J. 1975. *The Equilibration of Cognitive Structures: The Central Problem of Intellectual Development.* Chicago: University of Chicago Press.

Selman, R. L. 1980. *The Growth of Interpersonal Understanding: Developmental and Clinical Analyses.* New York: Academic Press.

Springer, L. 1995. "Do White Students Perceive Racism toward Minority Students on Predominantly White Campuses?" Paper presented at the Annual Meeting of the American Educational Research Association, San Francisco, April.

Thompson, M. C., T. G. Brett, and C. Behling. 2001. "Educating for Social Justice: The Program on Intergroup Relations, Conflict, and Community at the University of Michigan." In this volume.

Tiven, L. 2001. "Student Voices: The ADL's A WORLD OF DIFFERENCE Institute Peer Training Program." In this volume.

Treviño, J. 2001. "Voices of Discovery: Intergroup Dialogues at Arizona State University." In this volume.

Vasques Scalera, C. M. 1999. "Democracy, Diversity, and Dialogue: Education for Critical Multicultural Citizenship." Ph.D. diss., University of Michigan.

Yeakley, A. M. 1998. "The Nature of Prejudice Change: Positive and Negative Change Processes Arising from Intergroup Contact Experience." Ph.D. diss., University of Michigan.

Zúñiga, X., and R. A. Nagda. 2001. "Design Considerations in Intergroup Dialogue." In this volume.

Zúñiga, X., B. A. Nagda, T. D. Sevig, M. Thompson, and E. L. Dey. 1995. "Speaking the Unspeakable: Student Learning Outcomes in Intergroup Dialogues on a

College Campus." Paper presented at the Annual Meeting of the Association for the Study of Higher Education, Orlando, Fla., November.

Zúñiga, X., and T. Sevig. 1997. "Bridging the 'Us/Them' Divide through Intergroup Dialogue and Peer Leadership." *Diversity Factor* 5, no. 2: 22–28.

Zúñiga, X., C. M. Vasques, T. D. Sevig, and B. A. Nagda. 1996. "Dismantling the Walls: Peer-Facilitated Inter-Race/Ethnic Dialogue Processes and Experiences." Program on Conflict Management Alternatives Working Paper Series no. 49, University of Michigan.

Case Studies

Introduction

The twelve case studies that follow capture the efforts of practitioners from some of the leading organizations in the nation to implement intergroup dialogue programs. These cases demonstrate in their program descriptions the theoretical ideals and critical challenges of intergroup dialogue that have been outlined in the prior chapters and in the chapters that follow. Some of these programs have a local/regional focus, and others have a national outreach focus. Some of the cases are written by the directors and/or practitioners of these programs, and others by outside consultants working with different agencies and businesses.

The case studies are organized by intergroup dialogue programs located in K–12 schools, colleges and universities, community settings, and the corporate workplace. In a number of cases, the practitioners and/or their organizations cross naturally between these settings. In other cases, however, the distinctions, practices, boundaries, and challenges are unique to the particular setting, and there is little conversation across settings. Illustrative of these distinctions, the chapters represent in both the content and written style of their case studies the diversity of approaches to intergroup dialogue. We embrace this diversity of approaches and find much to learn from their common themes and also their different perspectives.

All of the authors of these case studies do address the following topics: (1) the institutional context for starting the program as well as its philosophy and rationale; (2) a description of the program components and program in practice; (3) a discussion of the methodology and process of the dialogues; (4) the successes and challenges facing the program and its intergroup dialogue efforts; and (5) evaluation data.

Tina Fernandez describes the multifaceted effort of Bridges to address through intergroup dialogue dramatic demographic changes that have taken place in Orange County, California, involving two elementary schools, thirty-five middle schools, and twenty-two high schools. Fernandez describes the carefully developed components of assessment, school-based human relations task forces, staff development, and schoolwide projects. However, the focus of the program and the chapter are highly effective intergroup dialogues that take place within human relations retreats held outside the school grounds.

The value and practice of peer training, students teaching other students, for intergroup dialogue is the focus of Lorraine Tiven's case study of the important Anti-Defamation League program involving school/ community collaboration. Tiven documents the successes and challenges for the eighteen hundred students who have participated in this intensive training in over thirty-five middle schools and high schools as well as in the Boys and Girls Clubs of America.

In contrast to the peer-training approach described by Tiven, Joseph McKenna and James Sauceda discuss Students Talk About Race, in which carefully trained college students facilitate dialogues with high school students. This very successful program has reached over twenty thousand students, and evaluative research has documented its practice as an intervention for prejudice reduction.

Jesús Treviño's discussion of Voices of Discovery moves the case studies' discussion to college-based programs. This dynamic and innovative program at Arizona State University provides college students with a structured opportunity to address in a substantive way various dimensions of intergroup relations through dialogue. Treviño thoughtfully describes the program's creation, growth, and development and the careful evaluative studies that point to successes and challenges.

The University of Michigan's program, perhaps the oldest university dialogue program in the United States, has served as the prototype for other universities planning to start their own intergroup dialogue program. Monita Thompson, Teresa Graham Brett, and Charles Behling describe the different program components, their stage approach to intergroup dialogues, and their training of peer undergraduate facilitators to lead the dialogues. This program is also noteworthy for its joint sponsorship by Academic Affairs and Student Affairs units at the university.

Intergroup Dialogue, Education, and Action is an exemplary model of a program developed to incorporate intergroup dialogue as part of professional training. Other professional schools will surely follow their lead in the future. In this case, undergraduates at the School of Social Work at the University of Washington participate in intergroup dialogues to prepare themselves personally and professionally for their careers. Biren (Ratnesh) Nagda and his colleagues have developed a careful evaluation of the program's impact on students and offer a detailed analysis of challenges they face.

Martha McCoy and Michael McCormick begin the discussion of case studies of intergroup dialogue at the community level by describing the nationally acclaimed efforts of the Study Circles Resource Center. This program has reached thousands of people in hundreds of intergroup dialogues organized in neighborhoods, towns, cities, counties, and states. The authors describe and analyze the complex task of working with communities to develop an intergroup dialogue practice best suited to the local setting and "owned" by the local participants, yet still compatible with the format and design of SCRC.

Hope in the Cities began its work in Richmond, Virginia, and, as a result of its highly successful approach, has expanded its work to cities across the country. Karen Elliott Greisdorf describes their six-stage sustained dialogue process that attempts to go beyond intellectual understandings of racism to moral and spiritual insights as well. She discusses HIC's attempts to balance its structured format with flexibility to meet community needs, and she analyzes the different expectations and responses of whites and people of color to the dialogue experiences.

Wayne Winborne and Allison Smith give the reader a firsthand view of intergroup dialogue through the experience of four regional intergroup dialogue efforts organized by the highly respected National Conference for Community and Justice. They describe their flexibility and skill in customizing intergroup dialogue to meet the needs of particular regions based on their unique histories and contexts. These approaches range from a multilingual emphasis in the Neighbors in Dialogue process in Los Angeles, to the Dinner and Dialogue Series in Birmingham, to the high school age focus of the Voices of Youth Initiative in Buffalo, to the living room and workplace dialogues of community members of the CommUnity Initiative in Cincinnati.

Rita Hardiman and Bailey Jackson introduce the experience of case studies of intergroup dialogue in the workplace. As consultants to corporations, they describe the complex dynamics of organizing and facilitating such dialogues and the risks and possibilities for those participating. The examples they offer provide valuable insights into the opportunity that intergroup dialogue holds for change for both individuals in the workplace and the corporation itself and, importantly, the structural and intergroup barriers that serve as impediments to change.

Gretchen Groth takes the reader through a probing analysis of the predominant models of intergroup dialogue in the corporate setting. She contrasts the common use of dialogue in corporations as an effort to advance the profit goal (among other goals) of the business with core principles such as justice and equity associated with intergroup dialogue. Groth also examines the corporate emphasis on dialogue on individual and interpersonal behavior rather than on intergroup behavior or organizational change strategies that are core principles associated with intergroup dialogue.

Maria Ramos and Cassandra Mitchell provide their thoughtful insights and analyses of an intergroup dialogue intervention at one corporation. They take the reader through the step-by-step details of this particular case, offering the reader an unusual firsthand look at the opportunities and challenges of this work. This chapter brings together consultant and corporate management perspectives to review and reexamine the intergroup dialogue experience.

Case Studies: School

Chapter 3

Building "Bridges" of Understanding through Dialogue

Tina Fernandez

Dialogue was the basis for the creation of the Orange County Human Relations Council's Bridges: A School Inter-Ethnic Relations Program (SIERP). We understood the power that people's words, experiences, and pain would have on each other. The need to be heard, to be listened to, is a most powerful one.

Eleven years ago we were called to work at a high school by the principal after a "racial incident" took place. The incident involved white cheerleaders who dressed up as African-Americans by painting their faces black, padding their derrieres, and putting on "Afro wigs" for a skit at an outdoor pep rally. They danced and lip-synched a song during the pep rally. They got a loud and positive reception from most of the student body, but the response by the few African-American students on campus was not the same.

The African-American students felt that they had been the objects of ridicule because of who they were and what they looked like. The white cheerleaders had not performed their skit with the intent to put down, demean, or laugh at the expense of the African-American students. The principal believed the effect on the school was serious enough to merit a response. The Orange County Human Relations Council (OCHRC) was called in. We asked the principal to bring together the students and parents who perceived themselves as the victims/aggrieved in the incident, as well the perceived perpetrators. Our staff acted as the facilitators in this meeting.

During this dialogue students were asked to describe the incident as they understood it, as it affected them. As each person had the opportunity to share his or her side of the story, it became apparent to all that everyone had a different perspective on what had been done, what their intent had been, and how people should have responded. Strong feelings of pain and betrayal were shared. Empathy and apologies were offered and accepted. Students did not feel that relations would ever be as they had been before, but they believed that this incident, which had affected some so deeply, could and should bring greater understanding among students.

The dialogues were expanded into "student human relations retreats." Student leaders, both official and unofficial—students who had influence over other students but had no official position—were identified and asked to participate. The group was representative of the school by gender and ethnicity. Students were told that they were special individuals who were believed to deeply care about their school.

Several of these all-day student human relations retreats took place outside of the school campus. The format for these dialogues empowered and engaged students to be the leaders on their campus who would make a difference, who would be role models of positive human relations because they had been witness to the pain, the fear, the anger, and the loneliness that comes with being prejudged, stereotyped, and discriminated against. These students would carry the message to the rest of the student body that racial animosity was not what their campus should be about. Students began planning for a school event that would bring the message they had heard to other students, to teachers, and to other school staff. All of these observations by our staff, the students, and the principal were the impetus for a process that would be used to approach schools in crisis situations, such as that found in this school, as well as schools that wanted to take a proactive approach to human relations.

From Reactive to Proactive

As our county grew more diverse over the following ten years, it became incumbent upon us to collaborate with communities and institutions to hold out the promise that tomorrow we could have a community where all are valued and included. In 1995, county demographics showed that the minority communities represented 41 percent of the total population, with African-Americans representing 2 percent, Latinos 27 percent, and Asians 12 percent. Our school demographics, however, showed our minority student population at 54 percent of total K–12 students. African-Americans represented 2.3 percent, Latinos 37 percent, Asians 14.1 percent, and American Indians 0.6 percent of all students. The most current school figures, September 1998, show that white students now, only three years later, make up 43 percent of all students.

Our organization, the Orange County Human Relations Commission, a county government agency, and the Orange County Human Relations

Council, a nonprofit organization, created six years ago to support the work of the commission, created a school program that fit the mission of both organizations, "to provide programs to foster mutual understanding among residents in order to make Orange County a better place for ALL people to live, work and do business." Both of these organizations are under one roof, sharing staff and other resources, and working together to provide a variety of community-based approaches to organizational change in the area of human relations.

We work closely and collaboratively with our county office of education and other human relations organizations, like the National Conference for Community and Justice, the Anti-Defamation League, and the Gay, Lesbian, Straight Education Network on various school-related projects. Schools and school districts approach us to provide human relations work through our Bridges: School Inter-Ethnic Relations Program. Through the OCHRC we also provide mediation services to parents, students, teachers, and other school staff working to solve educational disputes.

Our schools have experienced bias-related incidents that have prompted administrators and teachers to seek help building interethnic communication, cohesion, and a sense of community on their campuses. For the most part, this help has been found outside of the regular educational setting. Our organization has worked successfully with schools throughout Orange County to address these challenges with interethnic relations, conflict management, and violence prevention programs. We currently have human relations programs in two elementary schools, thirty-five middle or intermediate schools, and twenty-two high schools.

How "Bridges" Works

The mission of the program is to "improve inter-group relations on a school campus by enabling a representative group of school community members, students, teachers, parents, other school staff and interested community members to work collaboratively toward creating and sustaining a safe, inclusive school climate that is respectful of society's diversity." The program is uniquely designed to meet each individual school's needs and objectives by cooperatively involving the whole school community. We concentrate on training and encouraging students, parents, and teachers to use positive peer support to promote intergroup understanding.

In elementary schools, the program focuses on parent and teacher participation in a planning effort to build understanding and acceptance for people who are different. This can include adult human relations retreats, student human relations retreats with fifth and sixth graders, in-service training for teachers and other staff, and classroom presentations of age-appropriate curriculum. We offer a broad variety of curriculum and other resources geared for teachers and parent volunteers.

In middle or intermediate school, young people go through some of the most dramatic physical, emotional, and hormonal changes that human beings encounter in life. When this period of great inner turmoil is coupled with the rapidly changing diversity, we see challenging times for schools. Our middle school program begins with a "leadership consultation," an orientation and assessment done with the principal and his or her leadership team. A collaborative process then follows that includes all participants of the school community in building and implementing a multifaceted plan to promote interethnic understanding and a positive climate on campus. Parents, students, teachers, and other staff are also included in the process from the beginning.

The high school interethnic relations and violence prevention programs were developed over the last ten years to work to restore and develop a sense of understanding and school spirit inclusive of the diversity that exists. This age group requires a student-centered approach; thus the program focuses on positive peer pressure as well as working with parents, teachers, and other staff.

A comprehensive human relations program at Bridges schools includes the following components:

The *leadership team consultation* provides an introduction to the program that includes assessment of each school's needs and identifies objectives. It includes the principal, a teacher who will be our contact, a parent, and at times a custodian and a student.

The school's *human relations task force* identifies needs and establishes short-term and long-term objectives to improve the intergroup relations climate on campus by bringing together five teachers, five parents, five school staff—usually including the principal—and ten to fifteen students to dialogue for an all-day human relations retreat.

Twenty-five to thirty students participate in all-day *student human relations retreats* to increase student awareness, encourage dialogue about diversity issues, evaluate the school interethnic relations climate, and build enthusiasm for the task force efforts.

Staff development sessions are held with teachers and administrators in order to address the specific needs of the staff. These sessions can include building awareness, dealing with prejudice and conflict management in the classroom, and incorporating diversity into the curriculum.

The development of *schoolwide projects* comes out of the efforts of the human relations task force, student human relations retreats, and staff development sessions. School projects help the students and teachers convey their new understanding to the entire student body.

Currently our program employs eight professional staff, each of whom has responsibility for human relations programs at eight schools. Their assignments include a combination of middle and high schools. School programs include the five components previously described. During an academic year, the task force is scheduled within a month of the leadership consultation, usually in September or October. Three to four student task force retreats are then scheduled between October and January. Staff developments can take place at any time during the school year, but schools are encouraged to schedule these between October and March. Schoolwide projects are usually implemented during the spring, between February and April.

Our organization also provides a variety of support to our contracted schools, as well as to nonparticipating schools:

An annual middle and high school student symposium in intercultural cooperation, Walk in My Shoes, brings together more than eight hundred students and teachers from all over our county to foster greater understanding of the challenges and positive responses to the rapidly increasing ethnic diversity in schools.

A three-volume video series, *Stop in Your Tracks,* produced by OCHRC, addresses themes such as what makes us angry, why we fight, and how to manage anger. Through interactive and experiential activities, the curriculum engages students in dialogues about the conflict that they may face at school, at home, and in the community. Teacher training and classroom presentations are conducted.

A new youth campaign, What Do You See? features a series of four posters of local high school students to teach about stereotyping. An accompanying twenty-eight-minute video compliments the posters with powerful images of the consequences of prejudice. As in other program components, the purpose is to get students to talk about their individual experiences with stereotyping in order to create understanding and a commitment "to do something about it."

An annual Human Relations School Awards Ceremony recognizes elementary, middle, and high schools for their outstanding efforts in promoting, nurturing, protecting, and cultivating a safe campus climate that is respectful of their diversity. Fifteen local schools have been awarded this recognition in the first three years of the program. A monetary award is part of the recognition.

The Hate Crime Education Committee works in collaboration with our Hate Crime Network, to convene a countywide network of law enforcement, education leaders, and community groups to document hate-related crimes and incidents and publish that data. The committee provides support for hate crime victims and assistance to schools in responding to incidents. It works with school districts to develop policies and conducts training for educators, police officials, and community members on school hate crime protocol.

The Human Relations Leadership Institute is a weeklong summer training that provides high school and middle school students with advanced skill training, a deeper awareness of human relations, and a forum to participate in open dialogue. Fifty students participate in the program each year.

The Human Relations Associate Program, a new yearlong certificate and internship program, provides advanced leadership training in human relations issues and skills by having twenty students participate in dialogues, project planning, and mentoring with OCHRC staff.

The Parent Leadership Institute, an intensive fifteen-hour training program, builds the skills and abilities of non-English-speaking parents so they can be more effectively involved in their children's schools.

Since a school's human relations task force requires the involvement of a diverse group of parent leaders, this program prepares parents for this type of participation.

A variety of videos, curriculum materials, exercises, and books on human relations topics is made available to teachers and other school staff on a check-out basis. Other professional staff and volunteers are available as resources to schools and community members on intergroup tension and violence.

Listening to Others and Being Heard

Many of the components described above, including the supporting projects, use dialogues between students, between adults, or across generations. All of these are powerful methods to get people "to get into the shoes of the other" (Lippitt 1949).

The two components that allow for the most powerful use of dialogues are the human relations task force retreats and the student human relations retreats. Our staff works closely with our teacher contact and the principal to schedule the date, time, and location where these will be held. We encourage schools to secure locations outside of the school campus. This helps to create an environment different from the school's. It is quieter, participants cannot easily leave for short periods of time, there are fewer distractions, and it makes for a special event. We also work with the school to select participants to be invited based on a few guidelines: there should be equal numbers of boys and girls; traditional and "untraditional" leaders should be included; the ethnic diversity of the school should be represented; and participating students are expected to be active in improving the human relations climate on campus.

The retreats are designed to begin the dialogue; they are the beginning of a process. They give participants an overview of human relations and help them to explore and come to understand prejudice, stereotyping, racism, and discrimination with others who have been victimized as well as those who may have been perpetrators. From this point, participants can become actively involved in developing ways to combat discrimination.

The student human relations retreat goals are to (1) increase understanding about the diverse individuals that make up the school; (2) break down stereotypes that limit perceptions of others; (3) reduce intergroup tension and conflict on campus, and therefore build understanding among individuals and between different groups of students; and (4) develop action plans to improve the human relations climate at the school.

The retreats begin with the school's leadership, usually the principal, giving a brief introduction that includes the reason why the group has been assembled. The leader emphasizes that participants are a special group with an important task and makes a brief statement of his or her expectations. Our staff person continues with introductions and a review of the day's agenda. An "ice-breaker" follows to get students moving and interacting a little. The climate of trust and support is created by having the group agreeing to basic "community" guidelines for participation: be honest; speak for yourself; respect confidentiality; participate in risk sharing; listen—don't interrupt; try not to judge one another; and be open to different experiences, opinions, communication styles, and so on.

A "getting to know you" activity usually follows. One favorite has been an adaptation of "Family Search and Research" (Smith and Otero 1989). Students are asked to share something that is important to them about their cultural heritage. The activity helps students become aware of the diversity that exists in the group, increases their trust in one another, and involves them in an exploration of knowledge about their own culture through their families' history. In debriefing the activity, students make the observation that there are many differences among students but just as many similarities.

The next activity, "What Do You See?" begins the exploration of students' own prejudices. Using four posters of four local high school students, students are asked to work in small groups to identify characteristics about these four individuals just by looking at them. After a few minutes students are asked to share their stories about these young people with the rest of the group. It doesn't take too long before someone makes the observation that they have been making assumptions about these young people. They have been stereotyping. Discussions include prejudice, stereotyping, and the effects of these behaviors. The activity ends with the students getting very close to the posters to read each young person's story, which is not observable until you are only a few inches away from the poster.

In the last two activities, participants rate the intergroup climate at their school and suggest how to improve it. These activities concentrate on defining and developing action strategies to improve human relations at school campuses. Students explore possible action strategies, define and develop a specific course of action to improve their school's human relations climate, and name the next steps for their continued exploration of personal prejudices.

Before concluding the session, participants are asked if they are ready to make a personal commitment to improve the human relations climate on their campus. A go-around offers participants the opportunity to state one thing that they learned that day and one thing they will do differently.

The retreat can be staffed in a variety of ways. Our most common format is using one staff person as the facilitator and having at least two teachers from the school present. The size of the student group ranges from twenty to no more than forty students, with the ideal number being twenty-five to thirty.

The human relations retreats can be used and applied in many contexts and formats, depending on the setting and the time limitations. The key to an effective program is to maintain flexibility and adaptability. A little imagination and knowledge of the group's needs is vital. The more the content of the program focuses on the issues that reflect the participants' world, the more investment they will probably make, and the greater the degree of learning.

The cross-generational human relations task force retreats are very similar in format to the student human relations retreats. Students, parents, teachers, and other school staff work on comparable activities that support equal status dialogue. Participants are always amazed at how much they learn about each other.

Does It Work?

One of the questions raised with any form of human relations work is its effectiveness. We ask ourselves the following: Are we really changing behavior, or are people merely becoming more knowledgeable about their prejudices? We know that awareness is not enough, which is why our program is designed to follow up throughout the school year to see if behavior is changing. Assessment of the success of the schoolwide projects—how many students are involved in planning the event, how many students are reached through the awareness campaigns, how many teachers have changed their curricula or have addressed themes of intergroup relations in their courses—focuses on individual behavior as well as school behavior.

We continually work to relate our program design to the "essential principles" from the Program Design for Reducing Racial and Ethnic Prejudice (Hawley and Jackson 1995), developed by the Consensus Panel on Race Relations, Common Destiny Alliance. Researchers at the Common Destiny Alliance reviewed many programs and found that most only incorporated two or three of these principles. Our SIERP, established more than ten years ago, has nine of the thirteen principles at the core of the program.

The program addresses both instructional and individual sources of prejudice and discrimination in the contexts and situation in which the students learn.

Strategies seek to influence the behavior of individuals and are not limited to increasing knowledge and awareness.

Participants are included who reflect the racial, ethnic, and linguistic diversity and ensure cooperative, equal-status roles for persons from different groups.

Strategies include highly focused activities and efforts to ensure that positive intergroup relations are pursued throughout the school.

Strategies examine similarities and differences across and within ethnic groups.

Strategies expose the inaccuracies of myths that sustain stereotypes and prejudices.

Our trained staff works with a school team to implement the learning activities.

We work with the school to assess its needs and continually evaluate the program at each school.

We emphasize that prejudice and its consequences belong to everyone at the school, not just to ethnic minority members.

A key to the success of Bridges is our professional staff. Human relations specialists are assigned to work with several schools as facilitators. They have a good understanding of human relations and participatory decision making processes and have good facilitation skills. Awareness on a personal level of their own prejudices and assumptions is essential. The ability to analyze and describe racism on an institutional and cultural level is also important. To try to facilitate these dialogues without a good understanding and working knowledge of the dynamics of racism not only will cause the dialogue to be ineffective but also may perpetuate the participants' racism, as well as the facilitator's.

Human relations are complex and encompass a wide range of behaviors. Change sometimes comes slowly. Participants may leave the program with little or no apparent change in their perspectives, but in time they may begin to see themselves in a new light. Others may also be seeing them this way. Developing awareness, accepting and owning one's prejudices, and developing ways to change are difficult tasks. SIERP has been successful in helping participants take the first few steps in that process.

> Academic achievement suffers if there is not an ambiance of safety, comfort, appreciation and respect. The OCHRC are critical to the academic achievement of our schools ultimately. I'm very pleased to have the Bridges program in our community. It's made a difference in our junior high and high schools. It's making a difference in the community. It's not only worthwhile, but it's going to have some far-reaching effects. Bridges is a program that will impact all of us. (Dr. Janice Billings, Superintendent, Anaheim Union High School District, 1998)

During the eighth year of the SIERP a minievaluation was implemented in four middle schools in one of the county's largest and more diverse districts.

Instruments tailored to the philosophy and characteristics of SIERP were created for students, for faculty, and for parents. The Likert-type instruments were created jointly by SIERP staff and an outside evaluator contracted for this project. The student instrument was designed to produce data suited to the measurement of the outcomes that are produced by the program. Commitment, fairness, inclusion/access/affiliation, safety, openness/tolerance, and comfort were the identified factors. The final design was an attitude scale, probing beliefs and attitudes rather than knowledge.

The faculty instrument probed three levels of perception: the urgency of dealing with the realities of diversity; the policy currently in place to create and sustain a safe school climate that is respectful of society's diversity; and the value of certain strategies for creating and sustaining a safe school climate that is respectful of society's diversity.

The parent instrument probed two major areas of parent perception: what the parents have experienced personally in their relations with the school and what they have heard from their students with regard to issues of safety, prejudice, and inclusion.

The final report presented a description of the climate at the schools based on the data. The evaluator prefaced his report by stating the following:

> Does SIERP make a difference? Certainly it does. The differences are seen most clearly in the behavior of retreat participants. The unbiased observer is struck with the positive responses of students and adults alike. Differences are also seen in the school-wide projects. These are a direct result of the task force and retreat work (Piper 1998).

The students who were surveyed perceived the climate at the schools to include an active commitment to "creating and sustaining a safe, inclusive school climate that is respectful of society's diversity." They felt that they were being treated fairly, knew people from different backgrounds and got along fine, were willing to make friends with students from other countries and even appreciate their cultures, and for the most part felt safe. The faculty responses showed that teachers had positive views of policies in place "to create and sustain a safe school climate" and that strategies needed to be implemented, even though faculty could not agree on specific approaches. The findings of the parents' responses were inconclusive.

The Challenges

Observations by participants and members of the community are a great impetus for continuing our work. There are, however, some ways in which the institutionalization and continuity of the overall program could be strengthened. We have also struggled to find appropriate instruments to measure attitudinal change as well as behavior and institutional change.

A challenge the program needs to overcome is its dependence on the teacher contact. Some of our teachers are overwhelmed with classroom and other school responsibilities. It is difficult for them to take on another responsibility, but they do so because they are driven by passion for their work and caring for their students. They are truly amazing. The way kids relate to each other is important to them, sometimes for very personal reasons. Some of them see themselves in the stories of pain that students share. Their own experiences become strong motivators. This dedication and drive has caused the program at some schools to appear to be the individual teacher's rather than the school's. Colleagues may see the human relations activities as belonging to that one teacher and thus not take ownership of the human relations climate at their school, as something that belongs to all of them. If the teacher with whom the program is identified leaves the school, the program may leave too.

Another variable that is sometimes beyond our control is the internal "politics" of the school. It is important to pick the best possible candidate to be the school contact. It may be difficult for our staff to be involved in this administrative decision initially, when we have not identified key supporters or allies. Sometimes principals are transferred from school to school; we then lose our strongest administrative ally. Our principals usually do such a terrific job with the program that the district office often promotes them out of the school to a higher-level administrative job.

Other challenges to the institutionalization of our work include the highly mobile student population. In middle schools we have only two or three years to work with students before they are off to high school. Their new school may not have a human relations program, so that young persons' growth in unlearning prejudice and other "isms" will have ended unless their own initiative drives them to continue.

Our organization's dream is to have programs across grade levels and across schools, so this type of dialogue will be part of a students' entire school experience. Teachers, administrators, and other school staff should be encouraged to participate in ongoing awareness, knowledge, and skill building in human relations. Curriculum in all academic areas should have human relations strands woven throughout the year and throughout the grade levels. Derman-Sparks (1989, ix) says that the best way to do this is to ensure that the curriculum "enables every child: to construct a knowledgeable, confident self-identity; to develop comfortable, empathetic, and just interaction with diversity; and to develop critical thinking and the skills for standing up for oneself and others in the face of injustice."

The institution of the school will not "create and sustain a safe, inclusive climate that is respectful of society's diversity" if the individuals that make up that institution have not had the opportunity to dialogue, problem-solve, and work together toward that end. This does not happen magically just because the institution is a school. I once heard an educator state that it takes a decade for a new learning strategy or idea to be implemented in the educational setting. A few of our schools that have been "doing human relations work" for the ten years SIERP has been around are very happy with what they see. They are getting closer to their vision and ours.

REFERENCES

Derman-Sparks, Louise. 1989. *Anti-Bias Curriculum: Tools for Empowering Young Children.* Washington, D.C.: National Association for the Education of Young Children.

Hawley, Willis D., and Anthony W. Jackson, eds. 1995. *Toward a Common Destiny: Improving Race and Ethnic Relations in America.* San Francisco: Jossey-Bass.

Lippitt, R. 1949. *Training in Community Relations.* New York: Harper and Brothers.

Piper, Richard. 1998. "Student Inter-Ethnic Relations Program Report on a Small Evaluation Study Conducted in the Anaheim Union High School District." Typescript.

Smith, Gary, and George Otero. 1989. *Teaching about Cultural Awareness.* Denver, Colo.: Center for Teaching International Relations.

Chapter 4

Student Voices: The ADL's A WORLD OF DIFFERENCE Institute Peer Training Program

Lorraine Tiven

Peer pressure is one of the most powerful forces in the lives of young people. Peers influence each other's choices, at times leading to behaviors that may have long-lasting negative consequences that young people may lack the maturity to anticipate or understand.

When used to create positive change, however, there are few methods more effective than peer-to-peer education. Building on this concept, the Anti-Defamation League's A WORLD OF DIFFERENCE (Anti-Defamation League and A WORLD OF DIFFERENCE are registered trademarks of the Anti-Defamation League of B'nai B'rith)[1] Peer Training Program prepares young people to use the power of peer pressure to motivate other students to reflect upon their stereotypes and assumptions and take action against prejudice and bigotry in their schools and communities.

The Peer Training Program is a collaborative effort between the Anti-Defamation League (ADL) and secondary schools or youth service organizations. It includes comprehensive training for participating students and staff, ongoing consultation services to ensure program success, and an established structure for implementation. The program also initiates an ongoing process in schools that empowers students to help shape school cultures that are inclusive of all groups and other individuals. In the aftermath of the Columbine High School massacre and the school shootings of the last few years, an inclusive, bias-free school climate should be the goal of any secondary school.

The Peer Training Program is designed to actively engage young people to find the strength and skills to combat—peaceably—the prejudice they have encountered. It provides students with the facilitation and conflict resolution skills they need to effectively interact with their peers, adults, and other authority figures.

Background Information

The ADL's A WORLD OF DIFFERENCE Institute Peer Training Program was initiated in 1991 in response to the riots in the Crown Heights section of Brooklyn. ADL staff began working with a group of twenty-nine students at Clara Barton High School in Brooklyn to help these young people take on the challenge of combating hatred in their community and opening lines of communication among their peers.

Currently, thirty-five middle and high schools in New York state are participating in the Peer Training Program. Over eighteen hundred students have been trained as peer trainers, reaching thousands of additional students through workshops, club activities, and face-to-face peer interactions. The A WORLD OF DIFFERENCE Institute staff provides ongoing technical assistance and field consulting to school program sites, along with materials and manuals for the peer trainers and coordinators.

The power and efficacy of the Peer Training Program have been recognized by the New York City Board of Education, which has selected the program as a resource for cultural diversity training in its schools, and by the U.S. Department of Education, which selected the program's principal staff to provide a national workshop on their methods. School officials on site are uniform in their praise of the program. The Guidance Counselor of Middle School 141 in the Bronx remarked, "The program *works!* The kids love it. It can be *A WORLD OF DIFFERENCE* if you buy into it." The coordinator of student affairs at Clara Barton High School notes, "We have had several workshops conducted within the school for students who have taught the A WORLD OF DIFFERENCE message throughout our school and community. Not only is the message these students spread positive and constructive in and of itself, but those who have received the training gain a self-awareness and confidence in all their activities. They have truly become leaders." The program has grown to reach middle and high schools across the United States and in six countries overseas.

In 1998, ADL entered into a grant-funded multiyear collaboration with the Boys and Girls Clubs of America, creating an initiative that included peer training for teens enrolled in both urban and nonurban clubs across the United States. To date, this initiative has involved hundreds of disadvantaged youth, developing in them the skills to serve as positive role models and social activists against intolerance in their clubs and communities. These young adults have become leaders in the movement to combat prejudice and violence and have acquired valuable leadership and life skills in the process.

As young people begin the process of becoming peer trainers, they learn to identify personal goals and priorities and link their existing responsibilities and relationships with social activism. A summer internship program at ADL National Headquarters provides peer trainers with job skills and work-preparation training. An annual International Peer Training Conference unites peer trainers from across the globe at an educational forum to improve their skills and strengthen their own personal commitments to making justice and equity a reality in their communities. Peer trainers have also had opportunities to participate in additional ADL Education Division programs, including youth trips to the U.S. Holocaust Memorial Museum and ADL's Children of the Dream Program, which brings Ethiopian Israeli youth to U.S. high schools, sends U.S. students of color to Israel, and links diverse students in yearlong community service programs.

Goals of the Peer Training Program

Although the Peer Training Program is based on the premise that peer groups have tremendous influence on the behaviors and attitudes of their members, ADL recognizes that peer trainers need to develop certain basic skills and competencies to be effective. The Peer Training Program begins by having the students engage in activities that require them to examine and understand their own strengths and weaknesses, skills and limitations, attitudes and values. Since skill development is facilitated when students are first exposed to a body of knowledge and then given the opportunity to integrate that knowledge into their own experience, students receive a balance of experiential group activities and opportunities for practical application in their everyday lives (Ender, McCaffrey, and Miller 1979).

As peer trainers, young people learn a common vocabulary for discussing issues of diversity, bigotry, and discrimination. They begin the ongoing process of developing the capacity to recognize and challenge prejudice and discriminatory behavior in themselves and others. Once trained, these students lead antibias workshops that offer their peers a forum to explore the way bigotry manifests itself in their lives.

The peer trainers help their fellow students develop the skills and motivation to confront these experiences effectively in the future. As peer trainers, these students are simultaneously solidifying their own knowledge and skills while helping to disseminate these concepts to the wider school community.

Theoretical Framework

The ADL believes that a reversal of the exponential rise in hate crimes in schools and communities requires a coordinated strategy that includes direct intervention with the schools. "Schools are crucial to the resolution of hate crime because the young are the perpetrators and schools are the staging grounds" (Bodinger-deUriarte 1991). Schools will continue to bear the brunt of the challenge because they are the first and often primary agency to reflect the dramatic changes in U.S. demographics, and these changes—when unaccompanied by skilled intervention—can lead to increased tensions (Parker 1995).

Although shootings, arson, and other sensational acts attract headlines, many researchers and practitioners are as concerned about the much more commonplace precursors of violence and hate that occur on almost every school campus in the country. These are the more subtle and more prevalent verbal threats, personal putdowns, harassment, and neglect that injure many young people in an unrelenting manner (Dear 1995).

Phinney (1990) suggests that many adolescents face considerable challenges within schools and communities as they attempt to establish authentic and positive relations across their ethnic and peer groups. Often they must resolve at least two primary conflicts: *(a)* the existence of two different sets of norms and values between dominant and nonmainstream cultures, and *(b)* the negative views and images of ethnic groups that bombard American society. These conflicts create tensions in schools and foster inequitable learning environments. The Peer Training Program utilizes the successful techniques of institute trainings, which are designed to prompt participants to recognize their own biases, to value their own cultures and those of their peers, to hold high expectations for all (Brookover and Lezotte 1979; Levine and Stark 1981), and to examine closely school policies and practices "to insure that insofar as possible they promote equal status and cooperative interdependence between minority and majority-group members" (Banks 1995, 642).

Opportunities to explore their ideas, attitudes, and experiences in an open and nonjudgmental atmosphere promote reflective and thoughtful discussion and decision making about the significant issues and choices young people face daily. Existing secondary curricula, however, provide few opportunities for students to engage in meaningful dialogue about many of the issues that affect them most deeply. It is not surprising that a national study conducted in 1991 by Peter D. Hart Research Associates for People for the American Way found that many teens—particularly young whites—report that they have never been asked by a significant adult in their lives to take time to examine their own prejudices. Peers are often more effective than adults in facilitating this type of discourse as they share a common language, experience, and culture. As one peer trainer explains, "It's better for something to come from someone who's more like you than an adult. Adults have a certain amount of knowledge, but a person can relate better to someone who's closer and more like them. So if I'm talking to a student, in ways, I'd be more effective than an adult."

The Peer Training Program provides opportunities for such dialogue, and, because discussions are facilitated by peers, there is an absence of the social control and authoritarianism characteristic of many interactions between youth and adults. Peer education has the added benefit of being able to "reach beyond the classroom . . . [to influence] children's behavior in school corridors and yards, in their homes and in their community environment, bridging the traditional gap between school and the 'real world.' They reach where not only the teacher, but any adult cannot" (Topping 1996, 24). Gartner and Riessman (1998, 36) of the Peer Resource Center have identified peer education as one of the most powerful and underutilized resources available to schools: "Schools are all about kids and for them. But rarely are schools by them or even with them. They are being ignored as the prime constituency. The opportunity of using students as agents of change is being squandered."

The Peer Training Program gives voice to young people, involving and empowering them as leaders in a process that is at the heart of all school reform efforts, the creation of a school environment where all students can succeed.

The Partnership Framework

The Peer Training Program is a model of successful school-community collaboration that includes a recommended program structure of education and skill development, relevant materials and resources, training for participants, and ongoing consultation.

The program is coordinated by the *site-based coordinator,* a school staff member who oversees the implementation of the program in cooperation with the school's administration, faculty, and parents. The roles and responsibilities of the site-based coordinator include assisting in identifying a diverse group of students interested in becoming peer trainers; coordinating peer-training meetings, practice sessions, and programs; and providing opportunities for students to engage in positive and constructive feedback. Coordinators empower, coach, value, and validate young people, as well as acting as their advocates.

Administrative and faculty support is critical to insuring the success of the Peer Training Program. This support may include providing meeting times and places for peer-training workshops, securing funding for training and materials, and demonstrating a willingness to communicate support to the school community through such venues as informal conversations, meeting presentations, and newsletter or newspaper articles.

Peer trainers are typically a diverse group of students in grades 9 to 11 who are recognized as being among the formal or informal leaders in the school; demonstrate above-average responsibility for themselves and their peers; and communicate a willingness to promote the values of diversity, equality, and fairness.

The process of becoming a peer trainer begins with training sessions where students participate in activities designed to assist them in exploring personal assumptions and biases, in promoting dialogue and inquiry, and in establishing guidelines for open communication. The training process includes a variety of activities that explore issues of racism and other forms of oppression, cultural identity, language, generalizations and stereotypes, and discrimination.

Methodology of the Peer Training Program

The following is a description of a typical, initial peer-training workshop, which begins the process for students of becoming peer trainers. Sessions are scheduled over three days and are six to seven hours in duration per day.

Day 1

On this first day, peer trainers are encouraged to explore their own attitudes and beliefs—their personal identity and the role it plays in how they perceive others. They become conscious of the effects of stereotypical thinking and assumptions and reflect on the ways bigotry has affected them or others. Videotapes, small and large group discussions, role-playing, and other interactive methods are used throughout the program to accomplish these goals. Chief among the prejudice-combating skills identified by researchers that are stressed in institute workshops are critical-thinking skills (Byrnes 1988; Pate 1988; Walsh 1988) and cooperative learning (Gaertner et al. 1990; Erber and Fiske 1984; Rothbart and John 1985; Slavin 1990).

The day opens with an opportunity for the group to create a set of agreed-upon ground rules for their discussion. If conflict arises or an insensitive or offensive remark causes hurt feelings, the ground rules serve as a "safety net" and road map for more respectful dialogue. Each interactive exercise is followed by the opportunity to process the experience as a group. Students also begin to consider the qualities that will promote leadership as they gather in small groups on the floor around the room to "Build a Leader" on a large sheet of butcher paper. One group's depiction may possess oversized ears to represent the ability and willingness to listen, another a large scarlet heart to denote the quality of caring about others. Often the day ends with an opportunity to reflect on the experiences of the day in a journal. Journal writing is continued by the peer trainers in the weeks that follow the training sessions.

Day 2

The roles and responsibilities of peer trainers are clarified on the second day, and students receive a manual of training activities and resources that have been developed by the A WORLD OF DIFFERENCE Institute. Throughout the day, students are encouraged to begin to see themselves as facilitators of this process in their schools and communities. They have the opportunity to participate in many of the activities they will later facilitate themselves, and trainers share helpful tips throughout the day.

Peer trainers have their first experience speaking in front of the group as they begin to learn how to "think on their feet" in "Spontaneous Combustion." In this activity, peer trainers are asked to respond to a random question, standing and speaking for one minute about their topic to the group. Following this, students generate a list of typical incidents of bias that occur in their school. They then develop role-plays that include their ideas for the best ways to challenge the bias. The lively discussion that follows creates for the students a toolbox of effective responses and supports an Institute operating assumption, that the wisdom of the group is greater than any one person.

Day 3

The third day provides an experiential opportunity for peer trainers to practice their new role. Working in teams, peer trainers prepare and present training activities from their manuals and learn how to provide feedback that will assist them in improving and refining their facilitation skills.

Time is provided for group goal setting, a discussion of next steps, and an opportunity to brainstorm responses to difficult situations. Each peer trainer is asked to create an artistic rendition of his or her worst fear in becoming a peer trainer. As each student shares their drawing with the group, it becomes clear that these are common and shared fears and that working together, they can develop useful strategies. At the closing of the three-day program, the site-based coordinator, responsible for assuming the educational process in the weeks to come, speaks with the group about next steps, and all participants come together to reflect on their experience and what they hope to accomplish as peer trainers.

Program Implementation

As peer trainers, students need to develop sophisticated facilitation skills that include the ability to effectively process training activities, to maintain neutrality and confidentiality during group discussions, and to manage conflict. This process demands a significant commitment of time and energy and is accomplished through a series of structured weekly meetings. These meetings have two primary functions: to continue the educational and skill-development process and to provide opportunities to practice presenting and facilitating training activities. Approximately ten weeks of structured group meetings are required before peer trainers begin to conduct programs or workshops in their schools.

Peer trainers are students who have learned how to effectively respond when they hear racial slurs, name-calling, and put-downs. In addition to leading these workshops, peer trainers become models for their peers by personally challenging prejudicial attitudes and behaviors when they occur in the hallways, lunchrooms, and classrooms of their schools. As one peer trainer explained, "To walk through school with the attitude that I have to tune out what other people are saying is really the wrong attitude to go through school with. I'm trying to teach them not to ignore that someone is Black or White or Hispanic, but rather to see that and to accept it and then move on so they can see what's inside someone, because it's only then that you really get to know somebody."

Peer Trainers in the Classroom

As leaders in their schools, peer trainers need to have a voice in developing goals for their programs. Peer-facilitated workshops take many forms as they encourage other students to examine and challenge intolerance through the use of videos, role playing, small and large group discussions, and other interactive methods.

An example of a popular peer trainer–led activity is the "Lemon Exercise on Stereotyping."[2] Peer trainers first ask their peers to look at a group of lemons and to generate a list of qualities that all lemons have in common. Then, in small groups, students get to know one lemon as an individual, creating a unique and often humorous story about the lemon's life to share with the group. All lemons are gathered again and piled in the center and representatives from each group come forward to identify their lemon, a task accomplished without difficulty or hesitation. A discussion follows that connects the "lemon experience" with the tendency to make assumptions about other people based on group membership.

Other peer training activities include "The Rumor Clinic," which provides a firsthand experience of how rumors quickly distort the truth; video selections that explore name-calling and ethnic humor; and interactive games that develop empathy.

Successes and Challenges

To date, a comprehensive longitudinal evaluation of the Peer Training Program has not taken place. In two unpublished studies, however, data on the A WORLD OF DIFFERENCE Institute Peer Training Program was collected from a group of past and present peer trainers. The studies looked at the effect of the program on the beliefs and behaviors of the youth and the resulting effect of the program on the schools and communities. Data was gathered from a survey questionnaire developed by graduate students at Teachers College, Columbia University, and administered to fifty-eight peer trainers. In addition, in 1997–1998, in-depth individual and focus group interviews were conducted by an ADL staff member and administered to approximately forty peer trainers from high schools in San Diego, Los Angeles, Omaha, and Staten Island. These sites were selected because they were part of a federally funded pilot program, Stop the Hate, designed to reduce the levels of tension and violence at participating schools.

Successes

From the forty focus group interviews and in-depth individual interviews, it is apparent that students are generally positive about the Peer Training

Program. For many of the students, involvement in the program helped them believe in their abilities to institute change. Many students commented on how they wanted all—not just a selected few—of their high school peers to benefit from such a program. Many urged that it reach younger students at feeder schools as well.

A large number of students mentioned that in addition to increasing their self-esteem, the program provided them with a support group of peers with common interests and goals and helped them to establish a stronger connection to their schools. They valued opportunities to develop basic leadership skills such as public speaking, organizing a presentation, and working as a team.

Many young people discussed how much they had learned from participating in the Peer Training Program, an experience many claimed had changed them significantly: "This program showed me . . . I don't have to be like other people. I could be myself, and I could love who I am, what I'm for. It also made me put an emphasis on what I believe in, instead of other people's comments . . . and also gave me more respect for my peers."

The survey of fifty-eight former and present peer trainers corroborates the narrative above. In general, the results indicate that participation in the Peer Training Program had a strong influence on personal social development (an individual's ability and desire to critically reflect on social issues, especially as they relate to bias, as well as an increase in communication skills), as well as on strong support of social responsibility (an individual's action in response to social conditions, especially as they relate to issues of bias)—two constructs that support the qualitative data (see table 1).

Challenges

Although the survey and interviews illustrate that the majority of peer trainers are satisfied with the activities, content, and outcomes of the Peer Training Program, areas have been identified where improvement could be made.

In open-ended questions, only 58 percent of respondents reported that they would take active steps to challenge a slur based on the victim's sexual orientation. Thus, while participation in the Peer Training Program seems to strongly influence attitudes and reflections on bias (personal social development), it seems to have less consistent influence on participants' ability to take action against some forms of bias (social responsibility). One explanation for this is that students' responses to bias based on sexual orientation are often tied to individually held religious beliefs. Additionally, because schools must balance the interests of a wide variety of constituency groups, there is sometimes a resulting tendency to avoid discussion or curricular responses to harassment based on perceived sexual orientation.

During a peer-training retreat in 1997, the issue of sexual orientation bias arose with a group who shared a strong religious affiliation. Students supported their disapproval of homosexuality with quotations from religious texts. By encouraging them to imagine that they might be the targets of intolerance based on their religious beliefs, the facilitators succeeded in establishing an acceptance of the premise that respect for individual differences could exist independent of one's deeply held religious beliefs.

Second, despite the expectation that peer trainers will conduct many workshops over the course of their high school years, the survey data indicates that 14 percent of peer trainers led only five to ten peer-training ses-

TABLE 1. Influence of Peer Training Program on Social Development and Social Responsibilty

Type of Influence	Self-Evaluation by Peer Trainer
Influence on social development	84% agreed that the program increased confidence in their ability to prepare and organize a presentation
	89% agreed that the program made them aware of their own strengths and weaknesses
	86% reported that the program made them aware of their own biases
	86% agreed that the program gave them a better understanding about prejudice and discrimination in their school and community
Influence on social responsibility	43% of all employed respondents reported that involvement in the program was somewhat or very influential in their job choice
	61% of all respondents reported involvement in some type of community service
	88% reported that involvement in the program was somewhat or very influential in their involvement in community service

Source: Responses of fifty-eight former peer trainers to survey questionnaire administered, 1998.

sions and 12.7 percent led ten to twenty sessions. Additional opportunities to lead workshops would strengthen students' communication skills and ultimately increase their positive impact on the climate of the school. At times, however, the scheduling of peer trainer workshops necessitates having students miss classes, a reality that is understandably not received with enthusiasm by school faculty. Often this challenge can be met by providing opportunities for peer trainer workshops during students' free periods or during classes in which individual peer trainers are enrolled.

More importantly, greater recognition should be given to the valuable contribution being made by the peer trainers to the overall climate of the school. Often, the Peer Training Program is viewed as an extracurricular rather than educational activity; however, student participation as peer trainers can enhance multidisciplinary academic goals and can contribute to the fulfillment of learning standards in many content areas. For example, peer trainers learn to recognize, respect, and analyze differences in interests, values, and perspectives; they have opportunities to take, defend, and evaluate points of view that facilitate thoughtful and effective participation in public affairs; they participate in negotiation and compromise to resolve classroom, school, and community disagreements and problems. These are vital skills young people will need to live and work in an increasingly diverse society. A clearer understanding of these benefits for individual students and the community at large would contribute to the development of a supportive environment that provides ample opportunities for peer trainers.

Another challenge frequently faced by schools is identifying a time for meetings that supports high student attendance. Often, schools select students for the program that are identified leaders who typically have full extracurricular schedules. Some schools are able to designate time during the school day for peer-training meetings, but most rely on after-school hours that often conflict with students' prior commitments. The importance of the process of the weekly meetings cannot be overemphasized as key to the future success of peer trainers' efforts. The existing commitments of students should be given serious consideration in the recruitment process before the program begins.

Conclusion

Peer education programs will always present unique challenges for evaluation, because peer trainers' activities change and evolve over time and because of the difficulties in quantifying attitudinal change. Anecdotal evidence, however, continues to support the benefits of this methodology for both peer trainers and the school and community at large. The comments of one middle school principal are typical of administrators at schools that sponsor the program: "I think there have been changes, and sometimes they're hard to quantify, but we have a lot of new groups in the school. . . . We have kids who are working together on a project . . . that would not three years ago have been working together. So, it's funneling the energies toward something positive. And meanwhile, you're creating an atmosphere for kids to get to know each other and to appreciate each other's differences."

Perhaps the effect of antibias peer-to-peer education is best summed up by the following excerpt from a letter written by a sixth grader to peer trainers who had recently presented a program to her class: "You helped me learn how to be a better person, and accept myself and others! You taught me what I should and shouldn't do. I shouldn't spread rumors, judge people by appearance, and exclude others. I should be helpful to others, be respectful, include everyone, and be a leader. Now that I know what to do . . . you get my thanks. I hope you can do this again with other students!"

NOTES

Material for this chapter was provided by Marjorie B. Green, Lindsay Friedman, and Dr. Lucia Rodriguez.

1. The Anti-Defamation League (ADL) was founded in 1913 "to stop the defamation of the Jewish people and to secure justice and fair treatment to all citizens alike." Committed to defending democratic ideals and safeguarding civil rights through fact-finding, research, advocacy, and the monitoring of extremist groups, the ADL combats bigotry in every form. Proactively, the league develops programs to combat prejudice and promote the value of diversity. The A WORLD OF DIFFERENCE Institute is the culmination of the ADL's years of experience working with schools to promote intergroup understanding and our country's democratic ideals.
2. "The Lemon Exercise on Stereotyping" is used with permission and is adapted from Pfeiffer and Jones 1974.

REFERENCES

Banks, J. A. 1995. "Multicultural Education and the Modification of Students' Racial Attitudes." In *Toward a Common Destiny: Improving Race and Ethnic Relations in America,* ed. W. D. Hawley and A. W. Jackson. San Francisco: Jossey-Bass.

Bodinger-deUriarte, C. 1991. "The Rise of Hate Crime on School Campuses." *Phi Delta Kappa* 10:1–6.

Brookover, W. B., and L. W. Lezotte. 1979. *Changes in School Characteristics Coincident with Changes in School Achievement.* East Lansing: Michigan State University Institute for Research on Teaching.

Byrnes, D. A. 1988. "Children and Prejudice." *Social Education* 52, no. 4: 4–8.

Chang, E., T. Hausman-Kelly, M. Iwaki, and T. Jester. 1998. "A WORLD OF DIFFERENCE Institute's Peer Training Evaluation Report." Teachers College, Columbia University, New York.

Dear, J. D. 1995. *Creating Caring Relationships to Foster Academic Excellence: Recommendations for Reducing Violence in California Schools.* Sacramento: State of California, Commission on Teacher Credentialing.

Democracy's Next Generation: A Study of American Youth on Race. 1992. Washington, D.C.: People for the American Way.

Ender, S. C., S. S. McCaffrey, and T. K. Miller. 1979. *Students Helping Students.* Athens, Ga.: Student Development Associates.

Erber, R., and S. T. Fiske. 1984. "Outcome Dependency and Attention to Inconsistent Information." *Journal of Personality and Social Psychology* 47:709–26.

Gaertner, S. L., J. Mann, J. F. Dovidio, A. Murrell, and M. Pomare. 1990. "How Does Cooperation Reduce Intergroup Bias?" *Journal of Personality and Social Psychology* 59:692–704.

Gartner, A., and F. Riessman. 1998. "Turning Peer Pressure Inside Out." *Education Week,* May 28, 36.

Levine, D. U., and J. Stark. 1981. *Instructional and Organizational Arrangements and Processes for Improving Academic Achievement at Inner-City Elementary Schools.* Kansas City: University of Missouri, Kansas City.

Parker, J. J. 1995. *Hate Crimes in Los Angeles Public Schools.* Los Angeles: Los Angeles County Office of Education.

Pate, G. S. 1988. "Research on Reducing Prejudice." *Social Education* 52, no. 4: 287–89.

Pfeiffer, J. W., and John E. Jones. 1974. *Handbook of Structured Experiences for Human Relations Training.* Vol. 3. San Diego: Pfeiffer and Company.

Phinney, J. S. 1990. "Ethnic Identity Development in Adolescents and Adults: Review of Research." *Psychological Bulletin* 108:499–514.

Rothbart, M., and O. P. John. 1985. "Social Categorization and Behavioral Episodes: A Cognitive Analysis of the Effects of Intergroup Contact." *Journal of Social Issues* 41:81–104.

Slavin, R. E. 1990. "Research on Cooperative Learning: Consensus and Controversy." *Educational Leadership* 47, no. 4: 52–54.

Topping, K. 1996. "Reaching Where Adults Cannot." *Educational Psychology in Practice* 11, no. 4: 23–24.

Walsh, D. 1988. "Critical Thinking to Reduce Prejudice." *Social Education* 52, no. 4: 280–82.

Chapter 5

Students Talk About Race

Joseph H. McKenna and James Manseau Sauceda

Background

In 1990 People For the American Way Foundation (PFAW), a national constitutional liberties foundation with offices in Washington, New York, and Los Angeles, created the Students Teach and Reach program in North Carolina in part as a thirty-year commemoration of the Greensboro sit-ins. The Greensboro sit-ins, where college students engaged in civil disobedience for the sake of racial equality, helped galvanize the nation into positive action. Students Teach and Reach (STAR) was designed to similarly utilize the idealism and empowerment potential of college students. The program enlisted and trained undergraduates to act as peer mentors and role models for middle and high school students. In keeping with the theme of the Greensboro sit-ins, the topic of Teach and Reach was race relations.

In the early 1990s, through its Campus Intolerance Project (a technical assistance program in which PFAW helped college administrators, faculty, and students analyze and more effectively address intergroup tensions on campus), PFAW found a substantial "perception gap" in the ways white youth and young people of color view society. In 1992, PFAW published its findings on this cultural discrepancy in *Democracy's Next Generation II*, a study on young Americans' views on race, diversity, and discrimination. This work offered a fully detailed portrait of the racial views of children of the post–civil rights era. *Democracy's Next Generation II* provided compelling evidence that racial divisions among young people were widening and deepening. Specifically, the study found that, despite positive personal contact with peers of other races and ethnicities, young people often revert to negative stereotypes when asked to discuss these groups. From these findings, PFAW concluded that a comprehensive effort was needed to engage young people in discussions about race relations in America. It was then that PFAW decided to take the STAR program to Southern California. It was brought to Los Angeles and renamed

Students Talk About Race in the fall of 1992, just four months after the city had suffered the most costly and damaging racial unrest in a generation. From 1992 until 1995 the program operated out of California State University, Long Beach (with the trainings being provided by the director of the Multicultural Center), and three schools, reaching a few hundred students with several dozen college facilitators. In 1995 we took STAR to greater Los Angeles County, and there was an explosion of interest. In the fall 1995 semester alone over two hundred college facilitators from fifteen campuses brought the program to four thousand local students in twenty schools. This was more than a tenfold growth in three months. By January 2000, fifteen hundred L.A.-area college students from twenty-two campuses had brought STAR to twenty thousand students in seventy-six schools.

From 1995 to 1996 the program was piloted with great results in Atlanta, Reno, Seattle, Sacramento, and the San Francisco Bay area. Limitations in funding later necessitated closing the program at those sites. Since fall 1996 STAR has been operating only in Southern California. It is no longer under the auspices of People for the American Way but runs out of the Multicultural Center at California State University, Long Beach.

How STAR Works

STAR's mission is to provide a forum for youth to share their personal thoughts and experiences about diversity; to educate participants about racial and ethnic intolerance and tolerance; to encourage understanding, acceptance, and celebration of diversity; to help participants acknowledge the equal human worth of distinct groups of people; to assist participants in recognizing the personal and social cues of racism, discrimination, prejudice, bigotry, stereotyping, and scapegoating; to understand these attitudes and behaviors and the risks posed by them; to contribute to community-mindedness and volunteerism; to create a bridge between neighborhoods and local colleges and universities; and to explore strategies for the creation of a climate of civility in our schools and communities.

STAR utilizes college students to facilitate candid discussions on race with middle and high school students. At school districts, it secures the permission and endorsement of administrators to approach middle and high school principals and teachers with the program. Interested teachers then make their requests directly to the STAR staff. At colleges and universities, the program works with professors, administrators, and staff to identify and recruit college student volunteers. Students are selected through faculty recommendations and self-selection. The type of student who would be interested in this type of time commitment is usually always good.

College students receive an intensive professional training that introduces them to issues in diversity, to facilitation skills, and to the STAR discussion guide. The training is a professional diversity sensitivity training, conducted on weekends in the fall and spring terms. Each training is six hours long, and students must attend one of them. During the academic portion of the workshop students are introduced to the origin of the concept of race in antiquity; they review racist acts in U.S. history; and they discuss problems surrounding contemporary dialogue in race relations. The practical portion of their training includes role-playing eight of the lessons in the STAR curriculum guide and learning twelve facilitation skills. The eight lessons include activities and discussions on the following topics: race, ethnicity, racist acts in U.S. history, race as it impacts individual students in their choice of friends or dates, race as it impacts gangs, race as it impacts a large metropolitan area (the unrest in Los Angeles in 1992), and possible solutions to the problem of racial discrimination. The twelve facilitation skills are as follows:

Knowing your audience
    Adolescence
    Ethnic minority students
    Contacting your assigned teacher early and asking about
        her/his students

Working with a partner
    Being equal partners, each assuming responsibility
    Getting to know your partner, sharing ideas, talking on the phone
    Validating differences of style, opinions, and experience
    Planning a session together
    Working cooperatively and simultaneously during
        classroom sessions
    "Weather reports" ("How'm I doin'?")
    Airing grievances

Putting students at ease and encouraging candid conversation
    Allowing personal risk and vulnerability (admitting fears)
    Respecting students

Having a sense of humor about yourself
Using first names

Active listening
Being nonargumentative, nonjudgmental, and empathetic
Noting body language (theirs and yours)

Analyzing and synthesizing what you hear
Seeing the particular
Seeing the whole
Summarizing

Being comfortable with silence
The "freedom of silence"
Taming your impulse to speak
Structuring silence

Managing personal bias
Admitting personal bias (to yourself and to the students)
Staying cool when your ideas are being challenged

Mediating conflicts
Seeing the positive and constructive elements in conflict
Important issues are aired
New and creative ideas arise
Tensions are relieved
Identifying the "real" issue, getting beyond surface statements
Defusing intensity while retaining the message
Stopping the interaction at the point of abusive language, name-calling, yelling
Deferring to the teacher for any needed disciplinary action

Dealing with problem students (a rarity)
Defusing tension with humor
Spotlighting the heckler
Acknowledging a point without validating exhibitionism
Moving on, changing topics
Deferring to the teacher for any needed disciplinary action

Dealing with noncurricular topics
 Letting the students talk and explore their feelings on the subject
 Admitting the possible need for a lesson on this theme; getting
  back on topic
 Deferring to the teacher for school policy on such topics

Closing each session
 Summarizing
 Posing a problem, inviting a practical solution
 Staying available briefly after class

Closing the program (last day)
 Recapping the purpose of STAR
 Posing practical projects
 Fifteen-minute party at class's end (with teacher's permission)

After their training, college facilitators are placed in pairs in middle or high school classrooms in the neighborhoods of their college campuses. College students facilitate discussions one class period per week for eight weeks. (There are spring and fall programs.) College facilitators use a curricular guide for their discussions. Here are some questions that are used in week 3 to generate classroom dialogue:

Do you think about your skin color much?
When are you most aware of it?
Have you ever wanted to be darker or lighter?
Do you think of your skin color as a good thing or a bad thing?
Do your family and friends think of your skin color as you do?
How do you think people of other colors think of your skin color?
How do people of the same color view those who are lighter or darker
 shades?
Are most things (clothes, makeup, etc.) made for people of your skin
 color?
What is the normal skin color in the United States? In Los Angeles? In
 this school?
If you're the norm in any of these groups, do you think about your skin
 color?
If you're outside the norm in any of these groups, do you have to adjust
 your life in any way to the world of the norm?

In week 5 other questions are asked about ethnic groups:

Which group do you identify with most closely?
Which are you most comfortable with other than your own?
Which are you least comfortable with?
Which are you most knowledgeable about other than your own?
Which are you least knowledgeable about?
Which have you had the most conflict with?
Which are you most afraid of?
Which are you most curious about?
Which are you most aware of avoiding?
Which represents most of your friends?
Which would you date? (For high school students)
What or who influences your choices? Friends, parents, religion, television?
Are your choices based upon a stereotype, an oversimplified generalization usually citing negative beliefs about a particular group?
Are your choices based on personal experience of the group?

These kinds of questions never fail to produce animated discussions.

No one expects the college students to emerge from their training as experts or certified professionals in race relations. However, they do take from it a competence and a confidence to bring STAR's message of acceptance to middle and high school students. It is part of their appeal that they are not professionals but slightly older peers. We have on rare occasions had difficulty with the college facilitators. A few lack the discipline and confidence to facilitate the classroom discussions, and eventually they drop out. By and large, however, most of our facilitators have been extremely good role models and discussion guides. There is a process of self-selectivity at work: students who sign up for a program like this are usually very committed to its ideals, and their earnestness takes them a long way in the classroom.

After the volunteers have conducted their first few classroom discussions they are invited to a follow-up debriefing session in which they recount their in-class experiences and learn how to better handle specific challenges they faced.

From the outset, college students and their assigned secondary school teachers are encouraged to work together to set goals and create a schedule (sometimes weekly sessions may be modified due to vacation periods, testing, and other special events). In addition, we urge teachers to attend the facilitators' training sessions to learn more about the program and become better acquainted with the college students. During the training sessions, the teachers are invited to share information specific to their students and schools, helping prepare the volunteers for what they will encounter in the classroom. During the actual STAR team visits, however, the teachers are asked to observe but not participate so that the critical peer-mentoring dynamic is maintained. As they become aware of the issues raised, the teachers are then able to maintain an ongoing dialogue with their students—both between STAR visits and after that semester's program has concluded.

The program's implementation requires continuous administrative guidance. In any given semester the Southern California program deals with dozens of academics and administrators, scores of teachers, hundreds of college facilitators, and thousands of middle and high school students. In addition to those actually participating, there is another larger set of nonparticipants in each category who receive our promotional literature in the effort to bring more people into the fold. The administrative maintenance of the program entails updating and disseminating the program's literature (flyers, fact sheets, advertisements, Q&A sheets, pitch letters, teacher's facilitator-request forms, facilitator availability, postcards, and so on); communicating by fax, surface mail, e-mail or phone with past participant teachers and college contacts and all potential future participants and contacts; recruiting all participants; arranging trainings and debriefings and managing event logistics; coordinating the placements of all facilitators and teachers; and making site visits.

Facilitators

The program continues to have a profound effect upon the facilitators. One reason the program affects college students has to do with their ability and willingness to think reflectively on this experience. They are caught in a reverie of comparison: they are not far enough out of high school to forget how they were then; they compare their experiences then to that of the high schoolers in front of them now and gain insight into their past and present lives. We are always amazed at the level of seriousness the college students have toward this program. One student solemnly advised us to "Keep moving forward, recruiting more potential STAR facilitators and sponsors. This has got to be communicated because it's relevant. It matters." Others say that the program "opens up avenues for dialogue that simply do not exist otherwise." All agree that the topic is timely. One facilitator says that the issue of race among this age group is "something that is always present but hardly ever talked about." Facilitators are impressed with the forum and its aptness for "allowing the kids to speak their minds."

Teachers

We hear the most amazing stories from the teachers. All teachers tell us that their students eagerly await the arrival of the college facilitators each week. One teacher reported that a student who has never spoken in her class has opened up to speak to the college students in the sessions. Another teacher says that a ten-year-old problem between Mexican students and Armenian students is beginning to be resolved at her school through the intervention of STAR. One teacher told us that her students are making "wonderful connections from their fun and enlightening experiences working with STAR." Another said that "the STAR concept is excellent" and "encourages class unity."

Teachers report that overall the program has been very successful at getting their students to talk about these issues. Often a teacher's rating of the program stands in direct relation to the college facilitator's performance, so that the program is praised by praising the facilitator: "Barbara is excellent. She is a godsend. She works so well with students from all different backgrounds. She can get everyone involved and excited." And so on. Teachers report that the facilitators cause "a closeness and camaraderie within the class that was absent before." To date we have had no incidents of hostility during a session. The sessions can be, as one teacher said, "uncomfortable, but never hostile and always 'alive.'"

All in all we would like to see the teachers getting more involved in the program, but they need incentives to do so. We would like to see a separate teacher orientation. We would have to do this during the week, which means we would need money for release time. This idea could be a big hit; on the other hand, one reason teachers like this program is that it asks little of them other than their class time.

Students

We know intuitively that this program is having its intended effect on students, but it is difficult to scientifically measure this growth. Students nowadays are savvy. We have been amazed observing middle schoolers' analysis of social situations they have been in. We need to take them beyond what they know or what they think they know, which is why we need content—facts, dates, figures—in the curriculum. They can talk about race, but they also need to be informed about race. We hope we can give these students a lexicon and a conceptual framework from which to approach race matters in this state and in this nation.

Evaluation

To measure the program's effectiveness and gain further insight into how to improve it, prior to 1997 students, college volunteers, and teachers completed questionnaires evaluating their experience. Using before-and-after surveys, participants offered valuable feedback and information. Completed surveys indicated that after the STAR experience students have a heightened awareness of diversity and recognize the benefits of exploring constructive solutions to promote respect and tolerance.

For example, before experiencing STAR, when asked about different programs that were to be created at their schools, many students wanted more performing arts and computer programs. After STAR, more students' wish lists included programs on conflict resolution and intergroup relations, programs that encourage respect and tolerance among students and faculty.

Surveys collected from college volunteers and teachers show that they, too, consider the program valuable and important for the students with whom they work and for their own personal and professional growth.

In the fall 1997 and spring 1998 semesters, a team of professors at California State University, Northridge, conducted an exhaustive evaluation of the program, funded by the Charles Stewart Mott Foundation. The results showed that STAR met all five criteria that scholars have identified as constituting a successful prejudice reduction intervention. The five criteria are as follows: (1) participants are given equal status within the situation; (2) the contact is individualized, so participants get to know one another; (3) cooperation across groups is fostered; (4) positive interaction is promoted that weakens negative images or stereotypes and strengthens positive images; (5) support from authorities (teachers and facilitators) strengthens expectations that the group will interact positively.

Notwithstanding the program's success, we have always faced certain obstacles. The most persistent challenge has been receiving adequate funding. We have received support from some high-profile foundations such as Levi Strauss, Time-Warner, Packard, Mott, and others. But our funding is usually on a year-to-year basis. As such we have not been able to pursue a larger vision of STAR.

Growing STAR

The program is enjoying an increased national profile for three reasons: (1) in 1997 the Center for Living Democracy included the program in *Interracial Dialogue Groups across America: A Directory* (Statham 1997); (2) in 1998 The National Conference for Community and Justice (formerly The National Conference of Christians and Jews) cited STAR in *Intergroup Relations in the United States;* (3) in 1998 the President's Initiative on Race cited the program as a "Promising Practice" and listed STAR on the White House web page.

Potential growth for the program will involve exporting it to other cities. We are in the process of designing a start-up kit that will include detailed instructions on how college administrators can implement STAR. This kit could be sent to interested parties at universities and/or school districts so that they can run the program using their own resources. The kit will include step-by-step instructions on how to implement the program for both colleges and school districts and templates of flyers, forms, and press materials. We will also include a copy of the STAR curriculum for reproduction. Though it would involve more expenditure, a training video could also be a valuable tool. We are considering modeling the kit after the Southern Poverty Law Center's Teaching Tolerance materials, which have been sent to teachers in seventy-five thousand K–12 schools across the nation. We could similarly send packages to colleges and universities. Morris Dees, who founded the Southern Poverty Law Center, recently commended our program: "Students Talk About Race is a prime example of a community-based program that nourishes genuine cross-cultural communication. It would make an excellent complement to Teaching Tolerance" (1999).

A second option for exporting STAR to other sites would be the creation of a summer institute where in a weekend seminar we will teach others how to implement the program at their home sites.

Conceivably, STAR could be exported to dozens of cities. It might be as simple as dropping a start-up kit in the mail and watching STAR grow.

REFERENCES

Dees, Morris. 1999. Telephone interview and faxed statement.

Democracy's Next Generation II. 1992. Washington, D.C.: People For the American Way Foundation.

Du Bois, Paul Martin, and Jonathan J. Hutson. 1997. *Bridging the Racial Divide: A Report on Interracial Dialogue in America.* Brattleboro, Vt.: Center for Living Democracy.

National Conference for Community and Justice. 1998. *Intergroup Relations in the United States.* New York: NCCJ.

Sauceda, James S., and Joseph H. McKenna. 2000. "Students Talk About Race: Curricular Discussion Guide." Handout. Los Angeles.

Statham, M. A., ed. 1997. *Interracial Dialogue Groups across America: A Directory.* Brattleboro, Vt.: Center for Living Democracy.

Wittig, Michele, and Shelia Grant. 1998. "Students Talk About Race: A Program Evaluation." Report for the Charles Stewart Mott Foundation.

Case Studies: College

Chapter 6

Voices of Discovery: Intergroup Dialogues at Arizona State University

Jesús Treviño

Diversity at Arizona State University: Challenges and Prospects

Diversity on a college campus generates both challenges and prospects. Our institutions of higher education have not been immune to the challenges of a diverse student body and, consequently, have experienced a rash of incidents involving violence, hatred, prejudice, intolerance, and discrimination targeting members who identify with different groups. It appears that almost every issue of the *Chronicle of Higher Education,* the primary periodical of colleges and universities, includes a story about incidents involving misunderstandings, free speech versus hate speech, hatred, or intolerance targeting Jews, Chicanos, women, gays, lesbians, bisexuals, African Americans, Asians, American Indians, and other groups found on a college campus. The reasons for intolerance, hatred, misunderstanding, and intergroup conflict are varied and complex and include psychological, social, and economic explanations (Stephan and Stephan 1996). In light of the above, many institutions of higher education are struggling to develop strategies that address these incidents and improve the campus climate for diversity (Spitzberg and Thorndike 1992).

From a different perspective, having students, faculty, and staff from around the world on a college campus also poses prospects and opportunities for achieving cross-cultural, intergroup, and diversity-related educational outcomes. When students, faculty, and staff share their cultures, languages, and worldviews, the opportunities for achieving outcomes such as open-mindedness, positive intergroup relations, cross-cultural understanding, decreases in prejudice, harmony, cultural competency, and freedom of speech are maximized. Stated differently, diversity, if managed carefully, can be an asset in the pursuit of educational outcomes. This principle is supported by research in education (Hurtado et al. 1999) as well as in the business world, where organizations are realizing tremendous benefits of heterogeneous work groups (Cox and Beale 1997). However, to realize the benefits of a diverse student body, interaction between groups representing diverse backgrounds must first occur.

Arizona State University has not been immune to the difficult challenges that accompany a diverse community. In 1999, the University reached an enrollment of approximately fifty thousand students consisting of 10.7 percent Latino, 4.8 percent Asian American, 3.6 percent international students, 3.1 percent African American, 2.2 percent American Indian, and 71.5 percent White/Euro-American. Students come from throughout the world, the nation, and Arizona, representing a multiplicity of groups including race/ethnicity, religion, gender, sexual orientation, social class, and many other social dimensions. Like most campuses, ASU has been plagued periodically by incidents of violence and discrimination against women, ethnic/racial minorities, gays, lesbians, and bisexuals, disabled people, and other groups. To address issues and capitalize on diversity as an asset, in 1997 ASU created the Intergroup Relations Center, a fully funded and staffed entity designed to use different strategies to encourage intergroup interaction (e.g., intergroup dialogues, retreats, story circles, music, intergroup relations theater), address intergroup conflict, and provide intergroup relations education and training.

Although the Intergroup Relations Center is using a variety of approaches to structure interaction between groups, the purpose of this chapter is to describe those efforts to structure interaction between different groups specifically using intergroup dialogues.

Intergroup Interaction on College Campuses

One of the assumptions that colleges and universities have made related to campus diversity is that bringing large numbers of students, faculty, and staff from a multiplicity of backgrounds together on a college campus will in and of itself lead to intergroup interaction, cultural sharing, and intergroup harmony. History suggests (and most anthropologists agree) that this belief is erroneous (Winkelman 1993). That is, the exact opposite occurs. Cross-cultural conflict, misunderstandings, and intergroup tension are usually the outcome of groups that are in proximity to each other. There are several explanations for this. First, individuals are not easily persuaded to participate in and with other groups. We are all motivated to stay within our own groups. These allow individuals to enjoy camaraderie and celebrate, practice, and perpetuate culture. Moreover, some groups on college campuses provide students with a sense of safety and security from harsh campus climates that impact students from different backgrounds (Hurtado 1990). Second, whenever individuals from diverse backgrounds come in contact with each other, their different customs, traditions, languages, values, and worldviews are bound to clash, causing conflict and misunderstandings. In addition, intergroup processes such as stereotyping, in-group favoritism, anxiety, and intergroup conflict impede groups from interacting, cooperating, and understanding each other (Stephan and Stephan 1996).

In sum, our college campuses might sometimes be described as institutions with multiple groups living and studying in close proximity to each other with minimal interaction. Moreover, when interaction does take place, its depth and meaningfulness are questionable. That is, the discussions appear to be polite and relegated to safe topics primarily focusing on the personal aspects of an individual (e.g., favorite music, number of siblings, career aspirations) and shy away from the more difficult and controversial group topics (e.g., opinions about affirmative action, questions about group culture and group characteristics that include stereotypes).

There are several implications that emerge from the above. First, it is clear that as our institutions of higher education continue to diversify their student bodies, intergroup conflict and cross-cultural tension can only intensify. Second, diversity can be an asset, if colleges and universities harness the power of diverse groups (i.e., languages, cultures, customs, perspectives, talents, skills) in achieving educational outcomes. And third, interaction between individuals and groups from diverse backgrounds is not going to happen naturally and must therefore be deliberately structured (Hurtado, Dey, and Treviño 1994). Moreover, interaction has to be structured in such a way that will be meaningful and address the difficult issues related to diversity.

While there are various ways to structure meaningful interaction between groups on college campuses (e.g., retreats, story circles, institutes), one strategy that has been found to be effective and fruitful at ASU is to bring individuals from different groups together for dialogue. Intergroup dialogues are sustained (six weeks or more), honest, and face-to-face discussions between two or more different social identities. These dialogues are structured, purposeful, take place in small groups, and are guided by trained facilitators (Zúñiga and Nagda 1993). The groups take place within a context of safe space (i.e., students are not attacked or blamed for expressing themselves or asking questions), allowing participants to dialogue through difficult intergroup issues. Through the dialogue process, participants learn about and get to know each other by exchanging information and creating greater intergroup understanding.

Intergroup Dialogues at Arizona State University

Inspired and influenced by the University of Michigan's intergroup dialogue program (which was developed by its first director, Ximena Zúñiga), Arizona State University initiated an intergroup dialogue project during 1996 spring semester. Prior to 1996, ASU had been administering a number of intergroup relations initiatives (e.g., retreats, workshops, theater), but nothing like an intergroup dialogue program. In October 1995, representatives from the ASU Office of Student Life (Treviño and Geranios 1997) contacted representatives from the University of Michigan's Program on Intergroup Relations and Conflict and requested materials on their dialogue program. Next, a proposal was submitted to the ASU Campus Environment Team requesting a small grant for the implementation of an intergroup dialogue program. The grant was funded, and the ASU Voices of Discovery Intergroup Dialogue program was born.

Coincidentally, while the program was being piloted with about seven dialogue groups involving approximately one hundred students, Arizona State University experienced a series of racial incidents that sparked several weeks of student protests, negative publicity, and an overall disruption to the campus. The Students against Discrimination (SAD), a group formed to address the racial incidents, began to make recommendations and propose solutions to top-level administrators directed at improving the campus climate for diversity. SAD proposed several initiatives, one of which was the creation of a permanent, fully funded and fully staffed intergroup relations center to work year round on improving intergroup relations at ASU. Second, the students proposed extensive intergroup relations training for all incoming ASU students. And third, members of SAD proposed that ASU's newly created intergroup dialogue program, Voices of Discovery, be permanently funded and institutionalized. After the ASU Intergroup Relations Center (IRC) was created in 1997 as a permanent part of the Office of the Senior Vice-President and Provost, the intergroup dialogue program was moved out of the Office of Student Life and is now a permanent part of the center.

Mission and Goals of the Voices of Discovery Program

Voices of Discovery is an intergroup dialogue program designed to structure interaction between different groups on campus with the objective of increasing greater understanding around issues of race, ethnicity, sexual orientation, class, disability status, religion, and other social identities. The specific goals of the program are (1) to create greater understanding between different groups around issues of diversity; (2) to encourage intergroup interaction via intergroup dialogues; and (3) to proactively work to improve the campus climate for diversity at Arizona State University.

The Voices of Discovery program has several components to it. First, staff members from the Intergroup Relations Center determine the types and number of dialogue groups that will take place during the semester. The criteria for planning the combinations of dialogue groups include student interest in the dialogue groups, diversity of groups, the history of conflict and tension between specific groups on campus or in society, and the number of ASU students available from a particular group (e.g., the campus has a large Latino student population that supports several combinations of Latino/White dialogue groups). Essentially, the program relies on the diversity of the student body to create opportunities for intergroup interaction. Examples of intergroup dialogues that have been a part of the Voices of Discovery Program include African American/White; Latino/White; American Indian/White; Asian/White; gay, lesbian, bisexual/heterosexual; Latino/African American; disabled/able-bodied; Jewish/Christian; male/female; Greek/non-Greek; and women of color/White women. Recently, the program has expanded to include other types of dialogues including community service dialogue groups (which include participation in a community service project); female story circles (dialogue through the medium of storytelling); and a Latino/White/African American triad (dialogue among three groups). The program has also allowed for piloting intragroup dialogues including an African American intragroup dialogue and a White intragroup dialogue. Since its inception, the program has grown so much that during the fall 1998 semester approximately 280 students participated across fifteen different groups requiring approximately thirty staff and graduate student facilitators.

Second, once the groups are conceptualized, cofacilitators are recruited for each group. The facilitators are recruited to represent each of the social identities present. For example, an African American facilitator and White facilitator run the African American/White dialogue group. This is important because it signals to participants that their group is represented among the leadership of the group. The facilitators establish the time and days that the dialogue groups will meet, and students are recruited into those time slots. It is important to point out that, unlike the University of Michigan's program, Voices of Discovery does not utilize undergraduates as facilitators. Rather, the facilitators are either staff, faculty, or graduate students who primarily have backgrounds in social work, counseling, communication, anthropology, student personnel administration, higher education, or sociology. In the beginning it was necessary to train and establish a cadre of trained professionals on the campus who could teach courses and train others to undertake intergroup dialogue work. (Plans are currently under way to include and train undergraduates to participate in the program.) Presently, facilitators undergo approximately eight hours of training in facilitation techniques; team facilitation; history, theory, and philosophy of intergroup dialogues; group formation processes; conflict mediation; ingroup-outgroup dynamics; and social and personal identity theory. The facilitators also become members of a computer listserv and are required to report weekly on their group's progress. Two counseling psychologists from the ASU counseling center are also part of the listserv. The psychologists serve as a "safety net" and precaution in case severe psychological issues emerge from the dialogue process (e.g., a participant in the male/female dialogue group is reminded of a date rape that she experienced in the past). It is important to point out that, although the intergroup dialogues are not "therapy" groups, intergroup relations issues are fraught with conflict, tension, and emotion. Thus, even though the groups are led by trained facilitators who establish a safe environment, it is prudent to plan for the unforeseen.

Third, students enrolled in university courses addressing diversity-related topics (e.g., race and ethnic relations, multicultural education, women's studies, intercultural communication, anthropology) are recruited for participation in the dialogue program. Theoretically, these students are ideal for the program because they bring theoretical and research material that they receive in the classroom to the out-of-classroom intergroup dialogues. Participants accepted into the program are required to attend six two-hour sessions (once per week for six weeks) in addition to a closing ceremony. All the groups meet on the ASU campus during the late afternoon or evening hours in comfortable lounges or classrooms that are conducive to creating dialogue.

In recruiting students for the program, students are provided with two incentives. The primary one is credit (extra points for participation). More specifically, professors are asked to consider giving credit to students for participating in the program. Presently, the program has approximately twenty faculty members (several of the faculty teach courses that have over two hundred students) supporting the intergroup dialogues. In most cases, participation in the program is optional with students having several projects from which to choose (e.g., intergroup dialogues, community service project, research paper). Professors find the project helpful in that it supplements the theory and research presented in their classroom with actual face-to-face dialogue regarding the issues of gender, sexual orientation, ethnicity, class, and other salient social identities. The secondary incentive is food: pizza is served at each and every dialogue group. Conventional wisdom suggests that food is always a good motivator for bringing people together. The rationale for providing incentives for participation is that discussions about issues of sexism, heterosexism, racism, ableism, and other intergroup relations issues are difficult. Very few students are initially motivated to participate in such discussions unless incentives are provided.

Dialogue Process

The dialogue process is guided by a curriculum that serves as a guide for the facilitators. In some cases, facilitators follow the curriculum closely. In other cases, facilitators deviate from the curriculum and creatively use techniques and strategies for generating dialogue. The facilitators are instructed that whether they follow the curriculum or not, the primary goal is to create dialogue between the groups represented around intergroup issues. With respect to the suggested curriculum, the first session focuses on administering the pretest assessment instrument, establishing ground rules for dialogue, providing the students with the skills for dialogue (e.g., active listening, entering another person's worldview), and introducing the concept of personal identity (i.e., our identities as individuals). During the first session, the participants create name tags (that will be worn during the entire program) and participate in icebreakers designed to help them get to know each other in a personal way. The rationale behind the activities of the first meeting is that it is critical that the students bond personally before engaging in the more potentially volatile intergroup discussions.

During the second session, students are introduced to the concept of social identity (i.e., our identities within the context of groups). Participants also begin the difficult process of examining intergroup issues, conflict, and tension. Facilitators come prepared with a set of questions and activities designed to spark the dialogue. Ideally, the students should drive the specific intergroup issues discussed in the groups. Realistically, the issues are guided by both the participants and the facilitators, depending on how much students are willing to speak up.

The third, fourth, and fifth meetings are all devoted to intergroup discussions. However, they begin with short icebreakers designed to continue the personal bonding process. Again, this insures that the groups are able to overcome any conflict and tension that may emerge during intergroup discussions.

The final session focuses on closure and group affirmation. During this session, discussion of intergroup issues is not allowed. The groups are separated (separate rooms) and asked to think about an uplifting message of hope or understanding that they would like to share with the other group. In many cases, the students make statements about what they learned about the other group and also thank and affirm individuals in the group. Before closing, participants take the posttest and evaluation and are invited to a closing, celebratory ceremony.

At the closing ceremony, all groups are brought together and are asked to create a poster depicting their intergroup experience. They are then asked to briefly present their poster and talk about their experience. All participants receive a certificate for their involvement in the project.

Successes and Challenges

A critical assessment of the Voices of Discovery program suggests that the initiative has enjoyed success but also faces some challenges. On the positive side, student and faculty participation in the intergroup dialogue program has increased steadily from semester to semester. Students find the intergroup dialogues engaging primarily because they are ready for and desire intergroup interaction and learning. For many students, the intergroup dialogues represent one of the first opportunities for contact with and exposure to groups about which they know very little. Many students are also attracted to the intergroup dialogue process because it represents a break from the monotony of the traditional pedagogical approach: lectures. The dialogue process is much more participatory, dynamic, and democratic (Burbules 1993). For their part, faculty find the concept beneficial because it provides students with the opportunity to apply and process diversity-related concepts presented in the classroom. Stated differently, the theoretical material presented in the classroom comes to life in the intergroup dialogues and takes on greater meaning for the students. In addition, it is very difficult to replicate the intergroup dialogue process in the classroom, particularly when certain groups are not numerically represented (e.g., very small numbers of African Americans, Latinos, Jews, or other social identities).

On another front, the Voices of Discovery program faces several challenges. First, the program is only recruiting from courses and disciplines that deal with diversity-related topics. The intergroup dialogues have to expand to include students from other disciplines such as business, engineering, and other hard sciences. Second, the recruitment strategy has to be studied and modified to challenge students to grow and develop. Presently, it appears that White student participants are enrolling in what they consider to be "safe" dialogue groups (e.g., male/female) and avoiding more challenging groups such as those involving race and ethnicity (e.g., African American/White, Latino/White). Third, the gender discussion groups have proved to be a challenge because of the normalization of sexism. That is, sexism has become so "normal" and pervasive that it is difficult to build consciousness around these issues. This is particularly true when the females in the group collude with the males and support their sexist views (e.g., "What's wrong with being called a girl? I like being referred to as a girl"). A fourth challenge facing the intergroup dialogues is assessing the long-term impact of the program. Short-term assessment suggests that participants are learning about themselves and other groups. What is not known is whether the impact of the dialogue process lasts over time. A fifth challenge entails encouraging participants to take action to end intergroup conflict, misunderstandings, prejudice, and discrimination. All the consciousness in the world is not going to help end oppression unless participants are moved toward action.

Assessment

The Voices of Discovery program has been evaluated and researched using both quantitative and qualitative approaches. Using a pretest-posttest design, Geranios (1997) examined the impact that dialogue groups have on students' cognitive (e.g., knowledge about other groups), affective (feelings and attitudes about other groups), and behavioral outcomes. More specifically, she was interested in comparing two types of students on the outcomes outlined above: (1) students who took a cultural awareness course and participated in an intergroup dialogue, and (2) students who took a cultural awareness course only. The researcher hypothesized that students who participated in both, a course and the dialogue groups, would report greater increases in cognitive, affective, and behavioral outcomes.

Results of the study suggest that separately both approaches produce statistically significant cognitive and affective outcomes. That is, students increased their knowledge about, and awareness of discrimination toward, specific groups, such as Asians, African Americans, and Jews. Moreover, students reported a reduction in negative stereotypes toward African Americans, gays, lesbians, and bisexuals, Asian Americans, white males, and males in general.

Geranios compared the pooled cognitive, affective, and behavioral scores related to each approach (cultural awareness course vs. a cultural awareness course plus the dialogue program). She found that when the scores were pooled, there were no statistically significant differences between the two approaches. She did find that when the scores were compared along dimensions (e.g., the cognitive outcomes of a cultural awareness course alone vs. the cognitive outcomes of a cultural awareness course plus intergroup dialogue), "the number and intensity of the statistically significant individual cognitive, affective, and behavioral scores of those participating in the multicultural course and the Voices of Discovery Program exceed those of the multicultural course only participants" (1997, 129). She concludes,

> The findings confirm that a multicultural course in conjunction with the Voices of Discovery program produce greater outcomes than the course alone, although the increase in gain scores is not at a statistically significant level. Thus, the Voices of Discovery program enhances the outcomes provided by the multicultural course.

Maxwell (1997) examined the dimensions of students' intergroup awareness prior to engaging in dialogue. She specifically analyzed the responses of dialogue participants to the following question: Keeping in mind the dialogue group to which you have been assigned, what are three things that you don't understand about the other group that you would like to ask questions about or get answers to? In her study, Maxwell identified cognitive, affective, and behavioral dimensions related to what students do not understand and are seeking to know about each other. In the cognitive area, students appear to seek information (e.g., What are some traditions in the Hispanic culture? Why is the "coming out" process for gays so difficult?) as a way of understanding the others. With respect to affect, participants are also curious about attitudes toward and feelings (e.g., anger, guilt, frustration) about topics such as interracial dating, discrimination, and racism. At the behavioral level, participants are interested in taking action (e.g., What can we do to change things?) and examining a group's responsibility for intergroup conflict and tension. Maxwell's study of the program is important because it begins the work of identifying where the gaps in knowledge exist that contribute to intergroup conflict, tension, and misunderstanding. The program can target these areas in the future.

The Voices of Discovery program has also been evaluated to examine the experiences of the participants and to glean recommendations for improvement. The vast majority of respondents find the experience extremely beneficial and feel that the program should be required for all students. In some cases, they indicate that they learned more from participating in the program than from their courses. After six weeks of dialogue, most of the students request that the groups meet for two or three additional weeks to continue the process of dialogue. In their evaluations, they suggest that six weeks of dialogue is not enough.

Summary

As our institutions of higher education continue to diversify, new strategies must be employed to take advantage of the multiplicity of cultures, languages, worldviews, orientations, talents, skills, and perspectives that groups bring to the campus. Moreover, positive interaction between groups is not a natural phenomenon. It must be structured and encouraged. Intergroup dialogue is one effective approach to creating interaction between groups as a means of using diversity to achieve intergroup educational outcomes.

NOTE

I want to thank Christine Geranios for her work in establishing and coordinating the Voices of Discovery program. I also want to acknowledge the present coordinator, Kelly Maxwell, for her efforts in building and expanding the program. Special thanks to Kris Ewing, Erin Murphy, Joel Montemayor, Jennifer Hiatt, Sherrie Loomis, Kathya Hidalgo, Eva Fatigoni, Dondrell Swanson, Tonya Banz, and all the facilitators and faculty who have made contributions to the program over the last several years.

REFERENCES

Burbules, N. C. 1993. *Dialogue in Teaching: Theory and Practice.* New York: Teachers College.

Cox, T., Jr., and R. L. Beale. 1997. *Developing Competency to Manage Diversity: Reading, Cases, and Activities.* San Francisco: Berrett-Koehler.

Geranios, C. A. 1997. "Cognitive, Affective, and Behavioral Outcomes of Multicultural Courses and Intergroup Dialogues in Higher Education." Ed.D. diss., Arizona State University, Tempe.

Hurtado, S. 1990. "Campus Racial Climates and Educational Outcomes." University of California, Los Angeles: Unpublished doctoral dissertation.

Hurtado, S., E. Dey, and J. Treviño. 1994. "Exclusion or Self-Segregation? Interaction across Racial/Ethnic Groups on College Campuses." Paper presented at the Annual Meeting of the American Educational Research Association, New Orleans, April 4–8.

Hurtado, S., J. Milem, A. Clayton-Pederson, and W. Allen. 1999. *Enacting Diverse Learning Environments: Improving the Climate for Racial/Ethnic Diversity in Higher Education.* ASHE-ERIC Higher Education Report, vol. 26, no. 8. Washington, D.C.: George Washington University, Graduate School of Education and Human Development.

Maxwell, K. 1997. "Dimensions of Intergroup Consciousness: Preliminary Findings." Paper presented at First Annual Conference on Intergroup Dialogue on the College Campus, University of Michigan, November 13–15.

Spitzberg, I. J., Jr., and V. V. Thorndike. 1992. *Creating Community on College Campuses.* New York: SUNY Press.

Stephan, W. G., and C. W. Stephan. 1996. *Intergroup Relations.* Boulder, Colo.: Westview Press.

Treviño, J. G., and C. A. Geranios. 1997. "Promoting Positive Intergroup Relations at Arizona State University: Facilitator Handbook." Typescript.

Winkelman, M. 1993. *Ethnic Relations in the U.S.: A Sociohistorical Cultural Systems Approach.* San Francisco: West Publishing.

Zúñiga, X., and B. A. Nagda. 1993. "Dialogue Groups: An Innovative Approach to Multicultural Learning." In *Multicultural Teaching at the University,* ed. David Schoem, Linda Frankel, Ximena Zúñiga, and Edith A. Lewis. Westport, Conn.: Praeger.

Chapter 7

Educating for Social Justice: The Program on Intergroup Relations, Conflict, and Community at the University of Michigan

Monita C. Thompson, Teresa Graham Brett, and Charles Behling

The Program on Intergroup Relations, Conflict, and Community (IGRCC or IGR) is an interdisciplinary program that brings together faculty and staff from a broad range of academic backgrounds. As a unit in the Division of Student Affairs (DSA) that operates in partnership with the College of Literature, Science, and the Arts (LSA), IGR attempts to break down traditional barriers between academic programs and Student Affairs programs in order to create environments that integrate cognitive and affective learning. In doing so, we provide models of educational structures that effectively integrate the classroom and life experiences of students. IGR occupies a unique niche in higher education, and more specifically, in large research universities with a diverse student body.

The program uses research, theory, and practice from intergroup relations, sociology, psychology, and higher education student development to guide practice. Insights from the intergroup relations literature crucial to the program include the following:

- Contact between members of different social identity groups (based on race, ethnicity, gender, age, disability, class, sexual orientation, and religion) may be helpful in reducing prejudice and discrimination between those groups, but contact may also increase prejudice and discrimination.

- Determining the sorts of contact that have positive results and those that have negative results are empirical questions, and ones about which we already have much scientific knowledge.

- Productive contact is likely to involve relatively equal-status contact between group members, the perception of some shared goals among members, the provision of a safe environment for interaction, and contact sustained over time.

- Since honest, equal-status contact is likely to uncover long-standing conflict between groups, conflict should be seen as part of the process of developing positive group interaction, and as useful in building group bonds. Conflict should not be denied, avoided, or excessively managed.

- Teaching about intergroup relations is best done by following the principles of productive contact. Therefore, this teaching may require pedagogical techniques that are highly innovative and nontraditional. For example: there must be experiential teaching techniques as well as traditional techniques; status relationships in the classroom must be examined; conflict is to be expected and may be used as part of the process of learning.

- It is assumed that this sort of learning can be transformative in the lives of both students and instructors. While the program does not presume to tell students how to use their new insights in their lives as citizens, we act on the faith that persons educated in intergroup relations will have special contributions to make to the pursuit of social justice, even as those contributions differ and conflict in their specific political, social, and ethical operationalizations.

Program Mission

The mission of the Program on Intergroup Relations is to provide University of Michigan students with the opportunity to learn, cognitively and experientially, about issues of intergroup relations, explicitly focusing on the relationship between social conflict and social justice. The program seeks to offer and support curricular and cocurricular programs and services that facilitate student development and learning, and in doing so, to actively promote the building of more just communities. Our goals include bringing together students from various social identity groups through intergroup dialogue courses; developing a core of skilled student facilitators; and teaching other courses that address topics in intergroup relations.

Program History

IGR began in 1988 with a university Presidential Undergraduate Initiative Grant to the Pilot Program and to the Program on Conflict Management Alternatives (PCMA). The undergraduate initiative was proposed at a time of heightened racial and ethnic tension at the University of Michigan. IGR was developed with the purpose of both advancing students' understanding of and respect for diversity, and increasing students' skills in responding to intergroup conflicts in various settings. IGR was conceived with the vision of explicitly linking formal academic course work with cocurricular programming and students' social experiences.

Since its inception, IGR has worked closely with both academic and student affairs units to develop curricular and cocurricular activities that address social conflict, intergroup relations, and social justice. It has been the intention of the program to address these issues within the living-learning context of student life. Intergroup conflict is understood to encompass issues of gender, religion, nationality, socioeconomic class, physical ability, age, sexual orientation, as well as race and ethnicity.

The primary initiative of the program was the creation and execution of intergroup dialogues, which are structured interactions between members of different social identity groups over sustained periods of time (twelve to thirteen weeks). Accompanying the dialogues were workshops, training programs, and other activities.

Organization and Structure

Administratively, the IGR staff consists of two codirectors (one from LSA, one from the DSA); an associate director, program coordinator, and an administrative assistant (DSA); one lecturer (LSA); and three to four graduate and undergraduate student interns. This group has the primary responsibility of oversight of the program, including coordination of the first-year seminar faculty meetings and joint activities, placement of the students in intergroup dialogues, construction of course materials for intergroup dialogues, maintenance of the resource library, recruitment of faculty and students, campus workshops, public relations, and coordination of research and publications on the program.

There are four core faculty who teach regularly with the program: two tenured (one in sociology and one in psychology), and two lecturers assigned to the program (psychology). Although the two tenured faculty have committed to teaching with IGR, they must obtain approval from their respective departments in order to do so. The faculty work collaboratively with Student Affairs coteachers and the program to design the IGR course. They also take on administrative responsibilities for the courses they teach. Other faculty (numbering eight to ten) teach courses within the first-year seminars through their respective departments. Faculty teaching first-year students are independently responsible for the design of their course.

At its core, IGR believes that through systematic instruction, interaction, and dialogue, we will be able to prepare learners (including both students and instructors) to assist in the building of more just communities. Key to this philosophy is a set of values that includes sharing power and decision making, collaboration, self-reflection (as individuals and as an organization), and ongoing commitments to challenging hierarchies and power dynamics that reinforce traditional boundaries within society and the university. At the same time, we realize that we exist within a hierarchical and discipline-oriented research institution, that we must acknowledge the power structure inherent in the traditional university structure, and that we must be able to work within such a system.

The program, through the departments of psychology and sociology, offers four types of courses: Intergroup Dialogue, Training for Facilitation, Practicum in Facilitation, and Resident Hall Staff Training. In addition, First-Year Seminars are coordinated by the program and offered through various academic departments at the university.

Courses Currently Offered

First-Year Seminars

The program has offered first-year seminars since 1996. These seminars are organized as First-Year Interest Groups (FIGs). In this context, instructors from various departments offer seminars on different topics relating to social identity and social justice. Each seminar enrolls approximately twenty-five students for three academic credits. Instructors who wish to teach in this program apply to their home departments for permission to teach their seminar. Those home departments fund the seminars, usually as part of the university's first-year seminar program. In one year, as an experiment, two faculty included their junior-level courses in the FIGs group, and upper-class students joined the program. The faculty, both of whom had taught First-Year Seminars the previous year, wanted to continue the interdisciplinary collegial relationship and support of other faculty teaching a similar curriculum. The upper-division students felt the activities during the joint sessions were good for students beginning to learn about social justice issues; however, they were more advanced in their thinking and did not find the joint activities helpful for their level.

The teaching methods of the seminars vary from instructor to instructor, but traditional seminar methods that emphasize student conversation and interaction are the primary pedagogical techniques. However, almost all of the seminars also include some innovative experiential exercises, most of which are derived from the exercises developed or promoted by IGR.

There are several unique aspects of the FIGs seminars that are modeled after a first-year program at the University of Washington. The faculty, who represent a variety of disciplines, meet together regularly—biweekly in the summer and the fall—to plan the joint activities of the seminars (see below), but more importantly to exchange ideas across disciplines and to support each other in teaching about diversity. This faculty exchange has proven to be enormously appealing to the faculty, and in fact seems a primary reason that persons are eager to teach the program. Some faculty have reported that these meetings are one of the few opportunities for support and networking in teaching social justice courses. In fact, the faculty often continue to meet, even though the courses are over, as a way of continuing to exchange ideas and support across disciplines for teaching about diversity and social justice.

In addition to bringing together faculty in a supportive and intellectually stimulating atmosphere, the FIGs program also brings together students from the various seminars for periodic joint meetings. These joint FIGs occur three or four times during the semester of the program. Students engage in exercises, hear lectures, watch movies, and/or form discussion groups across seminars. A primary goal of the joint FIGs is to induce conversations across seminars, so that students, all of whom are studying some aspect of social diversity and justice, can exchange ideas from their various disciplinary perspectives. It is also hoped that students will form interest groups and will continue their conversations outside of the formal joint FIGs sessions.

Intergroup Dialogues (Psychology/Sociology)

Intergroup dialogues are the primary focus of IGR and are its most innovative contribution to education about intergroup relations. The original four-stage design by Ximena Zúñiga, Biren (Ratnesh) Nagda, and Todd Sevig in 1988 remains and has been expanded to fit the semester calendar. Dialogues meet once per week for two hours throughout the semester and offer two academic credits to students. The program constructs the dialogues as meetings between students from different social identity groups defined by ethnicity, race, religion, gender, sexual orientation, ability, class, age, or national origin.

Approximately twelve to sixteen students are admitted to each dialogue. Intergroup dialogues are structured around two identity groups, and students are assigned by the program to dialogues so that there is equal representation between the two groups. For example, if the dialogue is between people of color/white people, approximately half of the students in the dialogue identify as people of color and half as white people. Some dialogues are focused on exploring a particular identity or social group category such as white identity or classism. In these cases we strive to create diversity within the group but do not put an emphasis on equal numbers.

When students indicate their desire to enroll in the dialogue program, they complete placement forms, identifying their social group memberships if they wish, and indicating their top three choices for dialogue groups. The program then assigns participants to dialogues and is usually successful in placing students in the first or second of their preferred dialogues. We sometimes change the number or types of dialogues we had planned to offer to accommodate students' interests. In the dialogue courses, students engage in carefully structured interactions during class time, complete weekly reading assignments, write weekly journals and reaction papers, participate fully during in-class exercises and discussions, and write a final paper. Dialogues are facilitated by pairs of undergraduate students (and occasionally graduate students), paired so that one facilitator is from each of the social identity group represented in the dialogue. In the semester prior to the dialogues, the facilitators have been enrolled in an intensive training course in intergroup principles and facilitation skills (see below for training). While leading the dialogues, the facilitators are also enrolled in a practicum course that continues training. Each one of these courses provides three academic credits for the student.

Intergroup dialogues stress the viability of group identities, even as students are challenged to become aware of the ways in which their individual views are molded by social institutions. Students are challenged to new understandings of self and group identities by the identification of preconceptions and misconceptions shared between social groups, and by the exploration of attitudes about conflict and change that might inhibit dialogue. Exercises are designed to help students see both homogeneity and heterogeneity in each group. It is expected that participants will define areas of conflict between and within groups; whether that conflict is resolved or not, it is expected that participants will come to a greater understanding of the beliefs, feelings, and perceptions of those with whom they differ. As questions of social justice are brought to the fore, students may begin to reformulate their own communication strategies and may begin to reconceptualize alliances and communities across intergroup boundaries.

The dialogues follow a carefully planned structure of interactions or pedagogical framework, which may be revised by facilitators and supervisors in response to emerging needs and characteristics of the dialogue participants. This basic structure includes four phases of dialogue development, each requiring about a fourth of the semester's time schedule.

- Introduction: focus is on developing basic communication and listening skills; introducing and defining fundamental concepts and assumptions regarding intergroup relations; establishing initial group formation and ground rules for interactions.

- Inter- and intragroup processes: discussion centers on understanding social constructions of each group; recognizing multiple group identities; and exploring similarities and differences within and between groups.

- Discussion of concrete issues: Focus is on analysis and discussion of specific contemporary issues involving the groups. Because this is a period in which conflict often surfaces, the skills learned in the initial stages are likely to be tested. Students are confronted with questions of how (and whether) to promote social justice when groups conflict.

- Conclusion: The focus of discussion is on two important questions: (1) Where do we go from here? (2) What implications do the experiences and learnings of the semester have for social justice and the building of communities?

Training in Processes of Intergroup Dialogues

Students who desire to facilitate an intergroup dialogue must first successfully complete a three-credit, semester-long training course. The training course is offered in a variety of formats. For example, the course almost always includes intensive training periods in addition to the regular weekly class meetings. Depending on the methodology of the instructor, this might involve one or more weekend retreats, or one or more daylong seminars.

The course focuses on the teaching of basic principles of intergroup relations, using experiential pedagogical techniques, readings, journaling, and other written assignments. The course emphasizes learning about intergroup relations, not the explicit development of facilitation skills. Because the principles of intergroup relations are taught by the experiential methods of facilitation, students learn facilitation techniques by experiencing and participating in them. Toward the end of the course, students begin to facilitate class exercises themselves, and in doing so consolidate their ability to model the facilitation techniques used by the instructors of the course. Enrollment in the course is limited to twenty students. Registration is by permission and involves an application, group interview, and an interview by the instructors or IGR staff. As might be expected, a substantial number of enrollees are those persons who have earlier taken an Intergroup Dialogue course and/or FIGs.

At the end of the course, students continue the following term as Intergroup Dialogue facilitators. Some students may be deferred until later semesters or are offered other activities within the program. In addition to possessing a cognitive mastery of principles of intergroup relations, potential facilitators are expected to demonstrate the ability to manage conflict, be self-reflective, work collaboratively, and complete assignments on time.

Practicum in Facilitating Intergroup Dialogues

During the semester that student peers facilitate dialogues, they are also enrolled in a three-credit practicum. This course continues the training they received during the previous term and provides a forum for discussing issues and preparing for the weekly dialogues. Emphasis is placed on both the continued development of facilitation skills and continued experiential study of intergroup relations in general.

Practicum students complete readings, both for the practicum and for their dialogues, prepare weekly dialogue plans (which are reviewed and discussed with the practicum instructors), write weekly reports on the results of the dialogues, meet with their cofacilitator outside of practicum, read journals and reactions written by their dialogue participants, and complete periodic and final reports on the dialogue. In addition, the facilitators meet regularly for consultation sessions with practicum instructors and other IGR staff, and their dialogues are observed and evaluated by instructors and staff. Facilitators submit weekly records of attendance and participation by the dialogue students, and they are interviewed at the end of the term concerning the performance of each of the dialogue students. Grading of the dialogue students is done by the practicum instructors with the assistance of a graduate student grader, who reads all the final papers of the dialogue students.

Social Psychology in Community Settings: Resident Staff Training

An important development offers us the opportunity to reach, at least indirectly, many of the ten thousand students who live in university residence halls. The University Housing Office invited IGR to develop a new course to be required of all students who are hired as residence staff. Created by faculty and staff in Psychology, IGR, and University Housing, this course is called Social Psychology in Community Settings.

The course provides a foundational understanding of the dynamics of intergroup relations and applies these to the challenges inherent in building multicultural communities. It is expected that students will take the skills and insights learned in the course to the residence halls as they interact with student residents and as they plan cocurricular programming offered in the residence halls.

Offered to approximately 160 students each winter, the course combines large-group meetings (similar to FIGs) on intergroup relations with small discussion and experiential sessions. This course has twenty-four facilitators, including three lead instructors (a faculty member from Psychology, a senior housing staff member, and a senior member of the IGR staff) who have the responsibility of designing the curriculum and coordinating the facilitators. Each small group has two cofacilitators who may be either residence hall professional staff, students who are currently paraprofessional residence hall staff, or Student Affairs staff from units other than University Housing.

In addition to the formal classes, IGR staff, faculty, and student facilitators conduct a variety of one-time dialogues and workshops for various university departments and student organizations.

Strengths of the Program and Challenges Ahead

Effectiveness of Intergroup Education

The most important strength of the program is the success it has achieved in educating students about important and difficult issues regarding intergroup relations. Both the content of instruction and the techniques the program has devised for intergroup education are unique. Students are not likely to have many other opportunities to learn in this format. In methodology, organization, and effectiveness the program is innovative and successful. Another indication of effectiveness, and one closer to home, was revealed when IGR asked members of its undergraduate and graduate student staff to reach consensus about the program's strengths and continuing challenges. Strengths that staff included were these: providing valuable training, which is necessary and relevant to their lives; the commitment of staff and faculty; the diversity of the staff, including age and position at the university, and the unusual opportunity to work in a collaborative way with them. Weaknesses, which will be discussed in more detail in the section on challenges, included the wish for more linkages between student staff and student facilitators, consistency and continuity of staff, and activities across semesters.

Philosophy of Staffing

We believe that one of the innovations that has made the University of Michigan program so successful is its joint leadership by Academic Affairs (LSA) and the Division of Student Affairs. While LSA staff may have special training in the theory and methodology of Intergroup Relations, and DSA staff may have special training in interactive methods with students, Michigan is very fortunate in that LSA and DSA staff are rich in both kinds of experience and training. Drawing from both LSA and DSA greatly increases the diversity of the social identities of potential teaching teams, and often it is only by involving both units that we are able to achieve the identity balances we require. We know that learning occurs best when the classroom and the rest of the campus life reinforce each other and are integrated in the experience of students. We consider the merging of the concerns of LSA and DSA professionals as one of the primary strengths of the Program on Intergroup Relations.

Empowerment and Training of Student Facilitators

A primary strength of IGR is its use of peer facilitators in the dialogue courses. One reason that students, rather than faculty and staff, facilitate dialogues is to break down status differences that can often inhibit honest expression of opinions and experiences. The literature on intergroup relations clearly shows that dialogue experiences are richest when peers, not authority figures, facilitate sessions. IGR considers this a crucial part of its methodology.

Not only does the use of peer facilitators increase the effectiveness of dialogues, it also serves as a powerful means of empowering students to act on their learning. The training of facilitators builds a cadre of persons able to promote social justice and use conflict productively in a variety of settings. Moreover, the role models provided by the facilitators become important examples for the dialogue participants; they are enabled to see themselves not as passive learners but as persons who may act vigorously on the basis of their learning. Use of peer facilitators also provides an example of egalitarian decision-making between students, faculty, and staff. This in itself raises provocative questions and issues about ways to organize just communities.

Partnerships and Collaborations with Other University Programs and Units

The IGR staff, representing both LSA and DSA, has established a close, cooperative, and comfortable working relationship. Merging faculty's and Student Affairs professionals' interests and expertise has made for a highly creative and innovative environment. Steps have been taken to reach beyond LSA and Student Affairs to work with the School of Social Work, the School of Education, and the Rackham Graduate School. In all of this, the program provides models for collaborations and partnerships across units, and these models may be potentially beneficial for a number of programs on campus.

Challenges of Consistency and Continuity

As a necessity, IGR course offerings are continuously evolving. Intergroup relations is not a static field, but must be responsive and relevant to student experiences. As such, we must update course packs each year (if not each semester). This need to stay abreast of current issues can tax the program's limited staff. In addition, many students who take some of our courses also are accepted as residence hall staff; thus we must continually find and develop new ideas for course materials to eliminate redundancy across our courses.

Another challenge has been the lack of continuity in our training course. Although we have learned what is effective through each iteration of the course, each cohort of student facilitators has had a somewhat different experience. While the training course is centered on a framework, instruction is influenced by other factors: (1) the change of instructors from semester to semester; and (2) the consideration of specific needs of each group of students. We have not found student preparedness to be a large issue, yet by being responsive to each cohort, we admit that experiences do differ, and one group may have focused more on theory than skills, or on knowledge and awareness more than theory.

Follow-up after Dialogues and Resident Staff Training (Social Psychology in Community Settings)

The curriculum of the IGR program is focused on the early college experience for students. Theoretically, these students are likely to experience the most growth in their first encounters with social differences. We offer a rather extensive set of first-year seminars, and students may take dialogues (up to twice for credit) early in their careers. After this, however, interested students find it difficult to continue their study of intergroup relations. Only twenty may enroll in training and go on to practicum. The Resident Staff Training course is open only to persons hired as residence staff. Students who become interested in intercultural issues through dialogues and FIGs need advanced courses where they can continue their studies. It is true that the university offers excellent courses on culture and a variety of social issues in many departments. However, IGR offers a unique experiential method of instruction, and one that we believe teaches social justice information, which is different from many other courses. Students who become interested in intergroup relations and in our methodology should have more options of upper-level courses in order to continue their studies. As the program continues to develop, this expansion is crucial in order to be responsive to the needs of students.

Staffing

The staffing needs of IGR differ from those of many other programs. Although our philosophy of staffing is a crucial strength of the program, we do have problems in finding appropriate and available instructors to fulfill the needs of the program. Because of the nature of intergroup dialogues, training, and practicum, most of our courses must be team taught. The team members need to be of different social identities, as well as be familiar in both the theory of intergroup relations and in interactive, experiential techniques of teaching. The instructors need to be prepared for a time commitment that is unusually heavy and involves sensitive emotional interactions. The instructors should be able to work toward collaboration and equity between persons who are often given different status in the university and in society, and they must be able to deal with the conflict that this produces in a way that does not needlessly divert energy from the delivery of services to students.

These unique needs make the pool of available instructors somewhat limited. Our staff is small. Presently, some of the instructors best qualified to teach in our unique settings are those who hold nontraditional appointments, for example, lecturers. For various reasons, these instructors at Michigan may be the most frequently trained in experiential pedagogies, and they may represent a broader social diversity than other faculty. In the past, some university policies have made it difficult to gain permission for lecturers and other nontraditional faculty to teach appropriate courses for IGR. In addition, time is an important factor that can conflict with other faculty duties at a research university. Intergroup relations courses place special time demands on their instructors. Practicum instructors must not only teach a two-hour seminar, they must manage the intergroup dialogues. The instructors meet regularly with all facilitators outside of class for consultation sessions, they visit and observe dialogues; they grade dialogue participants, and so on. Training instructors also design and facilitate daylong and weekend retreats in addition to teaching the regular class meetings. All instructors meet regularly with their coinstructors to plan, coordinate, and design their class. If the program were able to appoint the same teams of instructors from semester to semester, some of the additional time required in coteaching the courses (discussion of course content, syllabi, grading criteria, etc.) might be lessened.

Perhaps most importantly, enormous time is required to deal with individual student needs that develop during intergroup experiences. Often students are very unsettled by the insights and conflicts that develop during the study of these extremely sensitive aspects of our culture. A great deal of unscheduled time needs to be spent responding to the needs of students who find themselves in need of support, conversation, and consultation. These individual meetings can be important teaching opportunities, but they cannot be done quickly.

Finally, since two of our core LSA faculty depend on annual negotiations with their departments for release time to teach in IGR, it is a challenge to maintain a reliable pool of instructors whom we know will be teaching for the program each year. At present, we function because of the generous support of the psychology and sociology departments. But when the chairs of these departments rotate, we are faced with the question of how to continue teaching intergroup dialogues if the new chairs are less interested in the program and are faced with the dilemma of finding new instructors when current instructors retire or move on. Despite our interdepartmental and interdisciplinary nature, departmental interests remain strong at a research institution with specialized programs.

What Have We Learned about Our Program?

Several studies have been conducted to assess student learning as participants of intergroup dialogues and with those who have facilitated these groups. A study by Lopez, Gurin, and Nagda (1998) revealed that compared with other students, those students who participated in an intergroup dialogue showed an increase in understanding of the social structural factors associated with racial inequalities and had a greater willingness to consider multiple perspectives. Nagda and Zúñiga (1999) looked at three measures of the impact of the process of intergroup dialogue: critical awareness, sustained dialogue, and bridging differences. They found an increase on all three measures and confirmed the overall goals of the dialogue: "to provide a setting for students to raise awareness, to talk about race with people from different racial/ethnic backgrounds and different viewpoints, and to strengthen the desire for cross-race exchanges and learning" (Nagda and Zúñiga 1999).

We have learned from other research that learning processes are different for dominant and subordinate groups, even when both are working on improving intergroup communication (Zúñiga and Sevig 1994); and that the change process can be both positive (improved intergroup relations) and negative (deteriorated intergroup relations) in the dialogue setting (Yeakley and Gutierrez 1999). Since the process of intergroup dialogue may have varied results for different individuals and groups, continued exploration may assist in understanding how and why these differences occur.

In order to assess long-term learning, Vasques Scalera (1999) studied the experiences of intergroup dialogue facilitators after college. In her research, former facilitators report and describe a deep and lasting impact on their self-awareness, understanding of issues of difference and intergroup relations, and their willingness, ability, and commitment to take action against social injustice in their personal and professional lives. This study was the first to explore impact after college.

Research and assessment are crucial to understanding how the program works and its impact on student learning. We will continue to support efforts that inquire into our processes of training facilitators and examining the experiences of students in intergroup dialogue. As a program situated in both Student Affairs and Academic Affairs at a research institution, we fully understand the importance of providing data to maintain continued support for our mission and for program expansion.

Plans for the Future

We believe IGR has a strong and promising future within the university and as a national model of intergroup education. Future plans call for expanding our offerings to provide more opportunities for intergroup education, including advanced courses for students who have facilitated, with the goal of offering a minor in intergroup relations/social justice education. We also see research and assessment as an important tool in our learning and in providing evidence to the sustainability of our program. As one of the first such programs in higher education, IGR maintains the goal of remaining a leader in intergroup relations and social justice education. We will continue to carry out the mission and goals that we have set forth, while we strive to overcome our current challenges.

REFERENCES

Lopez, Gretchen, Patricia Gurin, and Biren (Ratnesh) A. Nagda. 1998. "Education and Understanding Structural Causes for Group Inequalities." *Political Psychology* 19, no. 2: 305–29.

Nagda, Biren (Ratnesh) A., and Ximena Zúñiga. 1999. "Fostering Meaningful Racial Engagement through Intergroup Dialogues." Paper presented at the Annual

Conference of the Association for the Study of Higher Education, San Antonio, November.

Vasques Scalera, Carolyn M. 1999. "Democracy, Diversity, Dialogue: Education for Critical Multicultural Citizenship." Ph.D. diss., University of Michigan.

Yeakley, Anna M., and Lorraine M. Gutierrez. 1999. "Intergroup Dialogues for Individual, Community, and Organizational Change." Paper presented at the Twenty-first Symposium of the Association for the Advancement of Social Work with Groups, University of Denver, October.

Zúñiga, Ximena, and Todd Sevig. 1994. "Incorporating Multiple Learning Goals for Different Groups." Program presented at the National Conference on Race and Ethnicity in American Higher Education, Atlanta, June.

Chapter 8

Intergroup Dialogue, Education, and Action: Innovations at the University of Washington School of Social Work

Biren (Ratnesh) A. Nagda, Scott Harding, Dominique Moïse-Swanson, Mary Lou Balassone, Margaret Spearmon, and Stan de Mello

Social work education today is the nexus of many critical discussions about the role of the profession and educators in a period of demographic and societal change. As a profession, social work holds close the dual missions of social service and social change. The Social Work Code of Ethics calls on social work professionals to challenge social injustice: "to pursue social change, particularly with and on behalf of vulnerable and oppressed individuals and groups of people" (National Association of Social Workers 1996, 6). Current social reality, however, suggests that social workers are not always successful in balancing or integrating the goals of service and change. In fact, most often we incline toward one or the other (Franklin 1990; Gil 1998). In this era of welfare reform, managed care, and service cutbacks, social work graduates are more likely to take direct practice positions focusing mainly on providing social services rather than promoting social justice (Specht and Courtney 1994). Meanwhile, increasing social diversity and continued social injustices pose challenges to maintain the historic commitment of the profession to work with people and populations affected by injustice and oppression. A recent mandate from Council on Social Work Education (1992), the accrediting body for all social work programs, departments, and schools in the United States, emphasizes that the purpose of social work education is to prepare competent and effective social work professionals who are committed to practice that includes services to the poor and oppressed, and who work to alleviate poverty, oppression, and discrimination. In response, practitioners, scholars and researchers are compelled to innovate models of social work education that prepare social workers for multicultural practice, or what is more commonly referred to as culturally competent practice

(Sowers-Hoag and Sandau-Beckler 1996). In this chapter, we focus on the value of intergroup dialogues as a way of preparing generalist social workers for multicultural practice in a way that integrates a social justice approach to cultural competency work or working across differences.

Intergroup Dialogue, Education, and Action

The Intergroup Dialogue, Education, and Action (IDEA) effort at the University of Washington School of Social Work was started in November 1996 with funding from the Council on Social Work Education (CSWE) Millennium Project. As the national accrediting body for all social work programs in the United States, CSWE initiated the Millennium Project to foster educational innovations in schools of social work to advance the education of social workers for the changing societal context of the twenty-first century. One of the more urgent professional imperatives in this changing context is for social work educators to prepare competent practitioners who can work with an increasingly diverse clientele and embrace the profession's social justice mission.

The funding helped us to pioneer the integration of intergroup dialogues into social work practitioner education. Subsequent funding from the University of Washington Office of the Provost's Cultural and Ethnic Diversity Initiative and the William and Flora Hewlett Foundation's Pluralism and Unity Project has helped in institutionalizing both the intergroup dialogues and the facilitator training components of the program. Further funding from the University of Washington's Tools for Transformation and University Initiatives Fund has helped expand our efforts in graduate education and establish the Intergroup Dialogue, Education, and Action (IDEA) Training and Resource Institute.

The Institute's guiding philosophy draws from an understanding of three critical aspects necessary in forging alliances across differences for personal and social change.

> *Intergroup dialogue* provides a viable and transformative means of engaging across differences, especially when these differences are marked by both cultural and power differences. We believe that our ways of communicating and relating often replicate the same oppressive dynamics that are the content of our deliberations and the target of change. Thus, in the words of Margo Adair and Sharon Howell

(1997), through intergroup dialogue, we aim to "break old habits and weave new ties."

Education holds two parallel meanings for us. First, we view *education* from its Latin root, meaning "to draw out." We see our approach as closely aligned with Freirean dialogic education as opposed to banking education (Freire 1993). By using personal experiences and viewpoints as valid knowledge, we bring to the center participants' own lives and ways of being in the world. Second, education signifies our commitment to the learning *and* unlearning processes necessary in confronting oppression and injustices. Learning new information and skills, as well as unlearning socialized and prejudiced ways of being in the world, helps expand participants' capacity for critical consciousness—awareness about the impact of multiple levels of oppression and privilege in their lives, and agency to impact upon those systems.

Action refers to our belief that deep engagement in the intergroup dialogue and education processes can motivate and build participants' capacity for becoming change agents. We believe that these processes can facilitate both personal and social change and empower participants to act on the world around them in more just ways. While some action may involve direct interruption of oppressive speech, acts, and incidents, we also see action manifested in participants' interactions with others. In the context of social work education, this is particularly important as our students develop practice knowledge, attitudes, values, and skills to work with a diverse clientele.

Intergroup Dialogues in the Undergraduate Social Work Curriculum

We believe that intergroup dialogues offer both an innovative way of teaching about diversity and social justice, and an experiential setting for social work students to engage with people from different social and cultural backgrounds. The prevailing emphasis on working across differences in social work currently centers on culturally competent practice. A culturally competent practitioner is one who has *(a)* awareness and acceptance of cultural differences, *(b)* self-awareness of cultural values, *(c)* an understanding of the dynamics of difference in the helping process, *(d)* knowledge of a client's culture, and *(e)* ability to adapt skills to a client's cultural context (Cross et al. 1989). Criticisms of the cultural competence approach include the lack of explicit focus on inequality and social justice (Gutiérrez, Fredriksen, and Soifer 1999). More recent works embracing a social justice perspective add to this approach the dimensions of oppression, privilege, empowerment, and transformation (see Nagda and Gutiérrez 2000; Reed et al. 1997; Weaver 1999). Intergroup dialogues aim to bring such a perspective to educating social work students. Such dialogues represent a potentially powerful and effective way of engaging future practitioners to develop a social justice ethos in working across cultural differences.

In the next section we describe two main components of integrating intergroup dialogues in a social work curriculum: one, a required course in which students participate in intergroup dialogues; and two, an elective course for training facilitators for intergroup dialogues. Under each component, we also include the program evaluation methods and results.

Cultural Diversity and Justice Course

Since the spring quarter of 1997, intergroup dialogues have become an integral component of the undergraduate social work curriculum preparing students for entry-level generalist social work practice.[1] We have incorporated interracial/ethnic dialogues into the required Cultural Diversity and Justice course for undergraduates in the Bachelor of Social Welfare (BASW) program (table 1). We define intergroup dialogues as

> face-to-face meetings of students from different racial/ethnic groups. They [intergroup dialogues] are designed to offer a safe place where students from different groups can foster deeper understanding of diversity and justice issues through participation in experiential activities, individual and small group reflections and dialogues. . . . The intergroup nature of dialogue emphasizes open communication on justice issues, such as social group membership, identity, and positionality vis-à-vis structural and societal power. (Nagda et al. 1999, 437)

Students enroll in the Cultural Diversity and Justice course during the spring quarter of their first year in the two-year program. The overall learning objectives of the course are (1) to enable students to develop self- and other-awareness in relation to social group memberships and status in society, and (2) to explore professional values that support social work in a multicultural society (Nagda et al. 1999). The course seeks to enhance students' appreciation of the variety of differences based on social and cultural groups, awareness of ways in which these differences subjugate certain groups while privileging others, and understanding of power inequalities within many intergroup relationships, while also providing students with models of transformation that can counter negative intergroup relations and dynamics. As part of the course, students meet in lecture/discussion sections and separate intergroup dialogue sections. The lecture/discussion sections, with about twenty-two students each, meet for two hours and twenty minutes per week. This part of the course is organized using the developmental paradigm of difference-dominance-transformation. Requirements for this component include attendance at all section meetings, active participation, and a set of written assignments. The intergroup dialogue section, with ten to twelve students each, meets for one

TABLE 1. Design of Cultural Diversity and Justice Course with Intergroup Dialogues

Segment of Course	Intergroup Dialogue Session
1. Course overview and planning and review of critical concepts: conflict, difference, dominance, and change	Orientation to intergroup dialogue; group beginnings and getting acquainted
2. Groups and culture	Cultural chest: Sharing and learning about each other's cultures
3. Introduction to intergroup relationships	Reflecting upon and talking about racial/ethnic socialization
4. Oppression and dominance	Exploring advantages and disadvantages of racial/ethnic group membership
5. Racism, sexism, classism, and poverty	Talking about interracial/ethnic dating and relationships
6. Understanding gay men and lesbian women	Talking about affirmative action
7. Understanding ableism	Alliance building and action planning
8. On resistance and reform	Reflections on taking action and alliance building
9. Envisioning multicultural societies	Celebrate and speak out!
10. Where do we go from here?	

hour and fifty minutes every week. Student requirements for intergroup dialogue include mandatory participation in all sessions, and weekly reflection papers on their experiences in intergroup dialogues. Students also write a comprehensive paper at the end of the quarter that integrates their learning in the lectures and the intergroup dialogues.

The intergroup dialogues are cofacilitated by two peers—one student of color and one White student—who have undergone intensive facilitation training. The goals are

To develop a capacity for dialogue—deep listening, suspending judgments, identifying assumptions, and reflection and inquiry.

To reflect upon and learn about self and others as members of social group(s) in the context of systems of privilege and oppression.

To explore the similarities and differences in experiences across social group memberships.

To gain knowledge and understanding of the dynamics of difference and dominance at the personal and political levels.

To develop skills to work with differences, disagreements and conflicts as opportunities for deeper understanding and transformation.

To identify individual and collective actions for interrupting injustices and building alliances to promote greater social justice.

We adapted the four-stage intergroup dialogue model developed by Zúñiga, Nagda, and Sevig (2000) at the University of Michigan. The four-stage model, over a period of nine weeks (see table 1), involves getting acquainted and setting ground rules (sessions 1 and 2); learning about commonalities and differences (sessions 3 and 4); working on specific intergroup issues (sessions 5 and 6); and action planning and alliance building (sessions 7–9) (for elaboration of the model see Nagda et al. 1999; Zúñiga Nagda, and Sevig 2000). While the intergroup dialogues meet separately in small groups of about ten to twelve students, there are two collective meetings of all students. For one-half of the first session, all the students meet together so that we can impart shared expectations of intergroup dialogue and enhance the feeling of a learning community. We share our vision and goals of the intergroup dialogues, and some of the important building blocks necessary in this process. The facilitators speak about their own experiences, having gone through the intergroup dialogues just the previous year. Similarly, to celebrate our learning throughout the quarter, we meet as a whole group for the latter half of the final session. Each dialogue group documents or creatively portrays its collective learning in a collage that is shared with the other groups.

Program Evaluation of Student Experiences

From the beginning of the program, we have made a commitment to research and evaluation. The major goals for evaluation included documenting curriculum implementation of both the facilitator training and the actual dialogues, obtaining student feedback to improve the effort, and assessing student learning outcomes. We use both formative and summative evaluation methods. Student participants fill out pre- and posttest surveys and participate in individual and focus group interviews.

Over the first three years of the program, 177 students seeking bachelor's degrees in social welfare have participated in the intergroup dialogues. Most students were women (85 percent), and about half of the students identified themselves as middle class. The median age was twenty-two years with a range of nineteen years to fifty-four years. The racial/ethnic composition of the participants varied over the three years: in the first year, students of color comprised 50 percent; in the second year 38 percent; and in the third year 36 percent. Over the three years, approximately 7 percent of students were African American, 27 percent Asian American, 11 percent Latino(a), 8 percent Native American, and 59 percent European American/White. Most students also identified themselves as being heterosexual (93 percent) and without a disability (89 percent). Most of the students, about 86 percent, came from neighborhoods that were mostly racially homogeneous (67 percent from mostly or all-White neighborhoods and 19 percent from neighborhoods populated mostly or completely by people of color). Sixty-seven percent still live in mostly homogeneous communities (58 percent in mostly or all-White neighborhoods and 9 percent from neighborhoods populated mostly or completely by people of color).

In the posttest survey, we asked students about their learning experiences in the full Cultural Diversity and Justice course by indicating the extent of their agreement with a variety of learning outcomes (items adapted from Gurin, Lopez, and Nagda 1994). Some consistent themes emerged across the three years (also see Nagda et al. 1999). More than 83 percent of students indicated learning in four major areas, all of which are in line with the broad goals of intergroup dialogue. First, they thought more about the impact of social group membership on the person they were and about their own membership in social identity groups, and learned about experiences and perspectives of people from other social groups. Second, they became more aware of social inequalities. Third, they learned the difference between dialogue and debate, and also to value new viewpoints. And fourth, they thought more about taking actions to address social injustices.

In addition to completing the posttest survey, students were also required to write a final integrative paper in which they reflected more specifically on their learning from the intergroup dialogues. Many students remarked on the personal nature of intergroup dialogue, which put a "real face" to concepts that are talked about in class.

> This opportunity to hear individuals recount experiences and share their views made my learning so great. It is one thing to read about the concept of oppression and learn about the disadvantages and harmful effects it has on people. However, when you hear a classmate, someone who you know and respect, share an experience in which they were the disadvantaged, then the concept takes on an entirely new light. It is a perspective which can not be gained by reading from a book. Hearing the experiences of others makes the concept more real and hits closer to home. (Biracial [Mexican/White] woman)

> The dialogues gave me a human testimony which was much stronger than a book, because when I got uncomfortable I can put down a book, but you can't tell someone to shut up. (White man)

In line with the goals of intergroup dialogue, this process also encouraged students to reflect more deeply about themselves in a larger societal context. The process of understanding social identities and socialization evokes similar and different feelings for White students and students of color. For White students, the acknowledgment of misinformation and ignorance brings up feelings of anger.

> I was forced to look at myself, and decide if what I believed was true, was accurate, or if I was misinformed, or simply not looking at the issue. (White woman)

> I was mad a lot of the time. It pisses me off that I was even taught some things. And that I have to spend time reprogramming myself, but it's an excellent lesson. (White woman)

These challenges, however, are not absent for students of color. In fact, they too may face an ignorance of their racial/ethnic identity. The intergroup dialogue process and support allows them to validate identities previously hidden, ignored, and "silenced."

> This was a very sensitive issue for me, and at times I felt very uncomfortable, but the members and facilitators helped me to overcome my fears about my heritage. Because of this experience, I have lost a lot of fears I had about my identity of being Latino, and have gained a new confidence in my Latino side. (Biracial [Latina/White] woman)

> I was forced to confront and deal with both personal, family, and societal prejudices. The most difficult was dealing with past experiences of discrimination, racism, and oppression. Through my participation in the sessions, I was able to confront these past situations which I had never wanted to before due to all of the painful memories that I tried to forget. Thus, the dialogue session provided me with a safe place to speak out and begin the healing process. (Filipino-American woman)

Such healing can extend beyond the personal level. Speaking out and listening to each other's experiences also allows for new insights to emerge, such as the commonalities of being socialized with misinformation and stereotypes about various groups. This begins the process of intergroup healing and sows the first "seeds" to build alliances.

Students also spoke about developing very concrete communication skills that helped them work through differences and conflicts that arise in a discussion of controversial issues.

> The biggest thing I learned was being an active listener and just realizing that people have different sides to the same story and to be able to understand that person's story. I can't really put on their shoes and walk their life so it's important to listen to what their life has been like and to have that dialogue. (White woman)

> I am proud and amazed at the growth that I have noticed within myself! I now realize the importance of self-reflection, the sharing of experiences, and candid discussion as tools to recognize differences/similarities, personal identities, and to ignite social change! (African American woman)

Coupled with personal change, the intergroup dialogues also serve to engender a feeling of hopefulness to continue engaging across differences.

> What I learned is that people can discuss difficult subjects without hating each other and fighting with each other. So many people avoid hard subjects because of a fear of rejection, or anger, or of being misunderstood. While I know that I will still feel those fears, I now have a reason to believe that I will be heard, and

that not everybody will reject me, even if they don't agree with me. (White woman)

I think we learned more about building bridges. It was like our differences were laid out in front of us and we talked about those differences and then we came to some common ground and we started bridges. (Native American woman)

Students also talked about having developed an ethics of social justice through participation in the intergroup dialogues. They reported a new level of awareness and its importance in helping them engage in both personal and social change.

I think that I gained a better understanding of my unspoken and unnoticed racism. I can say that I'm not racist or sexist or whatever, but until I take a stand against it or make an effort toward change I'm still condoning it. (White man)

I've learned that I can't fight a color line, I can't fight an attitude about somebody's judgment of worth though I hope them equal. I can't fight that attitude in somebody else but I can fight for justice. So whether you're white or tan or brown I can collaborate with you and fight for justice on your behalf. (Focus group participant)

Building Competencies for Intergroup Dialogue Facilitation Course

In the first year of the program, intergroup dialogue facilitator training was conducted on a voluntary basis on the part of instructors. Students either volunteered or received independent study credit for their work. Student-facilitators were informally selected based on their interest and recommendations from faculty. In the beginning of the second year, we were awarded a Cultural and Ethnic Diversity Initiative grant through the University of Washington Provost's Office to formalize the facilitator training into a two-quarter course sequence.

Currently, in the first quarter of the course (winter), the class meets for seven three-hour sessions, and a weekend (Friday–Sunday) retreat. This course focuses on knowledge, awareness, and skills development. Topics covered include philosophy and principles of dialogic education and dialogic communication; intergroup communication; social identity development; principles of working with conflict; group dynamics, observation, and facilitation; team building among cofacilitators; and creating a support system among instructors and facilitators.

Students in the facilitation course are required to do several course assignments: (1) weekly "Learning Journal" to chart their own growth; (2) a "Taping Project I" to conduct an audiotaped, initial assessment of students' own ideas and attitudes about racism, and other issues related to interracial contact, dialogue, and facilitation (see Garcia and Van Soest 1997; Tatum 1992); (3) group observation to gain an understanding of group dynamics and processes; (4) adapt/design and implement an education module to give students a hands-on experience in implementing a structured experiential activity; and (5) "Taping Project II" to review students' responses on the first tape and write a reflection paper comparing these responses and their own growth through the quarter.

In all years of the program, we have had more students go through the facilitator training than available facilitator positions. We have used different strategies in selecting facilitators and offering other options to those not selected. We look for a commitment from facilitators to their own learning and contributing to others' learning, being a positive and constructive member of a learning community, awareness of social identities and oppression, and ability to work across differences. We use three strategies for assessment: (1) within the training course, we require students to demonstrate their skills by implementing a full educational activity with other facilitators-in-training; (2) the students write a self-assessment paper on their readiness for intergroup dialogue facilitation; and (3) as instructors we observe the students' development in facilitation over time in the training course. For those students not selected to be facilitators, we offer the option of being an observer so that they can still remain connected to the program while giving useful feedback to the facilitators, or they may continue their interest in the subject material through independent studies.

The second quarter of the training course is designed as a supervised practicum in intergroup dialogue facilitation to provide instruction, consultation, and supervision. The knowledge and skills developed in the winter quarter are examined in light of students' actual experiences facilitating the intergroup dialogues. The dialogue sessions meet on Friday afternoons, and the facilitator course meets weekly for two-hour sessions on Mondays. Weekly class sessions focus on comparison of facilitation experiences and consultations, troubleshooting with other facilitators, cofacilitator team building, and planning for upcoming dialogues. Further exploration of specific intergroup issues (such as affirmative action and immigration) and preparation for dialogues on these issues is also done.

The spring quarter also allows for continued team building among facilitators and instructors. Facilitator assignments include (1) facilitator process notes (twice during the quarter); (2) cofacilitator pair meetings with instructors (twice during the quarter); and (3) "Taping Project III," a reflection paper looking at their growth and development as facilitators over the two quarters.

Program Evaluation of Facilitator Skills Development

Student-facilitators play a critical role in other students' learning in the intergroup dialogues. One student noted:

> I think it was important to have facilitators in the group in order to have effective dialogue. The facilitators not only brought up the issues in which to discuss but also were there to help ease the tension which occurred during some sessions. I think that without them there would not have been a willingness to talk as openly because they enforced the idea of a "safe" environment and were there as a reminder that we were to learn about the diversity among us. If we had not had facilitators, [I] believe that as a group we would have let our emotions and strong convictions get between the learning process. (Focus group participant)

Program evaluation and assessment of facilitator skill development is also a key aspect of our work. Intergroup dialogue facilitators are asked to assess their knowledge, skills, personal awareness, commitment, and passion throughout their participation in the intergroup dialogue project. Facilitators participate in four different evaluation efforts: (1) they complete the "Intergroup Dialogue Facilitator Personal Resource Assessment Profile" at three points over the two quarters (beginning of winter quarter, end of winter quarter, and end of spring quarter); (2) they do the "Taping Project Assignment" (audiotape at beginning of winter quarter, reflection paper at end of winter quarter, and paper at end of spring quarter); (3) they fill out course evaluations at three points in the first quarter (after sessions 1–4, after the retreat, and after sessions 6–8); and (4) they participate in individual interviews and focus groups after the intergroup dialogues are completed.

Examining the data from the resource assessment profile, we find the greatest increase in facilitator skill development in the following areas over the two quarters:

Knowledge: principles and processes of intergroup dialogue, knowledge of dialogic pedagogy, and knowledge of intergroup issues

Skills: encouraging and facilitating participation from all group members, speaking in public, and facilitating a discussion

Personal awareness: awareness of their obstacles to awareness, of their own communication style, and of the impact of their communication style on other people

Commitment and passion: commitment to bring about social change, commitment on a professional level in working with others, and ability to share feelings with others

A facilitator says:

> I want to continue working in antiracist/oppression education in businesses and in schools. I will look for opportunities where I can facilitate group dialogues. I will continue my own learning to become familiar with current issues so that I can educate others wherever and whenever I can. When I see overt and covert acts of racism, I will continue to speak up. I will build alliances with all groups of people that want to work to overcome racial barriers and social injustices. (White woman)

Challenges

There are a number of challenges that exist in the implementation of intergroup dialogues.

Context

Two challenges became evident in relation to the professional and regional context. Since all the students are in social work, there is a strong professional ethical orientation that students are developing. The Social Work Code of Ethics encourages students to "treat each person in a caring and respectful fashion, mindful of individual differences and cultural and ethnic diversity" (National Association of Social Workers 1996, 5). While this is an asset in terms of enacting a dialogic process, some students have remarked that in many instances there is less disagreement and a sense of "preaching to the choir." The challenge in the dialogue then is to enable students to examine their personal values in the professional context and explore where the two may be at odds to open up a deeper inquiry.

The Northwest region poses a challenge because its population is still predominantly European American. The populations of color—Asian and Pacific Islanders, African Americans, Latino(a)s, and Native Americans—are present in different numbers but have great diversity within each of them (based on ethnicities, immigrant generation, and identification as people of color). All pose challenges in talking about race in the United States. It is important that dialogue opportunities offer the possibilities of examining these diversities in experiences, as well as the chance to explore commonalities and solidarities among people of color. Some of this work undoubtedly requires looking at intergroup issues among people of color. The Asian American and Pacific Islander population, in particular, has great diversity; some Japanese American students have been in the United States for over four generations while some Vietnamese American students have only recently immigrated. For European Americans who have grown up in mostly homogeneous environments, talking about race issues is a new undertaking. Acknowledging European ethnic roots is not always available through family histories. Thus, building trust and creating a safe atmosphere in the beginning sessions is crucial to initiate personal and individual sharing before examining commonalities and similarities both within and across groups.

Course

Students noted that one of the major challenges has been a disjuncture between the Cultural Diversity and Justice course and the intergroup dialogues. Topics discussed in the lecture sessions were not always continued in the intergroup dialogues. A second challenge relates to the role of the course instructors. Since they are not involved in facilitating the dialogues, nor are all of them actively involved in the training and support of the facilitators, there has not been a coherent effort to link the conceptual/theoretical learning in lectures to the dialogue experience in a way apparent to students.

To address these challenges, we conduct an orientation to intergroup dialogues in which we explain that the course is a broad introduction to issues of social identities, difference, dominant-subordinate relationships, empowerment, and social change, while the intergroup dialogues involve a deeper exploration of these issues as they relate to race and ethnicity. Course instructors now also read students' weekly reflection papers about their intergroup dialogues as a way of understanding student growth and development in the dialogues. In the future, we would like to have the course instructors more fully integrated in training and supporting the facilitators.

Facilitators

Given the complexity—cognitive, affective, and behavioral—of social justice education, facilitator training and preparedness remains a continual challenge. The facilitator role is indeed complex, and challenges remain in identifying the core competencies necessary for success. Currently, the intergroup dialogue facilitation class is open to any interested student. The challenge comes in selecting facilitators with sufficient skills for the actual facilitation. Some students may indicate passion for social justice education but need more development in self-awareness of social identities, group process and dialogic skills, and in implementation of educational activities. As the facilitators are continuing to deepen their own understanding of social identities, oppression, and empowerment, a strong support and consultation system is provided throughout the duration of the intergroup dialogues.

Many facilitators and students have remarked that a key facilitation challenge is in assessing when to let a dialogue continue and when to move to a different part of the agenda. Since the facilitators are given a detailed educational plan for each session, they often experience tension in accomplishing the entire plan. We stress that the facilitators should adapt the lesson plans according to the needs of the group that emerge throughout the dialogues. This need for flexibility raises another challenge—consistency of the student learning experience across the different dialogue groups. Therefore, the need for consistent monitoring and support for all groups is necessary, as is allowing for different processes and outcomes across groups.

Students

One challenge relates to the students' need for gaining skills for effective generalist practice; that is, they are concerned with concrete applications of their learning. One of the challenges has been to get away from a recipe approach of "these are the do's and these are the don'ts" toward an approach that facilitates students developing analytical perspectives and dialogic skills to apply competently and flexibly in practice situations.

Additionally, the student body is "nontraditional" in terms of the wide range of ages (nineteen to fifty-four years). Students come to the dialogues with different personal, direct practice, and working experiences on issues of diversity. On one hand, such diversity can enable more experienced students to be peer educators within the intergroup dialogues. By openly and nonjudgmentally sharing their life stories, such students can provide points of connection, support, and hope to students who may be less experienced. On the other hand, more experienced students may feel that they do not have much to learn from the dialogue experience, or that the conversation happens on a superficial level. Furthermore, the large age differences may pose challenges in creating a sense of equality in the dialogues. Older students may be perceived or perceive themselves to have more authority than younger students. They may be placed more in the role of a teacher rather than a peer. These dynamics may not only play out in student-student interactions, but also facilitator-student relationships. It is important not to lose the rich mutual learning that occurs when less experienced learners and the mature work together. This is an area that will require ongoing assessment and evaluation to better understand the underlying dynamics and respond thoughtfully.

Assessment

Given that the intergroup dialogues are part of a course, it is difficult to explicitly differentiate the student learning outcomes that are the result of the intergroup dialogues from those that are a result of the course. We are not able to do an experimental design because the course is required of all students. In addition, we still need to look at long-term outcomes and the incorporation of intergroup dialogue learning into the students' professional and continued academic endeavors. Future research will be directed toward understanding how students are able to transfer their learning in the course and intergroup dialogues to actual social work practice situations.

Future Directions

Intergroup dialogues have thus far been directed at training undergraduate students for effective social work practice at the generalist level. Students at this beginning stage often want an almost mechanistic step-by-step approach to solving complex human problems that confront them in their practice. Beyond developing good basic communication and interview skills, students must develop analytical perspectives that are supported by effective dialogic skills. Ideally, these should be tested in the day-to-day field practice. This requires training that is committed to dialogue at different levels of social work practice—individuals, groups, and large communities as well as the policy level. Moving from the individual to the community level, dialogues allow for a structured process to examine one's own awareness and internal strengths as well as the discovery and testing of powers and knowledge at increasingly complex levels of intervention. As Saleebey notes, "In dialogue we confirm the importance of others and begin to heal the rift between self, other and institution" (1997, 10).

It is our hope that the practicum, which is a yearlong field placement, and the concurrent seminar in the senior year of the social work program, can allow students to test concepts and approaches that were covered in the Cultural Diversity and Justice class during the junior year. Most specifically, we hope they can utilize and further refine specific social work competencies for working in a diverse society. The dialogues offer a unique opportunity to carry the skills and knowledge from the classroom and test them in the real world of social work practice. It allows the students a method of sustaining new ways of thinking beyond the walls of the university. For community agencies and the School of Social Work it provides a mutually enriching opportunity to critique and share new research and knowledge.

Many of the dialogue skills easily find immediate expression in and a logical fit with direct practice skills when dealing with difference. However, the application at the mezzo and macro level may also hold many equally promising possibilities. In a practicum setting where groups and communities are struggling with issues of community development such as collective problem-solving and social justice, students can offer new ways for groups rooted in different worldviews to share common meaning. Freire (1993) believes passionately that communities historically separated by mistrust, paternalism, and oppression can be brought together through this process, changing age-old patterns of entrenched thinking. "Founding itself upon love, humility and faith[,] dialogue becomes a horizontal relationship of which mutual trust between the dialoguers is a logical consequence" (72).

Field instructors have also expressed a keen interest in learning about and developing new and effective approaches to working with difference. Students, faculty, and community workers can find ways of bringing together hitherto alienated communities in a mutually caring and respectful manner. Dialogues in the practicum settings will both reinforce and further develop students' skills and competencies for working within a diverse society. The dual practice arenas available through the classroom and field placement will allow students to incorporate intergroup dialogues in a structured and supported manner in their daily social work practice. Ongoing evaluation of the dialogues will allow for critical reflection on the efficacy of this effort by both faculty and social work agencies.

In short, dialogues that are an integral component of the practicum experience can assist students in becoming effective citizens in both the classroom and community. They also provide invaluable skills for developing positive and healthy relationships with peers, supervisors, clients, and communities. This approach underscores the practical contribution that a school of social work can make in the community and shows how it can create enduring ties that are mutually supportive and enriching. The foundational experience provided by the intergroup dialogues as part of the Cultural Diversity and Justice class is indeed transformational, and students must be afforded opportunities to continue building on their newfound or reaffirmed commitments:

> This class has helped me in so many ways. I have learned the most important information yet [in] my educational career, as it is applicable not only to all my classes, but to my experiences in life. I desire to continue learning about culture and diversity issues through more readings, getting involved in affirmative action coalitions, volunteering with diverse people, and spreading around awareness and education. I will continue to be aware of my status in society and how it affects other people, avoid negative stereotypes and jokes, not back away from issues of discrimination or racism that are being discussed, and continue forming friendships with people who are different from myself. I will carry everything I have learned in [this class] into my career as a social worker as I attempt to enhance the quality of life for all individuals in society. (Filipino-American woman)

NOTES

Comments or inquires should be addressed to Intergroup Dialogue, Education, and Action (IDEA) Training and Resource Institute, University of Washington School of Social Work, 4101 Fifteenth Avenue N.E., Seattle WA 98105–6299. Telephone: 206–616–9083, fax: 206–543–1228.

1. Miley, O'Melia, and DuBois describe generalist social work as "an integrated and multi-leveled approach for meeting the purposes of social work. Generalist practitioners acknowledge the interplay of personal and collective issues, prompting them to work with a variety of human systems—societies, communities, neighborhoods, complex organizations, formal groups, families and individuals—to create changes which maximize human system functioning. This means that the generalist social workers work directly with client systems at all levels, connect clients to available resources, intervene with organizations to enhance the responsiveness of resource systems, advocate just social policies to ensure the distribution of resources, and research all aspects of social work practice" (1998, 9).

REFERENCES

Adair, M., and S. Howell. 1997. *Breaking Old Patterns, Weaving New Ties.* San Francisco: Tools for Change.

Council on Social Work Education. 1992. *Curriculum Policy Statements for Baccalaureate Degree and Master's Degree Programs in Social Work Education.* Alexandria, Va.: CSWE.

Cross, T. L., B. J. Bazron, K. W. Dennis, and M. R. Isaacs. 1989. *Towards a Culturally Competent System of Care.* Washington, D.C.: Georgetown University Child Development Center.

Franklin, D. L. 1990. "The Cycles of Social Work Practice: Social Action vs. Individual Interest." *Journal of Progressive Human Services* 1, no. 2: 59–80.

Freire, P. 1993. *Pedagogy of the Oppressed.* New York: Continuum.

Garcia, B., and D. Van Soest. 1997. "Changing Perceptions of Diversity and Oppression: MSW Students Discuss the Effects of a Required Course." *Journal of Social Work Education* 33, no. 1: 119–29.

Gil, D. G. 1998. *Confronting Injustice and Oppression: Concepts and Strategies for Social Workers.* New York: Columbia University Press.

Gurin, P., G. E. Lopez, and B. A. Nagda. 1994. "The Intergroup Relations and Conflict Study: A Four-Year Longitudinal Study to Assess the Impact of a Course on 'Intergroup Relations and Conflict.'" Paper presented at the Russell Sage Foundation Conference on the Social Psychology of Culture, Contact, and Conflict, Ann Arbor, Mich., September.

Gutiérrez, L., K. Fredriksen, and S. Soifer. 1999. "Perspectives of Social Work Faculty on Diversity and Societal Oppression Content: Results from a National Survey." *Journal of Social Work Education* 35, no. 3: 409–19.

Lewis, E. A. 1993. "Continuing the Legacy: On the Importance of Praxis in the Education of Social Work Students and Teachers." In *Multicultural Teaching in the University,* ed. D. Schoem, L. Frankel, X. Zúñiga, and E. A. Lewis. Westport, Conn.: Praeger.

Miley, K. K., M. O'Melia, and B. DuBois. 1998. *Generalist Social Work Practice: An Empowering Approach.* Boston: Allyn and Bacon.

Nagda, B. A., and L. M. Gutiérrez. 2000. "A *Praxis* and Research Agenda for Multicultural Human Services Organizations." *International Journal of Social Welfare* 9, no. 1: 43–52.

Nagda, B. A., M. Spearmon, L. C. Holley, S. Harding, M. L. Balassone, D. Moïse-Swanson, and S. de Mello. 1999. "Intergroup Dialogues: An Innovative Approach to Teaching about Diversity and Justice in Social Work Programs." *Journal of Social Work Education* 35, no. 3: 433–49.

National Association of Social Workers. 1996. *NASW Code of Ethics.* Washington, D.C.: NASW.

Reed, B., P. Newman, Z. Suarez, and E. A. Lewis. 1997. "Interpersonal Practice beyond Diversity and toward Social Justice: The Importance of Critical Consciousness." In *Interpersonal Practice in Social Work: Promoting Competence and Social Justice,* ed. C. Garvin and B. Seabury. Needham Heights, Mass.: Allyn and Bacon.

Saleebey, D. 1997. *The Strengths Perspective in Social Work Practice.* New York: Longman.

Sowers-Hoag, K. M., and P. Sandau-Beckler. 1996. "Educating for Cultural Competence in the Generalist Curriculum." *Journal of Multicultural Social Work* 4, no. 3: 37–56.

Specht, H., and M. E. Courtney. 1994. *Unfaithful Angels: How Social Work Has Abandoned Its Mission.* New York: Free Press.

Tatum, B. D. 1992. "Talking about Race, Learning about Racism: The Application of Racial Identity Development Theory in the Classroom." *Harvard Educational Review* 62:1–24.

Weaver, H. N. 1999. "Indigenous People and the Social Work Profession: Defining Culturally Competent Services." *Social Work* 44, no. 3: 217–25.

Zúñiga, X., B. A. Nagda, and T. D. Sevig. 2000. "Intergroup Dialogues: A Model for Cultivating Student Engagement across Differences." Typescript.

Case Studies: Community

Chapter 9

Engaging the Whole Community in Dialogue and Action: Study Circles Resource Center

Martha McCoy and Michael A. McCormick

> *Our democratic assumption is that we Americans, thinking, talking and working together, can solve our problems. . . . The building of diverse communities is hard but doable, and it is surely essential to a nation constituted as ours will be.*
>
> —Roger Wilkins

Intergroup dialogue conjures up a different image for each of us, depending on our own personal histories and experiences. As other chapters in this book demonstrate, intergroup dialogue takes many productive forms, varying with settings, intended participants, structures, and goals. At the Study Circles Resource Center (SCRC), we work with people and groups that are organizing democratic dialogue and action throughout a geographic community—whether a neighborhood, town, city, county, or state. In this chapter, we describe the evolution of the process communities are using to organize dialogue and action, its key elements, some of the results and outcomes, and some of the lessons of their work that can be applied to other communities. We pay particular attention to study circle programs that are addressing racism and race relations, since those programs most directly reflect the themes of intergroup dialogue in this volume, and because of the importance of race issues to other public issues.

SCRC was created by the Topsfield Foundation in 1989 with the goal of helping citizens take part in face-to-face democratic deliberation on critical social and political issues. We set out to create accessible, replicable processes and tools for communities that want to bring about opportunities for face-to-face citizen discussion and problem solving. Many people and groups that contact us for assistance believe that the key to making a difference on critical issues is for *all* citizens to have these opportunities.

Our work with these communities has led to a vision of citizen discussion that is quite different from typical political discussions. Instead, it is

Fun and productive. It gives people a chance to tell their stories, to discover personal connections to the issues and each other, and to build community.

Face-to-face and sustained over time. It gives people a chance to sit down with people different from themselves, to go beyond "sound bites," to really listen to one another, and to build trust.

Structured and facilitated, so that it gives everyone a voice and provides a place for all viewpoints to be heard with respect. Conflict and differences of opinion can be used to enhance people's understanding of the issue.

Inclusive of the whole community. Instead of the typical political discussions among just the experts, or just those who are already involved in community affairs, the conversations not only welcome everyone's participation but also actively work to make widespread participation possible.

Intentionally diverse—in terms of race and ethnicity, gender, age, educational background, and political beliefs. In most everyday conversations about public issues, we tend to talk with those who are most like us and most likely to agree with us. When public conversations are intentionally diverse, people can build relationships and work together across typical dividing lines.

Explicitly linked to opportunities for change and action that the participants create themselves. It validates action and change at all levels—personal, collective, institutional, and public policy—and allows people to choose how they can best make a difference.

Organized on a large scale. When citizen discussion is organized on a large scale, and when it leads directly to possibilities for community change and decision making, it results in new ideas for solving public problems. It also helps create new connections, policies, and energy for carrying out those ideas.

Ongoing and widespread. Public dialogue that connects to action can form the basis of how we work for social change and run our communities.

This vision provides the basis for the community-wide study circle process and for the study circle programs people are building in communities across the United States. Large-scale democratic discussion is taking hold in hundreds of places, in neighborhoods, small towns, and medium- and large-sized cities. In these places, diverse coalitions of community groups and individuals are bringing hundreds (and sometimes thousands) of people into study circles to deal with critical issues. The issues they address include racism and race relations, education reform, crime and violence, immigration and community change, criminal justice, youth concerns, growth and development, family concerns, building strong neighborhoods, and police-community relationships. SCRC provides direct assistance to these communities, learns with them, then synthesizes and disseminates the lessons back out to communities through various national, regional, and state networks.

Using Study Circles to Address Racism and Improve Race Relations

More communities have used study circles to address racism and race relations than any other issue. Early in our organizational life, SCRC staff heard from community leaders who were asking for tools to bring diverse people together for productive dialogue on race. Those leaders saw the need for large numbers of people to have the chance to form multiracial relationships and to dispel stereotypes. They saw that racial divisions underlie almost every other public concern, and so it was critical for people to have ways to work together to address those divisions. They realized that the issues of race, of great importance throughout our country's history, were becoming even more complex as divisions moved beyond the "black-white" paradigm. Because study circles help people form relationships, dispel stereotypes, *and also* take part in community problem solving, they seemed to be an ideal vehicle for addressing issues of racism and race relations.

At SCRC, we first began to work on this specific issue in 1992, after violence in Los Angeles reverberated across communities in every region of the United States. In 1993, we developed the first edition of our study circle guide on race. That guide, now entitled *Facing the Challenge of Racism and Race Relations: Democratic Dialogue and Action for Stronger Communities* (Flavin-McDonald and McCoy 1997), is in its third edition. Since the publication of the first edition, over eighty communities have organized large-scale, community-wide study circles on racism and race relations. Thousands of people have taken part. Some communities that have sustained study circle programs over several years have continued to focus on racism, while others (recognizing the relationships between racism and other issues) have begun dialogues on violence, youth, education, and economic development. In addition to community-wide programs, hundreds of congregations, schools, government agencies, unions, and workplaces have used the study circle process to engage people within their organizations in dialogue on racism and race relations.[1] Some of the specific outcomes that are coming from study circles on racism and race relations are included in the final section of this chapter.

Organizing Community-Wide Study Circles

The community-wide organizing process usually begins when a few people in a community see the importance of an issue and the importance of widespread public involvement for addressing it. Successful programs are organized by broad-based, diverse coalitions of community organizations and individuals. This is especially important when organizing a community-wide dialogue on racism and race relations. In a racism and race relations program, the organizing coalition must reach beyond the "choir" and engage the organizations, groups, and individuals not typically committed to working on race. The involvement of schools, businesses, newspapers, television and radio stations, neighborhood groups, and public officials helps people from all backgrounds and beliefs to see that issues of racism and race relations require the contribution of the whole community.

The organizing coalition must also be racially diverse. Such a coalition models the essence of the entire program and is the most important factor in recruiting racially diverse participants. To build such a coalition, initiators often hold "pilot study circles" for community leaders who are considering becoming part of the coalition. This firsthand experience helps people understand the value of the process and motivates them to join the coalition. In the end, community members will get involved when people they know and respect make it clear that their participation is important and that they will have a chance to make a difference on the issue.

It can take six months (and sometimes longer) for a coalition to take form and begin planning the full-scale program. A diverse coalition is the engine that drives successful study circle programs. Usually a smaller group within the coalition becomes the core working group. This core working group of leading organizations takes the heaviest program responsibilities, such as recruiting a wide range of community sponsors, recruiting and training facilitators, and setting up diverse study circles. It also works on fund-raising, setting up a kickoff event, evaluation, planning for action, and working with the media. Sponsoring organizations (a much larger number than the core working group) take responsibility for recruiting participants from their membership or networks, as well as other responsibilities, such as providing meeting sites or providing child care.

A typical "round" of study circles often involves hundreds of community members and is launched by a kickoff event that gains media coverage and galvanizes even more community participation. During a round, many diverse study circles happen at the same time across the community. Within each circle, a neutral facilitator helps group members abide by simple ground rules the members themselves established. Every study circle meets several times, for two hours each, usually weekly. The same group meets for several sessions, moving from a session on personal experiences with the issue, to examining different views about the nature of the issue and how to address it, and finally considering the actions they would like to take to make a difference on the issue.[2] At the end of the round, a large-scale action forum provides a chance for participants from all the study circles to meet as a large group and to find ways to work on the action ideas they developed in their individual circles.

For effective recruitment, organizers must explain that participants will have the opportunity for both dialogue and action. The dichotomy of "talking versus acting" is misleading with any public issue, but even more so when it comes to race. When there is a framework that leads the dialogue to possibilities for taking action, people can experience the discussion and action as parts of a continuum rather than as a dichotomy. People should know that the study circle process will not lead them to a particular viewpoint or require them to take action, but will provide *opportunities* to move to action of their own choosing.

A Few Notes on Methods

Community-wide study circle programs are based on an inclusive organizing model that connects each study circle to the whole community and that connects dialogue to the potential for action. Without the change-oriented organizing context, the small-group dialogues would not have as strong a potential for making a difference at the community level. The flip side of this is also true: without the transformational power of the small-group process, the large-scale program would not have the same kinds of impacts.

As described above, a diverse organizing group is at the heart of a successful program. Within its overall work to create a large-scale program, several processes are central.

The Small-Group Process

In a community-wide program, each study circle of eight to twelve diverse people generally meets weekly for five two-hour sessions. Group members are there because they have been invited to participate in a democratic, collaborative process to learn about the issue from each other, and to find ways to address it. They understand that their circle is one of many in a community-wide effort, and that they will have the chance to take their action ideas back to the community as a whole. During the course of the sessions, group members have the chance to uncover areas of agreement and common concern, but the study circle does not require consensus.

The group sets its own ground rules for the discussion. Facilitators begin by eliciting common ground rules from the group, which frequently include confidentiality, sharing "air time," speaking up if you are offended, refraining from personalizing disagreements, seeking first to understand and then to be understood, and speaking for yourself and not for others. Facilitators then review the agreed-upon ground rules at the start of every session, and the group members know that everyone shares responsibility for keeping this agreement. Throughout all their meetings, the facilitator helps move the discussion along and helps to ensure that participants have the chance to consider all points of view. The facilitator also refrains from disclosing her or his own point of view, in order to help group members feel safe in expressing their opinions.

Small-Group Facilitation

The most important factor in the effectiveness of the small-group dialogue is the quality of the facilitation. An effective study circle facilitator is one who remains neutral, is comfortable with diverse perspectives and the possibility of conflict, and can draw out quiet people or manage those who try to dominate the discussion. In many study circle programs, particularly those on race, organizers provide biracial cofacilitators for each study circle. This has been very effective in helping the group establish a level of comfort and honest expression (RKI 2000).

In some cases, organizers recruit facilitators from those people in the community who have facilitation or mediation experience. Facilitators are often drawn from clergy, teachers, professional or volunteer mediators, trainers, and human relations or organizational development specialists. However, previous formal training is not a prerequisite for being an effective study circle facilitator (RKI 2000). The best facilitators are good listeners and relate well to people of all backgrounds. With training and practice, this kind of person can make a good facilitator regardless of previous professional facilitation experience. In many communities, study circle facilitation has provided leadership opportunities for people who never previously thought of themselves as community leaders. Facilitators play a critical leadership role outside the study circle as well, since they often become "ambassadors" for the study circle program.

There is almost always an organization or person in the community with the skills and experience to take on the role of ongoing facilitation training, quality assurance, and support. SCRC works closely with this individual or organization.[3] SCRC has also developed additional facilitation tips for leading discussions about race (Flavin-McDonald and McCoy 1997, 45).

Large-Group Processes

When a round of study circles is about to begin, programs benefit greatly from kickoff events to which the whole community is invited. These events increase levels of participation and the visibility of the program. They usually include testimonials by people who have participated in study circles; recognition of sponsoring organizations; and endorsements by prominent people who are identified with the issue. For example, the community-wide program in New Castle County, Delaware, has had Maya Angelou, Cornel West, and Bernice King speak at separate kickoff events (RKI 2000). Usually, the kickoff offers a demonstration of a study circle and an opportunity to sign up as a participant. Often, these events draw media attention and help inspire community members to participate.

Another important large-group meeting is the "action forum," which culminates a round of study circles. In the forum, people have the chance to report on the action ideas that have come from their study circles, and to join with those who have similar ideas. At the forums, people often establish task forces around specific action ideas. By giving people a chance to speak to the whole group, and to reconnect with others who have similar visions of change, this large-group process carries forward the momentum that was generated in the small groups, builds on it, and connects it to the larger community.

Learning from Successes and Challenges

While the study circle process can seem fairly straightforward in this brief chapter, it requires a lot of hard work and visionary leadership to engage large numbers of diverse community members in face-to-face dialogue and action. At SCRC, we continually strive to learn with and from communities, to improve both the study circle model and our advice. Although each community faces unique challenges, no one should have to reinvent lessons already learned.

Accordingly, we work with organizers to help them build learning processes into their programs. In our largest formal learning collaboration with a community, SCRC and the YWCA of New Castle County, Delaware, coproduced a report on focus groups drawn from participants in the Delaware study circles on race (Flavin-McDonald 1998). In addition, we are working with various independent researchers who are conducting studies of study circles on race, examining their effectiveness and impact.

With funding from the C. S. Mott Foundation, the Topsfield Foundation contracted with Roberts and Kay, Inc., of Lexington, Kentucky, to carry out a two-year study of "best practices" in study circle programs. Within the "Best Practices" study (RKI 2000), there is an emphasis on documenting programs that address race, and examining the role that race plays in programs that address other issues. The multiracial research team is studying seventeen study circle programs in depth.[4]

The following analyses of successes and challenges are drawn from this varied body of research, including some preliminary lessons drawn from the "Best Practices" study.

Calling something a success is inherently a question of evaluation. Does the *process* live up to the goals and expectations of the organizers and of participants? Is it widespread, diverse, inclusive, and participatory? In terms of *impact*, does the process achieve what it set out to achieve—is it creating solutions at the community level? Is it addressing racism? Is it improving race relations? Is it addressing racial inequities? Even the most thrilling program successes are mixed with challenges, failures, and a need to learn from mistakes. Thus, an indicator of success is creating a learning process and applying the lessons learned to the next round of study circles.

The Process

Many study circle programs have succeeded in involving large numbers of diverse participants, of many racial backgrounds, educational backgrounds, neighborhoods, and income levels. As an example, in New Castle County, Delaware, thousands of racially diverse community members have participated in study circles on racism and race relations in the past three years. As of the spring of 2000, there have been over thirty-five hundred participants, and the program continues to expand.

Related challenges are the following:

> Many effective organizers face a great challenge in involving low-income participants. In one large metropolitan area, the organizing group began with high-profile corporate and political leaders. The high-profile sponsorship gave the program instant visibility and credibility in some sectors, including residents of the metropolitan region who had never participated in a community activity devoted to race. But it also made it difficult to include neighborhood leaders in the organizing group, because of long-standing mistrust and divisions between grassroots leaders and corporate leaders. The study circle organizers in this program are still working to help build enough trust so that neighborhood leaders will see the study circle process as a credible one that can make a difference on important issues.

> For some people, the opportunity for the dialogue itself is what draws them to participate: in general, whites are more apt to fall into this category. In many cases, they have had little direct exposure to explicit considerations of racism, and this is a unique opportunity to learn. For others, the opportunity to take action on racial inequities and divisions is the most important consideration: in general, people of color (who have had many more explicit opportunities to experience and talk about racism) fall into this category. Once people participate in a study circle program, almost everyone appreciates the value of the initial dialogue and the need for the action and changes that come from it, no matter where they started. Still, there is a real difference between people's beliefs about what would make the program ultimately worthwhile, with many people of color believing that without the action and change components, their participation would not be worth their time (Flavin-McDonald 1998). These are very important considerations for organizers to take into account as they describe the program in order to recruit participants.

The most successful programs have *begun* to get beyond the "usual crowd," by involving those who have never worked on the issue of racism before, or who have never had a conversation on race in a multiracial setting. In Syracuse, New York, organizers regularly attend different community and neighborhood functions to give people a chance to take part in a sample study circle. This has been an effective strategy for helping people overcome their fear or hesitation to take part.

Related challenges are the following:

> It can be difficult to organize the program in such a way that it draws people from all backgrounds and views, and lets them know that they can start "where they are." By naming the issue both broadly and specifically, people will know why they are participating, and what they can expect to come from the program. For example, in Syracuse, New York, organizers came up with an all-encompassing working title for the program—Community Wide Dialogue: Racism, Race Relations, and Racial Healing—which helped potential participants understand the purpose of the program (RKI 2000).

> Differing levels of knowledge and experience on racial issues between whites and people of color are evident in the study circles and can hamper the quality of the dialogue (Flavin-McDonald 1998). By creating study circles that are at least one-third people of color (some communities say it should be one-half) organizers have at least partially met this challenge (RKI 2000).

A growing number of programs are successfully linking dialogue to action. When program organizers plan deliberately to help link the study circles to action/change opportunities, success is much more likely. A good example is Decatur, Georgia, where program initiator Jon Abercrombie asked the city commission to invest in the study circles, participate as they could, and take seriously the outcomes. The commission promised their support and agreed to invest in the work. This made movement to change more likely, as well as helping to convince skeptical community members that the program was not window dressing or "just talk." Another good example is Springfield, Illinois, where program initiator Mayor Karen Hasara made an up-front commitment to work with community members to implement recommendations coming out of the study circles. Even in programs that did not have the benefit of such a commitment, the explicit connection to change has been key to diverse recruitment.

Related challenges are the following:

While numerous study circle programs have generated effective action, we (SCRC and the communities we work with) are still grappling with the challenges to effectively connect the dialogue to action and policymaking. The sheer amount of work it takes to bring large numbers of people into the dialogue can make it difficult for program organizers to plan the next stage of moving to action. Some programs are beginning to designate key people to deal just with the action phase. In Hartford, Connecticut, the program has hired a full-time "action coordinator."

A far greater challenge is whether action steps that come from the program should continue to be explicitly linked to study circles. There is a concern that this could compromise the neutral convening role of the program; and yet without the action connection, many people will not participate in the first place. This is of greater concern for some communities than for others. Some communities have seemingly met this challenge: they publicize or support the numerous action task forces that emerge, but (perhaps because of the great variety of those actions) still remain capable of bringing diverse participants to the table.

The Outcomes

Study circle programs are leading to changes and actions at individual, group, institutional, and community levels. Some of these outcomes are linked to the personal transformation that happens within the small-group sessions, while others are generated by the creation of intentional "actions" that happen after the dialogue sessions are completed. Still others come about because personal learning and new community connections generated in the circles helped to quicken or deepen change that was already under way.

Many individual participants come out of study circles with changes in personal attitudes and behaviors and a new commitment to work on racial issues. For example, participants in one study circle in New Castle County, Delaware, formed a summertime "buddy system" to continue their person-to-person effort to advance understanding among people of different races (Flavin-McDonald 1998). In Hartford, study circle participants joined with the local chapter of the National Conference for Community and Justice in the first annual Walk as One walk-a-thon, to raise money for youth leadership programs that will promote racial, religious, and cultural understanding (RKI 2000).

Many programs have generated new grassroots collaborations, a direct result of the diversity in the study circles and a process for developing new working relationships. In Lima, Ohio, an interracial community choir was one of the first outcomes of the study circle program. Also in Lima, participants got together to help expand the Daily Bread Soup Kitchen, by adding tutoring and recreation activities. Interracial teams of study circle participants from Springfield, Massachusetts, traveled to South Carolina to help rebuild a church that had been burned (Study Circles Resource Center 1998).

Programs lead to changes in local institutions such as police departments, school systems, the media, and businesses. Sometimes, the institutions change the way they connect to the larger community. For example, in Springfield, Illinois, the program has led to a strengthening of community policing. Sometimes, community institutions change their internal operations. Businesses often change their hiring policies (RKI 2000). In Fort Myers, Florida, the study circles led to a new minority recruiting and mentoring program in the police department. Also in Fort Myers, study circle participants helped push for the creation for a new shopping center in an underserved area of the community, on which planning had long been stalled. The ground for the new shopping center was broken in the winter of 2000.

Some changes take place at the level of local government. The city of Springfield, Illinois, has established a Race Relations Task Force, made up of study circle participants and public officials, to respond to racial incidents in the city.

The Ultimate Challenge: Taking the Risk

Sometimes, community-wide programs break down before they begin. This happens when initiators fail to reach out beyond the organizations that typically address race issues. When it happens, a program might never get off the ground or draw only a small numbers of participants. In other cases, initiators from one racial background may fail to form a multiracial coalition. Especially when initiators are white, this creates an insurmountable barrier to effective organizing. This can happen when people do not take the risk and time of beginning to communicate with others from different backgrounds. They may issue distant invitations for participation, which fail to bridge long-standing divides.

There is no substitute for personal, face-to-face trust building. A good example of this was Lima, Ohio, the site of the first community-wide study circle program. When the program was in its early planning stages, black and white clergy members knew they wanted to draw the community into dialogue, but didn't even know one another. The mayor first brought them together, but they had to find ways to create relationships and build on those relationships. This was very difficult at times, because they had never established trust with each other. This changed because of the mayor's leadership and the persistence of two trusted community leaders, one black and one white, who kept listening to everyone's fears and misgivings, bringing people back to the table, and helping the group build enough trust to work together. Eventually, they expanded to other sectors throughout the community. By now, thousands of city residents have engaged in study circles, with outcomes at all levels.

To return to Roger Wilkins's words at the beginning of this chapter, building diverse communities *is* hard and *is* doable. As we continue to learn with communities that are doing this difficult work and continue to disseminate their lessons, we believe there is continued hope for facing the challenges of racism and race relations, and for addressing seemingly intractable public issues.

NOTES

We gratefully acknowledge Molly Holme Barrett, Rona Roberts, and Scott Stiles for their comments and suggestions on this chapter.

1. The largest workplace applications of study circles have been organized in the Ohio Department of Health and Human Services, the Delaware Department of Labor, and the General Services Administration of the federal government.
2. The sessions from *Facing the Challenge of Racism and Race Relations* (Flavin-McDonald and McCoy 1997) are as follows: session 1: Race relations and racism: experiences, perceptions, and beliefs; session 2: Dealing with race: What is the nature of the problem? session 3: What should we do to make progress on race relations? session 4: What kinds of public policies will help us deal with race relations? session 5: How can we move from words to action in our community?
3. The Study Circles Resource Center publishes *A Guide for Training Study Circle Facilitators* (Campbell 1998) that includes the content of the training and tips for establishing a training program.
4. Some of the previous text refers to early drafts of these reports, but final reports are available. Please contact SCRC at P.O. Box 203, Pomfret CT 06258. Tele-

phone: 860–928–2616; fax: 860–928–3713; e-mail address: scrc@studycircles .org; web site: www.studycircles.org.

REFERENCES

Campbell, Sarah vL. 1998. A *Guide for Training Study Circle Facilitators.* Pomfret, Conn.: Topsfield Foundation.

Flavin-McDonald, C. 1998. *A Report on the Focus Groups.* Pomfret, Conn.: Study Circles Resource Center and the YWCA of New Castle County.

Flavin-McDonald, C., and M. McCoy. 1997. *Facing the Challenge of Racism and Race Relations: Democratic Dialogue and Action for Stronger Communities.* 3d ed. Pomfret, Conn.: Study Circles Resource Center and Topsfield Foundation.

Roberts and Kay, Inc. (RKI). 2000. "A Best Practices Report." Typescript.

Study Circles Resource Center. 1998. "How Have Study Circles Made an Impact? Organizers Report on Their Successes." *Focus* 9, no. 4: 2, 7.

Wilkins, R. 1997. "Building Diverse Communities." In *Governing Diverse Communities: A Focus on Race and Ethnic Relations,* ed. P. Reichler and P. B. Dredge. Annapolis Junction, Md.: NLC Publications.

Chapter 10

An Honest Conversation on Race, Reconciliation, and Responsibility: Hope in the Cities

Karen Elliott Greisdorf

There is a seeming paradox in talking about "a vision of community" coming from Richmond, Virginia, a city which for many years symbolized so much that is the antithesis of community. For some, the past conjures up images of Thomas Jefferson and Patrick Henry. For others, Richmond is the city credited with the debasement of blacks through its institutionalization of slavery and the abandonment of the school system by white families during the State of Virginia's massive resistance movement against school integration. It is a city where until 1977, when the first black mayor was elected, 50 percent of the population had no voice in the vital political and economic decisions affecting their lives.

But Metropolitan Richmond is a study of contrasts. Once the capital of the Confederacy, it became the home of the first elected black governor in the nation. The city's Monument Avenue has long showcased a proud legacy of Confederate heroes, but today includes a statue of tennis legend Arthur Ashe, who was once shut out as a black from playing on certain courts in the city. After decades of mistrust, the city and the county jurisdictions are taking the first tentative steps toward partnership. After two hundred years of race-based politics, there are signs that the regions may be moving in a new direction. In 1998, the black majority city council elected Tim Kaine, a white lawyer, as mayor. A year later, two of the majority-white surrounding counties elected black chairmen of their boards of supervisors.

"Virginia has always used a velvet glove approach to race relations," says Dr. John Moeser, professor of Urban Studies, Virginia Commonwealth University. "Code words are used all of the time. If you want to talk about race, you have to step out, make yourself vulnerable."[1] Hope in the Cities (HIC) is a national network based in Richmond whose very purpose is to talk about race, fostering an honest conversation on race, reconciliation, and responsibility. It grew out of recognition that failure to talk honestly about race was paralyzing efforts to address the social and economic needs of the Richmond region. Launched in 1990 as an effort to bring together political, business, and community leaders to address the matter of racial healing, today Hope in the Cities offers experience, resources, and a process to encourage reconciliation and responsibility for positive change on race relations.

Walter T. Kenney, former mayor of Richmond, Virginia, and an active participant in Hope in the Cities, has characterized the work of the organization as a "process for moving past and not getting stuck in the blame game," which is critical for real growth. He believes that "the mentality of victimhood or guilt-ridden shame anchors us in inaction. Hope in the Cities provides the arena for unselfish leadership and partnerships for building trust and hope" (Elliott Greisdorf 1997).

Key Elements to Nurturing Hope in the Cities

As Hope in the Cities has developed over the years, it has identified three key elements in the process of building hope: (1) everyone who has a stake in new community relationships must "come to the table" to be involved in the process of transformation; (2) there must be an honest acknowledgment of a shared racial history that can lead to forgiveness and a new level of understanding as individuals and as a society, so that all can work for change in relationships and structures; and (3) each individual must take personal responsibility for the change process.

As a pioneer in identifying the need for honest conversation, as a means to racial reconciliation and justice, HIC approaches the problem of racism as essentially moral and spiritual in nature. HIC views race as a human construct of the mind, often used to justify certain behavior for the maximization of profit, such as within the institution of slavery. Even in discussions of contemporary issues of economics and race or class and race, HIC views these issues as moral and spiritual at root. Therefore the conversation needs to engage participants at that level, not just intellectually. The work of HIC emphasizes the quality of relationships as a basis for structural change and the belief that individuals, working in teams, are the single most significant factor in bringing about effective community change in the area of race relations. In *Boundary Crossers: Community Leadership for a Global Age,* authors Neal Peirce and Curtis Johnson explore the new diverse "networks of responsibility" that are making a difference in several cities. They conclude, "There is no magical leadership structure—just people and relationships. In every case of successful leadership, it is not the structure that matters, but the way people work together to get things done" (1997, contents page). This emphasis on the individual and relationships over structure is founded on HIC's belief that if the concept and ills of racism were to be alleviated or improved simply by "tinkering with institutions," it would have happened by this time.

"While some organizations focus on an exchange of information through formal dialogue programs, Hope in the Cities focuses on the element of personal transformation through both our formal and informal dialogue initiatives," says Paige Chargois, national associate director of Hope in the Cities. Before exploring HIC's formal dialogue program, one must understand the foundation on which it is built. HIC's history of informal dialogue is drawn from over fifty years of international conflict resolution efforts of MRA: Initiatives for Change[2] (Johnston and Sampson 1993), which launched Hope in the Cities (Henderson 1996). HIC grew out of this faith-based process, whose roots are in the Christian tradition, but came to include a multifaith network. There was no thought of formal structure or organization, but rather a practice of seeking God's direction on reaching out to others by using home settings for informal dinners or one-on-one conversations. It was a conscious strategy of engaging "hard to reach" people; planning visits to the offices of key corporate executives or government officials and building a level of confidence with them; developing a sense of vision for the community; and identifying the "hinge issues" around which teams might be mobilized. These informal dialogues predated the structured dialogue program by several years and continue to be the backbone of the work. People spend casual time together, celebrate together, and respond to the needs and emergencies of others. In other words, they develop normal relationships. As Robert Corcoran, national director for Hope in the Cities, describes it, "They become an unseen, but vital network of friends who act as leaven in the life of the community."

National Outreach Leads to Further Local Development

Hope in the Cities was launched nationally with the conference "Healing the Heart of America: An Honest Conversation on Race, Reconciliation, and Responsibility" in 1993. The conference, cosponsored by the City of

Richmond, drew one thousand participants from fifty U.S. urban centers and twenty foreign countries. Through plenary sessions and small dialogue groups, it examined underlying racial issues that impact housing, education, police and community relations, and public policy as it relates to families.

A dramatic Unity Walk gave recognition to previously unacknowledged and unmarked sites and events in the city's racial history. Christopher Edley Jr., professor of law at Harvard University, who directed a White House review of affirmative action, wrote, "Hope in the Cities [has] discovered that appreciating shared history can be a catalyst to connect communities long divided" (1997, 5A). The purpose of the walk, according to Robert Corcoran, "is to tell everybody's story together and to honor everybody's experience in a way that is honest, inclusive and contributes to the healing of the city, the nation, and the world."

"Such a walk establishes an agenda for healing," says Joseph V. Montville, director of the Preventive Diplomacy Program at the Center for Strategic and International Studies in Washington, D.C. "Time does not heal wounds. Only healing, actively pursued, heals wounds" (Elliott Greisdorf 1997). Today, the once unmarked sites of the walk are well on the way to becoming significant educational resources for the region. The city has established an Historic Slave Trail Commission and is planning a major memorial to the contribution of slaves whose labor built Richmond and whose culture serves as a lasting legacy. Similar walks continue to take place in Richmond and provide an important foundation for the dialogue process in two ways. First, for the full potential of a walk to be realized, it must draw together the entire community—private and public, city and county. These participants are either drawn from or introduced to HIC's dialogue program. Second, the talk of reconciliation comes literally through a walk of recognition.

Suzanne Hall, director of community programs at the Virginia Museum of the Fine Arts, went on the first walk in 1993 with her family. "I feel it signaled a change for (all of us as) whites in Richmond," Hall says. "Out of it, you got a sense of who the people were that were committed."

Not only did the conference raise Hope in the Cities to a new level of visibility and action in Richmond, but elsewhere around the nation through participation from Los Angeles, Chicago, Portland, Hartford, Philadelphia and over forty other cities. Today, Richmond is partnering with teams in cities such as Selma, Alabama, Portland, Oregon, Dayton, Ohio, and Camden, New Jersey.

Over the next three years, while initiatives continued in Richmond, Hope in the Cities also nurtured teams in other cities. With a collective desire to place the discussion of race on the national agenda, Hope in the Cities issued "A Call to Community"[3] in May 1996 at the National Press Club in Washington, D.C. The program demonstrated an honest and respectful dialogue on race as it drew together participants across the political spectrum including Congressman Jesse Jackson Jr. and Paul Weyrich, founder of The Heritage Foundation, who commented, "Liberals and conservatives can come together on common ground in their belief that dialogue builds trust" (Reichler 1996, 1). The launch also created a network of over two hundred prominent individuals, national organizations, and partnering organizations to implement what the "Call" proposes. With the support of leaders such as former senator Bill Bradley, and partnering organizations such as The National Conference for Community and Justice, the National Council of La Raza, The YWCA, and the Study Circles Resource Center, it became clear to Hope in the Cities that there was a national basis for reinforcement of the work that HIC had been doing at the grassroots level in Richmond and elsewhere.

"In November 1996, when we made plans to launch the 'Call' in Richmond, we still were not sure what launching it there would mean," says Cricket White, national training director for Hope in the Cities. "We simply knew that we wanted to create a forum for conversation about the 'Call.'" The HIC team in Richmond soon discovered what it would mean when every seat sold out for the luncheon launching the "Call" at the Virginia Museum of the Fine Arts. While establishing what is now an annual event, Metropolitan Richmond Day, political, business, religious, and educational leaders came from across the city and surrounding counties to commit their personal and organizational support for "A Call to Community." These leaders spoke together in unexpected pairs, such as the directors of the Museum of the Confederacy and the Black History Museum, about their commitment to racial partnership. Participants at the launch were able to get a sense of what joining a dialogue group could be like when the luncheon table turned into a roundtable for discussion following a dramatic presentation on interracial dating performed by high school youth.

"The presentation gave the audience something to react to rather than reacting to each other," White recalls. "It was at a distance and was 'safe,' particularly for those Richmonders for whom talking about racial issues was still uncomfortable." Miriam Davidow, director of community services with the Jewish Community Federation, remembers there being "a real excitement and congestion in the space and that somehow created electricity." An ongoing dialogue participant, State Delegate Viola Baskerville, was on the city council at the time of the launch at the museum. "When I moved back (to Richmond), the racial polarization hit me in the face. Conversations didn't always start off about race, but it got back there." She continues, "There was something different about the dialogue, because it was happening in Richmond, where everyone builds artificial barriers."

Launching the Formal Dialogue Program Locally

As Hope in the Cities worked to bring down these artificial barriers, the community figuratively and literally responded to the "Call." The publicity from the event generated over one hundred phone calls from people wanting to join a dialogue group. The audience at the museum had also filled out cards strongly expressing a desire to continue the conversations they had begun that day. "A Call to Community" would very shortly become the basis for a curriculum to lead groups through a six-stage conversation.

According to the Richmond leadership, Hope in the Cities' goal, then and now, is to "provide an environment where isolated people become connected and involved; the frustrated or disillusioned find hope; and the alienated see those on the opposite side in a new light." This requires a "safe space" in which participants feel free to open up without fear of being "jumped on." Location becomes important: if participants do not feel comfortable in their surroundings, they are unlikely to open up. Each person is asked to come to the dialogue on the basis of working on the problem, not for the purpose of combating opponents.

Each dialogue series brings together eight to twelve participants and runs for six sessions. A group is allowed to determine how often they meet. One group believed so much in having all members present at each session that they took up to six months to complete the series, sometimes going as long as six weeks between meetings. Hope in the Cities also allows for flexibility in location. While other organizations hold dialogues in neutral settings, HIC encourages its groups to meet in each other's homes or places of worship, in the instance of two faith groups being paired. While some groups are formed of individuals, others are brought together organizationally, such as the Jewish Community Federation and the local chapter of the NAACP. Several alumni of the Leadership Metro Richmond program formed groups. Others were made up solely of men or women. "There's an energy with women," says Suzanne Hall, sharing her experience in a women's group. "There is a dimensional trust, and in an atmosphere of trust you can talk about little indignities that we don't talk about, but that perpetuate in society. We can do something about that."

Each group needs to be balanced racially, and everyone at the table is expected to become personally involved in the change process. For the process to be the most effective, the dialogue curriculum must be free of political bias or judgment and exclude any politically directed questions. The desire is for each participant to be there to learn and share, without the presupposition of teaching others. While it is not possible to completely control this aspect of the dialogues, it is the role of the facilitator, who is instructed not to interject his or her own personal political viewpoints, to move the conversation beyond the racial, social, and political boundaries that may exist in a group.

Talking through Issues Step by Step

The six-session series follows this order:

1. Beginning the conversation: why are we here?
2. Our experience of race and community: who are we?
3. Our experiences and history: can we come together?
4. Forgiveness and atonement: can we forgive? Repent?
5. Building hope for the future: what should our city look like?
6. Looking within: who are we now?

Each section of questions includes a homework portion to encourage individual reflection on various portions of "A Call to Community" and was chosen to reflect HIC's core values of getting everyone "to the table," recognition of history to be healed, and the commitment to personal responsibility. Throughout the six sessions, facilitators affirm the meeting and space in which it is taking place, as well as emphasize that "there are no enemies here" with a focus instead on *what* is right, not *who* is right, and that while discussing issues of race with a desire for reconciliation, each participant must take responsibility for his or her part in the process.

Facilitators come from throughout the community and always work in interracial teams and, where possible, are male and female. They receive sixteen hours of training from Hope in the Cities, which includes the facilitator trainees modeling dialogues within the class. As the program began, Hope in the Cities used training models of other organizations but ultimately decided to create its own curriculum that is focused toward its specific goals and its dialogue guide. Today, facilitator training includes key elements of HIC and its guide, as well as issues of personal styles of interaction, facilitating skills and techniques, and racial sensitivity, as well as conflict analysis and management. Because HIC is not always familiar with the credentials of those who volunteer to serve as facilitators, it is critical to start everyone out with the same framework.

"In facilitator training, we approach the whole person rather than trying to create race relations experts," says Robert Corcoran. "We don't just see it as training facilitators, but as developing leaders who will sustain a team." "The facilitator level of the community may be where the more lasting change occurs and where the change agents are created," says Cricket White. "If we have increased and ongoing contact with them, they spin off and have a great effect on the life of the community." The HIC office maintains contact with trained facilitators through special events in Richmond, informal one-on-one follow-up, and regular mailings. Despite this level of activity, HIC believes that future nurturing of relationships with facilitators is an area for development.

Eric Armstrong, owner of an Allstate insurance agency, speaks from his experience as a black facilitator and dialogue participant. "I'd never really talked about race. I just dealt with it. So to build a team, building common understanding helped me in terms of facilitating," Armstrong says. "The whole process was therapeutic. I still have a lot to work through, even as a facilitator."

Digging Deeper in Dialogue

Along with giving flexibility in dialogue location and series duration, Jane Talley, a black facilitator and director of Families First with the City of Richmond, appreciates the freedom HIC gives facilitators to use each session's questions most appropriately for the group. "You really have to learn to dig deeper from what someone says," Talley says. "You can't rigidly follow the guide book. You have to say 'tell me more.' You have to have a sixth sense, not so much an answer, but how it reflects more."

Sometimes the most experienced of facilitators, such as Pam Redd, a white facilitator and a seasoned trainer and consultant, have to give themselves permission to let go of the dialogue guide and previous experience.

While facilitating one of her first HIC dialogues, one of Redd's participants, a black man, began sharing a personal story. Another black man sitting next to him reached out and touched his knee while he spoke deeply of an experience. Redd remembers thinking that this was odd and saying to herself, 'White men don't do this.' Then the first man began to cry, and she realized that the man seated next to him could tell he was going to cry and that is why he had reached out. "I found that very humbling. Twenty years of experience told me to trust the process, to go with it and feel the pain," Redd remembers. "Ten years ago, I would've tried to stop it and redirect the group. But silence is important. You have to let the pain be out there."

Acknowledging such pain is often a private act, yet several organizations in Richmond have joined in partnership with Hope in the Cities and given A Season of Dialogue, the formal HIC program name, a public home. While Leadership Metro Richmond has formed many of its own HIC dialogue groups with its alumni, the Virginia Museum of the Fine Arts has provided meeting space since the launch of Metropolitan Richmond Day and the dialogue series. "There's a tremendous sea change which continues here at the museum as for many years we've been identified as a very upper class Caucasian institution," Suzanne Hall explains. "Because of Hope in the Cities, we've been buttressed in terms of effectiveness and in finding ways to reach the community. We've also been able to share assets with HIC. We have two great organizations that are moving in parallel directions."

Because Hope in the Cities is interested in fundamental and deeply rooted personal change, it is sometimes difficult to quantify or qualify the success of A Season of Dialogue. Yet in Richmond, where divisions and dichotomies are writ large, there is also no such thing as small change in the process of racial healing.

Signs of Success

A leading achievement of Hope in the Cities is the engagement of people from all sectors: government, religion, business, education, cultural institutions, media, and community organizations. It continues to provide the only forum in Richmond where people of conservative and liberal viewpoints talk honestly about race. Its goals have been formally endorsed by all city and county jurisdictions. People from largely white counties are now involved with HIC for the first time through the dialogue program, which has fostered a growing sense of community and interdependence. These new relationships have also provided a growing base of support for leaders to consider previously unimaginable partnerships between the city and counties, such as a "growth sharing" plan discussed by Chesterfield County supervisor Jack McHale and city councilman Timothy Kaine, now Richmond's mayor (Hickey 1996, A1).

Not only has HIC seen success in getting people to the table, but in fostering the type of experience that makes people want to come back for another series and maintain an ongoing relationship with the organization. Eighty to 90 percent of the participants have stated their desire to take a "next step" on the evaluation survey. There has been a particular desire for this on the part of the white participants, while black participants are somewhat more skeptical, though two-thirds stay involved with the process and complete the dialogues.

But some of the greatest gains come through in the stories of facilitators and participants, such as David Kalman, chairman of the Intergroup Relations Subcommittee of the Jewish Community Federation. "I've known Bernie and Steve [other participants from the Jewish Community Federation] since we were kids. I thought I knew them after twenty years, but I got to know them differently through the dialogue, because it wasn't about programs or goal oriented," Kalman recalls. The process also changed other perceptions: "I watched the news differently after the dialogue. I used to think that slavery doesn't fit into modern American life and that it is history. But I [now] know it's a reality, and I've been sensitized to why other people are still talking."

Meeting Challenges

While Hope in the Cities can identify successes in the process, it also squarely faces many challenges, both racial and programmatic. While Corcoran and his colleagues hold that "if talk is done well, that is action" (Dredge and Reichler 1998, 10), they are often asked, "Is this just more talk?" by many blacks who have been part of informal dialogues since the 1960s and have failed to see the level of change in society for which they would have hoped. Additionally, many younger blacks, who have experienced significant economic parity, are uninterested in going back to where they may have come from, either physically or psychologically, or are unwilling to examine the ways in which personal, systemic, and/or institutional racism has affected their lives.

Additionally, while black participants tend to be put in the position of telling their stories, whites tend to intellectualize the issue and react with either sympathy or disbelief asking, "Are you sure this is what really happened or was it in your imagination?" White participants have shown difficulty in connecting their heads to their hearts, which leads their black counterparts to challenge them by saying, "Unless you are serious and ready to do your own work, we are not taking part." Ultimately it is important for white participants to dig as deeply into their own experiences and ask, "What has racism cost me?" HIC is hoping to meet this challenge presented by a disparity of life experience by designing a questionnaire to better gauge a future participant's level of knowledge and experience; this is to encourage participation from those who feel they might be engaging in a level of dialogue not at their level. In recognition of the presence of issues for discussion within the black and white communities, plans are being made to include an intragroup dialogue component in the program. An interracial group would begin the six-week series together, have separate conversations in the middle, and join together to finish the series.

Regardless of the amount of training they receive, another ongoing challenge is for facilitators to be perceptive enough to deal with issues of reconciliation. It is not enough for them to be experienced in diversity issues; they must also have taken part in the dialogues themselves. In several cases, trained facilitators have become unintentional participants, because they had not worked through some of their own issues regarding race.

While HIC allows for flexibility in the scheduling for the groups, there is also the issue of time management within a given dialogue gathering. "There were a lot of intergroup dynamics in our group, and we didn't manage time well," says Miriam Davidow. "By session 3 or 4, we were just getting organized, and by sessions 5 and 6 we knew we were already winding down." To meet this challenge, HIC has designed an intensive residential weekend program covering the same six dialogue sessions, which are held in a retreat setting with built in times of guided silence and reflection.

Intergroup dynamics can also challenge facilitators and the gathering as a whole. Eric Armstrong, who facilitated a group and then became a participant in a second one, remembers. "There were all different levels of experience in that group," he recalls. "It got heated, but we decided to stay together despite differing educational backgrounds, religious experiences, and differences in experience between those who were far removed from racial experiences and those who were living in it every day. People from

Pittsburgh studied the civil rights movement. We lived it. They had to sit while we processed the more brutal and vivid of experiences." Today, HIC has moved from open enrollment to more carefully matching participants to avoid such an imbalance in which participants often do not connect with each other.

Evaluating the Experience

Dr. Amy Hubbard of Randolph Macon College in Ashland, Virginia, developed a survey to help Hope in the Cities better understand the experiences of all participants. Out of the fifteen questions asked of participants, six were demographic indicators. The remaining nine asked respondents to reflect on their experience, the goals of the program, the success of the group, a level of personal change, the design of the program, and key issues affecting race relations in Richmond. Over 90 percent of the respondents who answered a question rating their dialogue experience indicated that it was "very positive" or "somewhat positive." A majority of the respondents reported that their groups were successful, and nearly 75 percent of those participants who rated the overall success of their group gave it a score of seven or higher on a ten-point scale.

"A central theme which emerged from the open-ended questions was the importance of personal relationships in dialogue," reports Dr. Hubbard. "Several [respondents] recommended that the groups should have more than six meetings in order to get to know each other better, [and] a number of respondents stressed the importance of meeting in small groups in each other's homes, which also enhances personal sharing."

While Hope in the Cities emphasizes the role of the individual in the dialogue process, respondents defined their experiences as successful based on the development of the overall group in which they participated. White respondents did report an increased individual awareness, whereas black respondents reported that they had become less judgmental. While a group response can be limiting, HIC staff indicates that the broad response provides demographic data, which helps them understand who is taking part in terms of socioeconomic and educational strata. The next step of research will be to track a racially balanced group of individuals for over a year. This will be conducted by an independent research team, so that direct, honest, and helpful answers will be given to HIC staff to better determine how the dialogue series is affecting the individual participant.

While reflecting on race relations in Richmond, respondents indicated that "responsibility for the problems was shared equally by the races." Participants wrote that fear and ignorance and a "lack of integration" and "voluntary segregation" prevented blacks and whites from relating to each other more fully. Seventy percent of the black respondents described whites as being responsible for the state of race relations in Richmond; 74 percent of the white respondents described the same situation as being the responsibility of both black and white residents. There was also anecdotal evidence of how white Richmonders control the economy of the city and black Richmonders control the government.

Moving out of a Comfort Zone

At the close of the six-part series, many group participants ask, "What's next?" While some have informally begun their own second rounds, one group formed a book club, a second group worked through their respective churches to host a boys' choir from Florida, and a third, which brought together black and Jewish organizations, sought out common political issues on which to support one another and ways in which to bring together their young people. "You've got to protect what you've got [young people]," says David Kalman. "We can stop this [racism] with the next generation and make it different from my generation. Kids also take things home to their parents."

Youth have always played an integral role in the work of HIC in Richmond. They led the Unity Walk in 1993, during which time they took part in their own round of dialogues and were central to the launch of "A Call to Community" and A Season of Dialogue three years later. Today, Dr. Paige Chargois convenes youth dialogues, drawing on the HIC model. These dialogues also vary in locations, such as African American and European American history museums and black and white places of worship.

While young people gravitate to the process, adults seem to surprise themselves the most. Pam Redd says that as a white woman she is still amazed at the discrimination that blacks go through. One of the men in the group she was leading spoke of there "'always being pain right below the surface.' Having heard this, I feel I am now connecting to African American colleagues at work much better," Redd reflects. "Just being aware of people's experiences has helped me to not be quick to judge."

"This has been a growth experience—to see others' life experiences," says Jane Talley, a black facilitator. "I thought learning would be on the white side, but it was on the black side."

Today it is rare to find a community that is *not* taking part in some form of dialogue. In many ways, what sets Hope in the Cities' work apart from other programs is its balance between format and flexibility and the recognition that there are no quick fixes on the road to racial healing. Additionally, it emphasizes both bringing very diverse groups together in the expectation that sustained dialogue will result in effective team building and the role that *each* person can, and must, play in talking about and working for change in a community.

"I think one of the reasons people are willing to move forward past their own comfort zones is because we are willing to do that *with* them, as fellow travelers," says Cricket White. "We, as 'staff,' are working every day to form authentic, caring, and honest relationships with each other and everyone who gets involved with us. We are willing to be vulnerable, to open ourselves to the same scrutiny as anyone else in the program."

To some, a discussion of dialogue in terms of seasons might seem at best a one-time effort—an event for which there is a great buildup, a strong follow-through, and then an unresolved conclusion. But Hope in the Cities has moved beyond the code words and artificial barriers by which Richmonders used to navigate their city. For today *and* tomorrow, there is A Season of Dialogue, with each new season building on the last.

NOTES

1. Quotations not otherwise attributed are from interviews conducted during August and September, 1998.
2. Hope in the Cities is a program of Moral Re-Armament (MRA), an international network of people of different faiths and backgrounds working for reconciliation and justice, beginning with change in their own lives. MRA's long experience includes work in the area of race relations. Most notably, it produced a play inspired by the life of the African American educator Mary McLeod Behune, which was used to bring down racial barriers in Atlanta and other American cities in the 1950s. When a black majority was elected to Richmond City Council in the late 1970s, MRA worked to build bridges between the new political leadership and the white establishment. It was out of this ongoing work that Hope in the Cities emerged.
3. "A Call to Community," available at www.hopeinthecitys.org or by calling 804–358–1764.

REFERENCES

Dredge, Polly, and Patricia Reichler. 1998. "Partnership Inspires Hope in Twelve Cities." *Nation's Cities Weekly* (National League of Cities), October 5, 10.

Edley, Christopher, Jr. 1997. "In Confederate Capital, Shared History Leads to New Solutions." *USA Today,* February 27, 5A.

Elliott Greisdorf, Karen, ed. 1997. *Community Resource Manual.* Richmond, Vir.: Hope in the Cities.

Henderson, Michael. 1996. *The Forgiveness Factor.* Salem, Ore.: Grosvenor Books.

Hickey, Gordon. 1996. "Backers Hope for 'Growth Sharing.'" *Richmond Times Dispatch,* December 31, A1.

Johnston, Douglas, and Cynthia Sampson, eds. 1993. *Religion: The Missing Dimension of Statecraft.* Center for Strategic and International Studies. New York: Oxford University Press.

Peirce, Neal, and Curtis Johnson. 1997. *Boundary Crossers: Community Leadership for a Global Age.* College Park, Md.: Academy of Leadership Press.

Reichler, Patricia. 1996. "Coalition Urges National Dialogue on Race." *Nation's Cities Weekly* (National League of Cities), June 3, 1.

Chapter 11

Not Just Dialogue for Dialogue's Sake: The National Conference for Community and Justice

Wayne Winborne and Allison Smith

The National Conference for Community and Justice (NCCJ)[1] is committed to transforming communities through institutional change so that all people have access to our nation's opportunities. One way NCCJ creates just and whole communities is through facilitated dialogue that leads to collaboration and action. These dialogues foster new, respectful relationships informed by a deepened understanding of the role of prejudice and stereotyping in discriminatory behavior and characterized by personal commitments to fight against personal, cultural, and institutional racism. As such, they are dialogues with a purpose—improving our intergroup relations.

This chapter will focus on models of dialogue developed by NCCJ and implemented in local communities across the country. The flexibility of the conversation model allows great autonomy while providing a broad framework within which to organize specific activities. Thus, each dialogue project looks very different in each region, but is woven together by the thread of civil discourse between and among people who are very unlike one another yet share a desire to identify common ground. At the national level, NCCJ implements "event" type discussions, typically using well-known figures to provide sharply defined insights. These programs do not seek to change the hearts and minds of the discussants. Rather, the discussants serve as surrogates for the viewers, demonstrating the ability to express thoughts, beliefs, and ideas honestly, as well as providing insights into the issues being discussed. Moreover, the approach used at the national level, for example, functions as a theoretical framework for voicing and exploring differing opinions, as well as a practical example of such discussions. The regional models that will be discussed here are

CommUnity Dialogue Initiative, Cincinnati
CommUnity Dinner and Dialogue Series, Birmingham

Voices of Youth Initiative, Buffalo

Neighbors in Dialogue, Interracial Dialogue Series, and White Racial Awareness Dialogues, Los Angeles

NCCJ's Approach to Community Dialogue

Kelley and Olson (1993, 1) describe dialogue as "a new term for an old experience . . . the face-to-face meeting of minds in open and friendly confrontation. It is the frank and free discussion of what we believe in an atmosphere of mutual respect and trust." The authors also state that dialogue involves risk because it might result in change within us, and that this change and its direction cannot be known in advance. However, they also note that

> risks are the price of opportunity. Dialogue provides the opportunity for genuine reconciliation which cannot exist without communication between those who seek to become reconciled. There are things we need to say and hear, but sometimes they are so severely disturbing that we are unable to tolerate them under everyday circumstances. Only in the unusual openness of the dialogue can we—sometimes—accept the incision for the sake of the healing it might bring. (Kelley and Olson 1993, 6)

At NCCJ, dialogue is a purposeful conversation on a common subject between two or more people of differing views, undertaken so that each can learn from the other and each can change and grow. Designed to minimize the conflicts and communication breakdowns traceable to differences in style and mode of communication, the dialogue process fosters new, respectful relationships that are informed by a deepened understanding of the role of prejudice and stereotyping in discriminatory behavior. From these new relationships comes a commitment to fight against such behavior in one's self, one's life, and one's community. This commitment to action is critical, since it is only human action that can break down the walls that divide us.

The underlying philosophy of NCCJ's work in dialogue is the belief that before people from different identity groups can develop true understanding and respect for each other, a process of identifying and sharing differences in perceptions must occur. In NCCJ's model of dialogue, our differences need not disappear. Rather, they should be acknowledged and used to enhance understanding of the experiences of various groups within American society and, in so doing, inform our own experience. NCCJ believes that all people belong to a host of identity groups such as race, religion, age, gender, socioeconomics, and sexual orientation. All of these identities influence how each of us experiences the world and the world experiences us. Throughout this dynamic process, our opinions or our individual views of the world are created. Together, these variables contribute to the building of various cultures when people share similar life experiences.

The challenge of cross-cultural dialogue is how people of different backgrounds can listen and learn about someone else's life experience and worldview without invalidating that person's reality. Effective multicultural community collaboration will not occur until trust is developed. Trust is developed only when people begin to identify and share their own bias and prejudice with those about whom they hold the bias and prejudice. This process must be conducted in an environment of safety and be facilitated by trained and experienced staff.

Since intergroup cooperation has been rarely fostered outside of major social movements, the progression from public agreement, to honest dialogue, to awareness building, to developing action plans, takes time and commitment. A single session of dialogue will not achieve the goal of creating better communities through collective action. Discussing our similarities and differences, defining a common cause, and developing a strategy to achieve it are all tasks of the dialogue process. Similarly, a series of conversations alone will not automatically lead people to action.

It is important to emphasize what dialogue is not: it is not debate, lecture, or argument. Dialogue for the sake of mere conversation is not the goal of NCCJ. Rather, NCCJ views dialogue as a necessary first step in the purposeful movement toward collaborations and coalitions across cultural, racial, and religious barriers. And it is within the common space of collaboration and coalition that communities are transformed for the broader good. For NCCJ, the result of this purposeful movement toward collaboration is the gathering of resources, ideas, and energy from a range of communities to act upon issues of common concern.[2]

Most Americans live in geographic, cultural, and economic isolation from one another and need assistance in opening their hearts and minds to experience new ideas, feelings, situations, and people. Community dialogues provide the opportunity for the increased collaboration and involvement of a wide range of people in specific activities from parent-teacher associations, to local elections, to police–community relations boards. Achieving a successful outcome depends upon creating a suitable and safe arena in which communities can build trust, incorporate multiple points of view, develop flexible outlooks, and create a problem-solving process. Ultimately, the ongoing actions and interactions of diverse people in communities define the efficacy of the dialogue process.

NCCJ Regional Dialogue Models

Based upon NCCJ's dialogue philosophy, regional offices initiate dialogue projects customized to the issues and people in their local area. These initiatives utilize a variety of approaches to allow for the widest possible inclusion of individuals at all levels of awareness. The models used intertwine structured activities with discussion in order to meet the needs of the participants, in a flexible manner. There are several noteworthy NCCJ efforts under way that provide models for community dialogue and illustrate the potential of purposeful conversation for movement toward the identification of common ground. These models are represented here by the work of NCCJ in its Cincinnati, Birmingham, Buffalo, and Los Angeles regional offices.

Cincinnati: The CommUnity Dialogue Initiative

With fifty-two distinct neighborhoods within Cincinnati city limits and another forty to fifty in the surrounding region, the reality is that most people in the region do not often have meaningful interactions with people outside of their neighborhood. Some local residents feel isolated, and assumptions about people in the different neighborhoods abound. In 1994, the Episcopal diocese held a summit on racism in the area, which was also around the time of Cincinnati Reds owner Marge Schott's infamous, racist remarks about ballplayers. In response to these and other factors in their community, NCCJ's Cincinnati region began its CommUnity initiative,[3] the centerpiece of which is an ongoing series of dialogues. To date, approximately six hundred people have attended the living room dialogues, and fifteen hundred people have participated at their workplace.

The Cincinnati region's dialogue model is based on a monthlong, three-session curriculum. The committee working to design the model chose to have three three-hour sessions in the home of one of the participants. The three-hour length of the sessions was chosen so that participants could really get comfortable, engage in deeper dialogue, have time to answer any questions, and achieve some degree of closure.

Session 1 gives the participants a chance to get to know each other through a cultural sharing exercise, learn about each other as members of a neighborhood through an interactive mapping exercise, discuss experiences of being different, and learn about the process of stereotyping. Session 2 builds on the rapport the participants have developed and, using both reflective and interactive exercises, begins a dialogue on defining terms, the effects of societal prejudices in their community, and exploration of institutional racism. Session 3 focuses on the existing barriers to the creation of inclusive community and engages the participants in a dialogue to create processes to overcome these barriers and transform their community. Several of the dialogue groups have gone on to create an optional fourth session to explore further the issues facing their community and create action plans for future projects. Using a similar model, the CommUnity initiative also sponsors Community Leader dialogues and workplace dialogues.

Facilitators for the dialogues are recruited through NCCJ's volunteer network, dialogue alumni, corporate diversity practitioners, and NCCJ Cincinnati's partnership with Cinergy Corporation. These facilitators attend training sessions that include discussions of various topical readings, definitions of terms, and interactive exercises that address self-awareness and how to handle conflict. Participants are asked to complete evaluation forms after the closing session. Facilitators are also asked to evaluate the process and meet in focus groups to discuss possible modifications to the curriculum.

Another aspect of the Cincinnati region's CommUnity initiative involves a series of videos. Based in part on the "National Conversation on Race, Ethnicity, and Culture,"[4] the Cincinnati region has partnered with Cinergy Corporation and a local television station to develop a set of four videotaped panel discussions to be used as conversation starters for dialogue programs. The aim of each video program is to foster intergroup awareness, understanding, and cooperation through honest conversation on the challenging issues of race, ethnicity, and culture. Each of the thirty-minute videos focuses on one of the following topics: education, criminal justice, economic opportunity, and religion, and each comes with information sheets and questions for discussion.

One of the challenges facing the CommUnity initiative is recruiting a truly diverse set of participants, particularly regarding participants' socioeconomic class. To date, the participants have tended to be middle to upper class, and changes to the recruiting process are currently under way to address the issue.

Cincinnati's CommUnity initiative has been highly successful in creating opportunities for local residents to explore the difficult issues surrounding race and racism. The dialogue's focus on neighborhoods engages the participants in a process of breaking down the barriers that separate them and allows a space for personal and institutional change in their own community. Above all else, the CommUnity dialogues give people from different backgrounds the opportunity to see and understand that pieces of the human experience are common to us all. The results of this awareness can be a first step in the process of building a more inclusive and cooperative community.

Birmingham: CommUnity Dinner and Dialogue Series

The Birmingham metropolitan area consists of approximately one million people, one-third of Alabama's population. Since the 1960s, the relationships among the various racial and ethnic groups have shown steady growth of understanding and interaction. This is due to several factors including governmental intervention and the work of the nonprofit sector. However, several recent events (including the bombing of the New Women–All Women's Clinic, a KKK rally during Martin Luther King weekend, and most recently, the hate-motivated murder of a gay man— Billy Jack Gaither) continue to make programs such as NCCJ's Dinner and Dialogue Series relevant.

The Birmingham region of NCCJ initiated the CommUnity Dinner and Dialogue Series at the request of the participants in the region's Project CommUnity workshops who wanted to continue the dialogue on "building community." The participants also wanted a vehicle to break down the neighborhood barriers in Birmingham, a community that continues to struggle with racial tensions.

It is important to see how the Dinner and Dialogue Series grew out of an existing Birmingham NCCJ program, Project CommUnity, a daylong workshop and training whose workshops are held two times per year. The Dinner and Dialogue Series is held four times per year as a follow-up to Project CommUnity, and dialogues are scheduled to build upon the training provided in the workshop. The goal of Project CommUnity is to bring together adult leaders to foster community. The learning objectives are

To redefine community beyond our own streets and neighborhoods, and reintroduce civility as a standard of our relations

To provide a forum for adult members of our community to dialogue on human relations issues

To foster intergroup awareness, understanding, and cooperation
  through honest conversation on many challenging issues
To develop an understanding of inclusion/exclusion based on the systems of privilege present in our community
To build relationships with other members of our community through
  networking

The Dinner and Dialogue Series is an informal program held in different houses and neighborhood congregations to foster unity between very
segregated neighborhoods. The sessions include meals and informal sharing as an integral part of the program. Participants bring "cultural dishes"
and enjoy getting to know people on an informal basis, which allows for
the personal trust-building necessary for effective dialogue. The Comm-
Unity workshop targets forty as a maximum number of participants and
typically involves twenty-five to thirty-six individuals. A formal evaluation of Project CommUnity is currently under way.

NCCJ targeted leadership from a cross-section of organizations but
also invited the general public to participate. The first two Project Comm-
Unity workshops identified and recruited leadership from organizations
including Leadership Birmingham, Community Affairs Committee of
Operation New Birmingham, Coalition against Hate Crimes, National
Issues Forum, and the local NCCJ board. The third workshop specifically
targeted the Diversity Council of a statewide public utility and focused on
both personal and workplace issues. Indeed, the growth of the Comm-
Unity program in Birmingham is evident in that one of the workshop participants was the chair of the Diversity Council and decided to bring the
program back to his workplace. Another similar occurrence has taken
place, with a CommUnity workshop planned for the workplace of
another participant, a local college. At this site, the workshops will target
residence hall advisors and student leadership. The college hopes to
include a miniversion of CommUnity for the entire freshman class at
future orientations.

The evaluation process is less structured because of the informal nature
of the Dinner and Dialogue Series. However, participants are surveyed on
their reactions to, and satisfaction with, the program. With regard to the
short-term and long-term impact of the Dinner and Dialogue program on
individuals, participants report that friendships were made and that individuals have continued to meet outside of the programs. Participants have
stayed active in the Dinner and Dialogue Series and have brought new
people as guests. Indeed, the program has blossomed with new and vet-

eran participants, and the participants have become involved with other NCCJ programs, as well as with other community organizations.

As mentioned earlier, the CommUnity program expanded into a workplace as a result of a participant's interest. From a community perspective, the activities have created networks and friendships across racial, religious, socioeconomic, and geographic boundaries. The series has also prompted dialogue on relevant human relations issues between a cross section of community members. Additionally, there have been more collaborations between Birmingham's community organizations since this program was developed. Thus, the CommUnity program evolved to take the daylong workshop into workplaces, and the Dinner and Dialogue Series grew out of the CommUnity program, showing how one effective program can grow out of another if organizers pay attention to participants' suggestions and needs.

Buffalo: The Voices of Youth Initiative

Buffalo, a city with approximately one million residents, suffers from economic decline, tense police-community relations, and segregated neighborhoods. Race relations are strained, with many whites living in gated communities and several recent incidents of hate-motivated vandalism and harassment targeted at minorities. Through the concerted efforts of local nonprofits and coalitions of religious leaders, these tensions are being openly discussed and community-building initiatives are under way. In an effort to involve the city's youth in this process, NCCJ's Buffalo region began the Voices of Youth Initiative.

The Voices of Youth Initiative involves high school students (ages fourteen to sixteen) and runs through the academic year, from October through May. The program was developed to give youth an understanding of cross-cultural and cross-racial issues. The Buffalo NCCJ region has an adult dialogue called Buffalo Conversations, which was adapted to create this youth dialogue. Voices of Youth is a round-robin series of dialogues between students from African American, Buddhist, European American, Hispanic, Jewish, and Native American community centers. Students meet once a month throughout the academic year, visiting each other's community centers for dialogue sessions. Many times this is the young people's first visit to certain neighborhoods. In the program, which seeks to improve cross-racial and cross-cultural understanding, students develop an understanding of the effects of cultural identity on one's personal development. Learning objectives of the program include

Facilitating a more open, honest conversation about individuals and societal beliefs about race, ethnicity, culture, and religious differences and commonalities

Understanding the effects of language (verbal and nonverbal) across racial and ethnic groups

Understanding the history of diverse people in America and how history affects contemporary life

Increasing youth involvement in their own communities and other civic involvement through a range of viable activities

Staff from each community center choose participants for this program based on leadership skills, interest, and willingness to share information about one's culture. There are forty participants in the program, and they attend a program kickoff-orientation at the Buffalo Community Day Program. Students develop a series of cultural activities, icebreakers, and dialogue questions based on heritage, cultural traditions, values, and so on, throughout the academic year.

Over time, the control of the dialogue shifts to the students with adult staff used as a resource. Thus, the students decide what questions to ask and what the conversation topics will be. Finally, students maintain contact with one another after the academic year program. Evaluations of the program using a pre- and postattitude assessment Likert scale reveal that participants have an increase in cultural awareness and cross-cultural understanding after the program.

Los Angeles: Neighbors in Dialogue, Interracial Dialogue Series, and White Awareness Dialogues

NCCJ's Los Angeles region has been conducting community dialogues for over thirty years, beginning with interfaith dialogues between Christians and Jews. Today the various interracial dialogues conducted use the same format as their interfaith predecessors—a sequence of five meetings, with each two-and-a-half-hour session led by trained facilitators. The same participants are strongly urged to attend all five meetings. The model is structured, yet flexible enough to adapt to the specific needs of the facilitators and the participants. The number of sessions and the length of each session is determined primarily by the depth of the experience expected, as well as the session goals and objectives, the resources needed to convene people, and the ability of participants to attend. Based on their experience, NCCJ staff feel strongly that it takes at least eight to ten hours for true dialogue that can build bridges and respect strong enough to stand the test of time.

L.A.'s dialogue programs include Neighbors in Dialogue—an opportunity for neighbors to envision transforming their neighborhood into an inclusive community; the Interracial Dialogue Series (also called Working in a Diverse Environment, an Effective Process)—where an interracial group of adults who already have a working relationship discuss more deeply the issues of difference; and White Racial Awareness Dialogues—a forum for white people to come together to discuss issues of power and privilege and their role as allies in the movement for racial justice.

While NCCJ's Los Angeles region has a long-standing and well-established dialogue process and related programs, there are still challenges, including recruiting and training facilitators who are skilled technically and are aware of their own biases. L.A.'s dialogue facilitators must attend a five-session training. Over these five sessions, facilitators learn NCCJ's definition of dialogue, how to create a safe environment for the participants, the role of the facilitator, the dimensions of diversity, cross-cultural communication, how group size affects interaction, how to use and enforce communication ground rules, effective questioning methods, time management skills, group dynamics, and how to handle conflict. Also, throughout the training, facilitators experience the exercises that will be used in the dialogue sessions and have a chance to clarify their own values and ideas on race. It is extremely important that the facilitators recognize their own level of self-awareness with regard to issues of race, power, and privilege so they can better facilitate the dialogue. The facilitators also need to be clear on their role as facilitator: they are there to guide and help focus the discussions, not to work on their own issues, act as experts, or challenge participants who may hit on one of their hot buttons.

Other challenges include recruiting participants who can commit to attending all five sessions. This issue is heightened by the number of varied programs seeking dialogue participants in Los Angeles. For instance, in L.A. there are several organizations that advertise dialogue and mean different things by it. These organizations often overuse and misuse the term *dialogue.* For example, some of these "dialogues" are panel discussions with open mikes, some have a presenter who takes questions from the audience, some use a town hall model, and some are "speak outs." What they have in common is that they are one-time events. Thus, there can be confusion by prospective participants regarding what the L.A. region's five-session model is, and some prospective participants believe that attending one of these other one-day forums is all of the dialogue they need.

Language is one of the areas where NCCJ's Los Angeles region has sought to become an innovator and has adapted the dialogue process to fit a multilingual population. Due to the highly multicultural nature of Southern California language, the region has found that many of the people who want to participate in a dialogue process do not have English as their native tongue. Currently the dialogue materials—agendas, articles, worksheets—are all being translated into several languages. The Neighbors in Dialogue process is run multilingually through the use of on-site translators. Using such a multilingual approach allows the dialogue process to be truly inclusive.

With such a long history of dialogue in the region, L.A'.s innovative initiatives serve as models for other NCCJ regions. While there are many varied approaches to dialogue, the Los Angeles region strongly believes that although one-time events provide a taste of what it is like to break down the barriers and to communicate on a deeper level, it takes repeated interaction among participants to build trust. It is through these sequenced dialogues that participants are able to overcome communication barriers and develop relationships to disprove and discard stereotypes. The dialogues encourage participants to act within their own spheres of influence to combat racism. Dialogue alumni serve as a cadre of change agents in the Los Angeles region.

Conclusion

These examples are but a small sample of the varied dialogue efforts NCCJ is undertaking across the country. What these different efforts share is an understanding that the lack of dialogue and interaction between and among people in this country is detrimental to our communities and to the United States as a whole. NCCJ is committed to facilitating more inclusive public discourse. It seeks to promote cross-cultural understanding, reduce prejudice, provide the opportunity for civil dialogue on critical issues, and generate community-based problem-solving strategies. These approaches also are all predicated on the notion that focused, continued dialogue on issues that divide us is a prerequisite to identifying and moving toward common ground. This common ground, in turn, is the space where citizens of all races, ethnicities, and cultures can engage in strategies to build community and define the ways in which to have purposeful conversations. These conversations represent the continuing efforts of NCCJ to reduce bias, bigotry, and racism in America through open and honest communication.

NOTES

Portions of this research were supported by a grant from the Charles Stewart Mott Foundation. The authors also wish to thank NCCJ's President and CEO, Sanford Cloud, Jr., Scott Marshall, Director of Programming Strategies, and Renae Cohen, Director of Research, for their vision and leadership. And a special thanks to the staff of the Alabama, Greater Cincinnati, Los Angeles, and Western New York regions, for their gracious giving of time, expertise, and information.

1. The National Conference for Community and Justice, founded in 1927 as the National Conference of Christians and Jews, is a human relations organization dedicated to fighting bias, bigotry, and racism in America. NCCJ promotes understanding and respect among all races, religions, and cultures through advocacy, conflict resolution, and education.
2. It is important to emphasize that the participants in the dialogue have chosen to interact because of an interest in identifying common ground or attempting to do so. This process may work for people who do not want to participate in a dialogue, but NCCJ does not purport to be able to convert Nazis, for example.
3. The CommUnity dialogue model was originally developed by NCCJ's Tampa Bay region and then replicated in several NCCJ regions around the country.
4. The "National Conversation on Race, Ethnicity, and Culture" is an annual event cosponsored by NCCJ's national office and Aetna, Inc. that provides a forum for cross sections of national and community leaders to explore critical human relations issues.

REFERENCE

Kelley, Dean M., and Bernard E. Olson. 1993. *The Meaning and Conduct of Dialogue.* New York: The National Conference of Christians and Jews.

Case Studies: Workplace

Cultural Study Groups: Creating Dialogue in a Corporate Setting

Rita Hardiman and Bailey W. Jackson

This chapter describes an intergroup dialogue program in a corporate setting. The dialogue program was one of several interventions in the company to encourage learning about group differences based on race and gender, and about the presence and impact of discrimination, racism, and sexism on the lives of the participants in the group.

The Digital Equipment Core Groups: A Dialogue Model

This intergroup dialogue program is derived from a dialogue program started by Barbara Walker at Digital Equipment Corporation in the 1970s. Barbara Walker, an African-American manager at Digital, pioneered the use of this dialogue format, which continued in the company for several years. At Digital these dialogue sessions were referred to as *core groups:* "Core groups are . . . labs where people help each other explore their issues of racism, sexism and 'differentism'" (Walker 1986, 1). These groups were one part, perhaps even a major part of Digital's Valuing Differences strategy, which was directed toward understanding group differences such as race, culture, and gender and breaking down attitudinal barriers that impeded the potential of people of color and White women in the company.

The core groups were led by employees of the company, not necessarily people whose formal role in the company involved human resources or training. Any manager could start a group, but as Walker (1986, 9) wrote, the group leader needed to have the qualities of "openness, authenticity, self-acceptance, empathy, and be a serious student, invested in their own learning about issues of difference."

At Digital, the roles of the core group leader included logistical support (for example setting up times and places to meet), maintaining the focus of the discussion, and monitoring the group process so that participants felt heard and safe as they explored the issues.

The work of the core group was seen as bonding and critical thinking about the issues. As defined by Walker, "Bonding with people of difference enhances our ability to work interdependently with all kinds of people, broadens our perspectives on the world and enriches the quality of our work lives" (1986, 22). To the extent that this is achieved, it can change the corporate norm of "cloning"—managers promoting and choosing to work with those that are most like themselves, thereby continually replicating management groups of White men who are alike on many dimensions in addition to the two core ones of race and gender. Critical thinking about the issues of prejudice and stereotyping allows one to openly examine the prejudices and stereotypes one holds about all kinds of groups.

Core groups focused on race and gender differences and saw race and sex as a metaphor for all differences. By exploring these two difficult, charged issues, the core group could go on to more easily learn about or bridge other group differences. Core groups also explored the sources of disempowerment and self-victimization: an us-versus-them mind set, loneliness, the connection between rage and stereotyping, and collusion (Walker 1986, 33).

In the ABC Company we instituted what were called Cultural Study Groups (CSG), which mirrored the format of the Digital core groups, but with a number of significant differences. Before describing these groups and how they operated, it is important to first discuss the organizational context in which these attempts at dialogue were initiated.

Organizational Context at ABC

ABC is a Fortune 100 diversified company with numerous business units. It is a large company with global operations and several thousand employees. Like most U.S. corporations, its workforce, leadership, and company culture were White and male. In the late 1970s, the company began to hire more women and people of color into positions that previously had been open only to White men. While the company employed White women and men and women of color prior to this, they were typically hired into service roles such as clerical, secretarial, or maintenance jobs, or in entry-level positions in plants and factories. In the post–civil rights climate of the 1970s, the company began to implement affirmative action programs. As early as the late 1970s, the company began focusing on the impact that the influx of professional women was having on the company. Early diversity training programs primarily focused on gender issues and were designed to enhance collegial, respectful relationships among professional women and men and open up opportunities for women in the company. At the time the Cultural Study Groups were introduced as an intervention, the organization was pursuing change through training, primarily directed at changing individual awareness, and increasing sensitivity to the unique situations of women and people of color in the workplace.

A sometimes spoken, but often unspoken, strategy for change at ABC was to target high-ranking White males for awareness training in the hope that they would then translate their new awareness into action, hence creating more opportunities and paths to success for White women and men and women of color. A tandem strategy was to push for change from the bottom up by encouraging and enabling the formation of support groups and affinity groups for historically disenfranchised populations. In the early years of this change process, numerous women's networks emerged for different functions and levels. One of the larger and more influential networks was the Black women's network. As time went on, more groups emerged, including an Asian/Pacific network, a Hispanic network, and an affinity group for gay, lesbian, or bisexual employees and their allies.

Cultural Studies Groups and Multicultural Organization Development

The CSGs were one facet of a change effort that focused on the support building and leadership development aspects of our Multicultural Organization Development (MCOD) model (Jackson and Hardiman 1994). One of the key ingredients in creating change is to educate employees about issues and barriers that impinge on the success of White women and people of color in organizations. One of our assumptions in organizing the CSGs is that all of us suffer from ignorance and misinformation about groups other than our own, particularly historically disenfranchised groups such as racial minorities. This ignorance, coupled with stereotypes and distortions about various groups that are promoted by the media, produce a population that is inadequately prepared to work collaboratively in a diverse work environment. We also believe that correcting this ignorance is possible.

Another assumption that we make is that people can and want to learn, and can undo a great deal of the negative programming that afflicts them.

We can challenge our own assumptions, biases, and prejudices about other groups and learn to not only appreciate our differences but understand some of the forces that have led to our different life experiences and group histories. It is especially true that those in the dominant or privileged groups in corporate America—Whites, males, heterosexuals, Christians—frequently assume that the playing field has been leveled and miss seeing the sophisticated or more subtle forms of oppression that exist in the company culture. Through training events, dialogue groups, and other educational experiences, members of privileged groups can become more aware of the challenges facing their coworkers of color and White women.

Increasing awareness of issues that need to be remedied and building support for change is one important facet of Multicultural Organization Development. The dialogue groups also provide women and men of color and White women an opportunity to see where they have common concerns. This can also open up opportunities for coalition building for change.

Another component of MCOD is leadership development. This involves expanding the personal awareness of the leadership—helping them to recognize then reduce or eliminate their race and gender bias and become more aware of how that bias is present in the organization. Developing the leadership also involves helping the leaders become role models on diversity for their organization. This usually requires coaching and a willingness to be open to feedback from peers and consultants or trainers in and outside the organization. The CSGs were another opportunity for senior managers to fill in their gaps in knowledge about other cultures and social groups. It also provided them with an opportunity to hear about issues in their organization from which they are frequently far removed. Senior managers, unless they make a concerted effort to manage by walking around, are likely to be very isolated from the rank and file. The organizational hierarchy maintains layers of control between upper, middle, and lower levels of the organization, making it particularly unlikely that senior managers will be aware of issues and problems that impact racial and gender minorities.

As important as educational and support-building strategies are, they are of limited effectiveness unless coupled with efforts to root out institutionalized racist and sexist practices that are imbedded in corporate policies and practices. Other initiatives at ABC that focused on changing recruitment practices, compensation and reward systems, performance reviews, and other corporate systems were an important part of the total multicultural organization development work going on at that time. As

MCOD practitioners, the CSG leaders saw their role as one important component of the change process, but in no way the only one.

Intended Results and Desired Outcomes of the Cultural Study Groups

Our hoped-for results of the CSGs were as follows:

All participants would learn about the histories, struggles, cultural differences, and similarities of people different from themselves.

All participants would enhance their communication skills, especially listening skills and ability to engage in dialogue.

Senior managers would increase their awareness of issues affecting White women and people of color in the organization. They would also get to know people who represent the future workforce of the corporation.

Senior managers would transfer their awareness into action. They would be moved to take action to improve the organizational environment.

Mid- and lower-level employees would gain exposure to senior managers and would have more likelihood of finding a mentor or sponsor among the senior management group.

All employees would identify issues that they shared in common, thus increasing the possibility for forming coalitions across race and gender boundaries.

All participants would be motivated to continue their learning about diversity.

Leadership of the Cultural Study Groups

Each CSG was led by two facilitators, a man and woman of different race. The group leaders were frequently Black and White pairs, although other pairings also occurred. The social group representation of the leaders was an important consideration, in addition to the obvious consideration of skills and experience. As the focus of the CSG dialogues was on the impact of race and gender, it was seen as critical for the pairs to not only represent the racial and gender diversity of the group but to model shared leadership by women and men, and Whites and people of color. Unlike the model used at Digital, where the dialogue groups were not facilitated by trainers or consultants, at ABC each group's leaders were trained in the applied behavioral sciences. Most if not all facilitators had a Ph.D. in education, sociology, psychology, or related fields and were experienced in process consultation, conflict mediation, training design and facilitation, and personal growth laboratory training. In addition to this formal training, all facilitators were veteran consultants, having trained hundreds of employees in various companies throughout the United States. Each also brought to the work his or her own commitment to racial and gender justice and equity as well as experience in race relations, civil rights, and women's rights work. Finally, each trainer brought to the CSGs a bent toward learner-centered training and dialogue, taking the approach of allowing questions, issues, and understandings to emerge from the participants, in contrast to a "telling and selling" approach. Unlike some traditional classroom learning experiences in which the instructor communicates information that the learners are supposed to take in and remember, these groups encouraged the participants to be cocreators of the curriculum.

Facilitator's Role in the Group

The facilitators' job was to design the content and process of the CSG curriculum. This included selecting reading material, videos, and field trips and sequencing the topics. We also designed the process by which the dialogue groups would be conducted. However, the content and format of the CSG was also designed to emerge from the participants. Participants were encouraged to share resources including books and journal articles. They were active partners in selecting the cultural experiences—plays, films, concerts, and church services that the group attended. As the CSGs progressed through the "forming stage" of group development (Weber 1982), the participants also took a more directive role in creating the dialogue process. Through the interventions of the facilitators, group members saw and learned how to self-monitor their process. Early on in the life of the group, it was fairly typical for people to speak in parallel monologues, as distinct from dialogues. For example, Fred, a Black engineer, would describe a situation in his life that reflected something in one of the readings. His remarks would be followed by Jean, a White woman chemist, who would tell a story from her life that essentially said to Fred and the group: "Me too." Rather than responding to Fred by asking him a question, or stating how Fred's story impacted her, Jean and other group members would commence telling their own stories that either confirmed or denied the similarity of their experience with Fred's. In our group dynamics jargon, we refer to these remarks as "plops." Person A says something, and it goes unacknowledged or ignored: it "plops." Person B then tells their story and it falls down, "plop," in the middle of the group, and no one responds to it. In these situations, the facilitators' job is to intervene in the discussion and first name the group process, then attempt to redirect it. The facilitator would, for example, gently interrupt Jean and say to her and the other group members, "Before you go any further with your example, Jean, do you or any others want to respond to Fred? He just shared a personal example, and it feels like it is hanging out there in the air." This type of intervention and numerous others like it were part of the facilitators' job of enabling the group to create dialogue among its members, rather than a series of disconnected monologues where no one felt heard or acknowledged.

The facilitators' job also involved *gatekeeping*, encouraging participation from quiet members, while balancing the input of more vocal people; *probing* and encouraging people to explore deeper levels of thoughts, feelings, and beliefs to move beyond the surface level of superficial chat; *ensuring safety* by disallowing personal attacks or piling on; and *maintaining* the group boundaries of time, task, space, and curriculum.

Membership of the Cultural Study Group

Much as at Digital, the ABC Cultural Study Groups were assembled around senior managers who were willing and able to sponsor the group. This was deemed necessary because only those in leadership could create the conditions for the group to function. Senior managers had budgets to pay for the facilitators, materials, meals, and other expenses. They also had the ability to create opportunities for less powerful members of the organization to participate in the dialogues by securing release time for CSG meetings. Senior managers were motivated to sponsor CSGs and participate in them because their own job performance and compensation were tied to their work in diversity change efforts, of which the CSG was one activity or strategy, although several senior managers sponsored groups before this was a company policy.

The membership of the CSG was structured so as to include roughly half men and half women and no more than two-thirds Whites and no less than one-third people of color. The typical group was about fifteen people with six White men, four White women, and five men and women of color. The desired race and gender composition of the group was difficult to achieve given the demographics of the organization. Most of the White men were senior-level professionals, while the White women and women and men of color came from the mid- to lower-level ranks of the organization. No one in the group reported directly to anyone else in the group, although they may have been in each other's line of supervision, with several layers removed. To ensure diversity in the group, people sometimes crossed organizational units or lines to participate. At this particular time, there were a number of business units within ABC, which were initiating CSGs. To construct the right racial and gender representation in the groups, managers opened up participation to people in other organizational units. This also aided in the effort to keep people in direct reporting relationships out of the same group. The groups were also diverse by function as well as race, gender, and status in the hierarchy. They were generally comprised of a mix of managers, individual contributors, such as engineers and research-and-development specialists, and people from various functions such as human resources, marketing, or finance.

The CSGs were formed through the initiation of a senior manager, who served as the group sponsor. This manager sent out invitations to selected members of the organizational unit, factoring in race, gender, level, and functional differences. The invitations solicited voluntary participation, and no one was coerced to join the CSG. Letters were also sent to the managers of selected participants, explaining the group, its purpose, and the need for some flexibility and release time for the employee's participation. In addition to the formal process (letters), there was also a fair amount of behind-the-scenes strategizing and discussion about participation. The selection was not entirely random. Efforts were made to select participants who had expressed serious interest in learning about diversity issues in the company and were eager to engage with others; to select participants who were active in one or more diversity activities such as networks, or organizational task forces; and to select employees who, although they were not at senior level themselves, were confident and personally empowered enough to engage in frank discussion with those who outranked them. It was not unusual for there to be behind-the-scenes lobbying going on with regard to getting employees on or off the Cultural Study Group roster.

The expectations of membership in the CSG were attendance, doing the required prework, and active participation in the group dialogue. Participants were also expected to be open, willing to listen, and to entertain new, sometimes disconfirming, and even threatening, ideas. There were also expectations set by the groups themselves with regard to absences, confidentiality, and handling issues within the group rather than taking them out of the group.

For most of the possible risks associated with participation in this group, there were complimentary benefits that were possible as well. One of the risk/benefit possibilities was visibility. It was risky to participate in a group where one's ignorance or bias could be exposed, but the possible benefits of connecting with colleagues and senior managers and having one's enthusiasm and insights exposed was a significant opportunity. Another possibility was conflict among group members and the implications for one's career. Handled poorly, this conflict could damage careers; handled well, it could enhance them. One risk without an attendant benefit, however, was the reaction of others outside the group to those who participated. Occasionally jealousy and fear were two reactions from those around the participants. Managers whose subordinates participated in a CSG with a senior manager were fearful of exposure. What if their employees shared negative experiences or perceptions about him or her with others in the group? What if the employees showcased themselves as a shining star in the organization to the senior management? How might this affect their managers' own careers?

As an entity that functioned outside the hierarchical chain of command, the CSG created an opportunity for lower-level employees to have access to more senior managers and vice versa. Thus to a middle-level manager who was not part of the CSG, concerns about turf, face time with senior managers, and their own reputations were understandable. These concerns were less likely to occur when the members of the CSG were not part of the same business unit.

Structure and Curriculum

The CSG was designed as a yearlong commitment, with monthly meetings. Each meeting was designed as a four-hour session. Most sessions took place during normal working hours, but occasionally a meeting was held in the evening when the group attended a play or cultural event in the community. One group even met on a Sunday, when all the members attended a service at one member's church. Most sessions were held at the work site in a conference room. Each group began with a kick-off meeting that ran for a day or day and a half. In this extended session basic concepts related to oppression were explored, and the group members also had a concentrated period of time to get acquainted with each other and with the content and format of the meetings. Exploration of participants' hopes, fears, and expectations of the CSG were discussed.

As mentioned previously, the curriculum of the CSG was developed by facilitators with the understanding that it would change as the participants became more involved in the group and contributed their own ideas for material. Each group had assigned readings to do between meetings. Some of the meetings involved viewing a film or tape. But regardless of the medium, film, writings, or cultural events, the purpose of these inputs was to stimulate discussion and dialogue. The facilitators' role was to choose provocative material, then to focus the group on talking with each other about what the material evoked in them. The goal was not to thoroughly discuss all the assigned readings in an orderly fashion, but rather to engage in genuine dialogue with each other, using the readings or other stimuli as a jumping-off point.

The reading material covered contemporary issues of race and gender, some of which was first person or autobiographical, while some selections covered current research, for example a study on glass ceilings for women in corporations. Participants were encouraged to bring in suggestions for the group reading assignments or to recommend events in the community that the group could attend. Dialogue in the group also focused on social issues that appeared in the news. For example, the police beating of Rodney King occurred during one of the CSG's sequence of meetings. The event itself and the media reaction became a major focus of discussion over a series of meetings. With situations like this, the formal curriculum of the group was interrupted because the participants' energy and passion was directed at this significant social event, not the scheduled reading assignment for that month.

Dialogue took time to develop in these groups. As is typical in the "forming stages" of a group, most participants are reticent about personal information, are more inclined to discuss issues superficially, and are generally polite or averse to creating conflict (Weber 1982). As the groups matured, more honesty emerged. As the facilitators encouraged and modeled active listening, respect for individual points of view, and responsiveness to feelings as well as the sharing of ideas, more true feelings and conflict emerged. For example, in one of our CSGs, the topic of sexual harassment arose in the fifth or sixth meeting. Three of the men in the group treated the subject with dismissive comments, suggesting that it was "not an issue at ABC." These remarks prompted a number of reactions from the women in the group—from open-mouthed stares of disbelief, to loud sighs, and one outburst of "What planet do you guys live on?" This led, after some initial resistance, to one of the women sharing a very painful, personal account of her experience with harassment by a colleague, and the company's indifferent response to her situation. The facilitators took an active role in guiding this dialogue, because the initial response of the men in the group to this story was reminiscent of the response the woman received to her complaint: silence. As Carol came to tears in recounting her experience, a couple of the women in the group sat with her and encouraged her to speak. Other women responded nonverbally, but generally the response of the men was uncomfortable fidgeting and silence. They clearly were uncomfortable and did not know what to do when Carol finished talking. Their silence angered Carol and she became frustrated, saying that what was going on right there and then in the group was the same male pattern she found among her managers. The trauma of her experience was being re-created in the group. As facilitators our role was to help the group learn how to engage in true dialogue. One of our tasks was to allow for, encourage, and support Carol and those like her in "telling their stories." Another task was to help the other participants—in this case, the men—learn how to respond and participate in shared dialogue. This was easier said than done. We encouraged the men to make some response to Carol in any way they felt was appropriate, so that Carol knew she was heard. But the initial attempts at response made matters worse. Al, a middle manager in finance, asked Carol why she put up with the harassment so long and didn't report it sooner. This response infuriated Melynda, who replied that Al's comment smacked of "blaming the victim" and clearly showed that Al "understood nothing about what Carol and other women like her went through." We had to intervene numerous times to prevent a shouting match. Our interventions were focused at individuals, interpersonal dyads, and the total group. We directed them at various levels of behavior including the surface level (i.e., visible nonverbal gestures), intermediate level (i.e., group norms), and core level (i.e., individual defensive reactions) (Banet 1974, 187). We wanted to achieve learning on two levels—the content of what was actually discussed about the prevalence of sexual harassment in the organization, and the process—how to create dialogue, where mutual understanding and respect are achieved even if differences of opinion prevail. This incident turned out to be a significant milestone for the group. After this meeting, the discussion and sharing of experiences moved to a more personal level, and participants were able to intervene in their own process. They were able to identify when a statement "plopped" and stop the group from moving on, and they were able to identify when tangents occurred and redirect the focus back on track.

In another CSG, a significant turning point occurred as an outcome of a group exercise that involved teams working on a task where competition and collaboration were options for the groups to choose in playing the game. The facilitators set up two teams, one with all White participants, the other with all persons of color, all but one of whom were African American. The two teams approached the exercise very differently, with the Whites playing to win while simultaneously pursuing negotiation with the other group as a secondary strategy. The participants of color, on the other hand, pursued the negotiation strategy exclusively. The outcome of the exercise was that the White group won the game and then proceeded to distribute the winnings, in the spirit of charity, to both groups. The group's strategy and subsequent charity infuriated the African Americans and the one Asian American member of the second team. An emotional discussion ensued about how the game was not at all a game for the people of color, who indicated that the behavior of Whites in the group was no different from their real-life conduct in the organization.

Up to this point in the CSG, norms of honesty had been set but not tested. This discussion, where real feelings were shared and their White coworkers heard the anger of the people of color, was the first real experience of conflict and true dialogue that the group experienced. Subsequent sessions were marked by more honest expression of feelings, genuine responses, and closeness among group members.

Our experience as facilitators of CSGs in this organization was mixed. Some of the groups struggled with maintaining membership, and other groups never broke through intense defensiveness and achieved honest, open communication. Strong support and participation by key leaders in the organization, and consistent membership and regular participation by group members, characterized the most successful groups. They were also marked by a genuine willingness on the part of participants to have their thinking challenged on difficult issues. The participants in the most successful groups were overwhelmingly positive about the experience and felt that it was personally and professionally valuable, with many reporting positive impacts on their careers. An unexpected benefit to the male participants was better communication at home with spouses, daughters, and other significant women in their lives.

REFERENCES

Banet, A., Jr. 1974. "Therapeutic Intervention and the Perception of Process." In *The 1974 Annual Handbook for Group Facilitators,* ed. J. W. Pfeiffer and J. Jones. La Jolla, Calif.: University Associates Publishers.

Jackson, B., and R. Hardiman. 1994. "Multicultural Organization Development." In *The Promise of Diversity: Over Forty Voices Discuss Strategies for Eliminating Discrimination in Organizations,* ed. E. Y. Cross, J. Katz, F. A. Miller, and E. W. Seashore. New York: NTL Institute/Irwin Professional Publishing.

Walker, B. 1986. "Leading Core Groups." Typescript.

Weber, R. 1982. "The Group: A Cycle from Birth to Death." In *Reading Book for Human Relations Training,* ed. L. Porter and B. Mohr. 7th ed. Washington, D.C.: NTL Institute.

Chapter 13

Dialogue in Corporations

Gretchen Ann Groth

This chapter describes two main programs of dialogue in corporate settings, the Dialogue Group, cofounded by Linda Ellinor and Glenna Gerard (1998), and Fundamentals of Dialogue, with Sue Miller Hurst, plus one dialogue skill training by Deborah Flick (1998a).

Several dimensions influence dialogue in corporate settings as contrasted to educational or community groups. First, the questions asked to justify the initiation and use of dialogue often include these: "What can it do for the bottom line and our ability to generate or improve our profit?" and "How will it (and how quickly will it) make a difference in the ability of our work groups, employees, and/or management to work more effectively with each other?" Essentially, the values being promulgated are the profit goal, efficiency, and speed directed toward the end of generating a better product or service. Other values such as personal satisfaction, positive team interaction, a work environment that stimulates intra- or interpersonal growth, or a deeper understanding of differences may be espoused in some corporations, but these are often secondary to the primary values. As a result, the principles of dialogue may be seen as incompatible or irrelevant to the corporation's primary values, while dialogue groups are evaluated in terms of moving the corporation toward or, at a minimum, not "getting in the way" of these values.

The corporate context can skew or contradict some of the basic principles of dialogue. Most corporations present, and affirm as appropriate, a clear power structure. Although many organizations have been integrating self-empowered teams, matrix organizational structures, and other more "democratic" or inclusive forms of decision making, the precedent and backdrop remains a hierarchical model of power distribution. Privileges conditioned into the fabric of organizational interactions mean that those higher up the ladder of power can, legitimately, impose change on those below, are listened to and complied with more, define "reality" more accurately, and decide the group's directions, activities, and assignments, with or without input from others below.

These dominant corporate values and the power structure create a particular slant on intergroup differences. Differences tend to become "problematic" organizationally only when they clearly reduce the likelihood of maximizing the values (profit, efficiency) or threaten the power structure's ability to move in the stated directions. Up to this point, they may be dismissed as personality conflicts or differences to be ignored or tolerated rather than resolved. Turf struggles and functional unit differences, for example, marketing versus development, are typical intergroup conflicts that can escalate into problematic proportions. Resolution often begins with the next higher level attempting to define or coerce the difference out of existence. Subsequently, other methods to reduce the negative effects of the intergroup difference may be employed. Dialogue, in this context, implicitly is expected to meet an "outcome" that may not be wholly compatible with the traditional principles of dialogue.

Ellinor and Gerard: The Dialogue Group

In early 1990s, Linda Ellinor, coach and trainer to leaders at the Center for Creative Leadership, and Glenna Gerard, a corporate manager intrigued by methods to improve communication, collaborated to explore deeper possibilities of communication. Initially using the writings of David Bohm and Peter Senge and, later, the Quaker tradition, Carl Jung, the philosophies of Heidegger and Buber, and Native American traditions, they created the Dialogue Group. After many workshops with different organizations, they wrote *Dialogue: Rediscover the Transforming Power of Conversation* (Ellinor and Gerard 1998).

The "Living Technology" of Dialogue

For Ellinor and Gerard, the living technology of dialogue includes what are commonly referred to as the disciplines or fundamentals of dialogue, as well as some aspects they consider unique to their approach.

> *Suspension of judgment.* "There are often two types of judgments or thought forms we experience during a dialogue. The first is the yes/no, good/bad, or right/wrong variety. The second form is more complex judgments or assumptions about what is being said in the group. Of these two, the former, the good/bad variety, is death to dialogue" (Ellinor and Gerard 1998, 75).

Identification and suspension of assumptions. In dialogue, one learns not only to identify and suspend one's personal assumptions (those things we think we know), but also to (collectively) identify the shared assumptions of the group or organization. "By inquiring into our assumptions and listening for the shared meanings that emerge, we gain a vantage point from which we can observe ourselves in relationship to one another and the larger systems we are a part of" (Ellinor and Gerard 1998, 96).

Listening. Listening for Ellinor and Gerard is comprised of three levels: listening to another, listening to the self, and listening for collective shared meaning. "Listening for collective shared meaning assumes that what we each feel, see, hear, and perceive is one window on a common reality. If we listen for the interrelationships among the perceptions, the whole will become visible" (Ellinor and Gerard 1998, 106).

Inquiry and reflection. Inquiry and reflection require slowing down the process so that silence becomes the ground. "The capacity for collective inquiry and reflection is what leads to quantum leaps and breakthroughs in a group's thinking" (Ellinor and Gerard 1998, 122).

Nonverbal communication and dialogue. Ellinor identifies nonverbal communication as a particular contribution to dialogue: "Developing a capacity to listen through nonverbal channels helps groups get unstuck, integrate what they are learning, and listen for the collective meaning as it unfolds in the group" (Ellinor 1998). Four nonverbal mediums are highlighted: collective art, meditation and prayer, movement, and individually or group-created mandalas.

Guides for creating and sustaining dialogues. While hesitant to provide "rules" as they tend to be reframed as the "right" way to do things in dialogue, Ellinor and Gerard do discuss guides—intended to reflect the supports, attitudes, intentions, and behaviors that many diverse groups have found helpful.
- Focus on shared meaning and learning (rather than on what is right or best).
- Release the need for specific outcomes. The crucial word is "specific," which narrows the focus of conversation toward one outcome.

- Listen without resistance.
- Respect differences.
- Suspend role and status.
- Share responsibility and leadership.
- Speak to the group.
- Speak when the spirit moves you. If uncertain, simply sit and continue to listen.
- Go live. This is a simple reminder to speak from personal experience and stick with what one is thinking/feeling/wondering about in the present moment.
- Balance, inquiry, and advocacy. This guide reminds one to notice the intentions behind one's own inquiry and advocacy (offering own perspective as one of many), and to balance the two. (Ellinor and Gerard 1998, 142–53).

Form of Dialogue Workshops

Ellinor and Gerard recruit participants via two methods: by public sign-up workshops that generate attendees through advertising and large mailings of their workshop schedule and by internal organization workshops.

When dialogue is offered or requested by a specific corporation, the internal structure of the workshop remains essentially the same as their public sign-up workshops, but the before-and-after activities are different. One common model for corporate work is a "sign-up" within the organization, where individuals from different parts of the organization enroll in the dialogue course. Often the majority of participants are individuals who expect to use the skills with or teach them to other members of that organization (organizational development specialists, human relations staff). Sign-up workshops are similar to their four-day public workshops, except that subsets of the attendees often know each other, even though they probably will not use dialogue with each other as a group. With the sign-up model, intergroup differences arise from the particulars of the individuals attending, rather than from organizationally defined groupings, history, or differences.

The other model, for an intact group of fifteen to twenty people within an organization, is conducted as an overnight, off-site workshop ranging from three to four and a half days. The facilitators interview many of the participants prior to the workshop and prefer to schedule a half-day follow-up session within a month of the workshop. While the preinterviews generally elicit the active issues, conflicts, norms, and expectations within the group, the most critical preinterviews are with the leader. Leader interviews assess readiness for the changes dialogue engenders, and the facilitators coach the leader on how to become a "member" of the group rather than exerting one's traditional status. Inherent and implicit organization intergroup differences are likely to surface in this model.

Role of Facilitator

Ellinor and Gerard intentionally identify the role of facilitator in their model as profoundly transforming the power dynamics of the group. During the one- to one-and-a-half-hour dialogue sessions within the workshop, the facilitators participate as members of the group, rather than as facilitators who coach the group or intervene when the group seems to be struggling. Before any dialogue sessions, they explicitly discuss the intent to shift from traditional reliance on a facilitator to one where facilitators are participants and the entire group assumes responsibility for the ongoing direction and facilitation of the dialogue. Ellinor states (1998), "Our model of dialogue may not be as quick to learn as others, but we feel this is a small price to pay for the sense of shared leadership that takes place as the group takes active responsibility for the facilitation within dialogue."

Gerard (1998) indicates that the way Ellinor and Gerard conduct reflection, usually about twenty minutes following the dialogue sessions, uniquely adds to the learning of dialogic principles. During the reflection period, Ellinor, Gerard, or other participants may discuss the "process" of the dialogue session: raising questions or wondering about what happened, and what it might mean. Common concerns about whether this or that behavior is consistent with the skills or principles of dialogue may be discussed during the reflection period, whereas they might not surface in the dialogue sessions themselves. Reflection periods facilitate independence between the skill and process learning about dialogue and the actual dialogue sessions where the focus emphasizes everyone as equally responsible for leadership. This direct and intentional separation reinforces the collective responsibility of the group for its own facilitation and leadership.

Limitations to Dialogue

For Ellinor and Gerard, organizational readiness with intact groups is a major constraint: are the leaders and group prepared for the changes dialogue can initiate? Gerard states that dialogue is an absolute challenge to the status quo no matter what that status quo is. While certain skills such as listening or inquiry are not perceived as particularly threatening to the organization, the idea of "thinking collectively" will challenge any current organizational culture. To make visible "our" collective assumptions as a group about how we work together, our espoused values as compared to what we do, and how we make decisions raises basic questions about who we are and who we want to be. Since these discussions happen within the context of dialogue where everyone has responsibility for leadership and thus an equal voice, the conversations themselves might be seen as calling for a redistribution of power. If the leader or manager of the group attempts to define or give "the answer" to these explorations, it ceases to be dialogue.

It is extremely important to address these challenges up front with the leaders and the group, before the dialogue workshop even begins. This is why we initiate considerable coaching and exploration with the current group leader(s) to insure their willingness, readiness and commitment to the redistribution of power that inherently occurs with a commitment to ongoing dialogue. If the leadership is not ready for and open to this transition of power, we do not continue the contract and suggest they seek a different form of training, team building or skill development for their group. (1998)

Hurst Dialogue

Sue Miller Hurst served as one of the core facilitators with the Dialog Project, the Kellogg-funded research project of the MIT Center for Organizational Learning with Bill Isaacs. Hurst left the Dialog Project to expand and develop dialogue in her own way. For over eight years, she has been conducting a three-day workshop entitled Essential Conversation: Fundamentals of Dialogue for corporations and educational institutions.

Elements of Hurst Dialogue

Hurst's (1998) model aims toward deep listening, communication, and thinking: "Dialogue, as I envision it, works to evolve the mind so that I (and others) can see, deeply and clearly, how one's mind and the 'patterns of one's mind' limit one's thinking. Working with consciousness, not just behaviors or outcomes, opens up a process to let us recreate our world and transform culture. Most of us haven't seen the culture we want to create. Dialogue groups provide a glimpse of what a different culture could really look like."

Four elements characterize Hurst's model of dialogue (1998).

Personal mastery. All the ways a person needs to be or become master-ful can happen in dialogue: to listen deeply to each other, to be inti-mate, to be vulnerable, to recognize how "I am a product of the story I tell" (I am the scripter), to be open to change my own possibilities, and to confront myself. Personal mastery teaches people an increased capacity to love and a higher quality of caring.

Culture. Dialogue not only speaks to but allows members to experience a true learning environment, a safe place where I and others can truly be ourselves and deeply respect each other. This type of learning environment represents a cultural change from our ordinary reality. Hurst identifies three levels of cultural change: the individual, the group, and the field in which both the individual and the group oper-ate. This field—a deep learning field created like a web or nuance—is experienced as distinct from the individual or the group, yet it includes the unique awareness that any one individual at any moment can have absolute responsibility for that field. The individual is both recipient and giver of the field.

Thinking skills. Often called the fundamental discipline of dialogue (see "Disciplines of Dialogue" section), this element includes surfacing and identifying one's assumptions, questioning one's answers or con-clusions, looking anew at the nuances of how the system actually works, and regularly asking these types of questions, "What is it about this pattern of mine?" or "I wonder why I. . . ?"

Collective thinking. Dialogue has the potential for a group to *actually* think together, not just where each individual provides an own point of view and listens to other's views. The group actually creates together. The individual is not lost in this understanding of collective but is found.

Disciplines of Dialogue

Hurst presents five fundamentals or disciplines of dialogue.

Listen. Listen to ourselves and to others.
Suspend certainty. Begin to speak more provisionally and listen with more openness.

Hold the space for differences. So that any kind of difference can show up safely.

Slow down the inquiry. Leave space between our words so we can take in meaning.

Speak from awareness. Instead of positions, so we begin to be aware of the new thinking in us.

The three-day workshop gives the most attention and practice to the first three disciplines, as the last two can often arise from the first three.

Form of Dialogue Workshops

Hurst's three-day dialogues, while typically sponsored by a particular corporation, are usually open or "public" to other nonorganization individuals in the geographical area. Even when sponsored only for members of a specific corporation, the strong preference is for attendees to come from many different parts of the organization. She prefers a wide range of people to attend the workshop, indicating that this "increases the participation, freedom and thereby, perceived safety for all attendees" (Hurst 1998).

No more than 5–10 percent of Hurst's dialogues involve intact work groups. The history of, and accommodation to, working together often inhibits the ease and comfort for members who share feelings and experiences not previously shared in the group. As a result, more attention must be directed to "safety" issues. Also, prework with leaders may be necessary so that they can join the dialogue as a member, not as the group's "leader." She prefers an extra day for dialogue workshops with intact groups.

Similar to Ellinor and Gerard's public workshops, the intergroup differences that might present in Hurst dialogues arise from the particulars of an individual and are not prestructured into the criteria for participation. In fact, Hurst reduces the likelihood of such particular differences by seeking participants from different organizations or from multiple areas within any one organization. Thus, the strength of organizational membership groups such as sales, management, finance, or support staff is effectively eliminated. Other intergroup differences such as race, gender, sexual orientation, education, or geographical origins may "accidentally" appear by virtue of the mix in attendance. The extent to which these become salient within dialogue sessions arises from either the members' highlighting them themselves or from the facilitators' introducing the dimension or difference within the discussions.

Role of Facilitator

The facilitator, Sue Hurst, sees her role as creating a safe place where judgments are "kept out of the room" as much as possible. She uses "wonder questions" to help participants focus internally on their own processes and behavior rather than providing her perceptions of how the group is learning the principles of dialogue. Wonder questions might include "What are my learning edges?" "Did I interrupt or finish someone's thoughts before they did?" or "Where did I find my 'certainty' blocking my ability to listen to different points of view?" Another facilitation method Hurst employs is telling stories. By listening to the story, individuals can apply the point of the story to themselves, thereby personally adjusting their behavior or understanding of the dialogue disciplines.

Hurst does *not* encourage individuals to comment on the group process (collective assessments of the group dynamics, often introduced with "we seemed to . . ." or "we did . . .") or ask the group for feedback about their own behavior in the group. Although these types of interactions may be appropriate in other contexts, Hurst regards them as essentially asking for or giving "judgments" about the group or individuals, therefore counter to her emphasis on safety.

Whereas Ellinor and Gerard's facilitation intends to highlight the group experience, particularly shared facilitation or collective leadership, Hurst's facilitation aims to create a space of acceptance for each individual. With individual safety as the ground, individuals may then be able to experience the group more as a group. The difference is probably one of emphasis rather than contradiction.

Limitations to Dialogue

When asked about the areas or circumstances in which dialogue may be inappropriate or might generate problems, Hurst responded that although certain conditions may make the dialogue more difficult or require modifications in the internal structure or format of the dialogue workshop itself, there is *nowhere* she would not go or not do dialogue. Some conditions that make dialogue more difficult include participants being required to attend, or a situation where two individuals (or factions) are highly contentious and publicly locked into set positions, such as would be the case with, for example, a "President Clinton and Saddam Hussein." While individuals who behave resistantly, are haughty, or "refuse" to listen generate difficult dynamics within dialogue sessions, they can, if necessary, be handled one on one to reduce their disruption of the learning process for the other participants.

Flick's Understanding Process

Deborah Flick (1998a) defines the "understanding process" as fundamentally an interaction method for "entering into dialogue about any issue, especially difficult or controversial ones. This alternative to 'conventional discussion' or debate transforms our conversations in real and meaningful ways and fosters effective, lasting change" (Flick 1998a, 1). In her book *From Debate to Dialogue: Using the Understanding Process to Transform Our Conversations,* she contrasts the premises, goals, attitudes, focus, behaviors, role, and outcome for these two modalities.

Although Flick considers debate as the outcome to the conventional discussion process and dialogue as the outcome to the understanding process, I will use *understanding process* in the following discussion rather than *dialogue* to distinguish this form from the other forms of dialogue discussed previously. Flick also recognizes that the understanding process is different from, though philosophically consistent with, traditional dialogue. In fact, Flick (1998b) states that "traditional dialogue often takes on too much too quickly. The understanding process as dialogue serves as an entry into the framework and intent of traditional dialogue but is generally more workable for people."

Elements of the Understanding Process

Conventional discussion is based on the premise that there is one right answer or perspective and the interaction process is one of winning, selling, or convincing others of one's position (usually considered the "right" one) while criticizing, evaluating, or attending to "what's wrong" with the views, positions, or frameworks of others. In contrast, the understanding process assumes that in any given situation, there are multiple valid answers and perspectives and the interaction process aims to understand others' point of view from their perspective (understanding does not mean agreement), using a curious and open attitude to explore what can be learned, what is of value, or what is new.

Each process includes the behaviors of listening, inquiring, and advocating, but they function quite differently. In conventional discussion, one listens to judge, to find the errors and flaws, to accept nothing at face value, to plan one's own rebuttal, and to hear advocacy as a challenge to be met. In the understanding process, one listens for the other's "story," without judgment, to reflect rather than react, to accept the face value of statements as true for the giver, and to hear advocacy as an opportunity to deepen understanding. In conventional discussion, one talks more than one listens, whereas the opposite is true for the understanding process.

In conventional discussion, inquiry is interrogating the other person, often by asking questions that support your perspective and challenge the other person's view. In the understanding process, inquiry explores taken-for-granted assumptions, asks questions to clarify and deepen one's understanding, and aims to understand what another's ideas mean to that person. Advocating within conventional discussion asserts and justifies one's position, defends one's assumptions as truth, and describes flaws in the other perspectives; while in the understanding process, advocating offers one's ideas as only one's own and explores alternative points of view. The outcome for conventional discussion is debate, while the outcome for the understanding process is dialogue.

While the understanding process can be considered as a new behavior or a "technique," Flick (1998b) emphasizes that "a shift in mind set is what is most important; for then, we can experience our world, and ourselves in the world, differently."

Form of Workshop

Flick's workshops on the understanding process range from an hour to a full day. Many workshops are offered within a valuing diversity context. A typical one-day workshop begins by contrasting the understanding process to the debate mode, often using diversity content for the examples. Internal barriers, such as preconceived ideas, and external barriers, such as the expectation that debate will resolve differences, are highlighted by revisiting typical diversity conversations that became blocked. The afternoon develops some key competencies, such as how to identify one's unexamined judgments, how to elicit multiple perspectives, and ways to appropriately advocate one's point of view within the understanding process.

Limitations to the Understanding Process

In discussing the constraints to understanding, Flick (1998b) identifies internal and external factors or resistances. Internal resistances include "the habit of the debate culture, and for some, the attraction to the debate process; the position that 'it just won't work'; the fear that if we deeply understand someone, we will have to give up or lose something; and the sea of assumptions, judgments, and schemas constantly active which must be loosened or set aside in order to engage in the understanding process." External resistances include "the view that to survive in an organization, one must be proficient in the debate culture, therefore to use the understanding process at work effectively means 'I lose.'"

Interracial and Intergender Differences

Two questions about how these models address interracial and intergender differences can be asked: (1) does the model, or its facilitators, demonstrate any visible methods for "validating" attention to race and gender differences, or any other culturally weighted areas such as sexual orientation, class, education, disability?, and (2) how are race and gender addressed when they are not the organizing focus of the dialogue?

Since none of the models discussed so far have used race or gender as the overt definition or composition of dialogues, the first question can be reframed in terms of whether there has been any intentional inclusion of race and gender in the planning or conducting of dialogue, ranging from selection of facilitators to insuring that the participant mix is not highly imbalanced in race or gender. All models are currently facilitated by their authors (white females), although Ellinor and Gerard are currently training additional facilitators. Flick, when using the understanding process for diversity awareness workshops, often uses a cotrainer for a gender mix or, better, gender and race, gender and sexual orientation, or gender and disability. Participants self-select or are members of a predetermined organizational group; thus the opportunity to modify a racial or gender imbalance is minimal. No one discusses attention to race or gender composition in the selection process, instead working with whoever shows up. Except for the attention by Flick to selection of a different cotrainer when the focus is diversity awareness, none of these models attends directly or structurally to race and gender. Thus, the degree to which race and gender differences are validated within dialogue may be dependent on the depth of the facilitator's exploration and comfort with these issues.

The second question—how are race and gender addressed when they are not the organizing focus of the dialogue—can be examined explicitly (when someone brings it up directly) and implicitly (when the composition or assumptions within the group mirror the societal dynamics with respect to race and gender). Explicitly, each model handles spoken differences arising from race or gender as opportunities to practice the basic tenets of dialogue: suspend certainty or judgments, listen, use inquiry and reflection, and identify assumptions. To some extent, a race or gender difference may be seen as no different from any other "strongly held position," mind-model (Flick), or pattern of mind (Hurst).

Ellinor and Gerard and Flick address these areas directly. In the section "Creating Diversity as a Resource," Ellinor and Gerard (1998, 198) state, "Whenever people feel they are second-class citizens because of religion, race, sexual orientation, gender, cultural heritage, personal style or lifestyle, collaboration and partnership are the furthest things from anyone's mind. Dialogue provides a way for the group to talk about these difficult and important realities, to build the awareness needed for people to begin to take actions that promote respect for the differences present." Flick devotes a chapter to "Bridging the Diversity Divide," highlighting how the conventional discussion process (debate culture) handles, and hardens, diversity-based discussions, while the understanding process (dialogue) can open up new understandings: "Individual and collective consensus mind-models about who we are as blacks, whites, women, men, old, and young, and how we see each other can surface and be explored. Such dialogue creates the conditions for authentic healing" (Flick 1998a, 90).

Addressing the implicit race and gender dynamics or differences may be the weakest part of dialogue. To illustrate, I will use the example of a disproportionate number of women or people of color in a predominantly white or male group, a common occurrence within many corporate environments. This composition, "token" representation of women or people of color, often manifests a variety of race and gender dynamics: use of air time by, and interests of, the majority tend to dominate the group; the conditioning, privileges, and assumptions associated with being white or male tend to be largely unexamined; and the contributions of the tokens are often ignored or discounted. However, when race or gender does surface, the experiences of the "token" are often overly examined in detail, generalized as representing the entire group (race or female), or expected to be shared in greater depth so as to educate the majority group members—dynamics that often continue even when race or gender is no longer the topic. Whether subtle or blatant, these dynamics are often experienced as "normal," as not related to race or gender, and, thereby, are unnoticed except by those who have intentionally and actively explored the dynamics of racism and sexism in themselves and society. The question becomes:

to what extent does dialogue militate against the perpetuation of these race and gender dynamics, regardless of the clarity, astuteness, or background of the facilitator?

While dialogue intends to penetrate differences that are spoken, it is unclear whether unspoken dynamics that sit as the backdrop or structure underlying other conversations would be challenged by dialogue. Exploring the unexamined assumptions of how the group interacts with each other could identify some of the racial or gender dynamics mentioned above. The question, then, becomes whether the discussion markedly changes *if* these dynamics are labeled as race or gender inspired, as opposed to less "loaded" terminology such as work styles, mind-models, or patterns of thinking. The dynamic may be identified, and even modified, via dialogue, but if it is never understood within the context of race or gender, the learning or understanding is unlikely to transfer to other situations that parallel the underlying race or gender dynamics.

Level of Impact or Locus of Intended Change

Hurst's model—with its strong intention to help individuals understand their minds (patterns of thinking and perceiving, deriving meaning) and move toward personal mastery, and to provide a safe space of acceptance—essentially directs its locus of change to the individual and, secondarily, to the group. Her statement that "dialogue groups can give a glimpse of what an alternative, more affirming culture could look like" suggests that dialogue can facilitate a more concrete vision for change, but leaves open whether dialogue groups are, in fact, the agent of that cultural change or only the instrument for creating particulars of the vision.

Since over 90 percent of Hurst's dialogue participants are *non*intact groups and, by her preference, not from the same organization, the possibility for organizational change—whether culture, power, policies, or distribution of resources—results either from individual changes (transformations) that create a ripple effect of increasingly greater numbers being attracted to and wishing to learn dialogue, or from a significantly critical mass of organizational members having experienced dialogue, being personally transformed by it, and, almost by osmosis, integrating some dialogic principles within their own work groups. In either case, the potential organizational change, as distinct from the personal transformation, is effectively nonintentional and therefore subject to the usual status quo pressures, inertia, and resistances of organizational life.

In summary, with the Hurst model, dialogue may set a ground, aspiration, or backdrop for what might be possible or desirable in organizational life, but it does not intentionally adopt organizational change, whether represented by redistribution of power (democracy, self-directed teams, etc.), or modification of policies and procedures as its intended outcome. Individual change or personal transformation is the intended outcome, and only incidentally may other changes be activated as a result of that person's impact within his or her own sphere of influence.

Ellinor and Gerard, on the other hand, address directly the potential impact that dialogue can have on the power distribution within an intact group, as well as the damage a leader's behavior can do to a working group's experience and success with dialogue. Insofar as self-facilitation, a hallmark of their dialogue, alters the more common leader-group distribution of power, dialogue has the potential (and requirement) to transform the role and meaning of leader in the group in order for dialogue to be integrated as an ongoing part of organizational life. This organizational change, in a sense, is a by-product of how Ellinor and Gerard define and teach dialogue, rather than the purpose of dialogue itself.

Since they often work with intact groups and entire organizations, they conduct preinterviews to assess the readiness of both the group and the leader to create and maintain a self-facilitated and self-led (not "leader"-led) group. If the commitment is not evident, they will terminate the contract before conducting any dialogue workshops. To this extent, their model, while predominantly regarding the individual as the locus of change, includes direct attention to an aspect of organizational change, specifically the shift in power dynamics inherent for a successful, ongoing implementation of dialogue in a work group.

Some of Ellinor and Gerard's work with small organizations essentially subscribes to what I call the "critical mass" approach to change: everyone attends a dialogue workshop, and by virtue of the high number of people familiar with dialogic principles, organizational change, whether in cultural norms or decision-making methods, is presumed to occur. One difficulty with the critical mass approach is that familiarity with, or even personal implementation of, the principles of dialogue does not necessarily mean organizational implementation of these principles. Many times what occurs is a new, shared language with which to describe the same old events and perceptions.

Essentially, the primary focus and development of dialogue for Ellinor and Gerard is on individual and interpersonal behaviors within the context of a group, not on organization change strategies. The purpose for most groups in learning dialogue is to communicate with, respect, or listen to each other better, not to redistribute power, even though the redistribution of power may be an essential condition for an ongoing group regularly using dialogue. As Gerard states, dialogue is not about "fixing the organization," but about "creating a space where all of a person can show up and be present. In the long run this creates a healthier organization" (Gerard 1998).

Flick's understanding process—presented in the context of contrasting the conventional discussion method, debate, with the understanding process, dialogue—develops "micro" activities to highlight or help people learn specific competencies associated with the understanding process and with dialogue. The locus of change is the individual and the individual's particular understanding and skills related to listening, suspending judgment, or inquiry.

Conclusion

The three models of dialogue described in this chapter offer similar approaches to addressing differences within corporate settings. None of them overtly uses dialogue as the method for working with strong, predefined intergroup differences, whether they be polarization around a particular issue or differences arising from dimensions such as race, gender, or sexual orientation. In fact, in many cases participants arrive with little knowledge of each other and without content set by an agenda. If, however, these same differences are represented by an individual (a woman, an Asian, a transgendered person) rather than a group, they are explored as they arise within a dialogue session. But a dialogue populated about equally by two groups, that is, women and men, whose gender is the intended content for the dialogue, has not been the focus of Ellinor and Gerard's, Hurst's, or Flick's models.

REFERENCES

Ellinor, Linda. 1998. Interview by author. November 13.

Ellinor, Linda, and Glenna Gerard. 1998. *Dialogue: Rediscover the Transforming Power of Conversation.* New York: John Wiley and Sons.

Flick, Deborah L. 1998a. *From Debate to Dialogue: Using the Understanding Process to Transform Our Conversations.* Boulder, Colo.: Orchid.

———. 1998b. Interview by author. October 2.

Gerard, Glenna. 1998. Interview by author. November 9.

Hurst, Sue Miller. 1998. Interview by author. November 21.

Chapter 14

Dialogue throughout an Organization

Maria C. Ramos and Cassandra Mitchell

This case study will describe the intergroup dialogue initiative of Infinity Credit (not the real name). Infinity Credit was a very profitable, autonomous subsidiary of a large financial company that will be referred to as Corporate Bank. Infinity Credit had about five thousand employees in three office centers in the United States: a center in southern New England, one in the Mid-Atlantic, and the headquarters in the Midwest. The centers in New England and in the Mid-Atlantic were both in urban and racially mixed East Coast communities; however, the Midwest center was in a primarily white suburban community.

The Infinity Credit intergroup dialogue initiative was the primary process used in its organizational cultural change effort. The effort, which began in 1993, was launched at Corporate Bank. Corporate Bank had developed an interest in valuing diversity in the workforce. This interest evolved from its affirmative action efforts and from external studies of future trends that indicated an increasingly diverse workforce (these studies reached conclusions like those in Johnston and Packer 1987). Corporate Bank's affirmative action data showed that there were functions and levels throughout the organization where some demographic groups, particularly people of color and women, were underrepresented. This was especially true at the higher officer levels. The chairman was committed to turn this around for the present and future success of the enterprise. The company launched a large systems change strategy to embed in the organization's culture a core value for workforce diversity and to create a supportive work environment. The infrastructure for this would be Diversity Oversight Councils, which were established across Corporate Bank and all its subsidiaries, including Infinity Credit. The councils of highly ranked officers began their efforts to accept, value, and promote diversity by

Providing leadership in its human resource practices
Offering equal access to opportunities to all employees
Taking affirmative action when necessary to support protected classes
Providing developmental experiences to a diverse workforce

The Dialogue Group

The Infinity Credit Diversity Oversight Council was a demographically diverse leadership group. Its members consisted of eighteen leaders, including the senior leadership team of the business, specifically, the chairman–chief executive officer and the executive vice presidents of Human Resources, Operations, Marketing, Finance, Information Systems, and Credit. Key management of each center such as the assistant vice presidents and vice presidents of organizational development, affirmative action, and employee relations were involved. Finally, the vice president of diversity from Corporate Bank frequently participated. The members represented a diversity of social identity groups such as race, gender, religion, age, and ethnicity. For example, the initial council had as members seven white men, four white women, one Hispanic man, two black men, and four black women of various ethnicities, ranging in age from the late twenties to the late fifties, who were Christian and Jewish. The individual members of the Diversity Oversight Council changed over the five and a half years of work, yet the basic demographic configuration of the team remained similarly diverse.

The Diversity Oversight Council members began their work in the typical style of corporate committee meetings, stating objectives, problem solving, forming teams for various tasks, and so on. Yet they found that as they explored ways to identify and remove barriers to valuing diversity in Infinity Credit, they had to confront the varying perspectives in the group. Though they had been careful to select outspoken members at similar organizational levels to mitigate some of the power imbalance, it became clear that this work required a safer, more structured approach than they had in place. When Infinity Credit's Diversity Oversight Council came to this awareness, senior management agreed to bring in external resources to assist. Their willingness to hire a consultant had two outcomes. First, it was seen as an indicator that senior leadership was serious about creating diversity as a core value in the organization's culture. Traditionally, Infinity Credit did not like to depend on external talent; it liked to "grow its own," "build it themselves," and "get a bunch of smart people together and figure it out." Second, they got the support they needed and a framework within which to accomplish their mission.

Ramos Associates was selected to consult to Infinity Credit on this effort. Ramos Associates' approach was to collaborate with clients in the creation and maintenance of multicultural organizations that reflect the contributions and interests of a diverse workforce, clarify organizational values about diversity and social justice, and set the mission for their diverse members and stakeholders. This collaboration involves working with leadership and internal teams to develop and implement change strategy. Ramos Associates works with leadership to create a vision and performance expectations, create performance standards and rewards, develop personal awareness, and enhance the organization's leadership role in the community. External consultant collaboration with an internal team of diverse change agents is critical to develop an integrated, planned approach to organizational change efforts. Every organization has its own culture, which at once must be challenged and integrated with the selection, creation, implementation, and evaluation of a multiple intervention plan that is unique to the specific client organization. "The internal change team 'truly owns' responsibility for being a catalyst and leader of change" (Jackson and Hardiman 1994, 19). Of primary importance in Ramos Associates' work with organizations is the development of the organization's internal capability to ignite, direct, nurture, and renew long-term multicultural change efforts. The development of the internal change team is key to accomplishing this end.

Philosophy and Assumptions

The philosophy and assumptions that Ramos Associates brought to the change effort at Infinity Credit focused the intergroup dialogue. The basic premise is that valuing diversity is a leadership philosophy that sets the direction for organizational behavior, policies, and programs. Valuing diversity involves recognizing the many physical and cultural differences among human beings, as well as understanding the ways in which these differences are ranked, creating patterns of privilege, power, and dominance. Recognizing the manner in which some social groups are seen as "better" or more valued than others, and some social groups are seen as "deficient" or less valued than others, allows for a better understanding of the structural inequality in our society and organizations. Work environments have been created and are maintained where people in some groupings have more access to opportunities, authority, and authentic cultural and personal expression, resulting in the perpetuation of a variety of "isms" (e.g., racism, sexism, ageism). These work environments are fostered by creating arbitrary power relationships based on the behavior of dominant groups who consciously or unconsciously discriminate against other groups. Dealing with social differences and patterns of dominance means acknowledging that valuing diversity requires the eradication of all forms of social discrimination and domination.

Ramos Associates introduced the intergroup dialogue process in June 1994 when Infinity Credit engaged them to consult to its overall valuing diversity change effort. Ramos Associates provided the framework that Infinity Credit's Diversity Council needed to do their multicultural organizational change work. The intergroup dialogue initiative was the hub around which the team initiated all of its actions through April 1999. After some initial one-on-one interviews, Ramos Associates began the intergroup dialogue process with the members of the Diversity Oversight Council.

Through a series of half-day and full-day discussions, the consultants were instrumental in establishing and holding the group to the dialogue process. Intergroup dialogue became the core process in all of the developmental activities. The basic principle was that dialogue between the social identity groups of the Diversity Oversight Council would inform their actions leading to the desired change in the enterprise.

The members of the Diversity Oversight Council came to their work with varying levels of personal awareness, knowledge, and competence in the areas of social justice, valuing diversity, and organizational change. Some entered the work of valuing diversity reluctantly. They were engaged because of their positions of leadership and authority, yet they did not understand the purpose of a valuing diversity effort. Moreover, some did not personally believe in the need for the effort or the underlying principles of social justice and equal opportunity. Their inability to recognize the need for change and their reluctance to engage in change efforts had been tempered by a lifetime of privilege and ignorance of discrimination. On the other hand, some entered the work with a clear sense of the need for the valuing diversity change effort, its importance, and the benefits to be reaped from the change. These people usually had a personal passion that fueled their desire to initiate organizational change. Their passion had often been fired by a lifetime of fighting discrimination. Engaging this demographically diverse group of organizationally commissioned change agents in intergroup dialogue about the issues and their impact was a most profound method of deepening personal and organizational awareness. "When dialogue is done well, the results can be extraordinary: Long-standing stereotypes dissolved, mistrust overcome, mutual understanding achieved, visions shaped and grounded in shared purpose, people previously at odds with one another aligned on objectives and strategies, new common ground discovered, new perspective and insights gained, new levels of creativity stimulated and bonds of community strengthened" (Yankelovich 1999).

Dialogue at the Top of the Organization

From June 1994 through March 1995 the quarterly meetings of the Diversity Oversight Council included a time dedicated to intergroup dialogue. Members of the team represented their centers and their organizational units, but during the intergroup dialogue they represented their social identity groups first. It was clear to all the leaders involved that they were in a peer learning activity with the intent of prompting personal change as well as organizational change. As a microcosm of what they hoped the organization would look like at its multicultural best, they had to work at building bridges of understanding across their cultural differences.

In addition to the quarterly one-day sessions, the Diversity Oversight Council committed to participating in annual two-day sessions. These sessions focused dialogue on a specific topic area such as cross-gender relationships, sexual orientation, race relations, and so on. The requisite personal disclosure and interpersonal interaction resulted in intensely emotional dialogue. Team members expressed a whole spectrum of feelings relative to their own experiences and in reaction to others' experiences.

The Diversity Oversight Council learned to trust the process of intergroup dialogue. The council discovered that the process was strong enough to support the emotional well-being of each participant. The more the council members opened to each other, the easier it was to move toward a common goal. Tasks that initially seemed impossible became manageable for the group. These conflicting feelings of being overwhelmed yet empowered came with the realization that social justice is "bigger than me" yet "begins with me." This dynamic became an equalizer for the Diversity Oversight Council.

Council members were not beginning their work from a place of commonality. People of color on the council sensed the feeling of inequality and knew that it would only get better because of voicing their struggle. Many whites on the council believed that conditions were already equal; they were "confused, ignorant, and/or insensitive to minorities values, interests, and cultures, dominating in interpersonal as well as organizational relations, and guilty in interactions with minority group members" (Chesler 1981). The leadership of the chairman and the senior human resources manager, and the support of Ramos Associates were critical in sustaining the momentum necessary to continue this work. They facilitated the continuation of the dialogue between individuals and small groups in the intervals between the scheduled intergroup sessions to further the cohesion of the council and the learning of its members. This valuing diversity initiative was a long, often tedious, process that unfolded less visibly as organizational change and more visibly as personal change. The opportunity to dialogue gave everyone an equal voice, and this equality enhanced the quality of the council's work.

The council was now ready to begin moving the intergroup dialogue process throughout the organization. Team members were encouraged to engage in intergroup dialogue in their respective organizational units. Diversity subcouncils were formed in each center, mirroring the Oversight Council. The dialogues were conducted in a similar way each time, but there were variations in the topics, and the foci of the dialogues changed over time. The dialogues in the Diversity Oversight Council were facilitated by Maria C. Ramos, the consultant, and at times her associates. The dialogues of the subcouncils, which consisted of ten to twelve members at each of the three centers, were cofacilitated by Oversight Council team members located at the particular site. The Diversity Oversight Council intergroup dialogue sessions preceded the subcouncil intergroup dialogue sessions at the three centers. Therefore, the topics and methods that were demonstrated in the Diversity Oversight Council were mirrored in the subcouncils.

The Methodology

The methodology of the dialogues was consistent. The dialogues were typically two to three hours in length. A topic would be introduced to the team by the facilitator. Most often, the team members were asked to consider and share their thoughts, feelings, experiences, or attitudes regarding some aspect of the topic. This was either preceded or followed by a brief presentation of information on the topic by the facilitator or invited speakers. After the presentation applied the model, theory, or information to the personal experiences of team members, there was additional dialogue. Finally, the dialogue focused on the application of the learning to the organizational change effort.

The focus of the topics changed as the subcouncils became more cohesive, their members more knowledgeable, and changes began to occur in the organization. In the initial stages, the intergroup dialogue was about the basic assumptions and dimensions of valuing diversity and fundamentals of social justice. Topics included the "Meaning of Valuing Diversity," "Paradigms of Valuing Diversity," "Social Identity Memberships" and "Prejudice and Power." The next stage of dialogue focused on cultural differences and cross-cultural interactions. Topics included religion, anti-Semitism, white American culture, Asian American issues, African American issues, and men and women working together. Interspersed throughout these topics were dialogues about organizational diversity issues such as barriers to the upward mobility of people of color and white women, and diversity-related considerations in the selection of a new office site. An ongoing theme in the intergroup dialogue topic was race and gender differences in attitudes about the work environment. This led to an extensive organizational intervention that started with data gathering.

Gathering Data

Each year Infinity Credit surveyed employees. Indeed the survey indicated that for the most part job satisfaction levels among employees were slightly better than the industry average. However, the Diversity Oversight Council decided to examine the employee survey data more closely and discovered some significant differences between how people of different races and genders responded to items concerning employee satisfaction. All three centers discovered that men were more satisfied than women, and that whites were more satisfied than people of color. The critical employee feedback was surprising to some of the council's members, specifically the leaders from the urban mixed-race office sites. They had often taken the position that they had "open and inclusive work environments" merely by virtue of the fact that the majority of the urban centers' workforce was from "underrepresented" social groups, for example, people of color. Clearly, they had misjudged their employees' attitudes. To get beneath the data, focus groups were conducted to identify issues, concerns, perceptions, and expectations relating to the organization's efforts to value and manage diversity. These focus groups ultimately gave way to Leadership Listening Sessions that allowed employees to present their views to managers, who could hear and respond to their issues and concerns.

The results showed that Infinity Credit needed to focus more energy on creating an environment that was inclusive and individually supportive of all its members. Without exception, *all groups* felt that *other* groups received special treatment. The focus groups identified these additional problems.

Managers over- or undercompensated because of their own discomfort in managing a diverse workforce.

The lack of understanding of others' background, culture, value, and style differences resulted in communication problems.

There was a reluctance to bring issues out into the open for fear of retribution, offending others, having problems "blamed" on the person who revealed them, or being judged "oversensitive." In short, it was easier and safer to not risk a misunderstanding.

Career success was seen as being based on skills, experience, education, performance, and "politics." There were, however, differences of opinion along gender and racial lines as to the importance of each of these elements to career success. Each group identified numerous barriers to the success of "people like them" in the organization.

Most participants also acknowledged some degree of skepticism about management's willingness to follow through with positive action. The organization had a history that included lists of "quick hits" and long-term solutions to managing diversity. These activities and events stopped and started on assigned dates. It was already determined that this effort would require more pervasive and significant interventions. The Diversity Oversight Council, with support from the consultant, planned a five-year strategy of interventions designed to ensure lasting change. One of the interventions was to spread the intergroup dialogue beyond the Diversity Oversight Council and the three sites of subcouncils into the general employee population.

Preparing the Organization for Dialogue

The plan was to provide diversity knowledge, awareness, and skill/competency development in three stages. The first stage of diversity knowledge building had as the primary objective the preparation of the general employee population for intergroup dialogue. During this stage, one- to two-hour sessions of thirty to fifty employees each in groups mixed by gender, race, and level and departmental affiliation were conducted in all centers. Approximately thirty-five hundred employees participated in these introductory sessions. The objectives were to

> Have the chairman clarify goals and the business need for a valuing diversity effort, introduce the charter of the councils, and encourage employee participation

> Overview diversity as it related to the organization and the individual: what it is and what it is not

> Share the benefits of diversity

> Offer comparisons of diversity to affirmative action

> Provide an awareness-building activity

While these initial sessions did not meet all of the criteria for intergroup dialogue, they were a critical first step to announce the organization's intentions and "prime the pump" for future employee dialogue. Most importantly, the verbal and written feedback from these sessions was used to create further intergroup dialogue sessions.

From the participant surveys taken during these introductory information sessions, the Oversight Council was able to ascertain the major issues related to diversity, what employees wanted to know more about related to diversity, which organizational policies and practices would have the most positive effect on their quality of life, and which organizational policies and practices employees wanted to see changed.

Additionally, the development of the internal capability of Infinity Credit was extended through the training of a cadre of trainers to conduct these sessions. Eighteen facilitators paired across gender and race conducted the initial sessions. They were strong performers and influence leaders from each center who had previously been involved in affirmative action or diversity efforts. They were trained as trainers by Ramos Associates following an intense multicultural workshop.

Dialogue throughout the Organization

The second stage of diversity awareness was the actual intergroup dialogue process. Intergroup dialogue sessions of one-half day in length, facilitated by cross-gender/race pairs, were conducted for groups of eighteen to twenty employees mixed by race, gender, and level. Over 250 sessions were conducted across three centers during a twenty-four-month period. Close to four thousand participants attended the diversity intergroup dialogue sessions. To accommodate these sessions, thirty facilitators were initially trained and then thirty-five more were trained to meet the demand. In addition, about forty area coordinators were utilized from the various departments to schedule participants. Arranging time off away from regular job duties, scheduling dialogue rooms, and coordinating facilitators for this company-wide intergroup dialogue effort required serious coordination.

The dialogue sessions focused on understanding social identity and organizational discrimination. Participants shared with each other their experiences as members of various social identity groups: race, ethnicity, gender, socioeconomic class, religion, age, and physical ability. They also chose other areas that were critical to the shaping of their experiences such as sexual orientation and family status. This led to dialogue about the company's implicit and explicit practices and norms. The groups discussed how these practices and norms affected various social identity groups by sharing their personal experiences in Infinity Credit and other companies. Some of the insights gained from these intergroup dialogues were the following.

> Members of socially dominant groups (whites, males, middle and upper class, physically able-bodied, Christians, Northern European descent, heterosexual, English speaking, etc.) never really thought about their social identities and often had difficulty seeing them as significant.

> Members of socially subordinate groups (people of color, women, lower class, physically challenged, non-Christians, gays, English as a second language, etc.) often found the same social identity membership(s) both a source of pride and a discomfort in their experiences.

> Engaging in intergroup dialogue about the effects of social identity group memberships on organizational experiences was difficult, relieving, and helpful.

It was difficult because members of underrepresented groups felt vulnerable and sometimes angry, while members of dominant groups felt challenged and sometimes ashamed. The dialogues were a relief to many because the issues were lifted from underneath the table and put on the table to be dealt with by all. The dialogues were helpful in clarifying the direction of personal, interpersonal, and organizational action to make the work environment supportive of its diverse employee population.

Conclusion

The intergroup dialogues about diversity were structured relationship accelerators and led to changes in the practices at Infinity Credit. The process was open, confidential, and safe, and the content was highly personal, value oriented, and often controversial. This combination supported conversations at a much deeper level than is common in most lives and certainly in the workplace. The fact that intimate dialogue occurred in one's work setting, which is typically void of personal truths and emotional revelations, made it an even more valued process. Participants reported sharing their multicultural awareness with their family, friends, and colleagues. The commitment to continue the dialogue process made it possible to cascade multicultural learning throughout the organization by creating a variety of dialogue opportunities. Over time, the forums of intimate discussions begin to close cultural gaps. Clearly, those groups that were involved in ongoing learning and in-depth discussions for extended periods of time were able to build bridges and remove barriers more effectively than those groups that met one time or on a limited basis. In fact, one critical benefit of utilizing the intergroup dialogue process in a work environment is the depth of the relationships established. These relationships formed through personal, value-oriented, and principle-centered dialogue have proven to be excellent cornerstones in positive, productive working relationships. Individuals more readily trust "dialogue" partners with whom they have struggled for understanding.

The intergroup dialogues were often personally revealing, conflicting, and sometimes emotionally difficult. Therefore, high levels of trust were built among participants. It is common knowledge that trust is a critical component in strong, healthy relationships. This trust allows individuals to accept each other's shortcomings, more readily understand behavioral motivation, more easily forgive slights and unintended hurts, and have confidence in the congruence of another's words and deeds. Trust allows each of us to be more fully who we are, knowing we will not be judged too harshly and that we will be accepted despite our personal shortcomings. This trust then creates an environment where each individual feels "safe" in being her or his authentic self. In a work setting, this translates into the degree that people feel safe to bring who they are to the job. In valuing diversity, it is understood that by accepting each person's strengths and weaknesses, we are more likely to have a more satisfied and productive employee.

The partnership between the external consultant and the internal change team was a critical element in the success of the valuing diversity change effort. Their mutual trust and respect helped build a set of interventions that at once expanded the company's capacity for diversity, changed the norms of interactions, and honored the company's culture, while allowing it to change. It also prepared them for the final stage of the effort. In April 1999, Infinity Credit was subsumed by another company when Corporate Bank merged with another bank. The reality of the corporation is that change is constant. Within the organizational turbulence that resulted from the merger, the Diversity Oversight Council held a series of intergroup dialogues to "prepare for the termination and/or death of the coalition" they had formed (Chesler 1981). Members of the diversity subcouncils and the trained facilitators participated in several final intergroup dialogues. The relationships that had developed among the members helped them support each other as they individually faced uncertain futures. In parting, they vowed to continue their personal awareness development and promote valuing diversity wherever they worked and lived.

REFERENCES

Chesler, M. 1981. "Creating and Maintaining Interracial Coalitions." In *Impacts of Racism on White Americans,* ed. B. Bowser and R. Hunt. Thousand Oaks, Calif.: Sage.

Jackson, B., and R. Hardiman. 1994. "Multicultural Organizational Development." In *The Promise of Diversity: Over Forty Voices Discuss Strategies for Eliminating Discrimination in Organizations,* ed. E. Y. Cross, J. Katz, F. A. Miller, and E. W. Seashore. New York: NTL Institute/Irwin Professional Publishing.

Johnston, W. B. and A. H. Packer. 1987. *Workforce 2000: Work and Workers for the Twenty-first Century.* Indianapolis: Hudson Institute.

Yankelovich, D. 1999. "The Magic of Dialogue." In *Spirituality and Health.* New York: Trinity Church, Wall Street.

Critical Issues in
Intergroup Dialogue

Introduction

The power of the intergroup dialogue lies in its ability to evoke in participants the expression of deeply felt but rarely publicly spoken attitudes and viewpoints, to enable them to confront long-standing group conflicts, and to move them to address the structural barriers to social inequalities in society. The intergroup dialogue experience can transform communities of people to change group behaviors and effect institutional change, and it can enable individuals to emerge from the intergroup dialogue with new perspectives, insights, attitudes, and behaviors.

The critical issues described in this section represent far more than technical adjustments to the dialogue process. Rather, embedded in each issue of practice are the truly substantial issues of diversity, identity, social change, social justice, and democratic practice. In the practice of organizing intergroup dialogue, participants confront the deeper questions of how to conceptualize diversity, how to move forward a new society in both theory and practice, how to approach individual and social group identities, how to effect social change and for what purposes, and what all this means for a democratic society.

To achieve such positive results from intergroup dialogue requires attention to the very difficult and complex aspects of the dialogue process. The chapters that follow describe the careful and skillful balance of issues necessary to achieve such results. In the absence of such attention, the power of the intergroup dialogue described above can be negative and destructive, or the dialogue can be merely ineffective. The trust people put into the intergroup dialogue process must be honored with skillful facilitation and constant monitoring.

Ruby Beale, Monita Thompson, and Mark Chesler address the core issue of training dialogue facilitators in their critical issues chapter. They present their conceptual framework for approaching training and provide the practical components of their process. Finally, they discuss and analyze an extensive list of challenges they face in conducting training.

"Are we individuals or are we members of social identity groups?" is a predictable question raised by participants in intergroup dialogues. Diana Kardia and Todd Sevig address this question and help identify how practitioners can change it from a source of negative conflict to a constructive paradox. The authors offer a series of strategies in response to specific cases they have encountered within dialogue groups.

Ruby Beale and David Schoem address the value of carefully balancing both content and process in intergroup dialogues. They provide the reader with a detailed analysis of the benefits of both content and process, as well as the problems associated with an overemphasis of either at the expense of the other. The authors offer a series of strategies to achieve a desired balance of content and process.

Celebration of diversity is an important and compelling component of intergroup dialogue, but absent a thorough analysis and engagement of the issues of structure and power associated with diversity, dialogue is a shell of what it is intended to be. Stephen Sumida and Patricia Gurin model their different yet highly collaborative styles as they offer probing insights and experiences of approaches into the complexities of balancing both celebration and power issues.

Mark Chesler argues that as powerful as the intergroup dialogue can be for participants, its full potential for deeper understanding, transformation, and change is tied to action that is linked to the dialogue. Using examples from dialogue experiences in different settings, he explores the benefits of taking action as well as the potential risks for dialogue participants who choose to take action emerging from the dialogue.

Ximena Zúñiga and Biren (Ratnesh) Nagda provide a very useful and comprehensive analysis of the stages of dialogue across settings and type of dialogue that is helpful for theoretical understanding and practical use. They explore how different models structure and design the dialogue process, and some of the underlying orientations that influence how dialogues are designed.

There are a great many people who find themselves in settings in which organizing a full-fledged intergroup dialogue is not practical, yet they wish to utilize some of the intergroup dialogue processes. David Schoem and Shari Saunders offer specific ideas and concrete examples of how to incorporate dialogue processes into a variety of settings while still maintaining the integrity of the core principles and conceptual foundations of intergroup dialogue.

Chapter 15

Training Peer Facilitators for Intergroup Dialogue Leadership

Ruby L. Beale, Monita C. Thompson, and Mark Chesler

In this chapter we present the conceptual framework underlying the training of peer facilitators of semester-long intergroup dialogues. We also discuss a variety of the strategies and exercises used in the training program and review some of the challenges or problems that have arisen.

The Program on Intergroup Relations, Conflict, and Community (IGRCC) at the University of Michigan is uniquely characterized by its design of intergroup dialogues that rely on undergraduate peer facilitators. This choice reflects our intent to establish a relatively democratic instructional process, and to help distinguish the dialogue program from other, more traditionally academic efforts to teach about or improve intergroup communication. At the same time, the use of young and previously untrained students as facilitators necessitates a substantial investment in training and supporting these key players.

Conceptual Background

In the preparation and support of peer facilitators for intergroup dialogues we are concerned with helping these young people establish competence in two areas: (1) intergroup issues, including knowledge and awareness of their own and others' social identities and histories and structures of privilege and oppression, which impact on intergroup relations; and (2) small-group leadership, including the concepts and skills involved in providing instructional leadership to a group of their peers. To guide this work we have used a framework for multicultural competency training first developed by Bailey Jackson (n.d.).[1] It emphasizes four broad elements required for effective work in these arenas: personal awareness, knowledge, passion, and skill.

Personal Awareness

Personal awareness is defined as the awareness of self as a member of a community, of a particular social group identity, and of self in a social system marked by different levels of privilege and oppression. The willingness to engage in honest and critical self-reflection is vital to developing the capacity for this awareness. In the context of dialogue leadership, awareness enables facilitators to be conscious of the impact of their social identity group memberships on themselves and on others in the group. It also enables them to be conscious of their own facilitative or leadership style, and how this may interact with others' preferences. Above all, dialogue facilitators must be able to verbalize and act on that awareness, so as to be models for other group members' developing self-knowledge.

It also is critical for facilitators to be aware of their own "hot buttons," "soft buttons," and "blindspots." That is to say, facilitators must know their own hot buttons so that when something is said or done that triggers them, that makes them angry, they can use this knowledge to find a positive way out of such situations, rather than reacting with reciprocal anger and hurt or overly aggressive or defensive behavior. Similarly, when something occurs that triggers a soft button and would normally lead to withdrawal or passive behavior, this, too, can be overcome. Without adequate self-reflection, potential facilitators may be unaware of their own blindspots and therefore be blind to their own hot or soft buttons. Without sufficient awareness, facilitators may be so caught up in their own personal concerns, and what is happening to them in a dialogue group, that they become blind or insensitive to what is happening to others. Under these circumstances they may overlook or fail to respond adequately to members of their own social identity group or to others not of their particular background and status.

One example of the ways these issues work is the rather typical blinders that white people have with regard to the "invisible knapsack of white privilege" that accrues to them as an institutional advantage, above and beyond whatever they may have done to earn certain rewards (McIntosh 1989). Our experience is that many white people (young and old, dialogue participants and facilitators) view their privileged place in society as either an inalienable or an earned right, and not something that is preordained by the vagaries of class and caste in the United States. As a result, explicit discussions and personal explorations of the ways in which this society systematically provides both overt and subtle (material and symbolic) advantages to white people, and especially to affluent white males, may lead to new and unmanageable feelings of guilt and discomfort for young white students. In addition, some students of color are relatively blind to the way they internalize the oppressive messages this society holds about them (e.g., about their academic prowess, attractiveness, social skills). Explorations of the driving personal influence of these messages, and not just their abstract and impersonal existence, may have debilitating effects on their self-esteem and lead to anger and withdrawal. Still another example of a typical blinder is anyone's lack of awareness of the way his or her cultural style or interpersonal mannerisms (of talking, sitting, arguing, loving) may impact on others' comfort and on group dynamics. Raising and reflecting on such issues publicly makes them visible, hence more understandable, and therefore more likely to become a fruitful part of intergroup dialogues and learning.

A final issue of importance in this realm of awareness is an understanding of the role options available for facilitators of peer-led dialogue groups, and in particular ways to handle the issues of authority and friendship that may have to be renegotiated in this setting. An intergroup dialogue facilitator, peer or otherwise, must have and exercise a measure of authority in order to effectively help a group function. Many undergraduate students are not comfortable accepting or exercising such authority, especially with their friends and companions. Self-awareness of how these issues play out, intrapersonally and interpersonally, is a critical issue.

Knowledge

Knowledge is defined as the information people need to be able to see and act beyond their own individual experience. It includes myriad data about one's own and others' social identity groups' histories, traditions, and values. Knowledge is the fundamental basis for understanding the facts and theories associated with multiculturalism, intergroup dialogue, and the engagement of pluralistic thinking. Some of this information can be gained from books and articles, films and news stories. Some of it can be gained from the many academic courses on different group cultures available in college and university settings. Some of it can be gained by listening carefully to other people, both those within one's own social identity group and those in other groups.

Another kind of knowledge important in this setting is information about the nature of prejudice, discrimination, and institutionalized privilege and oppression. It is critical for facilitators to understand the differences between these terms, as well as the nature of the debates and struggles about their meaning. The examination of empirical evidence and scientific theories about discrimination, oppression, and privilege, in the society at large and within institutions of higher education (or within whatever institutions the dialogue is being conducted), is a vital background to understanding individuals' experiences and outlooks.

Knowledge of group and intergroup dynamics is also vital. This includes standard information about the processes of group development, from formation and membership rituals, through the establishment of patterns of communication and interaction, including potential struggles for influence and power, on through to productive work—effective and honest dialogue (sometimes characterized as stages of "forming," "norming," "storming," and "performing'—Weber 1982). When these typical patterns of group development are overlaid on a framework of intergroup relations, we can also expect competition, scapegoating, alliance building, and superordinate goal formation to be involved.

Finally it is critical for dialogue facilitators to be at home with various models, conceptual frameworks, and terminology about dialogue processes in general, and about intergroup dialogues in particular. This includes understanding—both in theory and in practice—the differences between a dialogue, a discussion, a debate, and a fight. Such knowledge helps inform and guide facilitators' work and can help group members gain an understanding of how they may be moving from lower to higher levels of awareness and skill in intergroup dialogue.

Passion

Passion refers to the deep personal reasons and commitments facilitators (or any of us) may have for caring about and doing this sort of work, as well as their ability to recognize and communicate these core motivations with others. Being in touch with and articulate about the roots of involvement in intergroup dialogue is an essential expression of personal authenticity and intellectual/emotional integrity. The ability to communicate and share such concern, compassion, and empathy is a powerful force that is too often unexpressed, or too often expressed only nonverbally (in facial expressions, body language, and paralanguage), and therefore understood less than fully—or often misinterpreted. Good communication of these feelings can help raise the level of authenticity, seriousness, and commitment group members feel in the face of personally risky and vulnerable dialogue encounters.

Different people may have different roots for their passions about multicultural and intergroup dialogue work. For some it may rest in love, for others in barely disguised or controlled anger, and for still others in sadness and pain. Most facilitators and most group members carry such feelings; being able to express them at appropriate times and in appropriate ways is the critical feature—they can shut down dialogue processes just as well as they can open them up. Some people have been taught that "strength and maturity" requires them to hide or mask such feelings when they are strong. Others have been taught to strongly emote such feelings as a valued demonstration of how serious and committed they are to an issue at hand. Both strategies have important impact on the progress of an intergroup dialogue, and both strategies are rooted in different cultural traditions (indeed, some would say that to understand and come to terms with these differences is one of the fundamental learnings possible in an intergroup dialogue). What is called for here is the ability to lead with both heart and head.

Skill

Skill includes the ability to facilitate opportunities for change in individuals and groups, managing critical incidents and developing the capacity for strategic analysis and action. This requires combining and applying the three other components—awareness, knowledge, and passion—in a timely and strategic fashion in order to enhance learning and growth opportunities for dialogue participants. Facilitators must be able to understand group dynamics, especially in an intergroup context, and create and manage group processes and agendas that increase multicultural learning. They also must be able to assess the impact of these agendas on individuals and on the group and make continual adjustments and interventions. Facilitators must learn to provide feedback in a direct and open manner, to solicit and receive feedback from group members, to take the risks to intervene in delicate or heated situations, to ask probing educational questions, and to address oppressive or inappropriate behavior in ways that allow others to hear about and alter their behavior.

Finally, since the University of Michigan's IGRCC program uses two facilitators in each intergroup dialogue group (one from each of the major social identity groups involved), facilitators must learn how to work effectively with a cofacilitator (Pfeiffer and Jones 1975). In the context of our training model, cofacilitators must be prepared and willing to provide and receive intimate information about their personal and social identities and history, including their awareness, knowledge, passion, and skill. It also requires cofacilitators to share power and control in ways that make the best use of two different people's skills and abilities, that permit them to both identify with and transcend identification with their own social identity group and thus build an effective multicultural leadership team.

As a template for helping peer facilitators assess their own competencies in these areas, and a working guide for the agenda of training sessions, we use the instrument shown in figure 1. This instrument is administered early in the facilitator-training process—its conceptual elaboration and discussion of students' responses helps to set personal and collective learning agendas. It is readministered at the conclusion of the training process, both to provide a basis for evaluating the training and each person's growth, and to remind potential facilitators of issues to which they need to continue to attend.

Supplementing the Conceptual Framework

In addition to the conceptual framework delineated above, we also design (and redesign) the training program on the basis of a series of practical assignments and activities, and solicit continuing feedback from students about their needs and concerns. Generally, their feedback has raised issues parallel to the framework itself. For example, trainees are asked early in the training process if they have questions about the intergroup dialogue. Their initial questions usually take the form, "What was the hardest situation to facilitate?" "Were you aware ahead of time what would be most difficult for you?" (personal awareness). "What if I don't know much about the culture and history of the other group—or of my own group?" (knowledge). "What do I do if I am really offended and made angry by something someone says?" (passion). Other questions have to do with skill-based issues, such as, "How do you get back to a question or answer that has gotten lost?" "What can I do when the room is quiet?" or "How do you deal with heated or explosive conflict in the group?" Most of the questions students have about intergroup dialogues can be addressed by training designs that are guided by the areas of knowledge, personal awareness, skills, and passion.

Another assignment generally asks students to work with a colleague of a different social identity, to gather a group of people and begin a group discussion on intergroup issues. The goal is to provide students with a supervised opportunity to learn about the process of cofacilitation, practice the skills necessary to facilitate group discussion, and gain an under-

Name: _____

Using a scale from 1 (low skill level) to 5 (high skill level) or "dk" (don't know), please indicate: A) where you are now (your current skill level) and B) where you want/need to be (what skill level you feel is important/necessary to be an effective group leader). In addition, fill out as much as you can in column "C" where relevant.

Facilitator Competency	A. where I am now	B. where I want/need to be	C. how/where I can get help to get to the skill level I want/need
Knowledge			
1. Knowledge of issues pertinent to the group I am interested in facilitating.			
2. Knowledge of difference between prejudice, discrimination, and institutional isms.			
3. Knowledge of my own group(s) culture and history.			
4. Knowledge of other group(s) culture and history.			
5. Knowledge of group process issues.			
6. Knowledge of intergroup issues.			
7. I can recognize isms.			
8. Knowledge of theories and terminology which inform and guide multicultural work.			
Skills			
1. I can work with people from different groups.			
2. I can challenge others.			
3. I am organized.			

Fig. 1. Facilitator Personal Assessment Chart

Facilitator Competency	A. where I am now	B. where I want/need to be	C. how/where I can get help to get to the skill level I want/need
4. I can speak in public.			
5. I can discuss issues.			
6. I can facilitate a discussion.			
7. I can write clear reports.			
8. I can accept others' leadership.			
9. I can utilize others' support.			
10. I can give and receive feedback.			
11. I can plan agendas.			
12. I can be on time.			

Awareness

	A. where I am now	B. where I want/need to be	C. how/where I can get help to get to the skill level I want/need
1. I am clear about my identities.			
2. I am clear about my values.			
3. Internally I am emotionally balanced.			
4. I am secure about my status and privileges.			
5. I can recognize my blinders.			
6. I am aware of the impact of my personal style on others.			
7. I am aware of the impact of my social identity group memberships on myself.			
8. I am aware of the impact of my social identity group memberships on others.			
9. I know my hot buttons.			

Facilitator Competency	A. where I am now	B. where I want/need to be	C. how/where I can get help to get to the skill level I want/need
Passion			
1. I have energy for this work.			
2. I can lead with my heart.			
3. I have deep personal reasons for doing this work.			
4. I have a commitment on personal and professional levels.			
5. I can demonstrate compassion.			
6. I have the ability to share feelings with others.			

standing of some of the real issues that arise in an intergroup discussion. Once students have had the opportunity to practice facilitation (and cofacilitation), new concerns, needs, and issues generally surface. The following are areas of concern compiled from students' reflective comments on their experiences facilitating an initial intergroup discussion.

Probing Deeper and Challenging Participants

I wish I would have asked more questions . . . that way I could have probed a little deeper into what B. was thinking.

Yep. We should have jumped on this one. Alarms should have gone off here. But we didn't (sigh).

But I think we should have explored more of this issue. Not just her feelings but the whole group's.

Looking back, I now see how as a facilitator my job should have been to probe them into the issues they just skirted around.

Dialogue Being Dominated, Addressing the Dominator

I didn't know how to cut her off. She was talking so quickly that I didn't know exactly how to get a word in edgewise.

I was getting frustrated with A's long soliloquies, but I didn't know how to ask her to be quiet.

Right now I think the discussion was one-sided with all the men talking. The men weren't dominating a discussion with the women but more just dominating the dialogue. We should have broadened it up more.

The Thin Line between Being a Facilitator and a Peer

I think my story of my learning about sex education and its relevance to me may have made the group look at me more like a peer, rather than an outsider not participating and just asking questions.

I wanted them to feel comfortable about asking questions and know that we will address them too. As facilitators, we aren't above the group.

It seemed okay for J. (my cofacilitator) to be offering his opinions, but I think we needed to ask the rest of the participants what they thought as well.

Communicating with Cofacilitator

It was like every time L. (my cofacilitator) spoke it was to try to bring some kind of real issues to light, except in a really nice and sometimes roundabout way. I think she was trying not to hurt her friend's feelings or to be offensive.

I was often confused as to some of the things he (my cofacilitator) said, and I was afraid to ask what he meant.

It would have been good here to ask S.C. why does he think that. . . . However, W. (my cofacilitator) asked another question to get others involved. But it would have been okay for me to be like, "Could we hold on to that question and ask this question to S.C.?" The reason why I felt that I shouldn't do that is because it makes us look unorganized.

The combination of the conceptual framework, supplemented by constant feedback from the participants, allows the training to be molded by both practical and theoretical considerations. Since the feedback has been so similar to the original framework, it has served as a validation/checking process for the appropriateness of the model. In the next section, we discuss the methods we use to address trainees' concerns and to prepare them for leadership roles in intergroup dialogue.

Structure and Content of Facilitator Preparation and Support

In the past ten years we have used several designs to prepare, train, and support peer facilitators. The current structure consists of two consecutive semester-long courses for which students receive academic credit. The first course focuses on prefacilitation training and involves students in the semester prior to their actual facilitation work. It typically begins with a two-day overnight retreat, off campus. The time and the location, supplemented by various activities and exercises, promote intense and concentrated work and bonding among participants. Subsequently, we meet once a week, for three hours, although the exact scheduling can vary from semester to semester. At times, several longer (four- to six-hour) sessions may be planned, as well as a full-day end-of-the-semester conclusion. The second course, which we label a practicum, meets concurrently with the students' actual facilitation work. It generally meets weekly in a two-hour session, and is designed primarily to provide support, debriefing opportunities, and ongoing in-service training.

Two experienced leaders of intergroup communication and interaction (trainers or instructors) are the facilitators for these training courses. In each case they come from different social identity groups (most importantly by race, gender and sexual orientation) and different status groups within the university community (faculty member and student affairs staff member).

Sequencing the Training Process

Students are selected to participate in this training program through an interview process that focuses on their interest in intergroup education and an assessment of their knowledge of key intergroup issues, their self-awareness, and their leadership abilities. Additionally, students need to commit to a yearlong process and/or other work with the program. Approximately twenty students are selected for each training course, with a priority on recruiting a group that is diverse in terms of race/ethnicity, gender, sexual orientation, and religion (the most common types of intergroup dialogues the program offers).

The training process begins with an orientation session, which provides an overview of the training and an introduction of members of the training team and the student group. Students complete a "social identity profile" (developed by New Perspectives Inc.), answer a series of questions about the meaning of their social identity group memberships, and then share these responses with others. This is followed by larger group sharing of general issues in social identity group memberships.

The concepts of "comfort zones" and "learning edges" are introduced, and this sets the stage for conversations about safety and risks, and the need for ground rules to provide a safe learning environment for participants. The importance of giving and receiving feedback effectively and appropriately is discussed, usually making use of the "JoHari Window" (Luft 1970). A variety of experiential exercises are utilized to portray and promote discussion of the roles people play in situations and social structures involving oppression and injustice/justice. A modified version of the Starpower simulation often is used to help participants experience and discuss the dynamics of power (Shirts n.d.). Debriefing the Starpower simulation usually includes reflection on and examination of the dynamics of stratification and oppression, the transition to resistance and empowerment, and the development of strategies that can be effectively used to address change and achieve more equitable allocations of power and resources. A series of interpersonal and small-group conflict resolution simulations also are used. These activities promote and reinforce the need for active listening skills and assist facilitators to recognize the usefulness of constructive conflict and the management of destructive conflict. Many practice sessions are included.

Throughout these sessions, and throughout the year, students read and discuss relevant scholarly and popular literature and commentary that provides them with a theoretical and conceptual background to intergroup relations issues and to small-group facilitation. Most of these readings come from the fields of psychology, sociology, intergroup relations, diversity training, communication, and social justice education.

At the end of the first semester training course not all students are quite ready for facilitation. They defer to another semester due to scheduling conflicts, or by instructor decision, they are assigned other tasks related to the program. Those selected proceed to the support sessions (practicum) accompanying their actual facilitation work.

Instructional and Learning Designs

Multiple formats are used to provide different learning experiences for the peer-facilitators-in-training. Many of these formats are similar to those the peer facilitators will use in the actual intergroup dialogues, so they are themselves learning about these issues at the same time they are learning how to facilitate others' learning.

Experiential exercises. In intergroup education we rely on experiential exercises to involve students in learning about issues on affective as well as cognitive dimensions. These exercises allow students to learn about their own and others' socialization, experiences with oppression, the nature of difference, institutional "isms," and roles and relationships within the broader society.

Large-group discussions. Large-group discussions are used to establish ground rules, debrief some exercises, examine intergroup issues and patterns developing among students and groups within the training course, and disseminate information broadly, and to discuss readings about data or core theories.

Small-group discussions and activities. Small groups provide a format within which students discuss their social identities and perform various collective tasks, such as making dinner, building a structure, or organizing a public event. When they perform these tasks in small groups, it is possible to view and discuss the processes of group interaction, creating opportunities for students to understand the practical meaning of concepts of group dynamics and to strategize techniques for facilitation and intervention in normative group situations. Such groups also are arenas within which students participate in actual intergroup dialogues, both to experience the dialogue process they will later be facilitating and to gain observer perspectives on the dialogue process. Often students are placed into caucuses with others of their same social identity, to explore the impact of these identities on their perspectives or experiences.

Minilectures. We make use of the standard instructional lecture, although generally try to make them brief (thus "minilectures"). This technique often is an effective way to present conceptual models, stories of group experiences in the United States, the meaning of particular terms, and emerging theory in intergroup relations.

Partnering. Risk taking is an integral part of all training and preparation. We use pairs of student partners to work closely together to share risks and deeply explore issues of personal awareness and passion in a relatively safe environment. As pairs of students work closely together, they share the meaning of their social group membership, explore areas of their life that are hidden or unknown to others, and reveal blinders and hot buttons. This format is also used for developing the skills in giving and receiving feedback. Partnering also serves as preparation for the teaming of facilitators as cofacilitators at a later date.

Practice. In order to provide experience with the dialogue itself, students in the training program are placed in a series of brief intergroup dialogues facilitated by the program instructors. Thus, if students have not previously participated in an intergroup dialogue they now get firsthand experience in the phenomenon. Indeed, not all potential facilitators have experienced a dialogue previously, although that is our preference. In addition, in order to gain experience with dialogue leadership, students are asked to accomplish two tasks: (1) to gather several persons of their own social identity group and lead them through a discussion of intergroup issues; and later, (2) to partner with another student of a different social identity group and gather several members of both those identity groups to participate in a brief intergroup dialogue that they facilitate. Journals, dyadic feedback monitored by the instructors, and total group reflection on, and debriefing of, the practice sessions help these potential facilitators examine the concrete issues they faced and might face in the future.

Personal time. It is important to allow students time in which to reflect on these activities and exercises by writing in their personal journals, sharing deeply with a close colleague, discussing reactions with an instructor, or meditating alone. Intimate intergroup exchange, let alone a substantial dialogue, is a rare experience for most students. As a result, many of the interactions central to the training program, and many of the concepts and skills central to their facilitative roles, are new to them. All students need time to digest, reflect upon, and decide how to integrate and make use of these new ideas, including testing how they resonate or conflict with previous beliefs and assumptions. Personal time also provides students with an opportunity to socialize with their peers outside of the instructional arena. Such relatively unstructured "free time" provides the opportunity for additional reflections and insights into individual personalities and group dynamics (perhaps even more so when conducted outside the presence and influence of the instructors).

Problems and Challenges in These Training Efforts

While we have found the use of peer facilitators of enormous value in the construction and operation of intergroup dialogues, it is clear that a number of problems have arisen in the training and development of young people for these roles. As we present these problems or challenges, we indicate some attempted solutions—other solutions obviously are possible.

One of the first challenges arises in the *process of recruiting and screening* students for the program. How do we find and select interested and skilled candidates? It has not worked to proceed with an open enrollment strategy, and to invite into the training effort anyone who is interested. As a result, over the years we have developed a screening system, whereby interested students submit a written application and participate in a series of interviews. The first interview is a one-on-one visit with a member of the training staff, in which we explore students' academic and social backgrounds and the sources and level of their interest in the IGRCC program. At that time we also explore the student's commitment to a two-semester activity—the first semester of training and the second semester of actual facilitation (it had occurred previously, and still does occur occasionally, that some students would undertake the training effort and then decide not to facilitate a dialogue). The second interview takes place in a small-group (four to six people) session, with other potential trainees, in which the candidates engage in a series of intergroup exercises designed to demonstrate their skills and understanding of the issues that are at the core of the training and facilitation effort. On these bases we have been able to gather more useful and relevant information about these students ahead of time and have substantially upgraded the effectiveness of the selection process.

On occasion it has been especially difficult to recruit males, especially African American males, and Native Americans of either gender, into this program. The small number of campus members of some of these social identity groups is part of the problem, but undoubtedly other issues in peer, intragroup, and intergroup relations are involved. We have not been able to solve this problem on a permanent basis.

A second challenge focuses on the *sequence of training goals and activities.* What should be the relationship (time-wise or energy-wise) between preparation in the substance of intergroup relations issues and in the skills of small-group instructional facilitation? The decision on this matter typically is made more difficult by students' anxieties and interests. At the beginning students are both keenly interested and highly anxious about exploring intergroup relations issues; they also often assume that small-group facilitation is a facile task. As time goes on, students begin to shy away from some of the intergroup conflicts typically generated by the intense contact involved in the exercises and at the same time to develop greater anxiety about upcoming facilitation tasks. Our solution has been to focus first on intergroup issues and in so doing model for students a variety of learning and skill development activities as well as our own facilitation styles. Through the use of the exercises, and the staff's modeling behavior, students gain a clearer sense of the strategies and skills that are involved in intergroup dialogue and in facilitating group development, while keeping the focus on intergroup learning.

A third challenge involves presenting the *content of intergroup instruction* and exploration. As suggested earlier, we use a variety of intellectual materials to help students explore the history and cultural traditions of different social identity groups, and the relevance of these traditions and experiences for resultant personal styles and behaviors. We focus explicitly on issues of domination and privilege, as well as on the appreciation of difference; and on structures and cultures of oppression, as well as on challenges to these patterns. Thus, the examination of interpersonal, intergroup, and societal-level conflict is an important ingredient of the training. While we emphasize differentiation and conflict, we also place a high priority on understanding communal or trans-identity group issues, and the history and tactics involved in efforts to form coalitions or alliances across particular identity groupings.

A fourth challenge involves decisions *about how deeply or intensively work should focus on issues of social group identity* and feelings/perceptions/behaviors with the student's own and other identity groups. The students are in late adolescent and young adult stages of identity development, for the most part, and their own identities may only be partially formulated. Moreover, given their own enmeshment (historically and currently) in backgrounds and communities that are segregated by race and class, most are on a steep learning curve with regard to issues of more or less intimate intergroup exchange and relationships. Many of them are still unclear about their gender identities and feelings about their own and others' sexual orientations. Thus, there is substantial psychological delicacy to the exploration of these issues. Moreover, to the extent that intrapersonal, interpersonal, or group-level conflict is part of the reality of intergroup interaction, it must be part of the intergroup dialogue process. Such conflicts, as they may be surfaced, generated, or explored in the context of facilitator training, adds to the psychological tensions and risks just noted.

A fifth challenge lies in the *nature of the incentives or rewards* used to make this venture attractive to students. What are the payoffs to potential facilitators? We have established the training program as for-credit courses in psychology and sociology. Clearly this is justifiable on intellectual or academic grounds, since a good deal of academic reading and discussion, as well as experiential exploration of intellectual issues, takes place. Only occasionally have we had to defend this proposition to university gatekeepers. However, as an academically creditable (and credible) course, it is graded, and this does raise questions about the kind of grading system that makes sense in a setting where safety, risk taking, vulnerability, and experimentation are much to be desired. Can anyone who makes a good-faith effort fail such a training course? Of course, not everyone who completes the training will be permitted to facilitate a dialogue; here different skill levels become quite relevant. But credit and grades are another matter—and a ticklish one. Generally we address these issues by establishing a floor grade for everyone who participates fully with their presence and attention, and who faithfully engages in the various learning opportunities available. Then we require students to write a series of papers, both analyzing intellectual material and their own experiences/reactions, and try to grade these papers on an individuated basis—with attention to students' learning and growth curves throughout the program.

A sixth challenge involves the *timing and location of such a training program*, given the level of attention, intensity, and bonding required for success. Where and when should it take place? After trying several alternatives, we have elected to conduct the initial portion of the program in a two- to three-day off-campus setting, in a live-in atmosphere, prior to or just at the start of the school semester. Under these circumstances, relatively free of external distractions, people appear to be better able to focus on their own and others' learning. This event is followed by a series of weekly or biweekly seminars, usually ending with a full-day session near the end of the semester.

A seventh challenge arises in the context of the intellectual, social, and emotional intensity of the training effort, especially in an off-campus live-in site. The challenges of meeting and dealing with new and often quite different groups of people, and with new ideas and insights, when combined with fatigue, often creates stress. This stress, taking place within an intensive bonding encounter, often raises the possibility of student use of alcohol, sex, and other *risk-taking behaviors as releases.* We have been careful to deal with these potential issues in two ways: (1) to make very clear ground rules about alcohol and drug use, and to raise warnings about other forms of risky behavior; and (2) to provide as part of the training design a variety of planned (games, competitions) and unplanned (parties, midnight swims) recreational activities that speak to the need for stress reduction or explosion. These ground rules focus primarily on the costs and benefits of different kinds of risk taking (e.g., with regard to openness in exploring intergroup issues as opposed to acting out tension reduction) to the IGR program and process and less on the moral judgments involved (though the two overlap).

An eighth challenge involves decisions about *what kind of "community"* we should help develop. Part of the training focuses on individuals' separate social identities, principally to help students better understand themselves and their own group. Another part focuses on helping students understand others' identities, and the cultures, social experiences, and outlooks of other groups. Both foci are part of an intergroup dialogue process. It is important for students to understand and appreciate one another and bond as a community that cuts across separate identity groups' interests, ideologies, or social locations. But it is important to do this in a real, impassioned, and committed way, not in a way that "paints over" important differences and inevitable conflicts. This dynamic also surfaces in actual intergroup dialogues, but it has a much more intense reality in the context of an intimate training program for group facilitators—especially on a weekend "away."

A ninth challenge involves designing a *continuing training program that supports and improves facilitators' skills and growth while they actually are facilitating intergroup dialogues.* Learning about social identity and intergroup issues is lifelong learning, a process that continually unfolds in greater complexity and is never complete. Given the normal pressures of collegiate life, the experience of the two- or three-day session starts to fade if not followed by continuing meeting and work throughout the semester. Moreover, sometimes the reality of what is involved in facilitating other students in an intergroup dialogue does not "hit" until they are involved in such work . . . then the opportunity for growth and development is truly great. Thus, we have designed a semester-long follow-up to the prefacilitation training program that continues to work with these students while they conduct dialogues.

A tenth challenge involves *how we, the instructors or trainers in this process, play out our own identities, roles, and personae*—with one another (as a team) and with the student "trainees." The instructional or training team usually is diverse itself—at least by race and/or gender and often in sexual orientation, age, academic status, or religion. We must figure out how to work together well, both in order to conduct the training effectively and to operate as a model for the student facilitators-to-be. We also must each manage these identities (and often significant age/developmental level differences as well) in interactions with students. The authority instructors or trainers usually carry in such situations is magnified by age differences and by our location in the credit-granting hierarchy of the academy. Moreover, since the University of Michigan IGRCC program involves a collaboration between the academic sectors and the Student Affairs sector of the university, the instructors/trainers who come from these different sectors must also struggle (within themselves, with each other, and with the student culture) with the attributions of greater expertise, authority, and aloofness often accorded to university faculty (and the corollary lesser status afforded student services personnel). Power differentials between faculty and student affairs staff, between tenured and non-tenured faculty, between faculty or staff and graduate students, are built into the structure of the university and inevitably impact on the training staff and student participants. The mix of skills and competencies required to train students in this program call for quite special faculty instructors as well, and often the low level of rewards and incentives for such faculty involvement make it difficult to regularly recruit instructors.

A final (for now) challenge involves the constant process of *sustaining the very life and structure/culture of such a training program within the context of the larger academic structure of the university.* Gaining legitimacy for course-credit work done in off-campus venues, as well as maintaining academic credibility for intellectual work accomplished through innovative pedagogies, requires constant communication and negotiation (and sometimes defense) with the surrounding academic culture and structure of the undergraduate college and relevant departments.

There is no question the Program on Intergroup Relations, Conflict, and Community, and its intergroup dialogue efforts, have been successful. Its success has largely been due to the high level of expertise and commitment evidenced by these peer facilitators. The program to train such facilitators often has permitted us as instructors to have access to the very "best and brightest" members of our academic and civic community. Moreover, we have been privileged to encounter and work with them at deep and meaningful levels of their own and our own learning about intergroup matters. In this sense it has called forth our own best efforts and afforded us some of our most exciting teaching-learning moments.

NOTE

1. This instrument was originally created by Mark Chesler, from a conceptual model developed by Bailey Jackson, and modified in a series of variations by Ximena Zúñiga, Todd Sevig, Ratnesh Nagda, Monita Thompson, and Mark Chesler.

REFERENCES

Jackson, B. N.d. "PASK: Framework for Multicultural Competency." New Perspectives, Amherst, Mass. Mimeograph.

Luft, J. 1970. *Group Processes: An Introduction to Group Dynamics.* 2d ed. Palo Alto, Calif.: National Press.

McIntosh, P. 1989. "White Privilege: Unpacking the Invisible Knapsack." *Peace and Freedom,* July–August, 10–12.

Pfeiffer, J., and J. Jones. 1975. "Co-Facilitating." In *The 1975 Annual Handbook for Group Facilitation,* ed. J. Pfeiffer and J. Jones. San Diego: University Associates.

Shirts, G. N.d. "Starpower: A Simulation Game." Mimeograph.

Weber, R. 1982. "The Group: A Cycle from Birth to Death." In *Reading Book for Human Relations Training,* ed. L. Porter and B. Mohr. 7th ed. Washington, D.C.: NTL Institute.

Chapter 16

Embracing the Paradox: Dialogue That Incorporates Both Individual and Group Identities

Diana Kardia and Todd Sevig

Are we individuals or are we members of social/identity groups? This question inevitably arises during the course of an intergroup dialogue as participants work to understand themselves, other participants, and the issues raised by the dialogue itself. Grappling with this question, and the individual and group conflicts it can generate, is one of the defining dynamics of an intergroup dialogue. During the course of the dialogue, this conflict can feel as if it will make or break the group, catalyze or destroy the possibility for change. As facilitators, we approach such conflict cautiously, reading the group, continually updating our sense of how (or whether) we'll make it through, how far we can push, and what the propensities for backlash might be. In this role, we are ever in need of strategies and perspectives that help us to avoid becoming entrenched in the conflict ourselves.

This chapter reflects strategies and perspectives we, the authors, have learned while facilitating dialogues and training undergraduate and graduate students to become dialogue facilitators. The scenarios and quotations presented here represent composites of our experience and the experiences of students.

Dialogue Interlude
The group has been quiet until now as we've moved through some basic introductions and definitions. There's at least an illusion of willingness to participate—after all, they all signed up for this dialogue voluntarily. But the quiet is revealed as being more akin to compliance when Julia raises her hand after we offer a set of definitions related to social group memberships. By the set of her jaw, it's clear that the question or comment she is about to contribute has lived with her awhile, nurtured by a general frustration with the terms of the conversation as she has known it. The feel of the room is that of a Western saloon town, this moment a showdown. The image is helpful primarily as a warning:

reminding us that we are not sheriffs here, nor is she an outlaw. Our goal is not to be the first gun out of the holster. We let her shoot, demonstrating that her words need not be fatal to our endeavor and that no defenses are needed.

Am I an individual or am I a member of some social group? Intergroup dialogues work toward moving beyond this question into an understanding of how we as individuals affect and are affected by our group affiliations. However, it is most often in a polarized form that concerns about identity, membership, and connection are first brought into the dialogue by participants:

> Being white isn't nearly as important as my personality.
> My ethnic identity matters much more than my gender.
> I'm tired of being blamed for racism. My family never owned slaves.
> I'm not homophobic—my best friend is a lesbian.
> Why can't we all just be friends?

These statements reflect the terms of the conversation in the world outside of an intergroup dialogue, where issues of identity and community are inevitably framed in dichotomies and battled with fervor across most of our social contexts. The job of an intergroup dialogue facilitator is to somehow bring these questions and concerns into the room and not allow ourselves or the group to be derailed by them—to honor this conflict for the reality it represents while also transforming the conflict into paradox.

Dialogue Interlude

When we don't rush into the void following Julia's words, Kyle steps in instead. He, like Julia, speaks from a place created by too many past frustrations. He hears her words as a siren, signaling that this conversation is likely to be just another dead end, another opportunity to be discounted and misrepresented. He is ready to pounce. Whether he will casually invalidate Julia's words, make an impassioned case for her to "wake up" to reality as he has experienced it, or angrily denounce her is not yet clear. The scene flashes to that of a courtroom, the prosecution poised to present closing arguments as if all evidence is in and the verdict is imminent. Again, this is a warning: do not accept the terms of the discussion as they currently stand. We are not judges here, and our goal is not to establish a single interpretation of truth—no single truth is possible in this discussion. But the burden of proof remains with us: to facilitate this dialogue so that multiple and conflicting truths can co-exist and be heard. In this way, we can begin to show that this conflict is why we are here, that in Julia and Kyle's exchange the dialogue has only just begun.

This chapter speaks to the strategies and skills that make it possible for a group to directly address and transform the conflict between individual and social identities into a paradox that is able to promote individual and group development. These strategies all incorporate one fundamental assumption about intergroup dialogue: any response or argument introduced into the dialogue needs and deserves attention. It is only by fully incorporating all aspects of the individual and group struggle that the paradox can be revealed. Otherwise, a polarized dichotomy necessarily remains in place as participants cling to a perspective that they feel deeply invested in having heard.

We start with a brief overview of the literature on identity development to provide a background for understanding the dynamics that emerge during the course of an intergroup dialogue. This is followed by an analysis of the specific ways in which participants revert to an over-individualized approach to dialogue. The subsequent section articulates a theoretical foundation for incorporating both individual and group identities into an intergroup dialogue. Finally, we share a set of basic guidelines and related strategies for responding to the individual and group dynamics associated with the individual/group identity conflict.

Identity Development as a Context for Intergroup Dialogues

Identity development, based on membership in certain racial, gender, or sexual orientation groups, can be an important variable in understanding intergroup dialogue process and content. Single group identity development models focus exclusively on one social identity group, and such models have been proposed for many diverse groups: Blacks or African Americans (Akbar 1989; Banks 1984; Cross 1971; Jackson 1975; Thomas 1971; Vontress 1971), Asian-Americans (Sue and Sue 1990), Latinos/Chicanos (Berry 1980; Keefe and Padilla 1987), White or European Americans (Carney and Kahn 1984; Hardiman 1982; Helms 1984, 1990; Ponterotto 1988; Terry 1977), women (Avery 1977; Downing and Roush 1985), and gay men and lesbians (Cass 1979; McCarn and Fassinger 1996). These models help elucidate the differential oppressive experiences of groups, different histories, different cultural traditions, and different cultural styles of these groups (Phinney 1992). Although unique terminology is used in the various models, the stages are noticeably similar (e.g., terms used to describe an "unawareness" first stage vary, yet all describe basically the same concept).

The "inclusive" models have incorporated these similarities across the identity development of minorities and oppressed people. The Minority Identity Development model (MID) of Atkinson, Morten, and Sue (1983), for instance, is applicable for different groups based on race, gender, ethnicity, and sexual orientation. Other examples of inclusive models include Banks 1984, with his work on racial/ethnic identity development among all oppressed racial groups, Sue and Sue 1990 in regard to cultural identity development for people of color, and Hardiman and Jackson 1992 in their description of racial identity development for Black and White people. These models have described a similar process across groups, although all have noted that the cultural context of the developmental processes obviously may differ. Finally, Myers et al. (1991) described a model applicable to all people in their Optimal Theory Applied to Identity Development (OTAID) model. The main tenets of this model include incorporating multiple worldviews, integrating spirituality into identity development, and focusing on allowing people to self-define (vs. being categorized only by others). The model has received support in the literature and there is now an instrument to help people assess where they are in their development according to this model (Sevig, Highlen, and Adams 2000).

The above literature helps us understand the processes and conflicts that people experience either within themselves or with other people around issues of identity. While terminology and emphasis vary, all these models describe the following process in some fashion. In an early stage, a person is unaware of her or his own identity and/or the impact of this identity on who she or he is as "a person." At some point, the person moves into a new phase in which an identity or identities start becoming salient. The person then proceeds through a widening and deepening spiral of new experiences, new insights, and new encounters with others, all of which contribute to making this new identity part of who the person is. Most models then include a phase in which people are very comfortable with the identity, can see connections with other identities and other oppressions, and so forth. While most of the above references are for stage or phase models, it should be noted some more recent work emphasizes styles, or "state-dependent" thoughts, feelings, or behaviors, as opposed to a more static stage or phase framework.

This literature base can be very useful for developing an understanding of intergroup dialogue content and process, especially with respect to the conflict between individual and group identities: the capacity of a dialogue participant to see beyond his or her individual identity is, in part, determined by where the person is in an individual identity development process. For example, a person who has not developed an extensive awareness of the various meanings and associations with an aspect of their identity will need to integrate a substantial amount of information before being able to effectively work with the paradox of identity. Such individuals might need more time, more reading, and more discussion with participants and facilitators than someone who has successfully proceeded through this work. In another example, someone newly integrating the reality of oppression related to the person's own group might have less capacity for a tolerant or compassionate response to someone else who is strongly emphasizing individual experience. We will refer more to ways in which this literature base can help later in this chapter.

We now focus on understanding why participants in an intergroup dialogue make the variety of claims and arguments that tend to be made during these discussions, and the responses we have found most useful for working through them.

Understanding the Conflict: The Tendency toward Individualism; or, "Why I Don't Want to Be Associated with 'My' Group"

The following set of responses represents a collection of typical statements made in intergroup dialogues as participants struggle with the role of social group identities in their lives. While these statements are separated into categories for the sake of discussion, these responses are actually overlapping and interconnected. It's important to note that the factors behind any participant's response are often complex and are typically intertwined with group and individual identity factors. The following explanations are intended to serve only as a reminder of the scope of possible underlying factors.

I've Never Been Oppressed/Been the Oppressor
I've never experienced sexism—it's never been a problem for me.
I'm tired of being blamed for racism. My family never owned slaves.

Recognizing oppression is painful. One of the strongest forces behind the assertion of individual realities is a defense against this pain—a defense that may be strongly interwoven with a participant's psychological structure. Dissociating from pain and an emphasis on positive life experiences may serve as a survival mechanism for individuals who either don't have or believe they don't have the resources to cope with pain directly. This is particularly true when facing destructive forces that permeate reality and cannot be easily changed. Refusing to acknowledge pain is characteristic of someone who has not done much thinking about what her or his identity means to them. Also, distancing from the pain of oppression may be a learned response. Key image makers, including parents, teachers, and the media, often buffer us from painful realities, even those realities associated with our specific individual experience. Without the skills to acknowledge and move through pain, denying or minimizing painful experiences is a common strategy utilized by many dialogue participants.

I've Never Been Oppressed/Been the Oppressor (Revisited)
I just demand respect, and then people don't mess with me.
I'm not homophobic—my best friend is a lesbian.

A resistance toward identifying oneself as an oppressor or as oppressed can also arise out of a resistance to or lack of experience with structural analysis. The emphasis in popular U.S. culture on "pulling oneself up by one's bootstraps" implies that individual experience is the strongest force in our lived reality, that we need not attend to what is going on around us as long as we ourselves are taking care of business. Again, as above, this way of experiencing the world can reflect a lack of thinking about the impact of group identity development, or a comfort with the status quo. Further, this emphasis on individualism is typically reinforced in the media and educational settings. Without an acknowledgement of the constraints and influences exerted by the institutions and systems in which we live, there is an automatic tendency to assume individual autonomy and to globalize individual experience.

I'm a Human and That's All That Matters
Being white isn't nearly as important as my personality.
I'm the same person I was before you found out that I'm gay.

Stereotypes can have a devastating affect on our lived experience. We know from elementary and high school that being associated with negatively stereotyped characteristics can lead to ostracism. We know from our own tendency to stereotype others that this process involves devaluing some characteristics while emphasizing others. Being associated with a group and related stereotypes also represents a lack of control over our lives. We resist being defined by others out of a fear that we are then unable to define ourselves—if you see me first as white or gay, then I will never be able to show you who I really am. Furthermore, once constrained by categories, there is a sense that we cannot change our life circumstances. If being white is most important, and being white has negative associations, and I cannot change being white, then my back is against the wall. Without a sense that a locus of control can be found even within a fixed identity, the most effective response can be to distance oneself from that identity.

I'm Too Different to Be One of Them
My ethnic identity matters much more than my gender.
I'm not white, I'm Jewish.

Oppression is experienced differently depending on the intersection of multiple factors, and our experiences can be many painful worlds apart from each other. This is especially true when we are asked to identify with a privileged identity that is offset by a less privileged aspect of our identity. During the identity development process, some aspects of our identity naturally take priority over others, while at other times, we readily identify with more than one identity at a time (e.g., a lower-class White male; an African American middle-class straight woman; for a cogent discussion on multiple identities, see Reynolds and Pope 1991). One of the strengths of the OTAID model mentioned above is that it allows for the self-definition process to naturally occur (including multiple identities). This self-defining becomes integral to an intergroup dialogue in order for participants to see the heterogeneity within groups while also helping people grapple and, at times, come to terms with their own identity/ies.

Shared identities are often experienced quite differently due to personal opportunities, education, and other differences in individual experience—so much so that the differences seem to wipe out any similarities within a group. The creation of intergroup dialogues rests on the assumption that there is a scarcity of opportunities for these different realities to be expressed. It is understandable that participants coming to an intergroup dialogue will focus first on the need to express these differences, and these differences are crucial to a full understanding of the complexity and meanings of social groups.

An emphasis on the differences within a shared identity can also be a defense against the possibility of pain—we may not want to identify with members of our group when such an association may set us up for further oppression related to our other, less privileged, identities. Without a reason to trust members of our own group, it is often safer to emphasize the differences between us.

> *If We Associate with Our Groups, Things Will Get Worse Instead of Better*
> Why can't we all just be friends?
> I don't need to spend time with my own group—what really matters is us all talking together.

A fundamental motivation for the creation of intergroup dialogues is the understanding that few of us have learned the skills or frameworks for attending to our differences and the truths of our experience in a manner that facilitates connection across social identities. In fact, we often get stuck in our development process or cycle through issues multiple times in part because we need multiple opportunities to get exposure to an issue, to start to think it through, to talk about it with others, to incorporate the issue into our heart, and so forth. Without these skills, many of us have learned that drawing direct attention to our differences can be uncomfortable and even destructive. Furthermore, many of us lack the skills for working through conflict in an effective manner—and conflict inevitably arises as we work together to create a shared understanding and new viewing points on each other. It is not surprising, therefore, that one response to intergroup work is the concern that it will foster divisions among us. This concern is particularly strong in contexts where a cohesive group identity is important outside the dialogue (e.g., when facilitating a dialogue among people who work together on a daily basis).

Transforming Conflict into Paradox: The Importance of Both Individual and Group Identities

When entering a classroom, it is typical to inform students of the basic learning goals, to indicate what students will know and be able to do when successfully completing a course. A similar approach applies to an intergroup dialogue. When approaching the conflict between individual and group identity, it is useful to start with an overview of why multiple experiences of identity are important to the basic goals of intergroup dialogue. This overview can clarify the destination to which we are traveling, reminding the group that, while we may stop along the way to more fully understand single aspects of identity, the intended goal is to keep moving until multiple experiences and facets of identity are integrated into the dialogue. From a facilitator perspective, the benefits associated with individual and group identity are multiple. It is important to include, address, and validate individual identities because

The individual is the primary locus for change—this is the place where social change agents are created. Journeying through the identity development process helps increase individual awareness and move us to a place of deeper and wider awareness of self, others, and the world around us. This journey can lead to a desire to participate in social change efforts that reflect the ongoing internal change being experienced.

The daily lives of individuals are the places where theory is understood and translated into practice. Participants need access to their individual experiences to fully test and understand the concepts discussed.

Discussion of identity groups often leads to hierarchical assumptions about the relative importance of various identities. It is only at the level of the individual where we can fully understand the complexity and the intersections of social group memberships. We may choose to focus on one group identity more than another in any discussion, but at any moment in time I am simultaneously all my identities— and being a White lesbian woman, for example, is similar to and different than being a White heterosexual man.

Attention to differences between groups can often be reductionistic, erasing or minimizing the differences within groups. The expression of individual voices moves the discussion beyond simplistic stereotypes and categorizations associated with any single social group.

Individual experience is the source of people's ability to engage in perspective taking and empathy that make an important contribution to intergroup dialogue. It is only through our multifaceted experience as individuals that we can begin to imagine what the experiences of others might be like.

For dominant group members who are grappling with the realities of oppression perpetrated by their group, individual identity may be the only obvious source of power, pride, or hope.

Focusing only on social group memberships circumscribes the discussion of community to the forms in which community historically has existed and been defined—which, in large part, has meant segregated communities, especially along racial/ethnic and class lines. Focusing on individual identity, choice, and agency is the means through which new visions of community and an integration of identities within such communities might be realized.

The group dynamics associated with an intergroup dialogue are strongly influenced by the particular life experiences and the identity developmental processes of individual participants. Providing opportunities for participants to represent themselves as individuals promotes self-reflection and can further the identity development process. It also provides information to facilitators about how to effectively design and facilitate the dialogue process so that it is responsive to the specific needs of those in the room.

It is important to include, address, and validate group identities because

Many social institutions were created to respond differently to specific social groups—a factor that has a significant impact on individual lives. By learning about the experiences associated with their own group, participants can often gain a better understanding of their own individual experience. By learning about the experiences associated with other groups, participants gain a framework for interpreting the perspectives and actions of individuals from these groups.

The history and resources associated with specific social groups are often radically different. In many instances we have been socialized to be unaware of these differences or to minimize them. Furthermore, the nature of individual experience, combined with social norms, myths, and the control of information, often obscures awareness of patterns occurring at group levels. This can perpetuate unrealistic expectations and inappropriate strategies and policies for social change. (The many ways in which affirmative action policies are represented and misunderstood are examples of this.) Providing information about social patterns and institutional influences makes it possible for individuals to make more informed decisions about how they live their lives and perceive and interact with others.

Membership in a social group is one of the places in which individuals get the support to take risks and make changes. In an intergroup dialogue, truth can be spoken across historic chasms of difference in large part because of the support provided by other members of one's own group in the room. Furthermore, in dialogues and in the larger world we often need the reinforcement provided by members of our own group to further the change process that can be initiated by an individual.

When intergroup dialogues occur in an academic context, the nonpersonalized aspects of the dialogue create much of the foundation for offering these dialogues for academic credit, including information on identity development theory and literature.

While a conscious awareness of these goals can benefit facilitators, it can also be useful to generate lists of this type with dialogue participants. Such a discussion might start with individual reflection on a sentence completion exercise: "Because I am an individual, I can contribute to this dialogue by . . ." and "Because I am a member of [social group], I can contribute to this dialogue by . . ." Based on this reflection, participants can work together to generate lists of benefits. Facilitators may elaborate on these lists based on some of the points articulated below, depending on the sophistication of the group.

Strategies for Embracing the Paradox

Understanding the tendency toward individualism and articulating the interlocking goals associated with individual and group identities provides a foundation for determining dialogue strategies. This section offers guidelines for the development of such strategies and describes a set of exercises that demonstrate these guidelines. These guidelines can also provide a framework for the ongoing development of new exercises and dialogue structures.

Intergroup dialogues are designed to provide new viewing points on previously entrenched ideas. The conflicts and concerns that participants bring to an intergroup dialogue are typically ones that have existed for years. Due to their longevity, these perspectives are quite practiced, often include distortions of information, and can seem overly polarized.

Ingrained dichotomies (such as the belief that we are either individuals or we are social group members) can be opened up through analogy or other strategies that cast the conflict in a new light.

Strategy: Normalizing the Individual/Group Split

Through writing or discussion, ask students to reflect on how they are both an individual in their family and how their family membership has relevance to their interactions both in and outside of their family. (This can also be applied to other group memberships—Girl Scouts, fraternities, etc.)

Behind every contribution to the dialogue, there is important information about participants and the current needs and potential of the group. Listen for this information and, when it is not immediately evident, provide additional opportunity for this information to become clear.

Strategy: Minute Papers

Many important concerns and perspectives will not be voiced during the course of the dialogue due to time, group dynamics, safety issues, and other factors. A basic classroom assessment technique called the "Minute Paper" (Angelo and Cross 1993) can provide an opportunity to gain insight into group and individual concerns that may not be readily apparent. At the end of a dialogue session, ask participants to respond in writing to a single question such as, "What is your biggest concern about this dialogue at this moment?" or "What is one important thing about your individual experience or perspective that is not currently being addressed in this dialogue?" These papers can be collected and read by the facilitators. The concerns communicated by participants can then be incorporated into subsequent planning or may be reported back to the group (either as a summary or in a manner that represents each contribution specifically).

Participants need to maintain a sense of control over their own actions and identity. The structure and facilitation of the dialogue need to promote willing participation, including a willingness to be uncomfortable, try new things, hear hard truths, and even be defined by others at some points during the course of the dialogue. This occurs by creating structures that promote safety, clearly expressing the intended goals of an exercise, being responsive to concerns as they arise, and providing a sufficient amount of integration and reflection time after each exercise and throughout the dialogue as a whole. In this process, it is useful to emphasize and define the difference between safety and comfort to indicate to students that having a sense of control is not the same as liking what is going on at all times in the dialogue.

It is also important to note that having a sense of individual control is not the same as controlling the dialogue itself. While it is sometimes appropriate to incorporate participants' ideas about modifying dialogue exercises or structure, an individual's effort to change the dynamics at the group level is often indicative of her or his need to reclaim an inner sense of control. Providing individuals with opportunities to express concerns and then regain a sense of agency (e.g., modifying their own participation or working through the basic assumptions related to an exercise using their own terminology) can often effectively address initial resistance to participation.

Strategy: Going to the Second Moment
Early in the course of a dialogue it is important to provide a general understanding of what it means to be in dialogue. "Going to the second moment" is a phrase useful for describing one of the basic dynamics involved in dialogue. In the course of a group interaction, there are a variety of moments when conflict breaks through to the surface. The first moment that conflict appears can often be volatile, filled with the classic fight or flight mechanisms, and can include feelings and actions that we feel we cannot get beyond (either as participants or as facilitators). During these "first moments" we may feel that it is impossible to be understood and that we have no interest in staying in the conversation any longer. These feelings may be very familiar from our interactions across social group identities outside of the dialogue structure. "Going to the second moment" (and third and fourth) is what dialogues are all about. Through facilitation, group exercises, and the intention and commitment of participants, intergroup dialogues help make it possible to create the follow-through with each other even during first moments that may seem insurmountable.

"Going to the second moment" can be specifically applied to the conflict between individual and social group identities. Any single moment may require that we focus more on one aspect of our identity than another. The principle of the "second moment" helps remind us of the continuity of time and the fact that no single moment need stand alone: I can represent an aspect of my experience that I share in common with others in my group in one moment and, in the next moment, make a contribution that speaks fully to the uniqueness of my individual experience. Sharing this principle with dialogue participants is a way to encourage us all to remember that we do not have to fear the single moment—the dialogue process is designed to help us all realize that ourselves and "the other" are more than what we seem at any one point in time.

Participants may enter a dialogue with a variety of reasons to avoid owning specific aspects of their identity, including pain, guilt, lack of information, fear, and the complexities associated with multiple group identities. The dialogue structure must take this into account while also facilitating a process in which these identities might be better understood and even claimed.

Strategy: The "Fishbowl" Exercise

The "Fishbowl" exercise is an extremely powerful and versatile tool that simultaneously demonstrates group differences, group similarities, and the differences within groups. Its structure promotes crucial listening skills and encourages a discovery approach to the dialogue. (See the description in Schoem, Zúñiga, and Nagda 1993, 326.)

Both the tone and the structure of the dialogue need to normalize conflict and pain, making room for these to be the beginning of a connection between us rather than an end. This can be accomplished by welcoming conflict and discussing its benefits with participants. It can also be useful to discuss the various responses individuals have to conflict and pain and the ways in which each of these responses can be appropriate in a specific context. This discussion demonstrates that responding to conflict is a skill, not a hardwired reaction, and that it can be useful to develop multiple kinds of responses in order to broaden one's choices in a conflict situation.

Strategy: "Multiple Roles and Multiple Choice" Exercise

This exercise helps participants to reflect on their own roles and styles while placing themselves in a larger context of roles, styles, and choices. (See the full description in Zúñiga and Myers 1993, 316.)

Trust between participants is a necessary, difficult, yet simple component of an intergroup dialogue. Participants will enter with many reasons not to trust each other—those imagined and those that are very real. Yet trust can enter surprisingly easily (even while it still remains fragile) as participants discover elements of their common humanity. The structure of the dialogue must direct participants toward this discovery. In doing so, it is helpful to think of trust as fluid and as welcome in any quantity.

Strategy: The "Four Corners of Oppression" Exercise

This exercise is designed to help participants realize that everyone participates in oppression in one form or another and that everyone is also affected by oppression.[1] It is effective at breaking through feelings of discomfort and shame associated with our own actions and for realizing the complexity and integrity of other participants. This exercise introduces pain and conflict into the discussion without polarization on the issues, training participants to listen well to the experiences of others and to combine stories across differences to discover common themes. It is ideally suited to a group of sixteen to twenty participants but can be adapted for larger groups.

Allow seventy-five minutes for the "Four Corners" exercise. To set up the exercise, put the following four questions on newsprint that will then be tacked in the four corners of the room (one question per corner):

Describe a time when oppressive comments or actions were directed toward you (based on any aspect of your identity).

Describe a time when you were the perpetrator of an oppressive act or comments.

Describe a time when you witnessed an act of oppression and did nothing about it.

Describe a time when you witnessed an act of oppression and intervened.

As a facilitator, prepare your own answers to each of these questions to be shared as you introduce the exercise. Choose answers that demonstrate that this exercise incorporates a range of identities. Since this exercise asks participants to be vulnerable with each other, also be aware of how your own examples model risk taking.

1. Arrange participants into groups of four or five with one group situated in each corner of the room (for larger groups, assign two small groups to a corner rather than increasing the size of the small group). Each group will rotate to all four corners but will start by sharing their answers to the question associated with their corner.

2. After introducing the exercise and sharing your own examples, each group spends ten minutes per corner with the facilitator acting as the overall timekeeper. Groups should also be instructed to monitor time internally so that all participants are able to respond to each question.

3. Debrief by asking participants what they learned as they considered and shared their own responses and what they learned from listening to each other.

While dialogue cannot happen without individuals bringing the specifics of their lives into the dialogue, it is not enough to build a dialogue on the foundation of individual experience. The structure of the dialogue must provide models for structural analysis—opportunities to understand the constraints and influences exerted by institutions and systems. If the facilitators and the dialogue structure do not provide this framework, entrenched conflict will erupt between participants as they pit individual experience against individual experience without a means for identifying the mechanisms that lie at the root of their different experiences.

Strategy: Guided Fantasies

Guided fantasies can help participants see institutionalized aspects of society by momentarily changing the terms of individual experience. See "Guided Fantasies: Exploring Issues of Homophobia and Heterosexism" (Lesbian–Gay Male Programs Office 1993, 329), as an example.

Conclusion

The conflict between individual and group identities arises in intergroup dialogues through many avenues: a refusal to participate in group activities, reticence expressed during the course of full participation in the dialogue, and reflections shared by participants as they integrate their dialogue experience. However this conflict arises, the answer is the same: we are individuals *and* we are members of a social group, many social groups. Intergroup dialogues operate on the basic assumption that our social group memberships cannot be ignored or denied. Yet a dialogue cannot occur without individuals who show up in all the uniqueness and complexity of their individual experience. Furthermore, dialogic interactions stem from "where people are at" in their own individual identity development process: how much they have thought about their membership in certain social groups (i.e., groups based on race, gender, sexual orientation, etc.) affects their views of themselves, of others, and of the sociological environment. All of these truths shape and inform what knowledge, assumptions, and gifts we bring to the discussion, what we need and desire from this interaction, and what choices we will make when presented with opportunities to stretch and grow. The great potential for intergroup dialogue lies in our ability to embrace the paradox of our separate, varied, continually evolving, and always connected identities.

As we have facilitated intergroup dialogues, we have developed effective responses to the many ways in which the individual/group identity conflict can arise by relying on the framework of "knowledge, skills, awareness, passion, and action" originally articulated by Bailey Jackson and Mark Chesler, and further described in Fukuyama and Sevig 1999.

What this framework and the preceding responses all stress is that an interest in, or commitment to, intergroup dialogue (passion) is not enough, nor is it sufficient to attend only to an informational level (knowledge) about social and group identities, nor is it enough to be an expert facilitator with all the right skills. As with any learning endeavor, intergroup dialogues must be structured to account for the specific skill and awareness strengths, deficiencies, and "everything in between" that participants bring to any dialogue. It is a skill to find ways to trust others when there are valid reasons for withholding such trust. It is a skill to articulate the specifics of one's own experience while also listening well to the experiences of others. And it is a skill to respond to pain, either within ourselves or in others, in a way that promotes healing rather than additional injury.

As we develop our awareness of ourselves and the world around us, these are skills that dialogue facilitators and participants can learn. As facilitators, we can encourage the development of participants' awareness and skills only if we normalize and understand that there are not yet nearly enough true experiences of intergroup dialogue in our society for us to assume that participants have these skills well in hand when they enter our dialogue. Therefore, we must be compassionately prepared for the various ways in which participants enter a dialogue and proactively create opportunities for individuals to learn new ways of interacting with themselves and each other.

NOTE

1. This exercise was first described to the authors and their colleagues by Mark Chesler at the University of Michigan and was based on a training experience that he had observed.

REFERENCES

Akbar, N. 1989. "Nigrescence and Identity: Some Limitations." *Counseling Psychologist* 17:258–63.

Angelo, Thomas A., and K. Patricia Cross. 1993. *Classroom Assessment Techniques: A Handbook for College Teachers.* San Francisco: Jossey-Bass.

Atkinson, D. R., G. Morten, and D. W. Sue. 1983. *Counseling American Minorities: A Cross-Cultural Perspective.* 2d ed. Dubuque, Iowa: Wm. C. Brown.

Avery, D. M. 1977. "The Psychological Stages of Liberation." *Illinois Personnel and Guidance Association Quarterly* 63:36–42.

Banks, J. A. 1984. *Teaching Strategies for Ethnic Studies.* 3d ed. Boston: Allyn and Bacon.

Berry, J. W. 1980. "Acculturation as Varieties of Adaptation." In *Acculturation Theory, Models, and Some New Findings,* ed. A. M. Padilla. Boulder, Colo.: Westview Press.

Carney, C. G., and K. B. Kahn. 1984. "Building Competencies for Effective Cross-Cultural Counseling: A Development View." *Counseling Psychologist* 12:111–19.

Cass, V. C. 1979. "Homosexual Identity Formation: A Theoretical Model." *Journal of Homosexuality* 4:219–35.

Cross, W. E. 1971. "The Negro-to-Black Conversion Experience." *Black World* 7:13–27.

Downing, N. E., and K. L. Roush. 1985. "From Passive Acceptance to Active Commitment: A Model of Feminist Identity Development of Women." *Counseling Psychologist* 13:695–705.

Fukuyama, M. A. and T. D. Sevig. 1999. *Integrating Spirituality into Multicultural Counseling.* Thousand Oaks, Calif.: Sage Publications.

Hardiman, R. 1982. "White Identity Development: A Process Oriented Model for Describing the Racial Consciousness of White Americans." Dissertation Abstracts International, 43:104A. University Microfilms No. 82–10330.

Hardiman, R., and B. W. Jackson. 1992. "Racial Identity Development: Understanding Racial Dynamics in College Classrooms and on Campus." *New Directions for Teaching and Learning* 52:21–37.

Helms, J. E. 1984. "Toward a Theoretical Explanation of the Effects of Race on Counseling: A Black and White Model." *Counseling Psychologist* 12:153–65.

———. 1990. *Black and White Racial Identity: Theory, Research, and Practice.* Westport, Conn.: Greenwood Press.

Jackson, B. W. 1975. "Black Identity Development." *Journal of Educational Diversity* 2:19–25.

Keefe, S. F., and A. M. Padilla. 1987. *Chicano Ethnicity.* Albuquerque, N. Mex.: University of New Mexico Press.

Lesbian-Gay Male Programs Office, University of Michigan, 1993. "Guided Fantasies: Exploring Issues of Homophobia and Heterosexism." In *Multicultural Teaching in the University,* ed. D. Schoem, L. Frankel, X. Zúñiga, and E. Lewis, 329–30. Westport, Conn.: Praeger.

McCarn, S. R., and R. E. Fassinger. 1996. "Revisioning Sexual Minority Identity Formation: A New Model of Lesbian Identity and Its Implications for Counseling and Research." *Counseling Psychologist* 24 no. 3:508–34.

Myers, L. J., S. L. Speight, P. S. Highlen, C. I. Cox, A. L. Reynolds, E. M. Adams, and C. P. Hanley. 1991. "Identity Development and Worldview: Toward an Optimal Conceptualization." *Journal of Counseling and Development* 70:54–63.

Phinney, J. S. 1992. "The Multigroup Ethnic Identity Measure: A New Scale for Use with Diverse Groups." *Journal of Adolescent Research* 7:156–71.

Ponterotto, J. G. 1988. "Racial Consciousness Development among White Counselor Trainees: A Stage Model." *Journal of Multicultural Counseling and Development* 16:146–56.

Reynolds, A. L., and R. L. Pope. 1991. "The Complexities of Diversity: Exploring Multiple Oppressions." *Journal of Counseling and Development* 70:174–80.

Rowe, W., S. K. Bennett, and D. R. Atkinson. 1994. "White Racial Identity Models: A Critique and Alternative Proposal." *Counseling Psychologist* 22:129–46.

Schoem, D., X. Zúñiga, and B. A. Nagda. 1993. "Exploring One's Group Background: The Fishbowl Exercise." In *Multicultural Teaching in the University,* ed. D. Schoem, L. Frankel, X. Zúñiga, and E. Lewis, 326–27. Westport, Conn.: Praeger.

Sevig, T. D., P. S. Highlen, and E. M. Adams. 2000. "Development and Validation of the Self-Identity Inventory SII: A Multicultural Identity Development Instrument." *Cultural Diversity and Ethnic Minority Psychology* 6, no. 2: 168–82.

Stone, W. O. 1984. "Multicultural Perspective of Career Development." In *Career Development Interventions,* ed. H. D. Bruck and R. C. Reardon. Springfield, Ill.: Charles C. Thomas.

Sue, D. W., and D. Sue. 1990. *Counseling the Culturally Different: Theory and Practice.* 2d ed. New York, N.Y.: John Wiley and Sons Inc.

Terry, R. 1977. *For Whites Only.* Grand Rapids, Mich.: William B. Eerdmans.

Thomas, C. 1971. *Boys No More.* Beverly Hills, Calif.: Glencoe Press.

Vontress, C. E. 1971. "Racial Differences: Impediments to Rapport." *Journal of Counseling Psychology* 18:7–13.

Zúñiga, X., and P. Myers. 1993. "Multiple Roles and Multiple Choice Exercise." In *Multicultural Teaching in the University,* ed. D. Schoem, L. Frankel, X. Zúñiga, and E. Lewis, 316–18. Westport, Conn.: Praeger.

Chapter 17

The Content/Process Balance in Intergroup Dialogue

Ruby L. Beale and David Schoem

The effort to achieve the appropriate balance between content and process in intergroup dialogue is one that theoreticians and practitioners have struggled with for many years. They are likely to continue to do so long into the future. Some, of course, believe they already have found the appropriate balance, favoring either a strong emphasis on content or a strong emphasis on process (*One America* 1998; *Promising Practices* 1997; Du Bois and Hutson 1997). Those who hold these fixed positions often are dismissive of their counterparts, and the two "camps" engage in verbal combat about which approach is better and why (Burbules 1993).

Our purpose in this chapter is to explore what contributes best to a successful intergroup dialogue experience. In doing so, we conclude that both process and content are of equal importance in facilitating effective dialogues. This is by no means a compromise position. Rather, by remaining focused on the vision and mission of intergroup dialogue and by strategically assessing what is needed and why, and what works and why it works well, we are persuaded that the most appropriate balance between content and process for intergroup dialogue is an equal balance (Stephan and Stephan 1996). This chapter, then, will explore the critical issue of identifying the appropriate balance between content and process and consider some useful strategies to achieve that desired end.

The Rationale for Equal Balance

Theory informs process. Process informs theory (Dukes 1996). The concept seems simple enough. The literature, theory, and empirical content about any particular intergroup dialogue topic help inform participants' thinking, ideas, information, and comments (Adams, Bell, and Griffin 1997; Schoem 1995; Sutton 1995; Lewis 1995). In turn, the interactive and engaging process of the dialogue group allows ideas, insights, and personal experiences (that are usually withheld) to be expressed and stimulates participants' interest in seeking more information and theoretical exploration and study (Dukes 1996).

A successful intergroup dialogue is one in which attention to the appropriate balance between content and process is achieved and monitored consistently. And while from session to session the balance may vary, the overall dialogue experience reflects a balance of equal emphasis between content and process.

The Benefits of Content

It provides information that goes beyond the scope of information known by participants in the dialogue (Aronson and Patnoe 1978).

It contextualizes the theoretical, empirical, and applied issues (Schoem et al. 1995).

It legitimizes the experience of participants as more than "just one person's experience" and worthy of research and analysis (Nagda, Zúñiga, and Sevig 1995).

It sheds broad and/or objective understanding about issues under discussion (Schoem and Stevenson 1990).

It offers a range of critical viewpoints about important ideas and information (Sfeir-Younis 1995).

It allows participants to read what others outside of the dialogue think, feel, and experience without having to deal face-to-face with the author and that person's pain, anger, or guilt (Schoem et al. 1995).

It allows readers to experience their own reaction to the issues under discussion without having to react or respond interactively or immediately to the author's experience and possible pain, anger, confusion, or guilt (Nagda, Zúñiga, and Sevig 1995).

It permits readers to have more personally honest responses (cognitively and affectively) because they are not having to "save face" or represent political viewpoints that might mask their own feelings and thoughts (Adams, Bell, and Griffin 1997; Schoem et al. 1995).

It provides readers with the opportunity for education of the mind (Aronson and Patnoe 1978).

The Benefits of Process

It allows participants to share their own real life experiences (or lack thereof), thereby bringing more personal awareness of that reality to the issues under discussion (Bosworth and Hamilton 1994).

It provides the group with the opportunity to hear and see multiple perspectives on feelings and issues raised in the readings, exercises, simulations, games, and films, thereby broadening the understanding of the issues as well as the dynamics of the group (Stephan and Stephan 1996).

It gives participants the opportunity to see personally how the emotional/affective component of issues (regardless of how expressed or not expressed externally) fuels the cognitive thoughts, paradigms, and behaviors/treatment of both issues and groups (Zúñiga and Nagda 1995).

It offers a framework to deal effectively with group dynamics, thereby making it more likely that the group process will work for and not against the growth of the group and the individual participants in the group (Dukes 1996).

It allows for the reasonable predictability as to where individuals and groups will be in relation to the intergroup experience when discussing a particular topic (Nagda, Zúñiga, and Sevig 1995).

It emphasizes the importance of having good skills in group process and facilitation so that the inevitable conflicts that arise, whether spoken or not, can be appropriately facilitated/managed for the growth and development of the group (Zúñiga and Chesler 1995).

It provides a legitimate opportunity for participants to discuss the importance of confidentiality and credible space to develop group trust and individual safety (not to be confused with comfort) (Schoem and Stevenson 1990).

It provides participants with the opportunity for education of the heart (Cox and Beale 1997; Schoem 1991).

The following example demonstrates the positive value of a balanced intersection of process and content. A dialogue group focused on men and women must be organized to develop trust so that all participants feel free to speak and share their ideas and experiences (Aronson and Patnoe 1978). Exercises and structured discussions are introduced to help elicit personal perspectives about particular topics. All of the participants' experiences with their own gender identity, including what they have been socialized to think about the roles of men and women, how their own thinking has been shaped, and the ways in which they have been treated or behaved based on their gender identity, bring a rich text of personal data about the subject matter. When this rich personal data set is offered into the dialogue context as a result of honest and open sharing by participants, it creates the vibrancy and dynamism that is unique to the intergroup dialogue process. However, when participants also are reading literature on the same topic, reviewing empirical studies on gender roles and socialization, analyzing data on studies of gender difference in school and the workplace, studying theory and viewing films adding perspective and nuance to the topic, and writing journals of their insights, then the value of the rich personal experiences is exponentially enhanced.

Problems Associated with an Imbalance of Content and Process

The effective balance and fusion of process and content are critical for awareness, understanding, and potentially long-term change of attitudes and behaviors of the participants. People participate in intergroup dialogue sessions for many reasons, but most come to dialogue sessions with either or both the emotional baggage of thoughts, feelings, and behaviors that they have experienced themselves and/or with incomplete, unexplored, and inaccurate information (Nagda, Zúñiga, and Sevig 1995). Getting caught up in the "chicken or egg" debate of process versus content does little to further productive discussion about the use of process and content. However, it also is detrimental to the achievement of desired outcomes of intergroup dialogue, which can lead to better understanding and willingness on the part of participants to engage in future opportunities for growth and learning in this area.

An overemphasis on process at the expense of content allows for the dialogue to be driven by misinformation, and for that misinformation to be reified as truth as it is repeated and reinforced through discussion (Schoem et al. 1995). It is a waste of everyone's time and worse for dialogue participants to use the dialogue session to discus topics that are based on falsehood. Further, a dialogue that is too heavily balanced on process gives disproportionate weight to the idiosyncratic experiences of individual participants. Clearly, the value of dialogue is to bring to the process the personal experiences of participants, but the absence of any contextualization in existing research and scholarship falsely exaggerates the generalizability of any single individual's experience (Schoem 1995). In addition, there is an increased possibility that participants will seek to transform the purpose of the intergroup dialogue into something more like a therapy group as the focus necessarily becomes personal and individualistic.

Liabilities of an Overemphasis on Process

See Schoem 1995; Guarasci, Cornwell, and associates 1997; Stephan and Stephan 1996.

The group focuses on issues that are idiosyncratic to participants in the group.

The group's understanding is limited to the experiences of the participants in the group.

The process is driven by certain strong personalities in the group.

More extroverted participants get heard and more introverted ones get silenced.

The dominant or the dominated group takes the process to a level that is not conducive to overall learning, growth, development, and progress of the group.

Participants believe that process is all about "feeling" and do not understand that there is content to process.

Participants use process as an excuse to avoid content and the social complexity of the issues.

Process becomes a mechanism for mere catharsis on issues that can be taken to the extremes and thus becomes counterproductive to the participants' and groups' learning and development.

Some participants mistakenly equate intergroup dialogue with a therapeutic support group, which is typically run by mental health professionals or paraprofessionals. Though the dialogue session(s) could have some personal therapeutic characteristics for individual participants, it is inappropriate for use as a therapy session.

Groups get stuck on "one" issue and try to resolve participants' or facilitators' reactions.

Equally problematic, though quite different, are the difficulties associated with an overemphasis on content at the expense of process. At one extreme is the use of the facilitator as lecturer or preacher, divesting wisdom through extended presentations to a passive audience of participants. Such passivity is the opposite of the desired engagement of participants in a dialogue. The overemphasis on content above process also can produce an intellectualization of the discussion, such that discussion of personal experience is dismissed and participants are able to hide honest and open feelings behind a presumed "higher" level of analysis. Again, discussion that is devoid of the personal, whether it is experience or values and viewpoints, does not approach the standard of intergroup dialogue. Further, the emphasis given to content at the expense of group process detracts from the opportunity to develop confidentiality and trusting relationships among the participants, so essential to producing the deeper and more honest and intense levels of discussion that are unique to the dialogue experience.

Liabilities of an Overemphasis on Content

See Adams, Bell, and Griffin 1997; Cox and Beale 1997; Zúñiga and Chesler 1995; Nagda, Zúñiga, and Sevig 1995.

It objectifies and distances the participants so far from life experience that they can dismiss, devalue, and discount the validity of individuals' experiences related to the issues brought forward for discussion.

It provides a crutch for the reader to believe that if it is in writing, then it is true and it is the *only* truth.

It simplifies the inherent social complexity of issues, and then it is used as an excuse to avoid process and complexity in the dialogue.

It provides an excuse for participants not to deal openly and honestly with the various dimensions of issues under discussion.

Discussion is limited by the selection of readings/topics to be discussed.

It suggests certain issues/topics as being the most important or primary issues in the discussion of difference by the selection or exclusion of what is assigned to be read in the text, article(s), or coursepack.

Participants can retreat to the readings when they feel that the process is too "hot" with conflict.

The publication source of the reading is interpreted as credible or not credible, valued or not valued.

Facilitator Background and Training

It is the skilled facilitator who holds the key to achieving the balance of content and process in any given intergroup dialogue. The facilitator should be knowledgeable about the content of the dialogue in addition to being well trained in group dynamics and facilitation skills (Sfeir-Younis 1995). Usually what comes into question is the issue of the facilitator's balance of expertise in both content and process. However, some researchers are confident that those with expertise either in the content area of the dialogue or in intergroup processes can be successful in leading an intergroup dialogue (Stephan and Stephan 1996; Chesler 1995).

Some argue that a good facilitator can manage a successful intergroup dialogue regardless of the topic. They believe that such a person will know how to develop trust, elicit discussion of personal experience and views, and be sensitive to maintaining a safe atmosphere. A skilled facilitator, however, must know what issues are particularly sensitive for each topic and what topics are better introduced at an early or later stage of the dialogue, depending on the group's developed level of trust. A good facilitator must also be able to know what issues to probe and when, and what issues to set aside for another time or leave tacit. A good facilitator needs to be able to discern when opinions are being put forward as fact, or when certain viewpoints are not being represented at all in the dialogue because of fear or ignorance. Only those facilitators who also have background in the dialogue topic will be able to successfully intervene, guide, and protect participants in these situations (Dukes 1996).

Others argue that a person expert only in the content area of a dialogue can serve as a good facilitator. They believe that such a person will be able to organize discussions in an appropriately sequential manner for greatest understanding and insight and will be most familiar with issues that are likely to be sensitive for participants. However, a good facilitator also must be able to build trusting relationships, to engage participants beyond theory and scholarship, and to evoke personal experience and perspectives. To do that in a manner that feels safe to participants requires significant skill in the process of intergroup dialogue. A facilitator also must be skilled in addressing and managing conflict, because conflicts do emerge in intergroup dialogues, and conflict avoidance is not desirable in such groups. In fact, appropriately utilizing conflict can help groups in having "breakthrough" experiences that lead to increased understanding and appreciation of the group's willingness to work through the tough issues and times (Zúñiga and Chesler 1995).

In terms of process, facilitators should have experience and training working with groups from backgrounds different from their own and with intergroup dialogues. The facilitators also should have experience reflecting personally upon intergroup issues, particularly issues of power between agent and target groups. Finally, the facilitators should have experience addressing conflict between individuals and between and within groups.

In terms of content, much like process, more is better. Facilitators should be well read in the topic area and, as a minimal standard, be able to identify fact from falsehood, be knowledgeable of pressing current and historical concerns, and be alert to sensitive and provocative issues. The facilitators should be familiar with resources available to guide self and participants for more information as needed and desired.

As is the case with intergroup dialogue itself, the focus on content serves as a springboard for continuing work and study in the topic area. The dialogue group should encourage more reading, more study, and even more course work in some cases. Theoretical and empirical learning ensures that there is a certain baseline of information for all participants. It assists in keeping the discussion focused and linked to understanding of social structures and social causation rather than allowing the dialogue to grow out of personal and idiosyncratic experience.

The areas of content and process in intergroup dialogue can be organized according to the following:

Content
   a. Personal learning (self-exploration)
   b. Experiential learning ("other"-exploration in action projects, community service)
   c. Theoretical and empirical learning (disciplinary and interdisciplinary understandings from readings, films, speakers, etc.)

Process
   a. Face-to-face interaction
   b. Interpersonal skills for community building and learning
   c. Engaging and managing conflict

The opportunity for achieving a good balance between content and process is readily apparent in both *a.* and *b.* above, in which personal learning is easily compatible with face-to-face interaction, and experiential learning fits neatly with community building and learning. Where the balance is more difficult to achieve is in *c.*, where the fit of theoretical and empirical learning with process is less obvious and the fit of engaging and managing conflict is less obvious with content.

Though the fit is less obvious between theoretical and empirical learning and engaging and managing conflict, it is a critical component. Since conflict is the interaction of interdependent parties who perceive incompatible goals and interference from the other party in achieving those goals, conflict areas will often come up around values, goals, perceived scarce resources, methods, preferences, and beliefs about facts. How might this play out in a dialogue session? When reading materials, viewing films, or listening to speakers, a person encounters facts and ideas. A person's values, preferences, and goals make up a worldview and fundamental assumptions about life and how things should be. In other words, people can form their own (sometimes) inaccurate theories. They, in turn, predispose a person to believe or not believe, accept or not accept the facts or ideas presented. Participants, thereby, may respond to this information in a variety of ways (interest-based vs. position-based strategies for win-lose vs. win-win strategies/solutions) that can bring positive or negative conflict to the dialogue. The conflict management skill of a dialogue facilitator should allow that person to know how to not merely tolerate but manage positive conflict when it allows participants to understand others and their points of view. Conflict can increase participants' involvement and allow them opportunity to change (their own theories) and grow (Zúñiga and Chesler 1995; Schoem 1995; Nagda, Zúñiga, and Sevig 1995). It is equally important to know when to intervene to resolve conflict that is negative and tears the group away from the group's goals, is polarizing, or involves personal attacks on the humanity or values of a person, group, or culture. Highly skilled facilitators who understand the benefits of effective conflict management provide the best chance for developing, maintaining, and improving relationships and can produce more understanding of issues and concerns in family, friends, community, and group. This is true whether one is talking about the dominant group or the dominated group.

Strategies for Achieving the Desired Balance between Content and Process

Readings, films, speakers, research, lectures, and presentations all serve as methods of presenting content that can be successfully linked to different group processes of learning, including writing, discussion, exercises, and dialogue.

Writing

Writing is a means of thinking, reflection and discovery. It provides enormous potential for individual and collaborative exploration and learning about self and theory.

Journals. Participants can keep personal, informal journals in which they record their personal reactions to new information, ideas, and analyses. These personal reflections allow participants to grow in their thinking between sessions and to bring new insights back to the next dialogue. Structured journals provide room for informal personal exploration, but they also give facilitators an opportunity to frame specific questions and topics for the participants to respond to in their writing. These questions typically link content learning with personal experience (Schoem and Stevenson 1990; Schoem et al. 1995).

Ethnic autobiographies and social identity group essays. The ethnic autobiography or social identity paper is a valuable tool for personal and collaborative exploration. Participants explore through writing their personal experience as a member of a social group, often as an exercise that takes place parallel to readings and discussions in the dialogue. The concurrent reading informs and stimulates participants' writing. As participants follow a writing outline for completing the assignment, they share their writing with fellow participants in the dialogue. Each participant thus learns not only from their own writing and exploration, but also from others as they read and offer feedback and questions to others in the dialogue (MacGregor 1995; Schoem 1991, 1995).

Multicultural organizational change papers. Another helpful writing assignment is the multicultural organizational change paper. As dialogue participants consider opportunities for taking their learning and discussions to a level of action and change, they will want to consider carefully how to be effective change agents. As participants watch films, read articles, or hear speakers discuss organizational change, they bring these ideas to their own considerations for change. The paper asks participants to do the following: (1) identify an organization, (2) chart its history in terms of multiculturalism, (3) define multiculturalism, (4) describe the organization as it would look were it multicultural, (5) offer concrete steps to move the organization from its current state toward a multicultural one, and then (6) indicate personal steps that the individual might actually attempt in order to change the organization. This writing project can be done individually or in groups, but it is very powerful to bring each of the papers before the entire dialogue group for analysis, feedback, and general discussion (Schoem 1997).

Exercises

Exercises provide participants with new and different ways of approaching concepts and ideas. Reading about class, race, power, and other social dynamics provides an extremely rich opportunity for learning. But many people find they uncover new and deeper levels of understanding about the same topic by using a range of approaches for learning. Safe, carefully structured exercises (though not always comfortable) can provide a path to new levels of insight and awareness about an issue that was previously not appreciated in its full complexity.

Exercises are a perfect complement to content-focused learning. They offer a chance to open doors to discussion about topics, personal and theoretical, that people find most difficult to discuss across groups or even to contemplate internally. They allow participants to bring nuanced insights and questions to empirical studies and analyses that might otherwise be overlooked or not openly discussed. They also, by necessity, bring dialogue participants together to discover new ideas and to share in learning through the experience of the various exercises. They can, at times, give participants the opportunity to walk in another's shoes without being judged. Specific and extensive suggestions for exercises have been presented elsewhere, and we urge readers to seek out those sources (Adams, Bell, and Griffin 1997; Cox and Beale 1997; Schoem et al. 1995).

In addition to exercises that can take place within the physical space of the dialogue group, there are other experiential learning opportunities that require participants to go out to different sites. Community service projects provide an outstanding opportunity for dialogue participants to experience firsthand content discussed in print and on film. Dialogue participants who work together on a project find they have a concrete experience upon which to build their own intergroup understandings, challenge preconceived notions, and explore new insights together. Field trips to museums, libraries, neighborhoods, and other sites also provide experiences that integrate new content learning in varied modes and forms that lead to better-informed and greatly enhanced dialogue.

Discussion

The intergroup dialogue can take many forms for discussion purposes. And discussing informed content is the most common approach for linking content and process. Most often a dialogue is physically arranged as a circle of people sitting on chairs facing one another. Though that may be the most frequent arrangement and the one to which the group ultimately returns time and again, there are many other approaches to consider along the way.

While the large-group circle discussion is an effective arrangement for many, some participants will always feel most comfortable engaging their peers in smaller groups of three or four. Certainly it's easy enough to arrange subgroups in the dialogue by randomly counting off, by assigning people to small groups, or by allowing participants to self-select their small groups. In small groups it is much easier to establish trust, enter the discussion, and build relationships, and there are fewer people who have to share the available airtime.

Beyond small groups, one-on-one conversations also are highly effective ways of engaging participants about both content and personal sharing. These conversations can be more highly structured, as in the case of formal interviewing of other participants. They also can be made very informal by matching people together randomly or systematically. A third approach is the use of rotating concentric circles in which participants are briefly matched with a wide range of peers but always on a one-to-one basis.

Finally, the large group can be organized into two circles, one inside the other, to form a fishbowl effect. The use of the fishbowl as a highly effective mechanism for dialogue has been described elsewhere (Schoem, Zúñiga, and Nagda 1995), but it also can be used to probe content. One of the unique features of the fishbowl is that it allows participants in the inside circle to feel as if they are talking in a small group, even while they are fully aware that a larger group of participants practicing good listening skills encircles them. As such, the fishbowl arrangement can recreate the rich intellectual vitality of a small-group discussion while opening the discussion for the entire group's edification.

REFERENCES

Adams, Maurianne, Lee Bell, and Pat Griffin. 1997. *Teaching for Diversity and Social Justice: A Sourcebook.* New York: Routledge.

Aronson, Elliot, and Shelly Patnoe. 1978. *The Jigsaw Classroom: Building Cooperation in the Classroom.* New York: Longman.

Bosworth, Chris, and Sharon Hamilton. 1994. *Collaborative Learning: Underlying Processes and Effective Techniques.* San Francisco: Jossey-Bass.

Burbules, Nicholas. 1993. *Dialogue for Teaching: Theory and Practice.* New York: Teachers College Press.

Chesler, Mark. 1995. "Racetalk: Thinking and Talking about Racism." *Diversity Factor* 3, no. 3: 37–45.

Cohen, Elizabeth. 1994. *Designing Groupwork: Strategies for the Heterogeneous Classroom.* 2d ed. New York: Teachers College Press.

Cox, Taylor, and Ruby L. Beale. 1997. *Developing Competency to Manage Diversity: Reading, Cases, and Activities.* San Francisco: Berrett-Koehler.

Du Bois, Paul Martin, and Jonathan Hutson. 1997. *Bridging the Racial Divide: A Report on Interracial Dialogue in America.* Brattleboro, Vt.: Center for Living Democracy.

Duke, James T. 1978. *Conflict and Power in Social Life.* Provo, Utah: Brigham Young University Press.

Dukes, Franklin E. 1996. *Resolving Public Conflict: Transforming Community and Governance.* New York: Manchester University Press.

Guarasci, Richard, Grant Cornwell, and associates, eds. 1997. *Democratic Education in an Age of Difference: Redefining Citizenship in Higher Education.* San Francisco: Jossey-Bass.

Lewis, Edith A. 1995. "Continuing the Legacy: On the Importance of Praxis in the Education of Social Work Students and Teachers." In *Multicultural Teaching in the University,* ed. David Schoem, Linda Frankel, Ximena Zúñiga, and Edith A. Lewis. Westport, Conn.: Praeger.

MacGregor, Jean. 1995. "The Ethnic Autobiography." *Washington Center Newsletter* (Washington Center for Improving Undergraduate Education), spring, 17.

Nagda, Biren (Ratnesh) A., Ximena Zúñiga, and Todd Sevig. 1995. "Bridging Differences through Peer Facilitated Intergroup Dialogues." In *Peer Programs on a*

College Campus: Theory, Training, and the Voices of the Peers, ed. Sherry Hatcher. San Diego: New Resources.

One America in the Twenty-first Century: The President's Initiative on Race— One America Dialogue Guide. 1998. Washington, D.C.: The White House.

Promising Practices—The President's Initiative on Race. Novermber 6, 1997. http://www.whitehouse.gov/Initiatives/OneAmerica/One America_Links.html.

Schoem, David. 1995. "Teaching about Ethnic Identity and Intergroup Relations." In *Multicultural Teaching in the University,* ed. David Schoem, Linda Frankel, Ximena Zúñiga, and Edith A. Lewis. Westport, Conn.: Praeger.

———. 1997. "Intergroup Relations, Conflict, and Community." In *Democratic Education in an Age of Difference: Redefining Citizenship in Higher Education,* ed. Richard Guarasci, Grant Cornwell, and associates. San Francisco: Jossey-Bass.

———, ed. 1991. *Inside Separate Worlds: Life Stories of Young Blacks, Jews, and Latinos.* Ann Arbor: University of Michigan Press.

Schoem, David, Linda Frankel, Ximena Zúñiga, and Edith A. Lewis, eds. 1995. *Multicultural Teaching in the University.* Westport, Conn.: Praeger.

Schoem, David, and Marshall Stevenson. 1990. "Teaching Ethnic Identity and Intergroup Relations: The Case of Blacks and Jews." *Teachers College Record* 91, no. 4: 579–94.

Schoem, David, Ximena Zúñiga, and Biren (Ratnesh) A. Nagda. 1995. "Exploring One's Background: The Fishbowl Exercise." In *Multicultural Teaching in the University,* ed. David Schoem, Linda Frankel, Ximena Zúñiga, and Edith A. Lewis. Westport, Conn.: Praeger.

Sfeir-Younis, Luis. 1995. "Reflections on the Teaching of Multicultural Courses." In *Multicultural Teaching in the University,* ed. David Schoem, Linda Frankel, Ximena Zúñiga, and Edith A. Lewis. Westport, Conn.: Praeger.

Stephan, Walter, and Cookie White Stephan. 1996. *Intergroup Relations.* Boulder, Colo.: Westview Press.

Sutton, Sharon. 1995. "Seeing the Whole of the Moon." In *Multicultural Teaching in the University,* ed. David Schoem, Linda Frankel, Ximena Zúñiga, and Edith A. Lewis. Westport, Conn.: Praeger.

Zúñiga, Ximena, and Mark Chesler. 1995. "Teaching with and about Conflict in the Classroom." In *Multicultural Teaching in the University,* ed. David Schoem, Linda Frankel, Ximena Zúñiga, and Edith A. Lewis. Westport, Conn.: Praeger.

Zúñiga, Ximena, and Biren (Ratnesh) A. Nagda. 1995. "Dialogue Groups: An Innovative Approach to Multicultural Learning." In *Multicultural Teaching in the University,* ed. David Schoem, Linda Frankel, Ximena Zúñiga, and Edith A. Lewis. Westport, Conn.: Praeger.

Chapter 18

A Celebration of Power

Stephen H. Sumida and Patricia Gurin

We come to this discussion of celebration and power from having jointly taught for several years a course at the University of Michigan called Race, Racism, and Ethnicity. This course has a special history. It was developed to be one of the courses that would meet a graduation policy instituted in 1992 by the College of Literature, Science and the Arts requiring students to take at least one course during the four years of college that would expose them to the meaning(s) of race, racism, and ethnicity. It is known as the R&E (race and ethnicity) requirement.

Intergroup dialogue was critical to achieving the goals of the course. All students participated in small-group discussions that comprised, as much as possible, equal numbers of students from different ethnic/racial groups. In these discussions, the students talked about readings, lectures, and films, took part in dialogue exercises, and used their own experiences to explore commonalities and differences among and between racial and ethnic groups in the United States. We each led a discussion group, as did eight graduate student assistants who formed our interdisciplinary, multicultural, and egalitarian staff.

We also have a unique history as a collaborating team. When Pat heard that Steve was joining the Michigan faculty, Pat called him at Washington State University to see if he would agree to teach this new Race, Racism, and Ethnicity course with her. We had never met. Steve did not yet know the intellectual scene at Michigan. He did not know the faculty who had pressed for the R&E requirement, or what role this course would have in the multicultural curricular reforms at Michigan. Still, we could both tell from the phone conversation that we would be able to forge an interdisciplinary collaboration that would work.

Our differences enriched our collaboration from that moment to this. We have different presentational styles, as is evident in these companion pieces. We brought obvious demographic differences to the classroom. Steve is an Asian American man, and Pat is a European American woman. Steve lived in his precollege years in Hawai'i, and Pat grew up in the Midwest. Steve is a humanities professor with a specialty in Asian American literature, and Pat is a social science professor with a specialty in social psychology. These different life experiences, categorical memberships, and disciplinary knowledge produced deep discussions and eventually a unified, interdisciplinary course of which we were both proud.

Subsequent to teaching the course, we volunteered to facilitate a discussion of relations between "celebration" and "power" for the conference "Intergroup Dialogue on the College Campus," held at the University of Michigan in 1997. This article reflects our continuing discussion and thoughts about issues of celebration and power, and it reflects our different yet highly collaborative approaches and styles. Steve Sumida's thoughts in essay form, "Celebration and Power," are presented first, followed by Pat Gurin's essay, "Power and the Idea of Structure."

Celebration and Power

Offering a point of departure, we presented these two items as opposites. But of course celebration and power are not necessarily opposites. Acts of celebration can be empowering and powerful. By "celebration" we had in mind events: events, for example, that people present to showcase their cultures, to honor their members publicly, to observe their holidays and hold their festivals, and to do so in ways that materially demonstrate their joy, belief, and commitment to their cause, community, history, and culture. Having stated this, we note already that words such as *commitment, cause,* and *community* connote politics and issues of power. By *power* we had in mind a concept that serves as a basis for a way of analyzing relations among groups in regard to domination and subordination, inequalities among the groups, as Pat Gurin explains in her companion essay. While at first glance relations between celebration and power seemed to us to be fairly simple, a binary on which to base a productive discussion in a workshop, to examine the matter even in a rather informal essay such as this one quickly leads to complications.

So close are relations between celebration and power that celebration is often associated with nationhood. Celebration of the Fourth of July is an obvious example, one that usually coincides with a dominant idea or narrative, a history, of the nation: the Fourth of July is construed as a distinctly "American" celebration of the nation, "America." But this uncontested sense of celebration too is not always so. During the era of protests against the American war in Vietnam, for instance, celebration and nation did not

naturally coincide in all Americans' hearts and minds. The symbolism of
the Fourth and the state of the nation—the links between the celebration,
the ideals it perhaps once stood for and celebrated, and the nation—were
questioned and contested in massive upheaval. Celebration, however, is
often associated with cultures considered "ethnic" and "minority," or
"subordinate," within the nation. Kwanzaa is an outstanding example of a
celebration that African Americans developed in the last quarter of the
twentieth century to honor and teach the community's and culture's
important values, in other words, to empower. Kwanzaa also teaches people of these times that celebrations are historical constructions, and importantly so: they are made by people to serve purposes of the people.

In the following comments, I try to assume and imply two points especially, among others, that tie my discussion to concepts and practices of
intergroup dialogue. First, as should be evident in my remarks above, in
writing about celebration and power I am writing about activities that
manifest, again as Pat argues, structural relations of and among groups of
people. My work on our interdisciplinary team was to include culture and
cultural expressions and productions into our course, Race, Racism, and
Ethnicity. We put it this way: while Pat led the development of analyses of
power and domination in our course, I was in charge of themes of resistance and cultural agency and how people in ostensibly subordinate cultures see themselves as human subjects, not simply victims and objects.
Recruiting me for the course, Pat recognized that there was a kind of
imbalance inherent in the conduct of social science: in analyzing power in
terms of domination and subordination, not only is it impossible by
definition and theory for the subordinate group to be dominant (in this
case, to be "racist"), but it also seems impossible for the subordinate to
have agency. This is an issue debated in literary and cultural studies, sometimes with such agonizing earnestness that it makes Hamlets out of all the
debaters. But cutting through to her purpose, Pat told me she wanted
someone to join her who could select and present "voices" in the course,
voices of writers and artists who identify with minority cultural groups
and in some measure demonstrate thereby the ability and power to have a
voice. The selection of literary and other "voices" was itself dialogical, for
the readings included ones standing in political and philosophical conflict
and controversy with others, as discussion in class and in writing made
evident to students, many of whom were encountering the authors for the
first time.

This aspect of our course, too, brought ideologies of individualism into question, as does the very term *intergroup dialogue.* Like a myth, culture is the creation and possession of a group of people, not just a single artist.

Second, my following narratives have to do with the ongoing construction of culture as it is historically and socially constructed, ever changing and dynamic—if, that is, it is "alive." Making the constructedness of culture apparent is directly related to what Pat ascribes to a social scientific inquiry into making society transparent to reveal its structures. The terminologies of "construction" and "structure" in this case are both metaphorically and practically related across our disciplines. Further, this way of conceptualizing culture not as things preserved but as processes of change frees people attempting intergroup dialogue from being frozen in postures of cultural determinism. Our arguing between determinism and constructionism, I should note, emphatically launched the course that Pat and I offered, when our colleague, the biologist John Vandermeer, would graphically demonstrate to the class how, according to the research of Richard Lewontin and others on mitochondrial DNA, there is no meaningful link between "race" and genetics. "Race" is a social construction and is extremely powerful for being one. It is not a genetic determinant, but it is also extremely powerful for being thought one.

The more "alien" a group is considered, the more static, preserved, culturally determined, and "objectified" the culture is usually thought to be. Aside from indigenous cultures of nations within the American nation— and the irony of indigenous alienation is immense—one of the strongest prejudices concerning alien nationality within the borders of the nation has historically and today been attached to Asian Americans. Celebrations of Asian American cultures are easily mistaken for celebrations of Asian nationhood rather than of American heterogeneity.

By the later 1990s, the Indian American Students' Association (IASA) became one of the strongest among student groups at large on the University of Michigan campus. Interestingly, IASA wielded political clout in student government as well as produced an annual cultural show, formerly called "Diwali" but later titled so as not to mask South Asian diversity with such a specifically Hindi name of a celebration. The cultural show packed the largest performance halls of the University of Michigan. The IASA presentation of the annual cultural night is obviously and immensely celebratory. Grandmothers and grandparents sit proudly, and perhaps in disbelief at the popularity of the event, alongside their children, the parents of the dancers, singers, stagehands, directors, musicians, and costumers. Little children are everywhere. The vast, diverse audience includes members of the general university community, teachers, friends, roommates, and so many others with some special interest and pleasure in the night's performances. In the fall of 1998, in Hill Auditorium where one night Yo-Yo Ma plays and another night IASA performs en masse, an ethereal voice rises from the stage, and dwarfing the singer is the live image of him projected on a huge screen. It is Amit Vaidya singing "Eh Ajnabi" ("Hey Stranger") from a film romance popular at the very same time, or only slightly earlier, in India and in all the places on the earth that the diaspora has taken families such as Amit's. Peering at the printed program in the dim light, I realize with a shock that it is he: Amit was a brilliant student in our course on Race, Racism, and Ethnicity the previous year. I had no idea he sings like a god. And leading the dancers animating the stage is Meera Eknath Deo, a law student, a graduate of Berkeley who was determined when she began her law studies at Michigan to be as involved in the community, both in celebration and in issues of social justice and power, as her time could allow.

The celebration in this case intensifies considerations of power. IASA and the other ethnically based student groups assert themselves through their programming; they demonstrate that they deserve recognition in United States society. They have to compete for funding to mount their events and carry out their purposes. They are part of the political structure of the campus and, in addition, have to struggle sometimes with the prejudice that they, being Asian, are not American, not entitled, and are alien to the very structures of power to which they are subject. The work of the associations in the 1990s was largely concerned with dis-alienating Asian American student groups, individuals, and the very concept of Asian Americanness. The South Asian American cultural night makes a powerful assertion about how the diverse grouping nowadays called South Asian American is integral to the United States.

Complicating the students' project, however, is a need to make a simultaneous and equally strong assertion that they and the cultures they are performing are related to postcolonial countries of South Asia that they are not simply acknowledging with their performances but are in some sense showing support for or the earned right to say something about. This right is earned by the students' great efforts to continue learning the songs, the dances, the foods, the literature, the politics, the narratives in such media as film, and the histories of the nations their parents, their grandparents, and, in some cases, they themselves came from. The celebration may intensify thoughts and feelings about relations between the person and the society, and two societies at that. "Eh Ajnabi," "Hey

Stranger," when performed by students in the United States carries themes and nuances meaningful to these performers, but not directly experienced by most of its audience in India, because the song is about the experience of being a person from India in America.

I observed the students. I saw the performers and producers of the cultural night as cultural agents: they make history, and they make culture. For a celebration to have power in the experience of one who is observing it, the observer too should have some idea, some basis for discerning, that the participants are cultural makers in their own right and not simply replicators.

Someone once insistently told me not to take culture and celebration for granted, as givens enforced by repetition. I first realized how deeply the celebration of the new year, O-Shogatsu, had rooted my life's rhythms when I experienced my first New Year's away from Hawai'i. I spent the holidays with a roommate and his family, in Brooklyn. On New Year's Day my stomach began speaking to me, and I understood that I missed something so natural to me that I could not immediately identify it. I realized as the day grew old that I wanted my *ozoni,* on New Year's Day: a soup that my mother happened to make with clam broth and other stocks, fresh vegetables such as *shungiku* (chrysanthemum leaves), *mizuna,* and decoratively cut daikon and carrot slices. In each bowl were a few of the clams and the glob of toasted *mochi,* a ball made from sticky rice pounded and formed into smooth cakes, that makes *ozoni* what it is—no matter that every region of Japan, indeed every family, seems to consider its own recipe, all of them different from one another, the authentic one. I had never realized until that New Year's Day in Brooklyn that I even liked *ozoni,* its taste so distinctive yet at the same time so bland, one serving of the soup to be eaten on that one day once a year for the mere sake of custom. Celebration in this sense is warmly personal while necessarily connected with greater contexts of culture and community; culture in this instance is as if trained into the human body itself. When I missed it that day, I realized that I had had an active relationship with that *mochi* soup all along; it was not just something that I passively received.

Partly because of the depth to which we experience our culture, it seems that the practice of culture too is beyond or outside of history and our own making. But over the years, my enthusiasm for holding our Shogatsu party with friends such as Pat, David Schoem, and their families has been sustained by what we learn along the way about the changes we take part in contributing to the cultural event. When my grandparents left Japan in the early 1900s, sugar was not plentiful there. They settled in

Hawai'i, where sugar was abundant. Shogatsu foods grew sweeter in Hawai'i than they were in Japan. Not found in the seas of Hawai'i, the customary red fish called *tai,* for celebration, congratulations, and good luck, in the Japanese observance of Shogatsu had to be replaced in America by varieties of locally available red fish. Meanwhile the poetry the immigrants wrote had to be finely sensitive to the local, not Japanese, environment: haiku, after all, is about the immediate perception of the natural world, and haiku of Hawai'i and North America meant the birth of new words to mark seasons never thus seen in the poetry of Japan. The same goes for how the immigrants adapted their celebration as well as poetry to conditions in places such as Seattle, San Francisco, Los Angeles, and, more challenging than these sites of some commerce with Japan, rural places such as the Yakima Valley of Washington and the Imperial Valley of California. The customary red fish was perhaps replaced by a roast of beef on some of the Shogatsu tables in farmhouses.

When students of usual college age engage in dialogue about their cultures, and when among them celebrations are talked about, in most instances they would be as I was that first time in Brooklyn, just beginning to ask about their own cultural customs. To celebrate Shogatsu as we do in the United States is most obviously not the same as in Japan because in the United States we observe the day with some awareness of cultural difference from what is predominantly "ordinary" or "normative" on New Year's Day in the United States. This is even so in Hawai'i, where the fact that peoples are of different ethnicities from one another cannot be ignored. Similarly, in intergroup dialogue difference raises one's self-consciousness about culture and its expression or embodiment in celebration. Debates about whose celebration is "authentic" may be entertaining and useful to the discovery of how individuals feel about and are invested in culture and custom. To go further by learning, however, how people contribute to the perpetuation, that is, the change and adaptation, of a celebration is to learn about powers of cultural agency.

Power and the Idea of Structure

The social structure of the teaching staff reflected the importance that we put on the idea of structure. We wanted to help students grasp that social life is more than the relationships of different *individuals*. Individuals are members of social categories that are ranked in our society's stratification system. These categories have *structured*—persisting and bounded patterns of—relationships. We used the concept of *power*, defined as the capacity of a category to control material resources (economic power), the decision-making apparatus (political power), and values (cultural power), as the major structural feature of category relationships. Power makes it possible for a category to create and perpetuate a dominant/subordinate relationship with another category.

Using the theoretical writing of Apfelbaum and Lubek (1979) and of Memmi (1968), we laid out mechanisms that a high power category typically employs to establish domination and subordination. The first step in creating a domination/subordination relationship is grouping—categorizing individuals on the basis of some feature that differs across individuals. But not all differences become involved in domination/subordination. The point of the Jane Elliot blue-eye/brown-eye experiment, which our students watched in video, is to show that almost any difference, such as eye color, can become a significant difference. The critical question is what differences dominant groups make significant in distinguishing themselves from other groups. The next step is evaluating, marking, or stigmatizing the differences. Closely related is the step of exaggerating the differences, a process that social psychologists have documented as a common result of categorization. Personalizing and generalizing also tend to follow so that members of derogated categories are led to believe that they are personally responsible for their devalued images, and that the negative qualities attributed to them characterize the whole category. These multiple processes that follow from categorization result in group stereotypes. In this part of the course, students read Adrian Piper's essay "Ways of Averting One's Gaze" (1988), in which she presents two critiques of her work that stigmatize her personally, one as neurotic, the other as stupid and malevolent. Piper ties the tendency of critics to personalize their criticism to a writer's structural marginality, in her case to her gender and racial marginality. They also read excerpts from Said on *Orientalism* (1978), a work that richly details how the Arab has become a sign of devalued human qualities. The final step of grouping is exclusion. The dominant group segregates itself from the devalued, subordinate group. The difference that served initially as the basis of mere categorization becomes the basis of stigmatization, is attributed to an entire category, and serves as a rationale for exclusion.

Dialogue in the discussion groups brought these mechanisms alive for the students. One in particular stands out from my own discussion group as especially effective. I divided the group into ethnic/racial groups, based on the identities that the students chose. Each of the identity groups was asked to list characteristics that they felt the wider society used to distinguish them from another group, and then to carry out four additional activities:

1. To evaluate how positive or negative each characteristic was
2. To describe how the characteristics have been used as bases for exclusion
3. To estimate the prevalence of each of the characteristics in another group of their choosing
4. To suggest a story, poem, essay, novel, or play that reflected voices within their groups that have resisted these characterizations, constructed new images, created culture, and celebrated the group and the human spirit

The work of the small groups was then presented to the whole discussion section to process how the mechanisms of domination had actually operated in the group experiences of students in the class. The exercise also connected the social science analysis of domination to the cultural analysis of literature—a constant thread in the course. For students who generally imagine that everyone is "just an individual," this intergroup dialogue dramatically illustrated both the existence of power and the operation of processes of domination and subordination that too often are hidden from perception in everyday experience.

Racism: A Troubling Concept

Although such exercises helped make the dynamics of power more transparent, we nonetheless encountered strong student resistance to the idea that racism is a domination mechanism, and thus should be used in reference to dominant groups, not to subordinate groups. The students understood Memmi's (1968) definition of racism: the generalized and final assigning of values to real or imaginary differences to the accuser's benefit and at the victim's expense in order to justify the former's own privileges. In the abstract they could see that this definition included all of the mechanisms of domination that they had already studied. They even grasped that the capacity to use these mechanisms came with economic, political, and cultural power. But they resisted the logical conclusion—that only racially dominant groups could be racist. We consistently provided other terms that could be ascribed to members of subordinate groups. They could be bigoted. They could be prejudiced. They could discriminate. But using the theoretical model of power and domination in the class, they could not be racist.

Why was this idea—that racism is a form of domination and is inherently connected to power—so difficult for our students? I believe that the idea of structured social relationships, and certainly the idea of power as a determiner of group outcomes, conflicts with the dominant ideology in the United States. Huber and Form (1973) describe the dominant ideology as involving the following beliefs: opportunities to get ahead are available to all; the position of individuals in the stratification system is determined by their personal efforts, traits, and abilities; therefore, inequality across individuals and groups is explained by individual or group differences in personality qualities, and not by the power of a group(s) over others.

Survey research confirms that Americans generally hold individuals rather than structural arrangements, such as power, responsible for inequality (Davis and Smith 1994; Kluegel and Bobo 1993). College education usually decreases the tendency to think individualistically about the causes of both racial and economic disparities (Kluegel and Smith 1986). It has much less consistent effects, however, on structural thinking. Kluegel and Smith found that the more educated actually offer fewer structural causes for both poverty and wealth than do less educated adults. Moreover, Kluegel and Bobo (1993) report that college education has little to no effect on what they call "hard" structural thinking about racial disparities—that is, attributing causes of those disparities to contemporary racism rather than only to the historical residue of slavery, and to political, social, and economic institutions rather than only to socialized attitudes of individuals.

We were not surprised, therefore, that our students had trouble grasping how power structures relationships between groups and that the dominating process (racism in the case of racial, ethnic groups) emanates from the group with greater power. Reading and listening to lectures were not sufficient for them to truly get the idea of structure. They needed to confront it in their own lives and through dialogue activities.

Learning about Structure in the Dialogue Process

How did we use the group discussions and dialogue process to foster the needed direct experience with social structure?

The very composition of dialogue groups—equal numbers of the members of different racial/ethnic groups—produces a class structure that fosters learning about social structure. Equality in group size is one way to achieve equality in group status, which was noted by Gordon Allport in the classic work *The Nature of Prejudice* (1954) as a critical condition for assuring positive outcomes from intergroup contact. Exercises that reveal the operation of social structure are the most effective teaching tools, however.

One that proved to be a compelling tool for teaching social structure is the "Line Exercise." Students were asked to stand together on one side of an imaginary line. I then asked them to cross that line if they belong in particular categories: "Cross the line if you are a man—are a member of a racial/ethnic minority—have traveled outside of the United States—are working to fund part of your college education—have a visible or invisible physical disability—grew up in the suburbs—grew up in a single-parent home—have witnessed racial insult to someone else and did nothing about it—have told a racial/ethnic joke—have had a close friend or relative die—have worried about getting into graduate school." (I used different phrases almost every time I taught the course.) This exercise taught two important lessons. First, students had to *see* categories in operation. They could not miss the fact that the class was divided in various ways by categorical memberships. They "got" *between group* differences in a visible way. Second, they could also *see* that these categories did not always overlap, and that the same students were not always on different sides of the line. They "got" *within group* differences in an equally visible way.

The last time I used this exercise, the first student to speak during discussion was an African American woman who grew up in a low-income family in Detroit. She spoke movingly: "I always knew that being African American meant having a whole different life experience. In some ways, this exercise confirmed that. I was often on one side of the line with other African Americans, like not traveling outside of the United States—at least not further than Canada which is right next door after all. But even that wasn't total—you, Jason, obviously grew up very differently from me. I also learned that I have a lot in common with the rest of you, much more than I usually think is true." A European-American man spoke next: "I dreaded this exercise. I thought it would be just one more time when my privileged status as a white man would make me feel put down. I *do* have a privileged position. I know it and it showed up here, too. It showed me how groups work—that I'm not just an individual, good ol' Alex. But it also showed me that this group thing is complex—that I share some experiences with women, some with African Americans. That's good to see." As a social scientist, I like to think of this exercise as a visible display of analysis of variance, the statistical technique that produces the probability that two groups (or more groups) are genuinely different by simultaneously taking into account *differences between groups and differences within groups.*

We also used a writing assignment to teach social structure. Students were required to do a structural analysis of their families of origin. We provided them census distributions that showed family incomes, occupational statuses, levels of education, and marital statuses for men and women of various ethnic/racial categories. The student was asked to interview his/her mother and father to obtain information about the family on these structural dimensions, and then to position his/her family within his/her ethnic/racial category and in comparison with some category. We asked the students of color to compare their families to European-Americans, and asked European-American students to compare their families to any other racial/ethnic category of their choosing. The most profound learning from this exercise was how privileged nearly all of the students were relative to national distributions for their own ethnic/racial categories. Of course, the second learning was the comparative one. However privileged most of the students of color were relative to their own racial/ethnic categories, their families generally held different structural positions than those held by the white national population. Obviously, the reverse was also learned by the white students. We asked students to share their papers, without names, so that everyone could learn something about the structural backgrounds of their classmates.

Education and "Hard" Structural Thinking

Colleagues and I have carried out evaluations of dialogue groups as part of the Intergroup Relations, Conflict, and Community program. They show that intergroup relations courses that cover structural sources of racial/ethnic inequalities can increase structural thinking among students (Lopez, Gurin, and Nagda 1998). We studied a course that first-year students take in this program. It included lectures, readings, discussions, and a ten-week intergroup dialogue. In one study of this course, students who took it were compared to a matched sample (matched on gender, race/ethnicity, in-/out-state residency, and Michigan residence hall) who did not take the course. Both groups were measured at the beginning and end of the semester. At the end of the semester, the participants offered a more structural analysis of racial and ethnic inequality. It is important to note this difference in structural thinking was valid even when we controlled statistically for any differences in thinking that the two groups exhibited at the beginning of the semester. (Those beginning differences were small in any case.) The participants were also more likely than the matched sam-

ple to offer a structural analysis of an intergroup conflict situation involving issues of sexual orientation. In the second study, we assessed the
impact of the course on structural thinking by comparing students who
took it at the beginning and end of the course. We found a significant
change in structural thinking about racial and ethnic inequality and also
for poverty. The students also became more structural in their causal
analysis of an intergroup conflict situation that involved ethnic issues
about language usage. A follow-up study of these students four years later
as seniors generally supported these findings. It showed that even long
after the students had taken the course there was evidence that the course
had affected the degree to which students could provide structural analyses of various intergroup disparities and conflicts.

These courses followed the same format as the Race, Racism, and Ethnicity course. They used many of the same dialogue exercises that I used
in the course with Steve Sumida. The goals of the courses were much the
same, as was the pedagogy to achieve them. The research shows that it *is*
possible to help students perceive and understand how social structure
shapes the fortunes of individuals as members of social categories in the
United States.

Power and Celebration

Steve Sumida tells many stories of celebration—how power structures the
life experiences of groups in America and how celebration of traditions
and creations of new ones empower members of racial and ethnic groups.
Some of these stories come from our class. Some come from his own life.

I brought to our joint teaching a different perspective—a social science
perspective on power and its relationship to domination and subordination. I haven't told the stories of the great impact that the literature—
poems, essays, short stories—had on our students. I have focused on dialogue exercises that directly taught about social structure. These exercises,
however, were taking place in the same discussion groups in which students sometimes read the poems that were assigned or acted out parts
from stories that were assigned. There is no question that the combination
of social science materials and materials from literature had enormous
impact on the students—just as Steve and I had hoped in forging our interdisciplinary collaboration. It is a strong collaboration that will continue,
despite separation now in different universities and the inevitable differences that take place in two people's life trajectories as I am about to retire
and Steve assumes even more academic responsibilities.

I end with my own celebration—not O-Shogatsu, which I have shared with Steve many times—but the celebrations that have taken place in my home as colleagues who have mounted multicultural reforms at Michigan and taught diversity courses in and across many disciplines come together to eat, talk, and laugh. The most recent of these took place in May 2000, when forty-nine colleagues, many of them new to Michigan, gathered for a faculty/graduate student seminar to take stock of what has been accomplished since the institution of the R&E requirement in 1992. For four days, colleagues shared literatures, research, films, discussion strategies, and exercises that have worked in engaging undergraduate students. We shared experiences with institutional barriers and richly rewarded opportunities as well. With so many new faculty, and so many graduate students ready to join the professoriate, the teaching about race, ethnicity, and racism will continue far into the future. There was much to celebrate. And so we did. Seminar participants, significant others, and children, including my two multiracial grandchildren, came together at my husband's and my home for yet another community event—to celebrate the power of a group of faculty that has had great impact at Michigan. It makes me proud.

REFERENCES

Allport, G. 1954. *The Nature of Prejudice.* Reading, Mass.: Addison-Wesley.

Apfelbaum, E., and I. Lubek. 1979. "Relations of Domination and Movements for Liberation: An Analysis of Power between Groups." In *The Social Psychology of Intergroup Relations,* ed. William G. Austin and Stephen Worchel. Monterey, Calif.: Brooks/Cole.

Davis, J. A., and T. W. Smith. 1994. General Social Surveys, 1972–1974. Database. Produced by National Opinion Research Center, Chicago. Distributed by Inter-university Consortium for Political and Social Research, Ann Arbor, Mich.

Huber, J., and W. Form. 1973. *Income and Ideology.* New York: Free Press.

Kluegel, J. R., and L. Bobo. 1993. "Dimensions of Whites' Beliefs about the Black-White Socio-economic Status, 1977–1989." *American Sociological Review* 55:512–25.

Kluegel, J. R., and E. R. Smith. 1986. *Beliefs about Inequality: Americans' Views of What Is and What Ought to Be.* Hawthorne, N.Y.: De Gruyter.

Lopez, G., P. Gurin, and B. A. Nagda. 1998. "Education and Understanding Structural Causes for Group Inequalities." *Political Psychology* 19:305–29.

Memmi, A. 1968. *Dominated Man.* Boston: Beacon Press.

Piper, A. 1988. "Ways of Averting One's Gaze." In *Adrian Piper,* ed. Michael Jones. Akron, Ohio: University of Akron Press.

Said, E. 1978. *Orientalism.* New York: Vintage Books.

Chapter 19

Extending Intergroup Dialogue: From Talk to Action

Mark Chesler

The promise of intergroup dialogue is that it may create better under-standing among people whose cultures and traditions differ from one another. It may also help people understand the ways in which traditions of cultural and material dominance, privilege and oppression, play out in dif-ferent views and experiences, access to important resources, and sustained inequalities in life opportunities. In addition, the hope of dialogue is that it will accomplish such objectives more coherently and at a deeper level than can traditional forms of educational instruction, consciousness-raising, and media dissemination of information. That is, the sharing of direct experi-ence, buttressed by intellectual inquiry and interpersonal intimacy, may bring such lessons home more forcefully—forcefully enough to penetrate the barriers of cultural fear, awkwardness, ignorance, or denial.

The limitation of dialogue is that it may *only* accomplish these objec-tives and, moreover, only accomplish them at an intellectual and some-what abstract level. If such new insights and understandings, about oneself and one's own cultural group as well as about others', are not translated into new personal and collective action, a major opportunity has been lost. When individual insights, new knowledge, and new social connections are not tested or acted upon in new behavior, they are not likely to be rein-forced. And when new individual behaviors are not translated into action with others, in forms of collective action, fundamental social structures maintaining privilege and oppression go unchecked.

Dialogue Participants: From Different Places, toward Different Goals

The desire to learn about difference, and to solve personal, interpersonal, and organizational problems, often is the stimulus for dialogue programs. But members of different racial and class groups in this society often have very little prior experience with one another. We grow up in neighborhoods and schools that are segregated on these social criteria. Moreover, these segregated backgrounds are marked by differential access to cherished social resources. This is the background of relative privilege and oppression that people bring with them into any form of sustained intergroup interaction—including dialogue.

Socialized and educated in different and segregated social settings, and having differential access to important social resources, has major impact on many aspects of life opportunities, both those of a structural or material nature and those of a symbolic or psychological character. As a result, people from different backgrounds (and therefore, social experiences) often come to the dialogue setting with different goals and motivations. For instance, several studies indicate that white people often come to an intergroup dialogue in order to learn things about others and to make new friends; people of color often come to an intergroup dialogue in order to teach things to others and to change the conditions of their organizational and societal lives. This core asymmetry may make it difficult for people of different backgrounds to share common dialogue objectives, let alone develop a common language or trust in a mutually satisfying enterprise. It certainly makes it harder for groups of people to feel together and think together, and it must make agreement on common actions difficult to obtain.

In addition, these different backgrounds, with their accompanying differential access to social resources, often create power imbalances in interpersonal settings. Members of traditionally privileged groups are used to dominating, in numbers as well as in "air time" and attention, interactions with people of color (and may be ill prepared for and resent/resist a sudden shift in expectations for their behavior). Reciprocally, people of color often experience exclusion or limitations on their interactive roles with whites and members of other dominant groups (a history they may well resent but new expectations they also may be unprepared for). Since the dialogue agenda explicitly attempts to counter these historic trends by creating more equitable discursive structures and hence interaction patterns, they require new learning on the part of all participants.

One result of people's different life experiences is that there also are different versions of the goals of intergroup relationships and of life in a multicultural democracy and its constituent communities, organizations, and educational systems. For instance, Chesler and Crowfoot (1997) and Sleeter and Grant (1994) identify several different forms of multiculturalism and multicultural organizations. One form stresses principles of *assimilationism* and proposes to help formerly oppressed groups "catch up" to majority members and to enter the lower rungs of mainstream organizations and communities. A second form emphasizes a *human relations* approach, stressing the majority's need to understand and respect cultural (and other) differences and perhaps to retrain organizational leaders in principles of tolerance, acceptance, and basic information about other cultures. This is perhaps the most popular approach and is a staple of many secondary and collegiate programs and most workshops designed for corporate leaders and members (Chesler and Moldenhauer-Salazar 1998). A third form emphasizes principles of *cultural pluralism* and structural integration, focusing on the education of minority/disadvantaged groups and opening up or altering currently exclusive educational and organizational structures (some scholars and practitioners have called this a transitional or affirmative action focus—Jackson and Holvino 1988; Katz 1988). All of the above approaches hold out the promise that "people of good will" will triumph, and that a general consensus for taking action can be achieved among people of different groups. Finally, a critical or conflict-oriented form of *multicultural education* and/or multicultural organizational development emphasizes the need to incorporate all the prior forms with the addition of a forthright identification of, and challenge to, the nature and practice of privilege and discrimination—in schools, organizations, and communities (Chesler 1994; Jackson and Holvino 1988; Vasques Scalera 1999). In this approach the goals include forming alliances or coalitions to take collective action to reduce institutional discrimination and expand the possibilities for social justice. Recognition of the pervasive nature of injustice, and of the existence of constituencies or interest groups committed to maintaining current organizational forms, requires actors to move beyond analyses of personal ignorance or prejudice. It emphasizes a focus on institutional structures and organized resistance to change. Thus, it is clear that any action taken in this framework involves partisan advocacy and the mobilization of power (people, ideas, money, etc.) with which to challenge existing institutional frameworks.

Understanding as a Prerequisite to Action

Many intergroup dialogue programs, especially those on college campuses, focus solely on education of the self. The very best of them link understanding of the self to understanding "the other" and place this search for knowledge in the context of historic and contemporary material conditions. This is an important form of education, stretching from the micro to the macro, from an expanded understanding of oneself and one's relationships with others to the nature of socially organized power and privilege. Such dialogue, such "racetalk," "gendertalk," or "classtalk," expands our horizons and plays an important role in the education, especially, of privileged persons who may have had little sustained or positive contact with peers from other cultures.

Increased understanding of this sort is essential for any action to improve the state of interpersonal relationships or the structures of power and privilege in our society that shape intergroup relations. However, if dialogue programs stop there, with personal talk and understanding, at the level of the assimilationist and human relations approaches discussed above, they have stopped short of the most meaningful forms of inquiry and exchange. As Isaacs notes, "Much of what is called dialogue . . . is rarely or never dialogue according to our definition . . . we are also seeing dialogue as a discipline of collective inquiry, distinct from the valuable yet individually focused learning processes that dominate fields of conflict resolution, mediation, organizational development, therapy and even 'team building'" (1996, 20–21). Individual exchanges and understandings must go beyond sharing personal histories and making personal connections to generating an understanding of collective experiences. Moreover, efforts must go beyond increasing understanding and awareness and be supplemented by collective engagement and joint action.

Thus, inquiry itself, while a valuable first step, is not the same as, nor does it necessarily lead to, action for change. It is not at all clear that increased knowledge about intergroup relations, or about oneself and others, leads to different behavior—not even if this is "deep understanding." In fact, there is a substantial scientific literature on precisely this "gap" between verbal attitudes and actual behavior, especially but not only with regard to racial/ethnic views and actions. The question then becomes: should dialogue programs attempt to stand alone and forgo action efforts? Or should they promise engagement in change efforts but leave action for subsequent programs? Or should personal and systemic change efforts be integrated into dialogue programs? And, if such change efforts (or the exploration and creation of change efforts) are integrated into a dialogue program, what form might they take?

Visions of Intergroup Action
Linked to Dialogue Programs

As we consider the possibilities for translating new information and attitudes into new behaviors, or actions for change, we can identify a number of different possibilities. First and foremost, we can distinguish between individual actions and group or collective/concerted actions.

Individual actions may take a variety of forms, beyond increased awareness or respect, including (1) decisions to participate in additional educational events, whether through formal classes or in informal community settings; (2) participation in different cultures' traditions and religious celebrations or rituals, and perhaps the creation of ecumenical Easter, Christmas, Hanukkah, Passover, Kwanzaa, or Ramadan events; (3) efforts to (re)reducate peers, as in challenges to the telling of jokes that disparage particular groups on the basis of their race/ethnicity, gender, religion, class, or sexual orientation. As one white student said about her postdialogue intentions to take action (Zúñiga et al. 1996, 15): "I feel I can be an ally of women of color by taking responsibility for educating my white peers and taking responsibility for issues of race and discrimination."

Beyond individual actions, and more powerful in terms of their potential impact on organizational and community structures, are collective actions taken by groups of people working together. Isaacs argues that dialogue programs have the potential to "produce coordinated action among collectives, and to bring about genuine social change" (1996, 20). Indeed, some dialogue programs conducted within institutions of higher education have attempted to go beyond the focus on learning as the only outcome and have attempted to help students engage in intergroup actions for change. Rhoads notes, "For students to see themselves as agents of social change, often it is necessary to have contact with diverse individuals and groups whose struggles might in some way connect to the lives of the students" (1998, 40). In the Washington, D.C., program, Rhoads's students engage in work with homelessness in ways that helps students "learn about the many ways that they might (help) alter the circumstances of homeless citizens beyond the obvious path of providing a hot meal or a warm place to sleep" (1998, 42). They also engage in programs that attempt directly to alter these circumstances or to reduce the impact of homelessness on people's lives.

In a similar vein, Chesler (1995) draws the distinction between community service learning programs that emphasize "service" to disadvantaged populations (such as the homeless), "education" of disadvantaged populations (such as tutoring incarcerated juveniles or tutoring failing elementary school students) or of privileged persons (such as enlightenment of the collegiate population), and "social change" efforts (such as advocacy work with the NAACP, lobbying for change in homeless people's access to shelters). These distinctions mirror the different forms of intergroup dialogue or multiculturalism discussed earlier, in their focus on maintaining the current shape of unequal and often unjust social systems with minimal changes beyond greater diversity and representation, versus focusing on efforts to challenge, reform, and remake existing forms of racial, class, and cultural privilege and oppression.

There are a number of examples from higher educational institutions of intergroup dialogue participants actively engaging in local change efforts. Sometimes these efforts are focused on community issues, such as homelessness or school failure, as indicated above. But sometimes they are focused on operational aspects of the collegiate institution itself, as in protests against racially limiting admissions and recruitment policies, campus harassment, or curricular narrowness. For instance, a recent protest movement at the University of Michigan involved a coalition of students from many racial/ethnic groups objecting to the existence of a secret student society that disparaged Native American names, traditions, and symbols. Students who had participated in the intergroup dialogues were among the leaders of this protest movement and, moreover, were in the leadership of efforts to maintain this protest as nonviolent and capable of negotiating with both the secret society and the university administration.

Several examples of corporate dialogue programs, including some of those reported in this volume, also move beyond understanding to the creation of intergroup action for change. In so doing, some of these programs had the advantage of working with "intact" groups, groups of people who were part of the same work unit or who worked closely together while they were engaged in the dialogue process, and groups of people concerned about organizational problems. As a result, they were able to learn together and move more quickly to collective action than those groups of "strangers" who first met one another as they were brought together for dialogue purposes or who initially engaged in dialogue for educational purposes. For example, Zane (1998) discusses an elaborate dialogue program initiated in "Eastern Bank," one that altered the nature of organizational discourse from a focus on "meritocracy" to a focus on "discrimination." As she notes, "By participating in dialogue in which white women, women of color, and men of color spoke candidly from their personal as well as their group-level experiences within the organization, the senior white men . . . were forced to recognize that the issues were systemic, and that there were patterns of discrimination throughout the organization that went far beyond individual experience" (1998, 34). While this description does not take us (or the participants) beyond new forms of verbal exchange and awareness, it is an example of the movement from individual understanding to collective insight and perhaps to alteration of the organization's culture. And in perhaps the clearest example of the links between dialogue and action in corporate settings, Learson describes a "diversity" program with Sandia National Laboratories that utilized "dialogue sessions, role plays, and small and large group discussions" (1998, 36). The long-term operation of this effort resulted in a number of procedural (more inclusive communication, greater solicitation of employee input and participation) and policy (child-care services, altered work-week schedules, elder-care programs, multicultural management competencies as an assessment metric) changes in the organization. By and large, few efforts at intergroup dialogue in the corporate sector, and few action or change efforts that flow from them, focus explicitly on issues of social justice and true multiculturalism; they are much more likely to be framed and implemented within the domains of cultural pluralism approaches (Chesler and Moldenhauer-Salazar 1998).

Community intergroup dialogues often include an element of action for change, partly because they also usually draw participants from intact neighborhood groups or from interest groups committed to rectifying their experience of oppression. Isaacs (1996) reports on a community dialogue in Colorado that led to community action that redesigned the entire local health-care delivery system. Similarly, Leighninger describes the "study circles" popular in several communities that have affected policies and programs of local schools, businesses, and media. Leighninger notes that "although study circle programs are designed to be a catalyst for action efforts, organizers can't predict what those actions will be" (2000, 6). But it is clear from their experience that study circle participants have gone on to work together to rebuild churches that had been burned, advocate and help plan new supermarkets in economically depressed areas, and otherwise alter community structures and cultures. Other examples, such as those reported elsewhere in this volume, are legion.

Elements of Intergroup Action for Social Justice–Oriented Change

I have argued throughout that "mere talk" among people of different social backgrounds, even with honest exchange of opinions and feelings, is not enough. The starting point for change is true and deep intergroup dialogue, complete with explorations of group-level histories, interests, privileges, and disadvantages, and current experiences—with one another and with the organizations and communities they inhabit. Moreover, such dialogue cannot be effective if it is a one-time or even short-term event. The development of trust and safety required for serious and productive inquiry requires continuing and long-term engagement and commitment to a dialogue process.

In addition, I have argued that even the best "talking dialogue" still falls short of meeting the criteria for educating and mobilizing people to work together for social justice objectives. Taking action together, taking action that entails risk and commitment to social justice objectives, is where we find out if we can truly "walk the talk."

There are many situations in which such work together can be accomplished. A particularly useful model of a formally organized intergroup change process, one that is in itself an ongoing intergroup dialogue, is the coalition. *Coalition* refers to the organization of more than one person or group, typically in (prior or current) separation or even conflict, working together to influence the operations of another group, organization, or social system. In this sense of the term, a coalition is a temporary social system. It works with, but does not seek to eliminate or ignore, differences and conflicts of interest. A coalition also may be made more permanent, as when this form of intergroup interaction is institutionalized in the workings of an ongoing economic or political organization or a community decision-making apparatus. For instance, recent discussions of multicultural organizations (in higher education, in the corporate world, and in community agencies) share this vision of a more-than-temporary coalition for social production, service provision, or community change.

What are some principles of coalition development and operation? Chesler and Crowfoot (1981) argue that coalitional work, especially cross-race coalitions, must (*a*) acknowledge that groups in conflict will continue in conflict, whether they temporarily cooperate with one another or not; (*b*) recognize everyone's embeddedness in societal/organizational patterns of racism, regardless of their majority or minority status; *(c)* provide arenas for everyone's continued learning about racial matters—through racial or intergroup dialogue; *(d)* organize on the basis of relatively equal power relationships among participating groups; and *(e)* establish leadership patterns that cut across racial lines and utilize culturally plural processes. Clearly, such coalitions will benefit from the kinds of intergroup dialogues currently in vogue; just as clearly they establish an action setting in which such intergroup dialogues can be sustained over time and where the learning that flows from them can be expanded and tested in action for change.

Problems When Intergroup Action for Change Is the Goal

The level of interpersonal risk escalates for participants as rhetoric is put to the test, and as talk takes the form of collective action that might encounter serious resistance. The form of risk may vary: it may involve material danger, such as loss of employment or even freedom (if powerful institutions utilize police action to resist change), or it may involve psychic danger, such as anxiety or loss of self-esteem, peer respect, or prestige. All of these risks are more likely to occur, and in escalated fashion, in intact groups and among people who know one another fairly well. When anyone takes action that departs markedly from expectations associated with her or his social status and identity groups, family and friends often express sanctions: they may isolate former intimates who are now behaving "differently" (e.g., counter to prior norms of racial or gender etiquette) or accuse dialogers of "selling out" or "going over to the other side."

Multicultural or social justice–oriented change efforts in the corporate arena may encounter resistance from the higher levels of the organizational hierarchy. In such settings, intergroup dialogues that encourage openness about past and present patterns of discrimination and advantage may not be the rule, and may even open the organization to unwanted legal challenge. Resistance may take the form of arguing that engagement in dialogues, and especially in collective change efforts that may flow from them, is "interfering with the work" and "affecting the bottom line" of what people were hired to do. Resistance from lower levels of the hierarchy also may be present, as such change efforts may be seen as the work of "well-fed liberals" and "elites."

Community agencies that are open to discussion of intergroup issues may not be supportive of change efforts that flow from these discussions, especially when such explorations are staffed or initiated by outsiders/volunteers, and especially when such action threatens well-established community values and norms.

In higher educational arenas, town-gown relations are complicated and may be threatened when university students—outsiders—attempt to change local systems, rather than simply rendering service to local agencies. And while collegiate dialogue efforts often are defendable internally as educationally valuable learning opportunities, as soon as they become involved in change efforts, especially collective change efforts deliberately planned by groups of people—inside the academy or in the local environment—the faculty usually surfaces concerns about objectivity, political correctness, and forceful impositions of values. Especially in these settings a critical question becomes, "Who decides what action will be taken?"—faculty members, students as a group, individual students? Thus there are three central reasons change efforts are less likely to flow from dialogues conducted within higher educational systems: they are less likely to be conducted with intact groups that can easily link people's common lives; they are less likely to start from a recognition and desire to act on institutionally based problems; they are more likely to be seen as strictly educational enterprises.

All organizations and communities resist change, especially around intergroup issues, because of loyalty to established ways of conducting organizational and community business, because of the time and energy constraints of most work situations, because of the defense of domains of power and privilege, and because of a lack of knowledge/vision of different futures. Thus, while we may expect support and engagement in talk sessions and awareness programs, we should also expect efforts to create change to surface or create resistance. Often resistance takes the form of misunderstanding, defensiveness, and outright sabotage of the program and its leaders and adherents. As Isaacs reports on his experience, "Introducing deep change in one part of a system became quite threatening to other parts" (1996, 28).

And Finally . . .

I have argued that intergroup dialogues have enormous potential both for individual change and for social change. I also have argued that the link between interpersonal or intergroup dialogue and collective action for social change is more likely to occur in community and corporate settings than in educational (secondary or higher) settings. Interestingly, the action link is likely to occur particularly in those settings where the stakes are more real and the risk level is greater. At the same time, the forthright linkage of intergroup dialogue to social justice objectives is more likely to occur in higher educational settings than in community or corporate settings, if only rhetorically. Interestingly, the social justice link is likely to occur particularly where the action potential is the weakest. Perhaps talk *is* cheap!

These cautions notwithstanding, intergroup dialogue clearly has great potential for transforming individual identities and increasing personal understanding of our own and others' locations in social and community settings. This is an enormous plus in a society where honest and direct conversation about matters relating to social identities is so stilted and rare. Shared disclosure of differences and commonalities also can create group-level understanding that permits and encourages collective action for change. The personally transformative power of dialogue is clear; what is untested but even more promising is its power to engage people in coalitions to transform the organizational, community, and societal conditions and structures of our lives.

REFERENCES

Chesler, M. 1994. "Strategies of Multicultural Organizational Development." *Diversity Factor* 2, no. 2: 12–18.

———. 1995. "Service, Service-Learning, and Change-Making." In *Praxis III: Voices in Dialogue,* ed. J. Galura, J. Howard, D. Waterhouse, and K. Ross. Ann Arbor, Mich.: OCSL Press.

Chesler, M., and J. Crowfoot. 1981. "Creating and Maintaining Interracial Coalitions." In *Impacts of Racism on White Americans,* ed. B. Bowser and R. Hunt. Beverly Hills, Calif.: Sage Publications.

———. 1997. "Racism in Higher Education II: Challenging Racism and Promoting Multiculturalism in Higher Education Organizations." Center for Research on Social Organization Working Paper no. 558, University of Michigan.

Chesler, M., and J. Moldenhauer-Salazar. 1998. "Diversity, Organizational Change, and Social Justice." *Diversity Factor* 6, no. 3: 13–19.

Isaacs, W. 1996. "The Process and Potential of Dialogue in Social Change." *Educational Technology,* January–February, 20–30.

Jackson, B., and E. Holvino. 1988. "Multicultural Organization Development." Program on Conflict Management Alternatives Working Paper Series no. 11, University of Michigan.

Katz, J. 1988. "Facing the Challenge of Diversity and Multiculturalism." Program on Conflict Management Alternatives Working Paper Series no. 13, University of Michigan.

Learson, B. 1998. "Sandia National Laboratories: Influencing Organizational Culture Change through Line Ownership of Diversity." *Diversity Factor* 6, no. 4: 33–39.

Leighninger, M. 2000. "How Have Study Circles Made an Impact?" In *Focus on Study Circles.* Pomfret, Conn.: Study Circles Resource Center.

Rhoads, R. 1998. "Critical Multiculturalism and Service Learning." *New Directions for Teaching and Learning* 73:39–46.

Sleeter, C., and C. Grant. 1994. *Making Choices for Multicultural Education: Five Approaches to Race, Class, and Gender.* New York: Macmillan.

Vasques Scalera, C. 1999. "Democracy, Diversity, Dialogue: Education for Critical Multicultural Citizenship." Ph.D. diss., University of Michigan.

Zane, N. 1998. "The Discourses of Diversity: The Links between Conversation and Organizational Change." *Diversity Factor* 7, no. 1: 29–39.

Zúñiga, X., C. Vasques, T. Sevig, and B. A. Nagda. 1996. "Dismantling the Walls: Peer-Facilitated Inter-Race/Ethnic Dialogue Processes and Experiences." Program on Conflict Management Alternatives Working Paper Series no. 49, University of Michigan.

Chapter 20

Design Considerations in Intergroup Dialogue

Ximena Zúñiga and Biren (Ratnesh) A. Nagda

Dialogue as a communication practice has been used in many traditions to encourage inquiry and explore shared concerns. For example, early Greek philosophers, Native Americans, and Quakers have used, or continue to use, forms of this practice. Perspectives on dialogue that have been developed more recently, such as Freire's (1972) critical dialogues, Isaacs's (1996a, 1996b) Dialogue Project, Norman's (1994) conflict mediation interethnic/-racial dialogues, and Study Circles Resource Center's (1997) study circles, show the extraordinary potential of this practice in varied contexts and for different purposes. These contemporary views and practices draw on the dialogue method to examine relevant questions, deliberate about policy issues, and develop positive relationships among estranged groups. In recent years, many efforts have used dialogue to forge understanding and build bridges among people with differing worldviews, cultural heritage, and social status. In fact, *dialogue* as a meaningful exchange among a group of individuals has been further expanded to *intergroup dialogue,* in which members of two or more social identity groups come together to address issues of difference across gender, sexual orientation, race, ethnicity, religion, nationality, and other social group boundaries (Du Bois and Hutson 1997; Zúñiga and Nagda 1993).

The purpose of this chapter is to identify and examine common and distinctive design elements among a wide range of dialogue practices. While most practitioners and theorists may agree on the definition of dialogue as a communicative process aimed at fostering mutual understanding and deeper relationships, they vary considerably in their methods and goals. We have approached this chapter with two critical questions in mind: How do different models structure and design the dialogue process? What are some of the underlying orientations that influence how dialogues are designed? We explore these questions by first briefly reviewing current dialogue practices and grouping them into four practice models.

Second, we define the concept of stages in dialogue and provide a rationale for sequencing the process of intergroup dialogue. We also describe four common stages of intergroup dialogue. Third, we examine two philosophical and practical orientations that, in our view, influence the design, breadth, and direction of the stages of intergroup dialogue. Last, we offer a set of questions to stimulate further reflection and dialogue.

Models of Dialogue

Du Bois and Hutson (1997) assert that more and more people in the United States, from all walks of life, young and old, are engaging in dialogues in schools, communities, and organizations. A review of the literature suggests that there are different models shaping the current thinking and practice of dialogue in these settings (see table 1). The four general models—which we named collective inquiry, critical-dialogic education, community building and action, and conflict resolution and peace building—vary in their purposes and the contexts in which they have been developed. While they are presented as distinct models, we recognize that some applications of dialogue may combine some aspects of two or more models in their practice. We describe the main characteristics of each of the models below.

Collective inquiry models posit that suspending judgments and assumptions is essential to find shared meaning among dialogue participants. This model focuses on nurturing participants' abilities to engage in collective thinking and inquiry for the development of synergistic and meaningful relationships (Ellinor and Gerard 1998; Isaacs 1996a, 1996b). Originating in the work of Bohm (1996) in England, this model is central in the work of Ellinor and Gerard (1998), cofounders of the Dialogue Group, and Isaacs (1996a, 1996b) and colleagues at the Dialogue Project, Massachusetts Institute of Technology. Variations of this model have been implemented in organizations and communities throughout the United States.

Critical-dialogical education models integrate sustained dialogue with consciousness-raising and bridge building across differences (Behling et al. 1998; Nagda et al. 1999; Treviño and Maxwell 2000; Zúñiga, Nagda, and Sevig 2000). The educational dimension of this model focuses on exploring group differences from a social justice perspective with a goal of both individual and systemic change. The pedagogy underlying this model draws from Freire's (1972) work on liberatory education. This dialogue

TABLE 1. Models of Dialogue

	Collective Inquiry Model	Critical-Dialogic Education Model	Community Building and Social Action Model	Conflict Resolution and Peace Building Model
Applications	Ellinor and Gerard 1998; Huang-Nissen 1999; Isaacs 1996a, 1996b	Behling et al. 1998; Nagda et al. 1999; Treviño and Maxwell 2000; Zúñiga 1998; Zúñiga, Nagda, and Sevig 1995, 2000	President's Initiative on Race 1998; Study Circles Resource Center 1997	Kelman 1978, 1990; Lederach 1995; Norman 1991a, 1991b, 1994; Saunders 1999

process, as applied in college settings, facilitates increasing awareness about social inequalities, intergroup understanding, and alliance building among participants (Nagda and Zúñiga 2000; Zúñiga and Sevig 1997; Zúñiga et al. 1996). This model was developed by Zúñiga, Nagda, and Sevig at the University of Michigan's Program on Intergroup Relations, Conflict, and Community (see Zúñiga, Nagda, and Sevig 2000 for model description). Variations of this model have been implemented in several college campuses across the United States.

Community building and social action models aim to involve a broad base of citizens in addressing community issues. Such an effort may bring together community members to talk about community concerns and build relationships among estranged groups before exploring the possibility of working together to effect change in their community. Other applications of this model are community efforts that invite citizens to participate in dialogue to mobilize around a specific action project. The most widespread effort of this kind in the United States is supported by the Study Circles Resource Center (Flavin-McDonald and Barrett 1999; McCoy and Sherman 1994). The practice model proposed in the President's Initiative on Race (1998) *Dialogue Guide* for conducting dialogues on race is yet another example.

Conflict resolution and peace-building models bring together members of conflicting parties to identify issues of conflict, generate action plans, and, if possible, achieve a workable agreement to conflicts or disputes. In this instance, the dialogue process is driven by a conflict mediation method that asks participants to acquire insights into the perspectives of the other group, to become open to the idea that mutual compromises may create a new situation, and to become responsive to the psychological needs and concerns of the other group (Kelman 1978, 1987). Applications of these models draw from national and international peace studies and conflict mediation movements (Kelman 1990; Lederach 1995; Norman 1991a, 1991b, 1994; Saunders 1999).

Most the models and applications described in this section bring together people from different social identity groups to address social and cultural differences. The collective inquiry model, however, does not always attend to issues of social diversity. We decided to include this model in our analysis because several dialogue efforts have integrated some of the guiding principles articulated by Bohm (1996) and Isaacs (1996a, 1996b) in their work, particularly in organizations (Ellinor and Gerard 1998; Huang-Nissen 1999).

The Concept of Stages in the
Design of Intergroup Dialogue

While the four models described above are sufficiently different from each other in terms of their purposes and the contexts in which they are applied, they are similar in that they envision dialogue as a process and not an event. Moving from polite conversations to meaningful and honest dialogue across race and other group boundaries involves a sustained process that takes time and commitment. In this section, we examine how the process of dialogue is organized and structured, and for what purpose, drawing from our analysis of various models and dialogue guides. We define the concept of stages in dialogue; present a rationale for sequencing the process of dialogue, particularly in the context of dialogues across race and other social group boundaries; and present a four-stage framework for designing intergroup dialogues.

Definition

In reviewing conceptual and descriptive materials about the models identified above, it is evident that practitioners organize and structure the dialogue process in order to achieve desired goals. Multiple meetings that take place consecutively over a period of time offer participants the opportunity to engage in sustained dialogue. The way in which meetings are structured, sequenced, paced, and facilitated to achieve specific goals concerns matters of design. In outlining the design of a particular model or practice, several authors refer to the established sequence as "stages" (Behling et al. 1998; Nagda et al. 1999; Saunders 1999; Stephan and Stephan 1996; Zúñiga, Nagda, and Sevig 1995, 2000), "phases" (Isaac 1996a; Norman 1991a; One America 1998), or "facets" (Lederach 1995) of dialogue. Other authors refer to the established sequence as numbered sessions (Huang-Nissen 1999; SCRC 1997; Treviño and Maxwell 2000). We refer to the sequence that is established to organize and pace the dialogue process as stages of dialogue. We see the stages of dialogue as a guide for facilitators (and participants) to keep the focus on the main goals of each stage, transition from one stage to the next, and guide the process toward the overall purpose of the effort.

Rationale

Meaningful dialogues across differences offer participants experiences that can be subtly or dramatically different from their usual way of interacting with people different from themselves at school, at work, or in their community. Regardless of the way in which the process of dialogue is sequenced, organizers of dialogue efforts must attend to a number of challenges in order to create a fertile environment for dialogue, be it to help participants get acquainted with each other, develop a more informed understanding of pertinent issues, or establish linkages between dialogue and action. We elaborate on three such challenges below.

Communicating with Strangers

Fostering meaningful dialogue requires nurturing a significantly different environment than most people are used to experiencing in everyday life. The process of communicating across race and other social group boundaries with people you do not know, or do not have meaningful contact with, can be particularly challenging because many people tend to rely on socially biased information in interpreting each other's behaviors or perspectives (Gudykunst 1998). Careful attention, therefore, needs to be given to how people come together and engage with each other in a dialogue group. A variety of opportunities can be structured to invite people to share and exchange experiences and perspectives that encourage equal participation and communicate the value of listening to all perspectives. For instance, Huang-Nissen (1999) proposes the practice of listening with *ting,* the Chinese word for listening—with our ears, mind, eyes, and heart—as a means through which the speaker and listener can acquire insight into each others' lived experience. Another method used to encourage active listening is the "Fishbowl" exercise. In this activity, participants from two or more social identity groups take turns sharing their own experiences of race, ethnicity, religion, sexual orientation, or other social identities, listening to the other group, and asking questions of each other (Schoem, Zúñiga, and Nagda 1993).

Bridging Conflicting Perspectives and Experiences

An environment for dialogue may involve more than *simply* good communication or goodwill. It may necessitate speaking "against the grain of status differences, and often personal histories of intolerance and harm" (Burbules 1993, 156). The process of naming how differences of power and privilege impact people's lives can be both emotionally and intellectually challenging. Bridging experiences and perspectives across power differences may require developing some common understanding about the relationship that exists between people's personal lives and social inequality (Zúñiga, Nagda, and Sevig 2000). For example, participants may need to explore the impact of group inequality on their own in-group biases and together examine the root causes of these biases and other forms of group differences in order to make meaningful dialogue possible. In other instances, bridging different perspectives on the impact of power inequities on peoples' lives may require developing a common language or examining common frames of references to codify and make meaning of the conflicting experiences of dialogue participants.

Participants' different experiences (and knowledge) of the impact of race and other social categories at the personal and interpersonal level may pose additional challenges to the bridging process. Racial identity development theories, for example, suggest that people go through a process from "unawareness" to "exploration" of the impact of race on their social group affiliation and then move toward internalizing and integrating this awareness (Hardiman and Jackson 1997; Helms 1990; Tatum 1992, 1997). Such a process raises important questions for participants to reflect upon individually and in dialogue: How do race and racism impact my experience? How do race and racism impact your experience? How do race and racism impact our relationships? How do I feel about people who are racially like me or different from me? What is my role in the struggle for racial equality? (Chesler 1995; Zúñiga and Nagda 1993).

Acknowledging Developmental and Dynamic Aspects of Group Life

Group development issues and the internal dynamics of group life will challenge a group's ability to sustain the process of dialogue over time. For instance, the developmental stages groups go through—sometimes characterized as "forming," "storming," "norming," and "working" or "performing"—can serve as general guideposts for group leaders to help them understand emerging group dynamics and provide direction to the process (Huang-Nissen 1999; Manning, Curtis, and Macmillan 1996; Weber 1982). Similarly, templates such as Schein's (1982) "What to look for in groups" are helpful in identifying important dimensions of group life (such as maintenance and task functions) that need attention. Though groups vary in how they move through their developmental stages and in their internal dynamics, there are specific things that leaders and participants can do to facilitate the group's evolution. For example, group leaders can help create a fertile environment for dialogue in the forming stage—by inviting participants to talk about their hopes and expectations for the dialogue process and allocating sufficient time for members to get to know each other (Zúñiga, Nagda, and Sevig 2000). In the storming or conflict stage, group leaders can model good listening skills by listening to all points of view and acknowledging conflict as an opportunity for learning and deepening the dialogue (Manning, Curtis, and Macmillan 1996).

The design of the four models of dialogue described earlier addresses these challenges in different ways. The following section identifies and describes the stages of dialogue that emerged from our analysis of various models and dialogue guides. In describing the stages of dialogue, we touch upon how various dialogue models and applications address some of the challenges described above in their designs.

Four Stages of Intergroup Dialogue

In reviewing articles about dialogue and intergroup dialogue, and examining dialogue guides of various models or efforts, we have identified four stages that appear to be common across the models (see table 2). We identify some of the main tasks and goals that need to be accomplished in each stage. In most models, the dialogue process begins by focusing on activities aimed at setting an environment for dialogue and concludes by inviting dialogue participants to consider ways of moving from dialogue to action. However, there is considerable variation in what happens between the first and last stages of the dialogue process. Several models include a second stage aimed at developing a common base. Typically the main purpose of this stage is to develop a common knowledge base to facilitate dialogue across social group differences. Most models then include a third stage of exploring questions, issues, or conflicts, which provides a structure for participants to focus in more depth on some of the issues that have surfaced.

The four stages of dialogue provide an organizing framework to better understand the core sequence of tasks involved in the design of a dialogue process. However, not all the dialogue or intergroup dialogue efforts follow this framework explicitly. For example, Norman (1991a) outlines six phases, while Saunders (1999) describes five stages. They both identify two core tasks related to action in order to move toward resolution or reconciliation—phases 5 and 6, or stages 4 and 5, respectively. In the proposed four-stage framework, we combine the two tasks into one stage, moving from dialogue to action. Other efforts do not refer to the sequencing of tasks as stages but as numbered sessions (SCRC 1997; Treviño and Maxwell 2000). Therefore, the four-stage framework, elaborated below, broadly extrapolates the intent of the main tasks, described by various models and dialogue guides, to organize and sequence the dialogue process.

TABLE 2. Stages of Intergroup Dialogue across Models and Applications

Stage	Collective Inquiry Model	Critical-Dialogic Education Model	Community Building and Social Action Model	Conflict Resolution and Peace Building Model
1. Setting an environment for dialogue	Build a "container" for dialogue for safety and trust issues to emerge Develop group consensus on purpose, mission, and structure	Develop guidelines for dialogue Begin relationship building	Discuss, clarify, and set ground rules Share personal beliefs and experiences about race and race relations	Orient group members Decide to engage in dialogue
2. Developing a common base	Explore beliefs and assumptions leading to public suspension of judgments Dialogue about personal, work-related, or general topics	Develop a common language Explore multiple social identities— commonalities and differences	Ask what the state of race relations in our community is. Ask what the nature of the problem with race is	Map and name problems and relationships Explore and clarify issues and group development

3. Exploring questions, issues, or conflicts	Increase suspension of judgment and trust in the dialogue process	Explore and dialogue about issues of conflict and social justice	Ask what the main changes are that participants would like to see in the community	Continue clarification of issues
	Inquiry and creativity flow in the container	Explore in/out group dynamics and issues	Ask what kind of public policies can help	Probe relationships to choose direction for change
	Dialogue about personal, work-related, or general topics			Build scenarios—experience a change in the relationship
4. Moving from dialogue to action	Assess experiences	Plan action	Ask what participants will do, as individuals and with others, to make a difference	Plan action
	Dialogue about transferring learning and skills into daily life	Envision and seek opportunities for action		Act together to make change happen
		Build alliances		Monitor and evaluate

Note: Based on dialogue guides for the applications listed in table 1.

Stage 1: *Setting an environment for dialogue* aims at developing a climate for meaningful dialogue. Most dialogue efforts start by clarifying the purpose of the dialogue. Guidelines for dialogue or expectations are developed that support sustaining a constructive dialogue process over time. Some models explicitly attend to the task of building interpersonal relationships among participants through sharing of expectations, fears, and hopes, and getting-acquainted activities. Other models focus on skill building, especially active listening skills, to develop the foundations for good communication (Huang-Nissen 1999). Still others attend to both relationship building and skill building (Nagda et al. 1999; Norman 1991a; Saunders 1999; Zúñiga, Nagda, and Sevig 2000). The number of meetings scheduled to set the tone and context for dialogue varies from model to model. Some efforts briefly attend to some of these concerns during the first session (SCRC 1997; Treviño and Maxwell 2000), while others spend one full session (*One America* 1998) or even two sessions (Behling et al. 1998; Nagda 2001; Zúñiga 1998) or more (Norman 1991a, 1991b; Saunders 1999).

Stage 2: *Developing a common base* seeks to establish a common base of knowledge—conceptual and/or personal—for talking across race and other social group boundaries. In some models, this may involve engaging at deeper levels of introspection and interpersonal sharing by inviting participants to share their own personal experiences with social discrimination, intolerance, and power inequities (Behling et al. 1998; Nagda et al. 1999; Norman 1991a, 1991b, 1994; *One America* 1998; Saunders 1999; Zúñiga 1998). In other models, this base is solidified through the development of a common language and frames of reference to assist with the examination of a particular question or issue of interest. For example, in some dialogue efforts, participants examine the underlying systemic conditions that impact upon race relations in a community or cognitive assumptions that guide our thinking and feeling (Ellinor and Gerard 1998; Isaacs 1996a; Nagda 2001; SCRC 1997; Zúñiga 1998; Zúñiga, Nagda, and Sevig 2000). In other practices, the development of a common base may involve identifying one point of collaboration in order to bridge a conflictual and volatile intergroup relationship (Norman 1991a). In most efforts one to three sessions are devoted to this stage, yet conflict resolution models may spend a longer period of time in this stage.

Stage 3: *Exploring questions, issues, or conflicts* strives to *focus* the dialogue on one or more questions, issues, or specific conflicts and to *deepen the dialogue*. It is usually designed to move the dialogue to attend to one or two issues with more depth. Participants are encouraged to use their awareness, knowledge, and skills to delve into a question, a relationship issue, or a policy concern. A consideration of multiple perspectives and identification of assumptions is important and emphasized throughout this stage. In some models, stage 3 involves delving more deeply into a creative inquiry process (Isaacs 1996a, 1996b). In other efforts, this stage encourages participants to explore more fully the direction they want to take regarding issues facing their community (*One America* 1998). It may probe more deeply the aspects of the relationship being examined in order to identify directions for change (Saunders 1999). Programs spend between one (SCRC 1997) and four sessions in this stage (Behling et al. 1998; Nagda et al. 1999; Zúñiga 1998; Zúñiga, Nagda, and Sevig 2000), while others may spend an indefinite amount of time depending on the emerging issues or needs (Norman 1991a, 1991b; Saunders 1999).

Stage 4: *Moving from dialogue to action* grapples with the question, "Where do we go from here?" Most of the models and applications reviewed focus on actions aimed at positively impacting the concerns addressed in the dialogue. Most efforts conceive this stage as an opportunity to facilitate individual and collective learning with social action. Some dialogue efforts invite participants to think about actions they can take to make a difference in the relationship between the groups (Behling et al. 1998; Nagda 2001; Norman 1991a, 1991b; *One America* 1998; Saunders 1999; Treviño and Maxwell 2000; Zúñiga 1998). Other efforts invite participants to consider taking a leadership role in future dialogue initiatives or to volunteer in the community (Nagda et al. 1999; SCRC 1997). Still other efforts engage participants in identifying specific action projects to be implemented in the community after the dialogue effort ends (e.g., SCRC 1997). Some models spend one to four sessions in this last stage, while other models may spend a longer period of time articulating and implementing an action plan.

The four-stage framework consolidates the core tasks described by various dialogue models and program efforts to guide the dialogue process over time, particularly in the context of dialogues across race and other social group boundaries. While not all models make explicit the structure of what needs to happen through a stage framework, it is evident from the materials reviewed that the sequencing and organization of tasks into "stages" or "phases" of dialogue is an important design element in intergroup dialogue practice.

Philosophical and Practical Orientations in the Design of Intergroup Dialogue

Whereas the concept of stages provides an overall structure and sequence to a dialogue effort, we also found that distinct orientations are implicit in how the dialogue process is designed. We refer to these as philosophical and practical orientations: philosophical because they suggest an analytical perspective or worldview of the central issues addressed in the dialogue; and practical because they have design implications regarding how an intergroup dialogue process is organized to meet specific goals in a particular context. Together, the orientations appear to influence the focus and scope—both breadth and depth—of the efforts. The two orientations can be described through these questions: (1) What is the conceptual lens used to examine social and cultural differences? and (2) What is the specific focus of the dialogue effort? Drawing from the models and dialogue guides reviewed, we identify two broad approaches within each orientation. These approaches to an orientation may represent dilemmas or tensions for practitioners concerning matters of design. Two caveats are necessary here. First, our thinking about and analysis of the models and applications are based on written material: conceptual papers, curricula, and guides. Our analysis does not, however, consider the specific in-the-field applications of these guides. It is possible that such field applications will modify the particular approach to meet the challenges of a particular situation. Therefore, while we have interpreted a certain model or program effort to espouse a particular approach below, in practice it may be modified to respond to emerging contextual needs. Second, we recognize that models and practice applications vary in the extent to which they incorporate the approaches to these orientations with consistency. In fact, a certain approach may be more prevalent in one stage of a dialogue process and less prevalent in the next stage. We elaborate on each orientation below and provide examples to illustrate how the two orientations inform the design of an intergroup dialogue effort.

The Conceptual Lens Used to Examine Social and Cultural Differences: Diversity or Justice?

While most models aim to explore race and other group differences, they vary in how they articulate and attend to differences in social identity and social status. One lens with which to examine differences emphasizes social and cultural differences as individual attributes that need to be acknowledged and valued in classrooms, organizations, and communities. This perspective may be termed the *diversity* approach; it acknowledges and values differences instead of suppressing or erasing them (Miller 1994). It recognizes that when relationships between people from diverse social groups become estranged due to a lack of meaningful interactions, a number of misunderstandings, stereotypes, and prejudices can evolve as barriers to positive intergroup relationships. These dialogue efforts aim to challenge prejudice and ignorance by bringing participants into face-to-face interactions and allowing for personal sharing, knowledge exchange, and relationship building. Reduction of prejudice and better opportunities for collaboration toward a common goal contribute to positive relations between groups. Examples of this approach include efforts by the Study Circles Resource Center (1997) and workplace dialogue groups as described by Huang-Nissen (1999).

A second distinct approach, focusing on social inequalities and social power relations as a context, may be termed a "diversity and justice" approach (Adams, Bell, and Griffin 1997; Miller 1994). This approach recognizes that racism, sexism, and other systems of oppression are endemic sources of protracted conflicts between social groups. It builds on the diversity approach but acknowledges that participants' experiences in the dialogue group, or in the larger community, will be impacted by status differences. This approach provides a different perspective to inquiry and dialogue. For example, the dialogue may focus on exploring internalized racism or sexism, on examining the racial and gender dynamics manifested by how people are engaging in the dialogue group, or on the roles people could take to effect change. Prejudice reduction, active interruption of injustices, and allied relations contribute to positive intergroup relationships. Efforts such as some of the college-based critical-dialogic education models (Nagda et al. 1999; Zúñiga, Nagda, and Sevig 2000) and conflict mediation and peace-building models (Norman 1991b; Saunders 1999) use this approach.

In both the "diversity" and "diversity and justice" approaches, participants may personalize the dialogue. This may occur through sharing stories of socialization experiences and uncovering the sources of misinformation, stereotypes, and prejudices (Behling et al. 1998; Treviño and Maxwell 2000). In the "diversity and justice" approach, however, these experiences and perspectives are further examined within the context of systems of privilege and oppression. A relevant distinction in terms of design between the two approaches is the use of affinity or caucus groups where participants examine how institutional discrimination impacts on

individuals or groups. The facilitators convene each of the parties participating in an intergroup dialogue to meet in groups of shared identities for
one or two sessions to talk, for example, about their own experiences with
privilege and oppression, and identify common concerns or needs. For
example, Norman (1994) reports asking Black and Korean dialogue participants to meet in affinity groups to "identify and set priorities on issues
and concerns of importance" (96–97). Similar methods are used in dialogues involving white people, biracial or multiracial people and people of
color, or men and women (Nagda et al. 1999; Zúñiga, Nagda, and Sevig
2000). Affinity-group conversations, therefore, can provide both a supportive and challenging place for inquiry and reflection before reconven-
ing as a total group.

Two particular dilemmas face organizers related to the conceptual lens
used to analyze group differences. On one hand, as a diversity approach
strives to affirm participants' experiences and perspectives of social diversity, it may alienate people from marginalized social groups as issues of
unequal power relations or internalized oppression are not fully
addressed. On the other hand, as a diversity-and-justice approach makes
more explicit differences in power and oppression in a dialogue group, it
may alienate participants who wish to take active roles against social injustice but feel discouraged because they feel blamed or excluded in a dialogue group. The important design implication here is that the particular
approach to difference may shape activities that attend to the similar
and/or different needs of the participants at different points during the
process of dialogue.

The Specific Focus of the Dialogue Effort: Public Issues or a Particular Group Relationship?

Most dialogue models and practice applications focus on specific questions, issues, or conflicts by the midpoint of a dialogue process. Some
models outline the dialogue topics beforehand in the dialogue guide (e.g.,
Nagda et al. 1999; SCRC 1997; Zúñiga, Nagda, and Sevig 1995, 2000),
while other models allow for the topics to emerge from the process
(Huang-Nissen 1999; Norman 1991b; Saunders 1999). The critical distinction here, however, concerns the extent to which the emphasis varies along
two approaches: *(a)* "issues" (for example, community concerns, policy
issues, or controversial topics); and *(b)* "relationship dynamics" (such as
group dynamics emerging from the dialogue process or conflicts in the
relationship). One set of models, focusing mostly on *issues,* appears to

consider public issues from a deliberative perspective. The SCRC model is perhaps the best example of this. In their guide for study circles on issues of racism and race relations, SCRC recommends using a public deliberation, choice-work approach based on the National Issues Forum (Kettering Foundation 1999). In a session on public policy issues, participants are given a number of different policy choices on changing race relations (ranging from conservative to liberal). In some cases, participants choose one that most closely resembles their own and then deliberate with others on the reasons for their choice. In other cases, they will consider all views at once, use them to stimulate thoughts about their own position, and often identify pieces of different views with which they agree or disagree. The ensuing dialogue revolves around understanding the different positions better rather than taking a more personal stand toward the issue being discussed. As the dialogue guide puts it: "the goal is to 'try on' various ideas and learn from each other's ideas" (SCRC 1997, 21).

A second set of applications focuses dialogue on both *issues and relationship*. This approach differs from "other public-policy discussions in focusing on the underlying relationships that cause divisive problems— not just the problems" (Saunders 1999, 258). In both Saunders's (1999) and Norman's (1991a) models to resolve intergroup conflicts, issues are generated by dialogue among participants. While they may start with each participant or group identifying a number of issues, the dialogue process is used to identify the most pertinent or urgent issues. Saunders recommends that each problem identified be probed for the underlying interests and relationships. The dialogue process involves a systematic outlining of the issues as well as a debriefing of the influence of the topic on the interactions among dialogue participants. In Norman's work, only common issues are identified for further dialogue. He states that this is perhaps the most difficult phase: while participants may agree on certain issues and trust each other in the group, they still hold on to a collective mistrust. The task of the facilitators is to point out and explore how these patterns of collective mistrust affect the dialogue process.

The approaches within this orientation affect the setting of the environment for dialogue. For instance, it appears that in issues-focused dialogues, the emphasis is placed on creating an environment that resembles collaborative group work—listening actively, being honest, respectful, and open to different perspectives, and maintaining confidentiality (Huang-Nissen 1999; SCRC 1997). These guidelines for dialogue are also present in other dialogue models. However, the distinction for efforts focused on issues and relationships rests on the specific consideration given to oppression dynamics and conflict de-escalation methods. First, some efforts specify guidelines to discourage participants from engaging in blaming behavior (Zúñiga, Nagda, and Sevig 1995). For example, Cannon (1990) suggests that when talking about issues of oppression based on race, gender, class, sexual orientation, it is helpful to ask participants not to blame people for their experiences of victimization. She also finds it valuable to ask participants not to blame people for being misinformed, but rather to take responsibility for their own learning. The ground rules of a dialogue group may also be further elaborated to include guidelines for mediating conflicts that may arise in the group (Norman 1994). Second, a midprocess check-in (perhaps as a transition between the second and third stages) is used in some models to lay the groundwork for deeper engagement as the dialogue moves from sharing views and perspectives to examining the underlying relationships that cause the problems (Saunders 1999).

In sum, the focus of a dialogue effort will shape the overall design in at least two ways. First, it shapes how the beginning stages of a dialogue group are structured to create a fertile environment for meaningful dialogue. While focusing on issues may require acquiring new knowledge and factual information about policy or economic issues, a focus on the relationship dynamics may make essential learning more deeply about each other's social identities, cultural background, and status differences. Second, the amount of time allocated to each of the stages in an issue-and-relationship approach to dialogue appears to be more than in dialogue groups that mostly focus on policy or economic issues. This is not surprising given that attention to relationship dynamics requires more time for them to emerge and be fully addressed. The two philosophical and practical orientations present practitioners with choices to weigh in designing and guiding a dialogue effort. As illustrated above, a particular approach within an orientation has different design implications. Particular approaches may be taken depending on the purpose of the effort, the social context, and the participants. Two other issues may also play a role: resource availability and examples of dialogue efforts implemented elsewhere.

In the conclusion, we build on these issues by posing a set of questions as a starting point for more dialogue among practitioners.

Conclusion

In this chapter we have explored two questions: How do different models structure and design the dialogue process? What are some of the underlying orientations that influence how dialogues are designed? In working with these questions, our own effort has paralleled some aspects of a dialogue process: a deeper inquiry to make tacit assumptions overt, to look for the strengths in the different models, and to uncover the interconnections—the commonalties and differences—among different efforts. In addressing these questions, we reviewed different dialogue guides, theoretical and conceptual papers, and our own practices. Two major considerations became evident. First, understanding the idea of dialogue as a process and not an event makes it imperative for practitioners to think about the sequencing, pacing, and structuring of dialogues sustained over time. Second, the idea that dialogue efforts reflect different philosophical and practical orientations challenges us to think about the underlying approaches within these orientations and ways in which they influence goals and design. In concluding this chapter, we ask ourselves another question: How can practitioners and theorists build on the analysis and integration offered in this chapter? We see our effort as being potentially useful in two ways: *(a)* for reflecting on implicit and explicit design considerations that guide intergroup dialogue efforts; and *(b)* stimulating a dialogue among practitioners and theorists to explore insights, challenges, and dilemmas. We have purposefully not provided prescriptive strategies to guide practitioners. Instead, in the spirit of dialogue, we offer a set of questions for further reflection and inquiry.

Philosophical and practical orientations: What are the guiding principles of your program philosophy? How clearly, and in what ways, are these communicated to participants and collaborators? What issues do you intend to address in your dialogue effort? Do the goals of your effort lean toward just dialogue, or dialogue and action?

Context: What is the social and historical context of your effort? What are the specific needs related to intergroup dialogue in your setting? Is your effort intended to respond to a crisis or volatile situation, or it a proactive initiative? Do the intergroup dialogues stand alone, or are they a building block in a multipronged change effort? How does the intergroup dialogue initiative fit in the context of other similar efforts taking place in your setting?

Participants: Who will be invited to participate in this initiative? What are the resources and needs—information, knowledge, skills, and experiences—of potential participants? How much diversity exists in your setting? How would you describe the relationship between diverse social groups in your school, community, or organization? What are the different pathways of continued involvement for participants after the dialogue?

Resources: What kind of resources—time, money, people, and facilities—do you have access to? How much time can participants commit to your dialogue effort? Do you have access to trained facilitators, or will you need to train facilitators? How are you planning to guide and sustain the dialogue process over time? What facilities do you have for dialogue meetings?

Linkages to other dialogue efforts: What aspects of your own initiative do you share with others? In what ways can you strengthen your efforts? What are pieces from other models or practices that you could adapt for your needs? What are pieces you can modify to fit your own reality? What are the innovations you need to develop, or are considering introducing, to enhance your own efforts?

As practitioners involved in this work, we are often challenged to question our own thinking in relation to issues of design, and reflect upon factors that influence how we organize a dialogue process. We continue to explore ways of aligning our conceptual models and dialogue guides with the complex nature of this work. We hope that this chapter and the concluding questions stimulate thinking about the challenges and dilemmas facing practitioners as well as an excitement about the breadth and potential of this practice.

NOTE

We wish to thank Adena Cytron, Mary McClintock, Jane Mildred, David Schoem, Nancy Shore, and Edwina Uehara for their insights and comments on earlier drafts of this chapter.

REFERENCES

Adams, M., L. A. Bell, and P. Griffin. 1997. *Teaching for Diversity and Social Justice: A Sourcebook.* New York: Routledge.

Behling, C., T. Brett, M. Thompson, D. Kardia, B. A. Nagda, T. Sevig, and X. Zúñiga. 1998. *Intergroup Dialogue Process/Content Outline.* Ann Arbor: University of Michigan, Program on Intergroup Relations, Conflict, and Community.

Bohm, D. 1996. *On Dialogue.* London: Routledge.

Burbules, N. 1993. *Dialogue in Teaching.* New York: Teachers College Press.

Cannon, L. W. 1990. "Fostering Positive Race, Class, and Gender Dynamics in the Classroom." *Women's Studies Quarterly* 18, nos. 1–2: 126–34.

Chesler, M. A. 1995. "Racetalk: Thinking and Talking about Racism." *Diversity Factor* 3, no. 3: 37–45.

Du Bois, P., and J. J. Hutson. 1997. *Bridging the Racial Divide: A Report on Interracial Dialogue in America.* Brattleboro, Vt.: Center for Living Democracy.

Ellinor, L., and G. Gerard. 1998. *Dialogue: Rediscover the Transforming Power of Conversation.* New York: John Wiley and Sons.

Flavin-McDonald, C., and M. H. Barrett. 1999. "The Topsfield Foundation: Fostering Democratic Community Building through Face-To-Face Dialogue." In *Enhancing Creativity in Adult and Continuing Education: Innovative Approaches, Methods, and Ideas,* ed. P. J. Edelson and P. L. Malone. San Francisco: Jossey-Bass.

Freire, P. 1972. *Pedagogy of the Oppressed.* New York: Seabury Press.

Gudykunst, W. B. 1998. *Bridging Differences: Effective Intergroup Communication.* Thousand Oaks, Calif.: Sage.

Hardiman, R., and B. Jackson 1997. "Conceptual Foundations for Social Justice Education Courses." In *Teaching for Diversity and Social Justice: A Sourcebook,* ed. M. Adams, L. A. Bell, and P. Griffin. New York: Routledge.

Helms, J. 1990. *Black and White Racial Identity: Theory, Research, and Practice.* Westport, Conn.: Greenwood Press.

Huang-Nissen, S. 1999. *Dialogue Groups: A Practical Guide to Facilitate Diversity Conversation.* Blue Hill, Maine: Medicine Bear.

Isaacs, W. 1996a. "The Process and Potential of Dialogue in Social Change." *Educational Technology,* January–February, 20–30.

———. 1996b. "Taking Flight: Dialogue, Collective Thinking, and Organizational Learning." *Organizational Dynamics,* autumn, 24–39.

Kelman, H. C. 1978. "Israelis and Palestinians: Psychological Prerequisites for Mutual Acceptances." *International Security* 3:162–86.

———. 1987. "The Political Psychology of the Arab-Israeli Conflict: How Can We Overcome the Barriers to a Negotiated Solution?" *Political Psychology* 8:347–63.

———. 1990. "Interactive Problem-Solving: A Social Psychological Approach to Conflict Resolution." In *Conflict: Readings in Management and Resolution,* ed. J. Burton and F. Dukes. New York: St. Martin's Press.

Kettering Foundation. 1999. *For Convenors and Moderators: Organizing for Public Deliberation and Moderating a Forum/Study Circle.* Dayton, Ohio: Kettering Foundation.

Lederach, J. P. 1995. *Preparing for Peace: Conflict Transformation across Cultures.* Syracuse, N.Y.: Syracuse University Press.

Manning, G., K. Curtis, and S. Macmillan. 1996. *Building Community: The Human Side of Work.* Cincinnati: Thompson Executive Press.

McCoy, M., and R. Sherman. 1994. "Bridging Divides of Race and Ethnicity." *National Civic Review* 83, no. 2: 111–19.

Miller, F. A. 1994. "Why We Chose to Address Oppression." In *The Promise of Diversity: Over Forty Voices Discuss Strategies for Eliminating Discrimination in Organizations*, ed. E. Cross, J. H. Katz, F. Miller, and E. W. Seashore. New York: NTL Institute/Irwin Professional Publishing.

Nagda, B. A. 2001. *Creating Spaces of Hope and Possibility: A Curriculum for Intergroup Dialogues.* Seattle, Wash.: IDEA Training and Resource Institute.

Nagda, B. A., M. Spearmon, L. C. Holley, S. Harding, M. L. Balassone, D. Moïse-Swanson, and S. de Mello. 1999. "Intergroup Dialogues: An Innovative Approach to Teaching about Diversity and Justice in Social Work Programs." *Journal of Social Work Education* 35, no. 3: 433–49.

Nagda, B. A., and X. Zúñiga. 2000. "Fostering Meaningful Racial Engagement through Intergroup Dialogues." Typescript.

Nagda, B. A., X. Zúñiga, and T. D. Sevig. 1995. "Bridging Differences through Peer-Facilitated Intergroup Dialogues." In *Peer Programs on a College Campus: Theory, Training, and "Voice of the Peers,"* ed. S. Hatcher. San Jose, Calif.: Resource Publications.

Norman, A. J. 1991a. "The Use of the Group and Group Work Techniques in Resolving Inter-ethnic Conflict." *Social Work with Groups* 14, nos. 3–4: 175–86.

———. 1991b. "Third Party Intervention in the Management of Arab/Jewish Conflict: A Case Study." *Journal of Multicultural Social Work* 1, no. 2: 51–64.

———. 1994. "Black-Korean Relations: From Desperation to Dialogue, or from Shouting and Shooting to Sitting and Talking." *Journal of Multicultural Social Work* 3, no. 2: 87–99.

One America in the Twenty-first Century: The President's Initiative on Race—One America Dialogue Guide. 1998. Washington, D.C.: The White House.

Saunders, H. H. 1999. *A Public Peace Process: Sustained Dialogue to Transform Racial and Ethnic Conflicts.* New York: St. Martin's Press.

Schein, E. H. 1982. "What to Observe in a Group." In *Reading Book for Human Relations Training*, ed. L. Porter and B. Mohr. Arlington, Va.: National Training Laboratories.

Schoem, D., X. Zúñiga, and B. A. Nagda. 1993. "Exploring One's Background: The Fishbowl Exercise." In *Multicultural Teaching in the University*, ed. D. Schoem, L. Frankel, X. Zúñiga, and E. Lewis. Westport, Conn.: Praeger.

Stephan, W., and C. W. Stephan. 1996. *Intergroup Relations.* Boulder, Colo.: Westview Press.

Study Circles Resource Center (SCRC). 1997. *Facing the Challenge of Racism and Race Relations: Democratic Dialogue and Action for Stronger Communities.* 3d ed. Pomfret, Conn.: Topsfield Foundation.

Tatum, B. D. 1992. "Talking about Race, Learning about Racism: The Application of Racial Identity Development Theory in the Classroom." *Harvard Educational Review* 62:1–24.

———. 1997. *Why Are All the Black Kids Sitting together in the Cafeteria? And Other Conversations about Race.* New York: Basic Books.

Treviño, J., and K. Maxwell. 2000. *Voices of Discovery: Facilitators' Handbook.* Tempe: Arizona State University, Intergroup Relations Center.

Weber, R. 1982. "The Group: A Cycle from Birth to Death." *International Reading Book for Human Relations Training.* Washington, D.C.: NTL Institute.

Zúñiga, X. 1998. *Exploring Conflicts and Common Ground: Facilitation Manual.* Amherst: Social Justice Education Program, University of Massachusetts.

Zúñiga, X., and B. A. Nagda. 1993. "Dialogue Groups: An Innovative Approach to Multicultural Learning." In *Multicultural Teaching in the University,* ed. D. Schoem, L. Frankel, X. Zúñiga, and E. A. Lewis. Westport, Conn.: Praeger.

Zúñiga, X., B. A. Nagda, and T. D. Sevig. 1995. *A Process/Content Outline for Intergroup Dialogues.* Ann Arbor: Program on Intergroup Relations, Conflict, and Community, University of Michigan.

———. 2000. "Intergroup Dialogues: A Model for Cultivating Student Engagement across Differences." Typescript.

Zúñiga, X. and T. Sevig. 1997. "Bridging the 'Us/Them' Divide through Intergroup Dialogue and Peer Leadership." *Diversity Factor* 5, no. 2: 22–28.

Zúñiga, X., C. Vasques, T. Sevig, and B. A. Nagda. 1996. "Dismantling the Walls: Peer-Facilitated Inter-Race/Ethnic Dialogue Processes and Experiences." Program on Conflict Management Alternatives Working Paper Series no. 49, University of Michigan.

Chapter 21

Adapting Intergroup Dialogue Processes for Use in a Variety of Settings

David Schoem and Shari Saunders

Many settings and activities offer excellent opportunities for incorporating aspects of the intergroup dialogue process when it is not possible to provide a full, stand-alone dialogue. Classes, workshops, training events, conferences, celebrations, staff development, and conflict management groups are just a few examples. Clearly, only a small number of people have as their primary work intergroup dialogue, but there are many with experience in intergroup dialogue who wish to bring into their daily work the conceptual underpinnings, processes, and techniques of dialogue.

There is an important distinction to be made between intergroup dialogue and the use of intergroup dialogue processes in other settings. Intergroup dialogue is a form of democratic practice and engagement involving face-to-face discussions occurring over time between two or more groups of people defined by their social identities. Certainly the skillful incorporation of intergroup dialogue processes into other settings will deeply enrich and enhance those activities. However, the intergroup dialogue itself is an intensive and extended process. Organizers should not be confused that they are providing intergroup dialogue, or participants that they have experienced the same, when, in fact, they have been part of what hopefully have been successful and moving, but limited, one-time workshops, discussions, training events, or town hall meetings. Done well, these activities can offer a rich intellectual and emotional introduction to intergroup dialogue, but they are distinct from the full dialogue experience.

Incorporating the Conceptual Foundations of Dialogue

Dialogue is a process, not an event or technique. Although there are exceptionally creative exercises and techniques associated with intergroup dialogue, any given exercise used in isolation from the underlying foundations of dialogue is without force and rendered relatively ineffective. Therefore, as one considers incorporating the dialogue process into a different setting, it is essential to consider the foundational principles that make dialogue distinctive and unique, setting it apart from other "diversity" work or group dynamics work.

Intergroup dialogue involves a commitment to democratic deliberation, careful listening, reflection, and constructive engagement with conflict. It requires an atmosphere of confidentiality as part of a broader effort to build trust among participants in face-to-face interaction. Participants focus on their group identity(ies) and their individual identity, exploring areas of difference and commonality. They confront issues of power, inequalities, and conflict about issues such as race, gender, class, religion, and sexual orientation. Burbules (1993) talks of dialogic learning as relational, and, as such, it must focus on individual and group interactions as well as elements of community building.

Within this framework there is much one can do to incorporate dialogue into other settings even before considering specific exercises. First, participants should be invited to the activity prepared to engage dialogic processes. At the outset, the well-trained group leader(s) will want to take time to have participants introduce themselves and begin a process of sharing and relationship building. Some people rely on ground rules to establish a basis for communication, but whether ground rules are laid out or not, the notion of respectful participation must be established. There also should be discussion of the difference between debate and efforts to "win" arguments on the one hand, and, on the other hand, the open and honest exchange of ideas and viewpoints with the goal of advancing awareness and understanding of different perspectives even when disagreement remains. Because active and focused listening is a skill most people need improvement in, dialogue activities require giving particular attention to this area.

As topics are raised in the workshop, class, meeting, or training event, the group leader(s) will want participants to engage with one another in an open and honest fashion. A setting that values active participation lends itself more easily to the dialogic process than one that encourages passive listening to presentations. An environment that works to establish equal status within the dialogue setting makes it easier for participants to speak openly without fear of being silenced or having their views dismissed than does one that emphasizes within the dialogue setting the hierarchical status of participants and leaders. A course or workshop that meets continuously over an extended period obviously provides a more appropriate context to build a sustained level of trust and engaged conflict than one that is limited to a couple of hours in a single meeting.

Incorporating Dialogue Exercises and Techniques

There are a variety of intergroup dialogue exercises and techniques that can be used in K–12, higher education, business, and community contexts. The exercises listed below represent just a few of the many outstanding and varied approaches for engaging participants in dialogue and reflection. Additional approaches can be found in a variety of books (Cox and Beale 1997; Adams, Bell, and Griffin 1997; Schoem et al. 1995). As much potential for good any exercise may have, whenever people are asked to engage openly and honestly there is opportunity for misuse and abuse of trust. Group leaders must be trained to use such exercises appropriately and effectively and must be skilled in handling the personal and intergroup issues that are likely to arise from the exercises.

The exercises and techniques that follow are illustrative of how intergroup dialogue between individuals and groups can be used in these contexts. We describe an exercise, LARA ("The LARA Method" 1993), emphasizing communication that facilitates dialogue between people with opposing positions; another structured technique, The "Closed Fishbowl" exercise (Schoem, Zúñiga, and Nagda 1995), to foster intergroup dialogue emphasizing both speaking and listening; a third exercise, the "Power Exercise" (Schulz 1995), developed to introduce discussion about issues of power; and, last, an ongoing process, the "Class (Group) Meeting" (Nalle 1994), that uses intergroup dialogue to encourage problem solving across differences.

Whichever techniques or exercises one chooses, they will have to be adapted to the particular context (educational, business, community, etc.). Some variables to consider include

Homogeneity and heterogeneity of the group of participants in terms of social identity characteristics, awareness, and understanding

Self-awareness of the participants in terms of social identity and issues of privilege or oppression related to their group identity

Willingness of participants to be involved in the dialogue process (identify what are sources of resistance and how they might be addressed)

Familiarity of participants with one another and the ways in which this might facilitate or hinder the dialogue process

Group dynamics in terms of issues of safety and trust that might arise in the dialogue process, and how they can be addressed

Participation in dialogues for the purpose of understanding or problem solving requires risk taking and trust. These can be difficult to achieve in environments in which power differentials exist (between teachers/professors and students, between supervisors and employees, between agencies and recipients of their services, etc.). It is essential that those who participate in dialogue activities be protected and not penalized for honestly expressing their views. To create a climate in which risk taking and trust can develop, several things should be considered before engaging in dialogues. The group should agree to some guidelines related to confidentiality; they should generate norms for participation; and those with the most power should put themselves in a position where they are the first ones who are publicly vulnerable. In some cases, it may be necessary to ask participants what it is they need in order to feel safe, and the outcome of this conversation should inform the subsequent discussions of confidentiality and norms. For individuals to receive the benefits of intergroup dialogue techniques and exercises in their settings, they need to create spaces for honest interaction.

The "LARA Method"

When people have passionate feelings about an issue (e.g., whether gays should have the same rights as heterosexuals), they are often more inclined to state their point of view than to listen to a person who has an opposing perspective. During these types of interactions, participants can find themselves becoming defensive or hostile in their responses to each other's comments and questions. The LARA method (*l*isten, *a*ffirm, *r*espond, *a*dd information) ("The LARA Method" 1993) is a technique that can be used when responding to questions (and comments) in a way that allows the individuals to feel connected in spite of their differences. It is likely to be most effective when participants with opposing views share a commitment to seeking greater understanding. This process helps participants find common ground across their differences as they switch roles multiple times.

The LARA method has four steps ("The LARA Method" 1993).

1. *Listen.* In this step, the listener listens to what the speaker is actually

saying as well as to what the speaker is not saying. To do the latter, the listener needs to consider what might be underlying the question or comment the speaker is making (frustration, anger, uncertainty, fear, etc.). Another important component of the listening process is being aware of the speaker's nonverbal behaviors and the ways in which these behaviors might inform the listener about the speaker's feelings. The ultimate task for the listener is to listen for something in the speaker's comment that resonates with the listener—a moral principal, feeling, or experience that might be shared with the speaker.

2. *Affirm.* This step begins with the listener expressing to the speaker the way(s) in which the listener connected with the speaker. The listener may have connected with a feeling, an experience, or the principle expressed by the speaker. When the speaker and listener have little in common in their views, it can be more difficult to find something to affirm. In these situations, recognizing that the person has strong feelings or cares deeply about an issue may be the only connection that can be made. Irrespective of how the listener chooses to affirm, the affirmation given should genuinely reflect the listener's feelings. In affirming the speaker, it is critical to convey that the speaker has integrity and therefore will not be attacked. This is a difficult step because it requires participants to listen carefully enough to be able to formulate an affirmation and affirming the comments of people whose opinions differ from their own does not come naturally to most people. Nevertheless, it is important not to skip this step, as it allows those in the communication process to sustain the dialogue.

3. *Respond.* The listener answers the initial speaker's question or issue raised. The listener can agree or disagree with the speaker's perspective on the issue. The key is to take the speaker's questions and concerns seriously and not to respond with defensiveness or anger. Responding with personal experiences that are relevant to the concerns and questions raised can be quite powerful. If the listener does not have an informed answer to the speaker's question, that should be said.

4. *Add information.* Even when the listener does not have an informed response to give, the listener might refer the speaker to resources from which she or he might obtain answers (books or articles, a person who is knowledgeable about the topic, an organization, etc.), or the listener can seek out the information from these resources and share it with the speaker at a later time. If the listener was able to respond but has additional information to share, this is where it can be done. In this step, the listener can correct errors of fact made in the speaker's comment and can recast the issue or question in a way that facilitates a more positive dia-

logue. If resources (people, materials, organizations, etc.) or personal anecdotes have not already been shared, they can be expressed at this point.

Examples of issues that can be discussed using the LARA method include

Exclusion of particular types of children from recess games or activities
Segregation of students in cafeterias and dining halls
Students "coming out" in college classrooms
Welfare versus work programs
Existence of the "glass ceiling"

The "Closed Fishbowl" Exercise

It is sometimes difficult for people to get an opportunity to speak with or listen to others who are different from them talk about their experiences as members of a particular social identity group. The fishbowl exercise is one effective means of providing participants with an opportunity to do just that. The process described below is adapted from Schoem, Zúñiga, and Nagda 1995.

The participants in the fishbowl exercise should be sufficiently diverse so that there can be two distinct groups that differ on some aspect of their identity (race, sex/gender, sexual orientation, age, ability/disability status, etc.). Participants are asked to divide into identity groups (e.g., Asian Pacific Americans and Latinos/as; men and women; lesbians, gay men, and bisexuals and heterosexuals).

One group (e.g., women) sits in an inner circle facing those within the circle while the rest of the session participants sit around them in an outer circle (e.g., men).

The group in the inner circle has a specified amount of time to discuss a set of questions among themselves. The amount of time available depends upon the number of people in the inner circle and the length of the session. Questions that might be discussed by people in the inner circle depend upon the identity group or focus. During a fishbowl, all of the questions pertain to one identity category, for example, race, gender, religion, class. (Our examples, however, use different categories to illustrate the flexibility of the questions for use with any identity group.) *(a)* What is it like to be [female/male] in this class, organization, community? *(b)* When did you realize that people of different [races/genders] were treated differently? *(c)* What are some of the advantages and disadvantages of being gay? and *(d)* What were your first experiences with ableism?

Norms guiding the participation during the fishbowl activity are discussed.

Only the people in the inner circle speak. The people in the outer circle silently observe. Depending on the time available, they may be given the opportunity to ask clarifying questions when the people in the inner circle have spoken for the allotted time.

After the first identity group is finished, the groups switch places, for example, the women move to the outer circle and the men to the inner circle. The process is repeated.

Immediately after the last group finishes or members of the outer circle ask clarifying questions, the session organizers facilitate the processing of the activity with the whole group. The whole group processing could include discussion of both content and process. Content questions might address (*a*) the ways in which awareness and understanding of another person's experiences were increased, (*b*) commonalities and differences between the different groups, and (*c*) areas of conflict. The questions about process might include (*a*) How did it feel to be in the inner circle? outer circle? (*b*) What was hard or easy about this process? (*c*) What were the strengths and shortcomings of the process? (*d*) What next steps should be taken to follow up on this activity?

Topics that might be discussed in a fishbowl include

Gender, sexism, social relations, and identity

Race, racism, social relations, and identity

Sexual orientation, heterosexism and homophobia, social relations, and identity

Disability, ableism, social relations, and identity

Class, classism, social relations, and identity

The "Power Exercise"

Talking about issues of power is difficult for most people. Where does one start the conversation? How does one approache the topic, and how can individuals discuss it without great defensiveness? Although issues of power are very much on people's minds, individuals experience power, both personal and social, in very different ways. Some people very much want to seize and hold power, others want to run from it, and still others want to share power. The "Power Exercise" allows participants to initially engage some of these issues, providing an opportunity for ongoing and more in-depth discussions over time. This exercise described below is adapted from Schulz 1995.

1. Prepare in advance one piece of paper for each group of three to four people. Each paper should have the word *power* written on it.
2. Ask participants to divide into groups of three or four, perhaps asking people to join groups with others they don't know very well.
3. Each person in the groups of three to four should grasp the piece of paper with both hands.
4. The facilitator says, "This is power. Do something with it." Give the groups about five minutes. The facilitator may instruct the participants to talk or not to talk during this time; either approach works well.
5. At the end of five minutes, ask each group to describe what happened in their group. Ask volunteers to describe what they were thinking in terms of their relationship to power as reflected in their actions during the exercise.
6. Next, ask members of each group what in retrospect they wish they had done with their power.
7. During the discussion period, try to draw out themes of power over, power with, power within, and people's different relations and reactions to power.
8. Questions can be modified to fit the particular participants and the context. For example, committees made up of people representing different levels and statuses could address the power issues that are relevant to their specific group composition.

This exercise is appropriate for

> K–12 students, teachers, and administrators
> College/university students, faculty, and administrators
> Clerical and secretarial staff, middle-level managers, high-level managers, and CEOs
> Service providers, clients, government and other funding agency administrators.

The "Class (Group) Meeting"

The "Class (Group) Meeting" technique is useful for talking across differences to solve problems. Nalle (1994) describes the success of this technique, which she routinely uses in her class. An example of an effective use of this technique occurred in her class when the request to bring pets to class as part of a sharing activity was met with different responses from students with allergies and those without them. There were students who had allergies and could not be in the same room as certain pets and students who loved pets and did not understand the difficulties experienced by the children who had allergies. After getting information from the school nurse, they were able to arrive at a consensus—furry pets could visit, but the visits had to take place outside in warm weather. The students with allergies could view the pet visits from the classroom window.

The class meeting can be used in any context in which participants see themselves as part of a community that operates in democratic ways. Within these contexts, people will sometimes have differences of opinion on issues that are partially informed by some aspect of their identities. The meeting process is a way to give people the opportunity to hear each other's perspectives on difficult or controversial issues and determine what additional information, if any, is needed before consensus can be reached on how the issue should be handled. Reaching consensus oftentimes means successfully dialoguing across differences. The process described below is adapted from Nalle 1994.

1. The group discusses the meaning of community in their context.
2. The group discusses the ways in which each member of the community is interconnected.
3. The group discusses the rights of community members to express their concerns related to participating in the community.
4. The group identifies a place where community members' concerns will be collected.
5. Community members with concerns place them (anonymously or signed) in the agreed-upon location.
6. The person whose responsibility is to schedule meetings does so when the first concern appears. These meetings should be kept short—about fifteen minutes.
7. The group sits in a way that allows all participants to see one another.
8. The group establishes ground rules that guide participation in the meeting.
9. A designated person randomly selects a concern and reads it to the group.
10. The group discusses the concern. If there is time, another concern is randomly selected and discussed.
11. A designated person records the topics discussed and the strengths and shortcomings of each idea generated in response to the topics.

12. A designated person facilitates the discussion (makes sure that participation is equitable, asks questions that clarify issues and concerns, and moves the discussion toward consensus).
13. The group reaches consensus or agrees to disagree and moves on to the next topic. Agreeing to disagree does not mean that the issue is settled. It can be revisited at a later time.

Issues that might be discussed during these meetings include

Name calling among students
Violence within the school setting
Equitable participation strategies in college classrooms
Ways that mothers living in poverty might earn a living wage
Diversity in hiring practices

Venues for Using the Intergroup Dialogue Process

The intergroup dialogue process can be used in K–12 schools and youth programs as well as in higher education, business and corporations, and community contexts. In all of these contexts there are a variety of opportunities for individuals with different identities to engage in situations that might lead to conflict. A variety of programs has emerged in these settings that allows for constructive dialogue across differences. In this section, we share examples of intergroup dialogue processes that are being used in programs in each of the above four contexts.

K–12 Schools and Youth Programs

Some of the best K–12 conflict management programs, such as the School Inter-Ethnic Relations Program in Orange County, California ("Bridges" 1999; Fernanadez 2001) and A WORLD OF DIFFERENCE ("A WORLD OF DIFFERENCE" 1999; Tiven 2001), have adapted intergroup dialogue approaches in recent years. In these programs, children and teachers often are brought together face-to-face to talk through individual and group issues; engage, address, and understand conflict in a constructive manner; and reach some settlement. Many school-based and youth programs such as Students Talk About Race in Los Angeles (Sauceda and McKenna 1999; McKenna and Suaceda 2001) and Seeds of

Peace (Seeds of Peace 1999) incorporate peer facilitation of direct conversations on race and intergroup relations in social studies/history classrooms or as part of special assemblies, performing arts, camps, retreats, and after-school activities. Certainly there is great opportunity to expand upon these activities that use dialogue processes to involve parents of students around issues of race, gender, class, and so forth. Teachers and administrators in the Samuel Fels Cluster Schools in Philadelphia ("Samuel Fels Cluster School" 1999), for example, find much value in structured engagement of similar issues with one another. Finally, students involved in ethnic youth groups or private religious schools would find opportunities to interact with their peers across groups in activities like Seeking Common Ground in Denver (1997) that incorporate dialogue group processes such as listening and speaking skills, or what they refer to as "intentional communication."

Higher Education

In colleges and universities, seminar classes, such as those at the University of Michigan (Schoem 1997) and St. Lawrence University (Cornwell and Stoddard 1997), are the most obvious setting for faculty to incorporate dialogue processes. The University of Michigan has a set of linked First Year Seminars, also known as FIGs, on intergroup relations in which dialogue processes are used (Thompson, Brett, and Behling 2001). For example, David Schoem uses the "Power Exercise" in his seminar Intergroup Relations, Conflict, and Community to introduce issues of power into discussions of topics such as race and religion. Shari Saunders uses the LARA method in her course, Diversity, Identity Development, and Change on American Campuses, to help students find common ground even as they express strong differences in their points of view about issues of race, gender, sexual orientation, or disability with peers within and outside the classroom. St. Lawrence University's living-learning program, the First-Year Program, emphasizes both content and communication skills in multidisciplinary seminars as a means of addressing social group conflicts (Cornwell and Stoddard 1997).

Dialogue processes are all about good learning practice, and the opportunity to emphasize substantial analytical reading and writing assignments in conjunction with close conversations about personal experience provides for an outstanding liberal arts experience. This is the case with courses offered through the Intergroup Relations Center at Arizona State University (Intergroup Relations Center 1997; see Adams,

Bell, and Griffin 1997; Schoem et al. 1995; Treviño 2001). In professional schools, such as the School of Social Work at the University of Washington (Intergroup Dialogue, Education, and Action 1997) and the School of Education at the University of Massachusetts ("Social Justice Education Program" 1997), training in dialogue processes serves as a necessary professional skill for future teachers and social workers. As professionals these people will as a matter of course work daily with issues of conflict and community around issues of race, gender, and class. Public health workers and business school and public policy students also will benefit from training in dialogue processes as preparation for their professional work with the broad issues facing our diverse society and global community. In many cases, community service learning programs, internship programs, and field agencies offer very limited if any training and preparation for the intergroup experiences that students regularly encounter as they present themselves in community settings far different from their college campuses. Again, intergroup exercises and approaches to learn about self and other, such as "Multiple Roles and Multiple Choice Exercise" (Zúñiga and Myers 1995) or "Concentric Circles Exercise" (Myers and Zúñiga 1995), developed at the University of Michigan, are critical tools for these activities. Finally, campuses with the traditional college population ages eighteen to twenty-two are ripe for students confronting personal and social development issues. The use of intergroup processes to encourage multicultural dialogue in the counseling centers at the University of California, Davis ("The UCD Multicultural Immersion Program" 1997) and the University of Illinois ("Program on Intergroup Relations" 1997) can be exceedingly helpful for students struggling with personal and group concerns regarding identity, relationships, power, and independence.

Community

Neighborhood associations are unhappy with their apparent lack of representation at city hall; a community group and new police chief strive to build closer ties between residents and police; local church leaders decide to organize an interfaith educational program for youth among Christians, Jews, Muslims, and Hindus following an anti-Semitic incident. All of these scenarios have provided good venues for community groups using intergroup dialogue processes. Organizations such as Hope in the Cities ("Hope in the Cities" 1999; Greisdorf 2001), Study Circles Resource Center ("Study Circles Resource Center" 1999; McCoy and

McCormick 2001), and the National Conference for Community and Justice ("National Conference" 1999; Winborne and Smith 2001) have been particularly effective in working with community groups to address a very wide range of issues on local and national levels, as described elsewhere in this text. Intragroup difference, such as those between Orthodox and Reform Jews, among Mexican Americans, Cubans and Puerto Ricans, or between Chinese and Indian students in a Pan-Asian organization, is the type of issue that has been addressed using dialogue techniques as one means of creating understanding and managing conflict. Long-standing racial hostilities in schools, perceived disregard for the city's poor among city council members, and controversy over an annual gay/lesbian rights parade are examples of the kind of issues that require skilled short-term and long-term management and for which community organizers have used intergroup dialogue processes for assistance.

Business and Corporate

Corporate leaders have for some time used dialogue techniques, focus groups, and performing arts as part of their diversity workshops and retreats for all levels of management and employees. Project Change ("Project Change" 1999) and the Common Way Institute ("Commonway" 1997) have used focus groups, vignettes, and newsletters among other approaches to address conflicts that result from histories of racial segregation. Human resource development staff may invite outside consultants (see Groth 2001; Hardiman and Jackson 2001; Ramos and Mitchell 2001) to train corporate heads and managers in intercultural communication techniques for international trade and in successful communication with a diverse U.S. employee base. Apart from the immediacy of a lawsuit, long-standing complaints about gender inequities in a city's business community or about exclusion based on religious affiliation are issues that can be addressed on a long-term basis using dialogue processes.

Final Thoughts

Intergroup dialogue processes can be adapted for valuable use in settings in which it is not feasible to have an ongoing, stand-alone dialogue. In doing so, it is essential to develop the kind of atmosphere that is needed for the effective use of dialogue processes. There are a variety of exercises that can be adapted for use in particular contexts and a variety of venues for the intergroup dialogue process.

The authors encourage interested readers to investigate further those programs, techniques, or exercises that seem relevant for their context and make the necessary adaptations. As one considers using dialogue processes, it is important to keep in mind the rationale, goals for process, expected outcomes, what is known about the participants and the context, and facilitation needs (internal vs. external facilitators, single vs. multiple facilitators, etc.). Because use of dialogue processes requires some level of risk, reflection, and self-awareness, it is important to create a supportive atmosphere in which all of these can occur. Using dialogue processes in any context can be quite challenging, but the rewards are great for those who are committed to the process and participate in it in authentic ways.

REFERENCES

Adams, Maurianne, Lee Bell, and Pat Griffin. 1997. *Teaching for Diversity and Social Justice: A Sourcebook.* New York: Routledge.

Aronson, Elliot, and Shelly Patnoe. 1978. *The Jigsaw Classroom: Building Cooperation in the Classroom.* New York: Longman.

Bosworth, Chris, and Sharon Hamilton. 1994. *Collaborative Learning: Underlying Processes and Effective Techniques.* San Francisco: Jossey-Bass.

"Bridges: A School Inter-Ethnic Relations Program." 1999. *One America—The President's Initiative on Race: Promising Practices.* http://www.whitehouse.gov /Initiatives/OneAmerica/Practices/pp_19980803.17218.html. March 24, 2000.

Burbules, Nicholas. 1993. *Dialogue in Teaching: Theory and Practice.* New York: Teachers College Press.

"Campus Week of Dialogue." 1999. *One America—The President's Initiative on Race: Promising Practices.* http://www.whitehouse.gov/Initiatives/OneAmerica /Practices/pp_19980406.html. March 24, 2000.

Cohen, Elizabeth. 1994. *Designing Groupwork: Strategies for the Heterogeneous Classroom.* 2d ed. New York: Teachers College Press.

"Commonway." 1997. Portland, Ore.: Common Way Institute.

Cornwell, Grant, and Eve Stoddard. 1997. "Residential Colleges: Laboratories for Teaching through Difference." In *Democratic Education in an Age of Difference: Redefining Citizenship in Higher Education,* ed. Richard Guarasci, Grant Cornwell, and associates. San Francisco: Jossey-Bass.

Cox, Taylor. 1993. *Cultural Diversity in Organizations.* San Francisco: Berrett-Koehler.

Cox, Taylor, and Ruby L. Beale. 1997. *Developing Competency to Manage Diversity: Reading, Cases, and Activities.* San Francisco: Berrett-Koehler.

"Cultural Diversity in Education Program." 1999. *One America—The President's Initiative on Race: Promising Practices.* http://www.whitehouse.gov/Initiatives/OneAmerica/Practices/pp_19980729.3448.html. March 24, 2000.

Duke, James. 1978. *Conflict and Power in Social Life.* Provo, Utah: Brigham Young University Press.

Dukes, Franklin. 1996. *Resolving Public Conflict: Transforming Community and Governance.* New York: Manchester University Press.

Fernandez, Tina. 2001. "Building 'Bridges' of Understanding through Dialogue." In this volume.

Greisdorf, Karen Elliott. 2001. "An Honest Conversation on Race, Reconciliation, and Responsibility: Hope in the Cities." In this volume.

Groth, Gretchen Ann. 2001. "Dialogue in Corporations." In this volume.

Hardiman, Rita, and Bailey W. Jackson. 2001. "Cultural Study Groups: Creating Dialogue in a Corporate Setting." In this volume.

"Hope in the Cities." 1999. *One America—The President's Initiative on Race: Promising Practices.* http://www.whitehouse.gov/Initiatives/OneAmerica/Practices/pp_19980729.6787.html. March 24, 2000.

Intergroup Dialogue, Education, and Action. 1997. Seattle: University of Washington.

Intergroup Relations Center. 1997. Tempe: University of Arizona.

"The LARA Method." 1993. Portland, Ore.: Love Makes a Family, Inc. http://www.divanw.com/lmaf/.

Leary, Robin. 1997. "Clinton's First Town Meeting on Race Set to Convene in Ohio." *Philadelphia Tribune* National On-Line Edition. http://www.philatribune.com/120297-2-P1.html. March 24, 2000.

McCoy, Martha, and Michael A. McCormick. 2001. "Engaging the Whole Community in Dialogue and Action: Study Circles Resource Center." In this volume.

McKenna, Joseph H., and James Sauceda. 2001. "Students Talk About Race." In this volume.

Myers, Patricia, and Ximena Zúñiga. 1995. "Concentric Circles Exercise." In *Multicultural Teaching in the University,* ed. David Schoem, Linda Frankel, Ximena Zúñiga, and Edith A. Lewis. Westport, Conn.: Praeger.

Nalle, Kathy. 1994. "A Democracy of Third Graders." *Teaching Tolerance* 3, no. 2: 54–57.

"National Conference." 1999. *One America—The President's Initiative on Race: Promising Practices.* http://www.whitehouse.gov/Initiatives/OneAmerica/Practices/pp_19980728.3214.html. March 24, 2000.

"Principles of Community." 1999. *One America—The President's Initiative on Race: Promising Practices.* http://www.whitehouse.gov/Initiatives/OneAmerica /Practices/pp_19980930.5792.html. March 24, 2000.

"Program on Intergroup Relations." 1997. Urbana-Champaign: University of Illinois.

"Project Change." 1999. *One America—The President's Initiative on Race: Promising   Practices.*   http://www.whitehouse.gov/Initiatives/OneAmerica /Practices/pp_19980729.6563.html. March 24, 2000.

Ramos, Maria C., and Cassandra Mitchell. 2001. "Dialogue throughout an Organization." In this volume.

"Samuel Fels Cluster School." 1999. *One America—The President's Initiative on Race: Promising Practices.* http://www.whitehouse.gov/Initiatives/OneAmerica /Practices/pp_19980729.4690.html. March 24, 2000.

Sauceda, James, and Joseph H. McKenna. 1999. *Students Talk About Race: Curricular Discussion Guide.* Los Angeles: People for the American Way Foundation.

Schoem, David. 1997. "Intergroup Relations, Conflict, and Community." In *Democratic Education in an Age of Difference: Redefining Citizenship in Higher Education,* ed. Richard Guarasci, Grant Cornwell, and associates. San Francisco: Jossey-Bass.

Schoem, David, Linda Frankel, Ximena Zúñiga, and Edith A. Lewis, eds. 1995. *Multicultural Teaching in the University.* Westport, Conn.: Praeger.

Schoem, David, Ximena Zúñiga, and Biren (Ratnesh) A. Nagda. 1995. "Exploring One's Background: The Fishbowl Exercise." In *Multicultural Teaching in the University,* ed. David Schoem, Linda Frankel, Ximena Zúñiga, and Edith A. Lewis. Westport, Conn.: Praeger.

Schulz, Amy. 1995. "The Power Exercise." Email correspondence, May 17.

Seeds of Peace. 1999. http://www.seedsofpeace.org/mission.htm.

Seeking Common Ground. 1997. Spring, 2.2.

"Social Justice Education Program." 1997. Amherst, Mass: University of Massachusetts.

Stephan, Walter, and Cookie White Stephan. 1996. *Intergroup Relations.* Boulder, Colo.: Westview Press.

"Study Circles Resource Center." 1999. *One America—The President's Initiative on Race: Promising Practices.* http://www.whitehouse.gov/Initiatives/OneAmerica /Practices/pp_19981014.5847.html. March 24, 2000.

Thompson, Monita C., Teresa Graham Brett, and Charles Behling. 2001. "Educating for Social Justice: The Program on Intergroup Relations, Conflict, and Community at the University of Michigan." In this volume.

Tiven, Lorraine. 2001. "Student Voices: The ADL's A WORLD OF DIFFER-ENCE Institute Peer Training Program." In this volume.

Treviño, Jesús. 2001. "Voices of Discovery: Intergroup Dialogues at Arizona State University." In this volume.

"The UCD Multicultural Immersion Program." 1997. Davis, Calif.: UC Davis.

Winborne, Wayne, and Allison Smith. 2001. "Not Just Dialogue for Dialogue's Sake: The National Conference for Community and Justice." In this volume.

"A WORLD OF DIFFERENCE." 1999. *One America—The President's Initiative on Race: Promising Practices.* http://www.whitehouse.gov/Initiatives /OneAmerica/Practices/pp_19980728.3201.html. March 24, 2000.

Zúñiga, Ximena, and Patricia Myers. 1995. "Multiple Roles and Multiple Choice Exercise." In *Multicultural Teaching in the University,* ed. David Schoem, Linda Frankel, Ximena Zúñiga, and Edith A. Lewis. Westport, Conn.: Praeger.

Chapter 22

A Directory of Intergroup Dialogue Programs and Organizations

Jonathan J. Hutson

Before President William Jefferson Clinton called for a great national conversation on race and reconciliation in June 1997,[1] thousands of people across the United States were already engaged in facilitated dialogues across differences. People were gathering in school dorms, public libraries, houses of worship, workplace cafeterias, and homes for honest, healing discourse about prejudice, bias, and institutional racism. However, since the President's Initiative on Race spotlighted grassroots efforts aimed at interracial understanding and cross-cultural collaboration, the practice of intergroup dialogue has gained broader recognition and popularity.

Intergroup dialogue is an open and honest forum that brings diverse people face-to-face with the aid of trained facilitators to share personal stories, express emotions, affirm values, ask questions, clarify viewpoints, and propose solutions to community concerns.[2]

Although there are many models for shared communication across differences, the organizations found here define dialogue not as a casual exchange, nor as a one-time event, but as a formal, facilitated, and inclusive process. This directory presents contact information for a wide variety of programs and organizations that use the dialogic process to build interpersonal and intergroup relationships as a basis for transformative community action. This list is not intended to be exhaustive, but illustrative of a variety of principles and practices used by dialogue organizers and facilitators in the United States.[3]

The author has compiled a database at the Western Justice Center web site, which provides a more comprehensive list of more than 430 organizations that provide resources, training, and experience in intergroup dialogue in the United States and abroad. The on-line database, www.westernjustice.org/orgs.cfm, is searchable by location and by focus area(s). It includes contact information for regional offices, partner programs, and affiliates of several national resource organizations listed here.

These include the Anti-Defamation League, Community Relations Service of the U.S. Department of Justice, Hope in the Cities, National Coalition Building Institute, National Conference for Community and Justice, Operation Understanding, Project Change, Study Circles Resource Center, and YWCA.

The Abraham Fund. 477 Madison Avenue, Fourth Floor, New York NY 10022. Phone: 212-303–9421 or 800–301–3863. Fax: 212–935–1834. Email: abrahamfund@aol.com. URL: www.coexistence.org/. The Abraham Fund has an affiliate office in Jerusalem.

ACTS (Active Compassion through Service) Ministries. Tenth Presbyterian Church, 1701 Delancy Street, Philadelphia PA 19103. Phone: 215-735-7688. Fax: 215-735-3960. Email: dapple@tenth.org. URL: www.tenth.org.

ALANA (African American, Latino, Asian, Native and American) Community Organization. 47 Williston Street, Brattleboro VT 05301. Phone: 802-254-2972. Fax: 802-254-0075. Email: acs@together.net. URL: www.alanacommunity.org.

All One Heart. 240 Perris Boulevard, Suite A-141, Moreno Valley CA 92557. Phone: 909-247-7699. Fax: 909-924-1882. URL: www.allone heart.com.

Arizona State University, Voices of Discovery, Intergroup Dialogues Program. P.O. Box 871512, Tempe AZ 85287-1512. Phone: 480-965-1574. Fax: 480-965-1347. Email: jesus.trevino@asu.edu. URL: www.asu.edu/provost/intergroup.

A WORLD OF DIFFERENCE Institute. Anti-Defamation League, National Office, 823 United Nations Plaza, New York NY 10017. Phone: 212–885–7800. Fax: 212–490–0187. Email: sterc@adl.org. URL: www.adl.org. ADL affiliate offices offer this program in Atlanta, Boston, Chicago, Cleveland, Ohio, Costa Mesa, Calif., Dallas, Denver, Fort Lauderdale, Fla., Houston, Las Vegas, Los Angeles, Miami, Fla., New Haven, New Orleans, New York, Omaha, Philadelphia, Phoenix, San Diego, San Francisco, St. Louis, Seattle, Southfield, Mich., Syosset, N.Y., Washington, D.C., West Hills, Calif., West Orange, N.J., and West Palm Beach, Fla.

Bahá'í National Center. Public Information Office–Chicago, 1233 Central Street, Evanston IL 60201. Phone: 847-869-9039. Fax: 847-733-3578. Email: publinfobnc@usbnc.org. URL: www.us.bahai.org. The National Spiritual Assembly of the Bahá'ís of the United States coordinates and stimulates Race Unity activities of local Bahá'í administrative bodies across the country.

Beaver Race Initiative Development Group. 924 Seventh Avenue, Beaver Falls PA 15010. Phone: 724-847-1352. Fax: 724-773-7472. Email: mveon@pahouse.net.

Blacks and Jews in Conversation. Law Department, Criminal Court, 100 Center Street, Room 324-B, New York NY 10013. Phone: 212-374-8441.

Bridges: School Inter-Ethnic Relations Program. Orange County Human Relations Council, 1300 South Grand Avenue, Building B, Santa Ana CA 92705. Phone: 714-567-7470. Email: ochrc@jtpa.csa.co.orange.ca.us. URL: www.oc.ca.gov/csa/hrc/html/sierp.htm.

Building Bridges: Overcoming Racism. New Mount Olive Baptist Church, 2 Herman Avenue, Asheville NC 28801. Phone: 828-253-0749. Fax: 828-253-0421.

Center for the Healing of Racism. P.O. Box 27327, Houston TX 77227. Phone: 713-520-8226. Fax: 713-526-3037. Email: cfhrlg@juno.com.

Citizens Project, P.O. Box 2085, Colorado Springs CO 80901–2085. Phone: 719-520-9899. Fax: 719-520-0118. Email: citpro@jgiex.net. URL: www.citizensproject.org.

Coalition for Mutual Respect. Temple Israel of New Rochelle, 1000 Pinebrook Boulevard, New Rochelle NY 10804. Phone: 914-235-1800. Fax: 914-235-1854. Email: tinr@aol.com.

COLORS (Christians Offering Love to Overcome Racism in Society). All Saints Episcopal Church, 132 North Euclid Avenue, Pasadena CA 91101. Phone: 626-796-1172. Email: cheneyn@usc.edu. URL: www.allsaints-pas.org.

Committee of 100. Greensboro Human Relations Commission, P.O. Box 3136, Greensboro NC 27402. Phone: 336-373-2038. Email: roslyn .fullwood@ci.greensboro.nc.us. URL: www.ci.greensboro.nc.us/ humrel/.

Community Cousins. 140 Encinitas Boulevard, Suite 220, Encinitas CA 92024. Phone: 760-944-2899. Fax: 760-632-1128.

Community Relations Service. U.S. Department of Justice, 600 E Street NW, Suite 2000, Washington DC 20530. Phone: 202-305-2935. Fax: 202-305-3009. URL: www.usdoj.gov/crs/crs.htm. CRS maintains field offices in Atlanta, Chicago, Dallas, Denver, Detroit, Houston, Kansas City, Mo., Los Angeles, Miami, Fla., New York, Philadelphia, San Francisco, and Seattle.

Days of Dialogue. Community Partners, 606 South Olive Street, Suite 2400, Los Angeles CA 90014. Phone: 213-439-9640, ext. 26. Fax: 213-439-9650. Email: dodialogue@aol.com. URL: www.cityofla.org /COUN CIL/cd8/dod/htm.

Facing History and Ourselves. 16 Hurd Road, Brookline MA 02445. Phone: 617-232-1595. Fax: 617-232-0281. Email: margo_strom@facing .org. URL: www.facinghistory.org.

Faith and Politics Institute. Congressional Conversations on Race, 110 Maryland Avenue NE, Suite 304, Washington DC 20002. Phone: 202-546-1299. Fax: 202-546-4025. Email: FAITHPOLI@aol.com. URL: www.faith-and-politics.org.

Fellowship of Reconciliation. P.O. Box 271, Nyack NY 10960. Phone: 914-358-4601. Fax: 914-358-4924. Email: for@forusa.org. URL: www .forusa.org.

FOCUS St. Louis. Bridges across Racial Polarization, 1910 Pine Street, Suite 200, St. Louis MO 63103. Phone: 314-622-1250. Fax: 314-622-1279. Email: fslstl@focus-stl.org. URL: www.focus-stl.org.

Forum on Race. Urban Enterprise Center, 1301 Fifth Avenue, Suite 2400, Seattle WA 98101-2603. Phone: 206-389-7337. Fax: 206-389-7288. Email: lynnc@seattlechamber.com. URL: www.seattlechamber.com/uec /initiatives/race.htm.

Global Kids, Inc. 561 Broadway, Sixth Floor, New York NY 10012. Phone: 212-226-0130. Fax: 212-226-0137. Email: globalkids@igc.apc.org. URL: www.globalkids.org.

Green Circle Program. 1300 Spruce Street, Philadelphia PA 19107. Phone: 215-893-8400. Fax: 215-735-9718. Email: ntlgcp@aol.com. URL: www.greencircle.org.

Hapa Issues Forum. 1840 Sutter Street, San Francisco CA 94115. Phone: 415-273-7275. Email: hif@hapaissuesforum.org. URL: www .hapaissuesforum.org. The name of this national organization comes from the Hawaiian term *hapa haole*, which means "half white/foreigner." Once considered derogatory, it is now a simple way to describe a person of partial Asian or Pacific Islander ancestry. HIF has chapters in San Francisco, Southern California, at the University of California, Berkeley, and at the University of California, Irvine.

Healing of Racism Institute. Starr Commonwealth, 13725 Starr Commonwealth Road, Albion MI 49224. Phone: 800-837-5591. Fax: 517-629-2317 Email: institute@starr.org. URL: www.starr.org/training/.

Healing Racism in Anchorage. 2106 Castner Circle, Anchorage AK 99517. Phone: 907-272-2369. Fax: 907-272-7511. Email: ppartnow@alaska .net.

Hope in the Cities. 1103 Sunset Avenue, Richmond VA 23221. Phone: 804-358-1764. Fax: 804-358-1769. Email: hopecities@aol.com. URL: www.hopeinthecities.org. This interracial, multifaith organization has established partnerships or regional contacts in seventeen U.S. cities, plus an informal network in Australia, India, Israel, South Africa, Switzerland, and the United Kingdom.

Institute on the Arts and Civic Dialogue. 69 Dunster Street, Cambridge MA 02138. Phone: 617-496-9672. Fax: 617-495-9121. Email: dialogue@arts-civic.org. URL: www.arts-civic.org/.

Interfaith Action for Racial Justice. 325 East Twenty-fifth Street, Baltimore MD 21218-5303. Phone: 410-889-8333. Fax: 410-889-5719. Email: iarj@bcpl.net. URL: www.bcpl.net/~iarj/Welcome.html.

Interfaith Conference of Metropolitan Washington. 1419 V Street NW, Washington DC 20009. Phone: 202-234-6300. Fax: 202-234-6303. Email: ifc@interfaith-metrodc.org. URL: www.interfaith-metrodc.org.

Jewish-Palestinian Living Room Dialogue Group. 1448 Cedarwood Drive, San Mateo CA 94403. Phone: 415-574-8303. Fax: 415-573-1217. Email: Ltraubman@igc.org. URL: www.igc.org/traubman.

Moral Re-Armament. 1156 Fifteenth Street NW, Suite 910, Washington DC 20005. Phone: 202-872-9077. Fax: 202-872-9137. Email: mrawash@aol.com. URL: www.mra.org.uk. MRA is an international network of people working together across differences in ethnicity, nationality, class, or religion. MRA has centers in twenty-five countries.

Multicultural Institute for Leadership (MIL) Forum. One Park Plaza, Sixth Floor, Irvine CA 92614. Phone: 949-852-4477. Fax: 949-852-4478. Email: elaninter@worldnet.att.net. URL: www.milforum.org.

National Coalition Building Institute. 1835 K Street NW, Suite 715, Washington DC 20006. Phone: 202-785-9400. Fax: 202-785-3385. Email: ncbiinc@aol.com. URL: www.ncbi.org. NCBI has some sixty campus affiliates, fifty-five city-based chapters, and more than ten organizational affiliate chapters in the United States, Canada, and Europe.

National Conference for Community and Justice. 475 Park Avenue South, Nineteenth Floor, New York NY 10016. Phone: 212-545-1300. Fax: 212-545-8053. URL: www.nccj.org. Through sixty-five regional offices in thirty-five states, NCCJ provides resources and training in intergroup dialogue facilitation.

National Multicultural Institute. 3000 Connecticut Avenue NW, Suite 438, Washington DC 20008-2556. Phone: 202-483-0700. Fax: 202-483-5233. Email: nmci@nmci.org. URL: www.nmci.org.

Operation Understanding D.C. 3000 Connecticut Avenue NW, Suite 335, Washington DC 20008. Phone: 202-234-6832. Fax: 202-234-6669. Email: cedorsey@juno.com. URL: www.oudc.org. Operation Understanding has affiliate offices in Philadelphia and San Diego.

Project Change. Tides Center, P.O. Box 29919, San Francisco CA 94129-0919. Phone: 415-561-4880. Fax: 415-561-4875. Email: pcsanfran @projectchange.org. URL: www.projectchange.org. Project Change has affiliated programs in Albuquerque, El Paso, Knoxville, and Valdosta, Ga.

Public Conversations Project. Family Institute of Cambridge, 46 Kondazian Street, Watertown MA 02472-2832. Phone: 617-923-1216. Fax: 617-923-2757. Email: info@publicconversations.org. URL: www.public conversations.org/. PCP has conducted trainings in dialogue facilitation in nine states, from coast to coast.

Samuel S. Fels Cluster of the Philadelphia School District. Philadelphia. Phone: 215-335-5037 or 335-5963. URL: www.philsch.kl2.pa.us /clusters/clusterpages/fels/.

Search for Common Ground. 1601 Connecticut Avenue NW, Suite 200, Washington DC 20009. Phone: 202-265-4300. Fax: 202-232-6718. Email: awind@sfcg.org. URL: www.sfcg.org. This decentralized organization sponsors roundtables and other conflict resolution activities on four continents, with offices in nine countries.

SEED (Students Educating Each Other about Diversity). Catholic Secondary Schools, Grand Rapids MI 49503. Phone: 616-458-1500. URL: www.remc8.k12.mi.us/cathsec/seed.htm.

Seeds of Peace. 370 Lexington Avenue, Suite 401, New York NY 10017. Phone: 212-573-8040. Fax: 212-573-8047. Email: info@seedsofpeace.org. URL: www.seedsofpeace.org/.

Seeking Common Ground. 51 Grape Street, Denver CO 80220. Phone: 303-337-8433. Email: bbfpeace@aol.com. URL: www.ajp.com /scg/.

Shreveport Community Renewal. P.O. Box 4678, Shreveport LA 71134-0678. Phone: 318-425-3222. Fax: 318-425-8999. Email: shvcom-ren@aol-com. URL: www.shrevecommunityrenewal.org.

Southern Institute for Education and Research. Southern Catalyst Network, MR Box 1692, New Orleans LA 70118-5555. Phone: 504-865-6100, ext. 3. Fax: 504-862-8957. Email: so-inst@mailhost.tcs.tulane.edu. URL: www.tulane.edu/~so-inst.

Students Talk About Race (STAR). Multicultural Center, California State University, Long Beach, Long Beach CA 90840. Phone: 562-985-8150. Fax: 562-985-8149. Email: mcc@csulb.edu. URL: www.csulb.edu /web/centers/mcc/.

Study Circles Resource Center. P.O. Box 203, 697 Pomfret Street, Pomfret CT 06258. Phone: 860-928-2616. Fax: 860-928-3713. Email: info@studycircles.org. URL: www.studycircles.org. SCRC has provided resources and training to more than 186 community-based programs in thirty-nine states.

Television Race Initiative. 2601 Mariposa Street, P Floor, San Francisco CA 94110. Phone: 415-553-2841. Fax: 415-553-2848. Email: tunein@pov.org. URL: www.pbs.org/pov/tvraceinitiative. The Television Race Initiative teams national nonprofits, local and national media, educational institutions, community groups, interfaith groups, and public television stations from across the United States to create sustained community dialogues on race relations.

University of California, Davis. Counseling Center, 219 North Hall, Davis CA 95616. Phone: 530-752-0871. URL: www.counselingcenter .ucdavis.edu/.

University of Illinois, Urbana-Champaign, Program on Intergroup Relations. Counseling Center, Student Services Building, 610 East John Street, Room 110, Champaign IL 61820. Phone: 217-333-3704. Fax: 217-244-9645. URL: www.intergrouprelations.uiuc.edu/.

University of Massachusetts, School of Education. 383 Hills South, Amherst MA 01003. Phone: 413-545-0236 or 545-0918. Email: xzu niga@educ.umass.edu. URL: www.umass.edu/education/.

University of Michigan, Program on Intergroup Relations, Conflict, and Community. 3000 Michigan Union, 530 South State Street, Ann Arbor MI 48109-1349. Phone: 734-936-1875. Fax: 734-647-4133. Email: igrcc@umich.edu. URL: www.umich.edu/~igrc/.

University of Washington, School of Social Work, Intergroup Dialogue, Education and Action. 4101-15th Avenue NE, Seattle WA 98105. Phone: 206-543-5640. Email: ratnesh@u.washington.edu. URL: www .depts.washington.edu/sswweb/.

NOTES

1. In his commencement address at the University of California, San Diego, in LaJolla, California, on June 14, 1997, President Clinton stated: "Over the coming year, I want to lead the American people in a great and unprecedented conversation about race." *Public Papers of the Presidents of the United States: William J. Clinton, 1997* (Washington, D.C.: U.S. Government Printing Office, 1998), 739.

2. Adapted from P. M. Du Bois and J. J. Hutson, *Bridging the Racial Divide: Interracial Dialogue in America* (Brattleboro, Vt.: Center for Living Democracy, 1997), 11. The federal government adopted this definition of dialogue in 1998. U.S. Department of Justice, *One America Dialogue Guide: Conducting a*

Discussion on Race (Washington, D.C.: U.S. Dept. of Justice, Community Relations Service, 1998), 1.

3. There have been three previous attempts to catalog dialogue groups. The Center for Living Democracy produced the first directory, with funding from the W. K. Kellogg Foundation. M. A. Statham, ed., *Interracial Dialogue Groups across America: A Directory* (Brattleboro, Vt.: Center for Living Democracy, 1997). This annotated directory described sixty-five dialogue groups representing thirty-five states and the District of Columbia. The following year, the National Conference for Community and Justice issued an annotated directory of more than three hundred organizations that focus on intergroup relations among various age groups, sexual orientations, ethnic groups, political stances, and programmatic methodologies. However, many of these groups practice cross-cultural collaboration, but not a formal process of intergroup dialogue. National Conference for Community and Justice, *Intergroup Relations in the United States: Programs and Organizations* (New York: National Conference for Community and Justice, 1998). President Clinton's call for a national conversation on race and reconciliation resulted in a third directory of 124 interracial organizations, including many dialogue groups. However, that directory does not provide mailing addresses. The President's Initiative on Race, *Pathways to One America in the Twenty-first Century—Promising Practices for Racial Reconciliation* (Washington, D.C.: U.S. Government Printing Office, 1999). Available at www.westernjustice.org/resources.htm.

Contributors

David Schoem is Faculty Director of the Michigan Community Scholars Program and Adjunct Associate Professor of Sociology at the University of Michigan. He also has served as Assistant Vice President for Academic and Student Affairs and as Assistant Dean for Undergraduate Education. He is cofounder of the University of Michigan's Program on Intergroup Relations, and his intergroup work dates back to his school days in racially divided Philadelphia in the 1960s. Schoem is editor of *Inside Separate Worlds: Life Stories of Young Blacks, Jews, and Latinos* (University of Michigan Press) and coeditor with Linda Frankel, Ximena Zúñiga, and Edith Lewis of *Multicultural Teaching in the University* (Praeger).

Sylvia Hurtado is Associate Professor and Director of the Center for the Study of Higher and Postsecondary Education at the University of Michigan. She is involved in a national project to examine how institutions are preparing students for living in a diverse democracy, including research on skills that can be achieved through intergroup dialogue. She is coauthor of *Enacting Diverse Learning Environments* (Jossey-Bass) and is author of numerous articles on improving the climate for racial and ethnic diversity in higher education.

Mary Lou Balassone, DSW, is Associate Professor and Associate Dean for Professional Degree Programs of the School of Social Work, University of Washington. She has a strong interest in undergraduate education, especially in the education of generalist social workers.

Ruby L. Beale is on the faculty in the Department of Psychology and the School of Business Administration at the University of Michigan. She is a specialist in multicultural programming and the training of trainers to successfully implement programs with a diverse audience. Dr. Beale is the coauthor of *Developing Competency to Manage Diversity: Readings, Cases, and Activities* (Berrett-Koehler Publishers, 1997).

Charles Behling is Codirector of the Program on Intergroup Relations and Adjunct Professor of Psychology at the University of Michigan. He is the recipient of awards for both teaching and social justice from the University of Buffalo and Lake Forest College.

Teresa Graham Brett has a juris doctor from the University of Arizona. She is Associate Dean of Students and Codirector of the Program on Intergroup Relations at the University of Michigan.

Mark Chesler is Professor of Sociology at the University of Michigan. He works with the Intergroup Dialogue Program at Michigan as a trainer-educator of the dialogue facilitators. He also is active as an organizational consultant on processes of antiracism-antisexism and multicultural transformation with public (higher education, community groups) and private (corporate) agencies.

Stan de Mello, MSW, MPA, is Lecturer and Practicum Coordinator at the School of Social Work, University of Washington. He is also a Faculty Associate with the Intergroup Dialogue, Education, and Action (IDEA) Training and Resource Institute. He has extensive experience in community development work with First Nations people in Canada.

Tina Fernandez is Program Director for Alternate Dispute Resolution and the School Inter-Ethnic Relations Program at the Orange County Human Relations Council. Since 1988, she has been working on the commission's mission: "to address inter-group tension and foster mutual understanding among residents, in order to make Orange County a better place for ALL to live, work, and do business."

Karen Elliott Greisdorf is an award-winning video producer and feature writer who lives in Bethesda, Maryland. Following work with the BBC, NBC, and FOX News Service, Ms. Greisdorf launched Cornerstone Communications with the mission of telling stories of individual and community change. Her work focuses on issues of racial reconciliation, urban renewal, and youth development.

Gretchen Ann Groth received her Ph.D. in Organizational Psychology and has been a diversity and organizational development consultant with corporations such as Lucent, DuPont, Hewlett Packard, Proctor and

Gamble, and AT&T for over twenty years. She has participated in several dialogue initiatives.

Patricia Gurin is Professor of Psychology and Women's Studies at the University of Michigan. She is also a Faculty Associate at the Center for Afroamerican and African Studies and the Research Center for Group Dynamics. In the 1990s, she teamed with Steve Sumida to teach a course in the study of race, racism, and ethnicity. She has been research coordinator, instructor, and a core member of the University of Michigan's Intergroup Relations Program.

Rita Hardiman is an adjunct faculty member at the School of Education, University of Massachusetts at Amherst. She is also a partner in New Perspectives, Inc., a firm that specializes in providing training and consultation on social justice and social diversity in organizational settings.

Scott Harding, Ph.D., is Assistant Professor in the School of Social Welfare at the University of Kansas. His research focuses on poverty, inequality, and social problems, gentrification and displacement, housing, and social welfare policy. He worked in a teaching and research capacity with the Intergroup Dialogue, Education, and Action effort at the University of Washington.

Jonathan J. Hutson, J.D., is Communications Director of the Trial Lawyers for Public Justice Foundation in Washington, D.C. He is coauthor, with Paul Martin Du Bois, of *Bridging the Racial Divide: Interracial Dialogue in America.* Along with Tom Grubisich, he designed and launched "Dialogues Online: Racial Healing in Our Communities" on America Online/Digital City, Inc., in 1999.

Bailey W. Jackson is founding faculty member of the Social Justice Education Program, School of Education, and currently Dean of the School of Education, University of Massachusetts, Amherst.

Diana Kardia, Ph.D., has facilitated a variety of models for intergroup dialogue with college students, faculty, and staff at the University of Michigan and as an independent consultant. She is now the Associate Director for the university's Center for Research on Learning and Teaching, where she works with faculty and graduate students to develop effective curricula and pedagogy for a diverse student body.

Michael A. McCormick, Program Director at the Study Circles Resource Center, has worked for over twenty-five years in community organizing and conflict resolution. He served as the Director of the Center for Conflict Resolution at Salisbury State University, and Lecturer and Director of the Mediation Clinic at the University of Washington School of Law. He holds an MSW in Community Practice from the University of Michigan.

Martha McCoy is the Executive Director of the Study Circles Resource Center and Executive Vice President of the Topsfield Foundation. She and her staff work with a growing network of local, statewide, and national organizations that are creating opportunities for citizen dialogue and action.

Joseph H. McKenna directs the STAR program and lectures in Religious Studies at the University of California, Irvine.

Cassandra Mitchell has had over twenty years of industry experience as an organizational development professional with a diverse set of clients from education, health care, government, and financial services. As First Vice President of Employee and Organizational Development for the credit card subsidiary of Bank One, she has spent the past eleven years providing training and performance support interventions.

Dominique Moïse-Swanson, MSW, is a doctoral candidate in the School of Social Work at the University of Washington. She has worked with the Intergroup Dialogue, Education, and Action effort in both a research and a teaching capacity. Her research and teaching interests include cultural diversity, social justice, and community practice.

Biren (Ratnesh) A. Nagda, Ph.D., is Assistant Professor and the founding Director of the Intergroup Dialogue, Education, and Action (IDEA) Training and Resource Institute at the School of Social Work, University of Washington. His teaching and research interests focus on cultural diversity and social justice, intergroup dialogue, and multicultural- and empowerment-oriented social work practice with individuals, groups, and organizations.

Maria C. Ramos, Ed.D., is President of Ramos Associates, a training and consulting firm. She has experience in the United States and abroad in organizational development, executive coaching, training of trainers, career development, and valuing diversity. Dr. Ramos has worked for organizations such as DuPont, First Card, FMC, Siemens, Cigna, and Yale University.

James Manseau Sauceda is the STAR trainer, Director of the Multicultural Center of California State University, Long Beach, and Professor of Speech Communications there.

Shari Saunders is currently the Coordinator of the Transforming Communities Project in the Division of Student Affairs at the University of Michigan. She was also Assistant Professor of Teacher Education for five years and Coordinator of Multicultural Teaching and Learning at the Center for Research on Learning and Teaching for four years. She earned her Ph.D. in Education from the University of Virginia in 1990.

Todd Sevig, Ph.D., is the Clinical Director at Counseling and Psychological Services at the University of Michigan. He has been involved with the Program on Intergroup Relations, Conflict, and Community at the university as a teacher, trainer, and program administrator. His most recent publication is *Integrating Spirituality and Multicultural Counseling,* coauthored with Mary Fukuyama and published by Sage Publications.

Allison Smith is a freelance writer specializing in Web site content. Prior to this she was a Program and Policy Research Analyst at The National Conference for Community and Justice, where she authored a comprehensive directory of over five hundred programs and organizations that seek to improve intergroup relations in the United States.

Margaret Spearmon, Ph.D., is Clinical Associate Professor and Director of Field Education at the School of Social Work, University of North Carolina, Chapel Hill. She is also president of Interface International with over fifteen years of experience consulting in the areas of cultural diversity, developing multicultural organizations, team building, and staff development in public education and human services.

Stephen H. Sumida is Professor and Chair of American Ethnic Studies and Adjunct Professor of English at the University of Washington, Seattle, where he teaches and researches in Asian/Pacific American and comparative American ethnic literatures and interdisciplinary American studies.

At the University of Michigan in the 1990s, he teamed with Patricia Gurin to teach a course in the study of race, racism, and ethnicity.

Monita C. Thompson has worked with the Program on Intergroup Relations at the University of Michigan since 1993 as a facilitator, peer consultant, research assistant, and trainer. She is the Associate Director of IGR and trains peer educators in dialogue facilitation and is one of the developers and lead instructors of the residence hall staff training course.

Lorraine Tiven is the National Director of Peer Training for the Anti-Defamation League and the Project Director for ADL's A WORLD OF DIFFERENCE Institute in New York State. Ms. Tiven has directed antibias education programs for educators, students, and community groups in New York State and developed ADL's A WORLD OF DIFFERENCE Institute Peer Leadership Program for youth service agencies.

Jesús Treviño, Ph.D., is the Director of the Intergroup Relations Center, Office of the Senior Vice-President and Provost at Arizona State University. He has both a B.A. and an M.A. from Eastern Michigan University. In 1992, Jesús received his Ph.D. from UCLA in the area of higher education. He has been with Arizona State University since 1993 and was formerly in the capacity of Assistant Dean for Student Life.

Wayne Winborne recently joined the Prudential Insurance Company as Director of Strategic Data Analysis in the Equal Opportunity/Diversity division. Prior to this he was Director of Program and Policy Research at The National Conference for Community and Justice, where he was responsible for national research activities, evaluation, the National Conversation on Race, Ethnicity, and Culture, and the Community Dialogues project.

Ximena Zúñiga, Ph.D., is Assistant Professor of Education at the University of Massachusetts, Amherst. She has coedited *Multicultural Teaching in the University* (Praeger) and *Readings for Diversity and Social Justice* (Routledge). Dr. Zúñiga publishes articles and teaches courses on multicultural group processes, racism in the United States, student development in social justice education, and cross-race/ethnic and gender dialogues.

Index